Partnership For All

John Spedan Lewis

Published by John Lewis plc

171 Victoria Street
London
SW1E 5NN

www.johnlewispartnership.co.uk

First published 1948
Reprinted 2014
© John Spedan Lewis

ISBN: 978-0-9928871-0-0

PREFACE

1. THE subject of this book includes many matters that at their cores are easy to distinguish but at their edges melt into several others, so that they are difficult to keep apart and to arrange satisfactorily. At least I have found it so. But I hope that the book will serve well enough its two main purposes, first, to answer certain questions that after my own time may arise within the Partnership and, second, to answer questions outside the Partnership in the minds of those considering whether to join it or how to advise someone else about that or who are for some reason students of such matters. Some of them perhaps may be thinking of starting other partnerships or may have already done so.

2. I hope the index will prove good. Paragraph-numbering has been used in case further editions of all or some parts of the book may have a different size of page. The plan is set out in the Table of Contents.

The book describes an experiment of which the design was complete by October of 1910 and has been developing ever since, that is to say for nearly forty years.

The experiment may be summed up as an attempt so to organise and conduct a business that all the advantages whatsoever of owning it shall be shared as fairly as possible by all who are working in it and that the qualification for having a position in it shall be ability (without overstrain) and will to fill that position in a way reasonably first-rate for the service of the general community, the service by which the business has to live.

OPINIONS OF PARTNERS

3. The experiment had been in progress for a good many years before, in March of 1920, the organisation, to which step by step it had given rise, was first called a partnership and its members partners. That name was welcomed with a promptitude and unanimity that seemed to me highly significant of the strong desire of the Managed in the modern business-world for such a change of Status, standpoint and mental atmosphere.

What impression the Partnership makes on some of its members may be judged from this passage from a letter written by one of them in 1942 when he was going on War Service. The writer had graduated at Cambridge with first-class honours and, before his eight years in the Partnership, had spent four in another large organisation in the retail drapery trade.

"I have been really happy, as I never previously thought it was possible to be in business life, from my very first days in the Partnership but at first my feelings were, so to speak, passive. I was happy because I seemed to fit and liked the work and because everyone with whom I had to deal was pleasant and congenial, in much the same way as an adopted child will from the first feel happy in a really kindly family.

"But, as I grew to be and feel part of the family, the nature of my feelings has changed, without my realising it till I stop now and look back, with the growth of an intense and I hope active affection, not for any particular person or persons but just for the whole thing, the entity we call the Partnership, not only among ourselves but to outsiders, in a way that confidently assumes that there exists no other partnership worthy of the name.

"I am grateful not only for this happiness but also for the intellectual stimulus and satisfaction I have derived from increased perception of all the implications of your great experiment. I read Professor Barker's book 'Reflections on Government' and in at least two places he might have been writing about the Partnership in the ideas he puts forward of how democracy may hope to meet the challenge of these times."

1932

At least equally significant, at least it seems so to me, was a remark made before the war by a middle-aged salesman. A special committee had been appointed to collect opinions and ideas upon the perennial problem of the pay of the Selling Staff. Should it be a fixed rate or should there be some system of incentives and, if so, what?

Among the thirty-nine witnesses, to whom the committee gave a hearing, was this particular salesman because of his many years of experience of similar employment in the West End of London.

The member of the committee, who told me of this; said that the witness appeared to be the sort of man who rather prides himself on being hard-headed and not easy to humbug. At the close of his talk with the committee he said that he would like to take that opportunity to express his personal opinion that the system of the Partnership affects really importantly the happiness of the worker by the feeling it gives him that he is not suffering the humiliation of being exploited but really is getting the whole fruit of his own work.

The speaker said that he for his own part would hesitate to leave the Partnership for other employment in which he had a good prospect of making another ten shillings a week but in which he would not have the satisfaction of feeling that whatever he was getting was really all there was to have. That is to say that he was not being exploited.

I am quoting from a conversation of quite ten years ago and my informant is dead. I am not suggesting that the word "humiliation" was

4

used or that the speaker had that idea at all clearly in his mind. I dare say he himself would have said that the word "annoyance" would better express his feeling. But for my own part I have very little doubt that the discomfort of what is really a sense of humiliation was the true cause of his saying, as to my clear recollection I was told that he did, that to him this consequence of the system of the Partnership was "worth ten shillings a week".

Here it seems to me we have the real core of the problem of getting rid of ca'canny so as to achieve the enormous increase that is now so desperately needed in our national income.

Feelings of this same kind are shown in the fact that more than one newcomer with experience of the general business world has said after some time in the Partnership that he had "never known before what it was to be glad that it was Monday morning".

GENERAL FRIENDLINESS

4. Another thing, that very commonly strikes newcomers, is what they feel to be the remarkable general friendliness that they encounter, the general atmosphere of welcome. A couple of years ago a particularly well qualified judge told me that in comparison with his previous experience of the business-world he had been struck by the Partnership's freedom from an atmosphere, to which he had been accustomed, of jealous competition. I have heard this before but the friendliness of reception of newcomers is mentioned much oftener. In literally, as I hope, my last hour of work upon this book, that has taken most of my leisure for several years, I feel that I must insert here a quotation from a letter that reached me less than a week ago. The writer, a graduate of Cambridge, is in his late thirties and newly retired from the Indian Civil Service. In his letter he was telling me that in the course of an experimental start in the Partnership he had made up his mind to join it. He says: "My provisional decision to join the Partnership has been a good deal strengthened by what I have seen in the past ten days—and not the least by the universal and apparently instinctive ability at all levels to make a newcomer feel welcome".

Another frequent comment is that the Partnership strikes newcomers as remarkably free and easy but also—and for this last reason surprisingly—hard-working. We do, of course, avoid regulation as far as we can. Fixed hours of attendance, for example, are never required in cases where there seems to be no real need.

EFFECT ON MINDS

5. Another comment, that is made now and again and that was made to me once with great seriousness by one of the Partnership's ablest members, is that its supreme attraction for the most intelligent and

cultivated of those, whom it does in fact attract, is not its social and political implications or the intellectual interest of business upon such a scale "but simply the extraordinary number of extraordinarily nice people that there are in it".

When that was first said to me, I heard it, of course, with acute pleasure but I said then and I have thought ever since that, so far as it is true, it is certainly not wholly and perhaps not even largely the result of any exceptional efficiency in recruiting. To at all events a substantial extent the real explanation, I believe, is that a great many people have it in them to be thus pleasant and prefer to be so but ordinarily in the business-world certain vexations and apprehensions draw out and develop their worse side, primarily in mere self-defence, though with, in many cases, a more aggressive intent as habit grows.

Of course there are people who will allow themselves to be pushed to a very great extent to the wall rather than forgo what are to them the pleasures of courtesy and of generosity. Presumably an organisation, that tends to be specially congenial to such people, will rarely lose any of them whom it has the luck to get and, since birds of a feather certainly do tend to flock. the proportion will gradually grow.

When however, this was first said to me a good many years ago, I thought and to-day I think still that what those speakers were saying (and it happens to have been written again very lately by a lady who with considerable experience of the world came into the Partnership for a short time and wrote this upon her marriage and retirement) was and is true but that the main cause was and still is that in a profit-seeking undertaking, in which there is no exploitation and a constant aim to achieve in all things as much fairness as possible, there develops to an important extent a general good temper and kindliness that draws out and fosters the better side of those who in very different conditions would be to a really important extent very different persons.

These things are perhaps worth mentioning here, though it is obviously possible to doubt their genuineness and also to doubt whether, even if they are genuine, they are sufficiently typical to have real importance.

POSSIBLE VALUE TO THE NATION

But suppose for a moment that upon these lines it is really possible to have enough of the psychological advantages of small-scale ownership and yet to have at the same time genuine teamwork on any scale necessary for efficiency. Might that not increase enormously the efficiency of British industry, enlarge its output, diminish the wastage and altogether raise the national income as that income must be raised if we are to have henceforward a good living?

A FRESH TRY AT AN OLD PROBLEM

6. As the ideas indicated by the adoption of this word "partnership" arose and their implications were gradually worked out, it became plain that the undertaking had developed into one more of the many attempts, that there have been and still are, to make a practical success of the idea of the Self-Governing Workshop or Cooperative Society of Producers.

Of those previous attempts one of the most famous was Robert Owen's a hundred and forty years ago. His early results at New Lanark attracted world-wide notice but in the end they came to nothing.

This present experiment owes nothing to Owen or to any other practitioner or theorist. The main lines of the plan were completed with no knowledge of that kind either from books or from personal contacts. This is not said for the sake of claiming originality but to make plain the fact that the whole thing has been a gradual, natural growth from practical efforts to solve the problems of one particular business. Many at all events of the ideas, that the experiment embodies, are very obvious and, if in the whole thing there is something of real importance, that something must presumably be original, for otherwise one or more of the previous ventures of the same sort, Owen's or another, would presumably have succeeded. This is not to say that all of them have come to nothing. "A survey of profit-sharing and co-partnership schemes in industry" published very lately with the title "Co-partnership To-day" mentions several such organisations of which the scale seems to be large.

But it is an obvious fact that as yet the idea of the Self-Governing Workshop or Cooperative Society of Producers or, as we call it in our own partnership, the idea of Partnership on the Scale of Modern Industry, has had no results at all comparable with those of the idea of the Cooperative Society of Consumers.

ENDING CA'CANNY

7. Opinions will of course differ whether the written constitution, as it stands at present, of this particular partnership goes about as far as at present is really possible towards reducing in modern large-scale industry excessive inequality in the distribution of power, income, sense of security and the other satisfactions of ownership.

But it surely cannot be denied that genuine adoption of these proposals themselves would be a considerable step towards a world far more reasonable, more decent, better for the real happiness of all of us? Perhaps it might suffice to produce such a general inclination to do one's best as we have now got to achieve somehow if the productive work of our country is to give us all a good living or even any living at all. In these, however, and in a multitude of other respects the system, that this book describes, for substituting partnership for exploiting employment, can be varied according to the ideas of those who create particular partnerships or come somehow into control of one. As I have repeated here and there in it, this book does not contend that the John Lewis Partnership is the best or one of the best of the forms that might be given to the general conception of partnership for all. Our particular venture has been and is still truly experimental. Its aim has been and is still simply to find out and to demonstrate what happens if certain things are done.

A SEVERE TEST OF TOUGHNESS

8. I have been trying to give some idea of what in this particular case has happened so far but perhaps enough has not been said upon one point, the toughness and resilience that the Partnership showed under the test of this war. That test was searching. The Partnership was bombed very severely indeed. Its achievement under that test and certain other symptoms, such as the type of recruit whom it has long shown and still shows itself able to attract, may perhaps be thought to indicate that the general plan is sound.

ABOVE PARTY POLITICS

9. How far, if sound, it is in harmony with the ideas of our time was shown amusingly in an item headed "Politics" in THE GAZETTE of 1946, reprinted here under "Journalism" (paragraph 644). It indicates incidentally the length to which the Partnership is able without any disadvantage—indeed, I believe, with substantial advantage to discipline and general efficiency—to carry a democratic freedom of speech but it is reprinted in this book as evidence that partnerships of this general type are agreeable to the ideas of members of all of our four political parties, Conservative, Liberal, Socialist and Communist.

IRREVOCABLE SETTLEMENTS

10. By April of 1929 this experiment had reached the stage of giving rise to what lawyers call an irrevocable settlement in trust but this was not in itself a complete foundation for the Partnership. It secured that, so long as the business should not be wound up, its profits must go to its workers but I felt that, until the results of this first step should seem to be solidly satisfactory, I must retain power to bring the whole experiment to an end. There had to be some years of further development before that first settlement could be supplemented by a second. That maturity was really reached somewhere about 1940. But for the war, the making of the second settlement and the writing of this book would have come then. Difficulties, that have hindered now the making of the second settlement, are indicated in paragraph 502.

RESULTS PRESENT AND PROSPECTIVE

11. On the latest count the present number of the Partners, that is to say the whole-time workers in the Partnership's business, is almost exactly twelve thousand. The Partnership would have been well worth creating if it had merely made the working lives of a good many of that community as happy as I am told and believe that it has. But some of us, who have devoted to it our working-lives or a considerable part of them, have hoped that it would do more than this. We have hoped that upon some problems of great urgency and importance in our modern world it would throw light useful in the development of public opinion and perhaps to legislators. Whether that hope was well founded must be judged from this book. The financial consequences to the Partners are given at the end of Part III.

COPYRIGHT AND AUTHORSHIP

12. The copyright of this book belongs to the Partnership and I wanted the authorship to be ascribed to its Council.

A time may come—and perhaps quickly—when partnership of this general type will be an idea so familiar and a practice so general that there will be little need of care lest any particular venture of that kind may be supposed mistakenly to be a partnership in name rather than in reality.

But at present it seems desirable to be extremely careful of everything whatever that may contribute appreciably to prevent any such mistake and on the other hand to build up and maintain a general sense of team-work, a general feeling that the Partnership does not depend upon any one person or group but is a true democracy, a true community of all its members.

In the course of years the John Lewis Partnership has come to be the work of many minds and of many hearts and I hoped that a special committee of the Council could play in the production of this book a part that would justify that ascription of its authorship. Such a committee did collaborate with me for a considerable time and gave valuable help but in the end they felt so strongly that the book, in ceasing to be my own personal utterance, lost vitality that I felt that I must give way.

The writing has taken some years. It has had to be done largely from memory that has kept on suggesting additions awkward to fit into the text as by then it stood. The work needed continuous effort from a fresh mind. It has had to be done at odd times and with a tired mind. My own share in the management of the Partnership's business has always been very much a whole-time occupation and this book has been written in fact in irregular snatches under the strain of the position of chief individual responsibility for such a business in the latter years of the war and in the hardly less harassing subsequent conditions up to this present time.

SOMETHING TO SHOW

13. The publication of any book was delayed deliberately until the Partnership should be able to show such results as now it can. Because of the war they are far smaller than otherwise they might have been by this time but even before the war, when they were very much smaller still, they seemed to be already just about large enough. The distribution of Partnership Benefit had exceeded a quarter of a million pounds. The number of members exceeded five thousand. The total capital ran into millions and the system seemed to be sufficiently mature, sufficiently completely and firmly settled.

In 1938 a large publishing company suggested that some such book as this should be written about the Partnership and but for the war this book would, I think, have been in existence upwards of five years ago. It was of course always obvious that, if the experiment persisted, a book about it must be written sooner or later. Delay, however, until actual results should have reached the general scale, that I have mentioned, seemed desirable. Ideas of this kind must have some savour of Utopianism and have generally come to nothing. For this as well as for other reasons they are apt to encounter a rather too ready scepticism, a rather too prompt and obstinate confidence that "it is too good to be true". In our own partnership it has happened repeatedly that newcomers, especially if they had joined *en masse* and, as it were, involuntarily by reason of our taking over some business in which they were already employed, have, upon finding themselves getting what they felt to be "something for nothing", enquired at once "What's the catch?" They could not believe that this was not a new device for exploitation. Such scepticism tends of course to secure its own fulfilment. If the minds of those, whose cooperation may be necessary to the success of an innovation, are closed against it, it may come to nothing not inevitably but because they do not take it seriously.

Accordingly in this case publication was delayed deliberately until the innovation could be put forward as a matter not of theory but of practice, not as a plan, an intention, but as something that in actual experiment had been tried out sufficiently.

14. The 22nd of next September (1948) will end the forty-fourth year since on my nineteenth birthday I entered my father's business. For over forty of these years I have been consciously thinking out this set of ideas and trying to build up from them an organisation that would be really a living thing, capable of maintaining itself and of growing quite independently of any particular person or family.

1908

The work has always seemed to me to be really a new form of political career. As a matter of fact in my own case it involved declining in my early twenties a number of invitations to stand for Parliament, including a very attractive one from the Whips of the Government of the day. I had no financial motive for remaining in the business-world. My father had given me already a handsome independence. Moreover, he told the Whips in my presence that he was sure I should find it impossible to combine a public career with retention of the business but that he was entirely willing that I should accept their invitation and I felt no doubt that, if I did, I should inherit a great part and very probably the whole of so much of his fortune as he had not given by that time to me or to my brother—between whom and my father there had been subsequently a complete breach.

Passionately fond, as I have been, of various sports I should rate above all others the fun of speaking upon matters on which feeling runs high—especially of impromptu speaking and of repartee—and I have never ceased to feel wistful hankerings for what might perhaps have been. But I felt then and I have felt ever since that there is in the modern world very great need of far-reaching practical experiment to show what does in fact happen if certain things are done, experiments that in some cases, as in this one, may be upon the scale of thousands of workers, millions of money and perhaps more than one lifetime.

I felt that the supply of such practical experimenters was as yet too small—indeed, so far as I knew, there were as yet hardly any—while on the other hand there was no shortage of theorists or of publicists and advocates of theories or of people willing and more or less well qualified to serve as legislators, seeking to coerce others to proceed in certain ways. The results of any particular experiment may be merely negative but, even so, they may still be very valuable light to other experimenters or to theorists or to legislators.

A LONG SLOW JOB AND AT BEST A GAMBLE

15. My father reached the age of ninety-two and never retired. That exceptional chance crippled for upwards of fifteen years this partnership's development. Ten years later the approach and advent of this war crippled it again for upwards of seven years more, to say nothing of all, that we lost and are losing still, by our special bad luck in being so heavily bombed. But for these happenings our present stage, that barely amounts to maturity, would have been reached long ago and we should have made much further progress towards strength of every kind.

All living things, however, even the toughest, are at the mercy of chance. Only within narrow limits can they survive calamity. Time alone can show whether this particular partnership has already, as I hope, become independently alive or at all events will do so.

Whatever its vitality, whatever its toughness, it may of course encounter calamity that it will not survive as it has survived the tremendous disaster of its bombing in 1940.

Even if in its design or otherwise it has no fatal flaw, it may be overwhelmed nevertheless by some mere mischance. In either case it will not be, as I have always hoped and as I hope still, a fairly impressive demonstration of certain possibilities, a practical example of which the influence may be perhaps strong.

IF THIS EFFORT FAILS LET OTHERS BE MADE

16. But, whether or not that particular hope is disappointed, there should be, I believe, much further experiment in this general direction, the direction of the Self-Governing Workshop, the Producer Cooperative, the direction in which Robert Owen achieved for a time so much and in the end so little.

Partnership is justice. Better than justice, it is kindness. It is harmony with what some people call the Nature of Things and some the Will of God. All civilisation is movement this way. The goal seems very far off but let us make here and there whatever beginnings we can. If, as our scientists tell us, we are still in the very early infancy of mankind, we must have patience and hope.

FOUR INVITATIONS

17. Criticisms and suggestions, either for the development of the Partnership or for a possible re-editing of this book, will be welcome. They should be addressed to the Editor, THE GAZETTE, John Lewis and Company Limited, Oxford Street, London, W.1, or to me at the same address.

Enquiries from anyone, who may be inclined to offer to join the Partnership or to advise someone else to do so, should be addressed there to the Director of Personnel.

Enquiries from anyone interested in the financial structure of the Partnership should be addressed there to the Director of Financial Operations. The Stock that has been distributed to the Partners as Partnership Benefit is the 7½% Cumulative Preferred Ordinary Stock of John Lewis Partnership Limited. In recent years each unit of this stock has been issued in respect of 30/- of new capital and the Stock is entitled in certain circumstances to 30/- a unit in a winding up. Some amendments to the Trust Settlement of 1929 will come before the Court of Chancery in October 1948. If they are approved by the Court, the Stock will be issued thenceforward at 5% instead of at 7½% and each unit of Stock will be issued in respect of 20/- of capital instead of 30/-. Many of the recipients want to sell it, so as to use the capital in some other way. It is a great feature of the whole plan that they shall be quite free to do this. The Stock was created in 1929. For the next ten years the dividend was paid punctually each half year. The flow was stopped by the war and the bombing of five of our businesses including the largest and most important but the dividend was cumulative. Payment began again in 1944 and by 1945 all the arrears had been paid off. We hope and believe that the half-yearly payments will be as punctual henceforward as before the war they always were.

Enquiries from anyone, who is connected with a business of almost any kind and of almost any size and in almost any country and who may be able and inclined to bring that business into the Partnership, should be addressed there to the Director of Expansion. In such cases the Partnership's main principles must of course be accepted. Among other things this means that the operations of its Branches must be combined to any extent that may be of important advantage to the quality and value of the goods to be produced or distributed or to the service that can be given in other ways. But within these limits there can be a very high degree of local self-government. Present leaders of any business brought thus into the Partnership could probably continue as long as they liked up to seventy-five years of age, the Partnership's limit for any tenure of authority. But any such arrangement must be terminable from the side of the Partnership by the payment of a definite sum of money. The sum may be large but to that extent the Partnership must be safe against finding that it has got into its team one or more people with whom that team as a whole cannot work satisfactorily.

J. SPEDAN LEWIS.

CONTENTS

PART ONE

FORTY–FOUR YEARS OF EXPERIENCE
1904–1948

CHAPTER 1
BUSINESS AS IT USED TO BE

18. TOWARDS the end of my time at Westminster, my parents said to me that I ought to be making up my mind whether, when I left school, I would go into the business or to Oxford. My mother added that, if I really wanted to go into the business, I ought in her opinion to give up the idea of going to Oxford, for she thought that it was virtually certain that, if I delayed to that extent, my father would be obliged by the decline of his health (he was then nearly seventy) either to sell the business or to take a partner.

THE STILL LIQUID CORE OF THINGS

I chose the business upon a vague idea that the business-world was the still liquid core of things, in which as yet there had been little crystallisation, little wearing of grooves, and in which there was corresponding freedom and scope for initiative.

My knowledge of life was extremely narrow. In my preparatory school and at Westminster I had always been a day boy and our private circle could scarcely have been smaller. My father practically never entertained at all and my brother and I had hardly ever stayed in any house but our own home and the house of our aunts at Weston-super-Mare. So far, however, as I can judge, no difference in these respects would have prevented my going, as I did, in 1904, on my nineteenth birthday, into the business that my father had started in Oxford Street forty years ago in one little shop. It was and always had been wholly his property.

OPPORTUNITY MISUSED

19. At home we had regarded him as a superman, virtually infallible in matters of business. I had not expected in the very least to find that his business was in fact no more than a second-rate success achieved in a first-rate opportunity. But that is what I did find. Fate had given my father an occupation that did not suit him. His abilities, especially his industry and thrift, had enabled him to make a very handsome fortune. At this time it was about £300,000. But this achievement, great as it was, was very far short of those of some of his contemporaries, Mr. William Whiteley, for example, Mr. Frederick Gorringe and Mr. Owen Owen of Liverpool.

For the next ten years of my life one of the most important of my occupations was an effort to see where my father had been right and where he had been wrong. I came to the conclusion that his ideas were absolutely sound. I think so still. But his practice was a very different matter.

FALSE ECONOMY AND ITS CONSEQUENCES

20. In theory he was perfectly willing to pay enough to get the right worker for a given post. In practice he could never believe that any particular post was worth more than a very small figure. He constantly preached the doctrine: "Praise in public and blame in private". In practice he blamed in public at the top of his voice and hardly ever praised at all.

He often said that the most frequent cause of failure in business is omission to keep sufficient accounts and to pay sufficient attention to them. "The Counting House", he was fond of remarking, "is a clock. You should be guided but not ruled by it". In practice the insufficiency of his figures and his inattention to them were almost unbelievable.

The audit was in charge of the junior partner of a certain small firm whose total remuneration for the audit and for keeping the private books was one hundred pounds a year. On, I think, almost the first occasion of our being alone together, this gentleman told me that he was very glad that one of the family was coming into the business "for", said he (I cannot, of course, guarantee that these are his exact words but I am absolutely sure that they are very nearly so), "no one knows what is going on here. Your father makes our firm keep the private books. I produce the accounts year after year and take them in to him. He takes them out of my hand, starts to talk to me about the Land Laws, unlocks a drawer in that desk, puts the accounts into it and locks them up. I know perfectly well that he will never look at them and, if anything went wrong with the business, our position might be very awkward."

To a certain extent things did go wrong. Both the head of my father's Post Order Department and the head of his Counting House robbed him for years on a great scale. One got eighteen months' hard labour. The other absconded to New Zealand.

Because of my father's inattention to figures there was in many of the departments an astounding accumulation of stale stock and there was also a shocking waste of floor-space that on such a site was of course extremely valuable. A great deal of it was not used at all. The whole of the third floor served simply as a stockroom. It had been fitted out at great cost with a vague idea of doing a wholesale trade but nothing had come of that. Two rooms on the second floor and the whole of the basement ran at a loss and at the north end of the basement two great rooms were completely empty except for some lumber.

21. Altogether it was glaringly obvious even to such a beginner as I was, that, however great had been at some past time the general efficiency of the business—and in earlier years it certainly must have been very great indeed—my father had by this time got himself into the position of being the captain of a big ship much under-engined and with those engines much under-fuelled. As a whole his staff were not nearly good enough and they had no sufficient motive to do their best. My father was more or less conscious that great parts of the floor-space were idle or nearly so and, so far as he was conscious of it, of course the thought vexed and worried him. But that consciousness was almost unbelievably small. As was shown by his amazement, when he read in newspapers the fortunes that had been made in some other careers like his own, he was extremely out of touch with what was happening outside his own business.

22. When, after a year, my brother, who was a little younger, came likewise into the business, he began after a while to concentrate upon the Counting House and there he found the same astonishing inefficiency. He found it in the method of the investment of the surplus of my father's income over his private expenditure and the slowly growing requirements of the business. He found it also in the management of these investments after they had been made. They were almost all in house or shop-property and by this time there were more than a hundred of them. With a view to this recurrent need to find some use for spare capital my father watched the property-advertisements in the newspapers. When he saw one, that attracted him, it would be snipped out with the scissors, kept for that purpose beside his armchair, and it would be put into the drawer of an inkstand that is before me at this moment. If anything particularly attractive caught his eye, he might move at once towards making the purchase but as a general rule he would wait until the manager of his Counting House bothered him again about the accumulation of surplus funds in the bank. Then he would look at the accumulation of advertisements and pick out one of the more recent. If the property in question was not too far off and he was not too busy and he was feeling energetic, he would drive to see it but sometimes he would bid (the purchases were largely made at auction) without having seen the property and without any surveyor's report or similar precautions.

23. His general knowledge of property-values brought him among these purchases some real plums and he would refer complacently to the fact that in Cumberland Place he had a property that paid him eleven per cent. and that in Rathbone Place he had another that paid ten per cent. and so on. But, just as it never occurred to him to have separate profit and loss accounts of the several departments of his business, so it never occurred to him to ask himself what was the overall yield of this considerable total estate.

If a property fell vacant or was so when he bought it, his various agents used to lament that, except, perhaps, when it had been empty for a long time, they could never get him to accept any but the somewhat optimistic rental to which, when he made the purchase, he had looked forward.

My brother now took it upon himself to ascertain the overall yield of all those separate properties. He found that it was three per cent., and in my hearing he announced that discovery to my father with intent to go on to urge certain changes of policy in the general direction of the advice of the agents and of the manager of the Counting House and of other people who had some acquaintance with this side of my father's affairs. The conversation did not go so far. My brother was promptly and energetically rebuked for intruding upon matters that did not concern him and upon which it was not possible that his opinion should have value.

WHO SUFFERED BY THIS WASTE OF OPPORTUNITY?

23.   But, when all was said and done, from a very small beginning long ago my father had made a great fortune. He had always been very thrifty but, though he had lived quietly, he had, I think, from very early days lived comfortably. For upwards of twenty years be had had on the edge of Hampstead Heath a commodious house with a fine garden. He drove a good pair of horses and, when he took to motoring, he got as a matter of course a Rolls.

At the same time his customers had been served extremely well. His fortune had been made by no sort of trickery but by the genuine efficiency of those comparatively few departments of his business that were properly developed and that occupied almost all of the ground floor and about half of the first. The great reputation of the business had been made by them. The others did not amount to much. But, as a whole, the shop, had it been closed down suddenly, would have been a serious loss to thousands of people. They would not have been able to find anywhere else either the convenience of the large stocks, constantly very complete in their variety, or such value as my father endeavoured to give in all of his departments and succeeded very notably in giving in all those that were well developed.

What then did it matter if as an unconscious hobby my father had been keeping the rest of his floor-space and capital unused or nearly so? If he had made so ample a fortune and at the same time his customers had been well served, what did it matter if a good part of his capital and of the floor-space of the business had been in a real sense wastefully idle?

The answer was that it mattered to his staff—and that to them it had mattered terribly.

THE DIVISION OF THE EARNINGS OF THE BUSINESS

25. It was, I think, in 1908 that the figures came first to my own knowledge. By that time my brother and I had each been given on our twenty-first birthdays a capital of £50,000 (one quarter of the capital in the business) and a partnership carrying one quarter of the profits after five per cent. had been paid upon the capital.

From first to last my father lost a very great deal of money by going to law. For all his great ability and success in business he could not, it seemed, grasp the idea that the law might not be whatever he thought that in that particular case it ought to be.

In this case he thought the law should and would allow him to avoid Estate Duty (commonly called Death Duty) by making such gifts as these in his lifetime but leave him free to revoke at any time the gifts of capital and to declare that the partnerships did not exist. He knew that the legal term of such a partnership was a "partnership at will" but he was quite sure that that must mean simply at his will.

All this became clear within a few months of my brother's twenty-first birthday but up to that time the business had three owner-managers.

TOO MUCH FOR THREE—TOO LITTLE FOR THREE HUNDRED

To them it was yielding altogether about twenty-six thousand pounds a year but to all the other people, who were likewise giving to it the whole of their working-lives, it was yielding only about another sixteen thousand pounds. When I say "all the other people", I am not including those of the Workroom Staff who were paid weekly but I am including all the senior people in the Workrooms and the whole of the staff of all the rest of the business. It must be remembered that of the three owner-managers one had reached an age at which he would have ridiculed the idea of employing anybody else. Physically he himself was lively. From the standpoint, however, of business efficiency he was by no means young for his age. He was, in fact, very much "behind the times". As for my brother and myself we were green beginners.

26. Of all the other people, who were making their living out of that business, only four were drawing more than two hundred and fifty pounds a year. Of them, one was getting one thousand, the other three much less. No one else was getting as much as five pounds a week and very few were getting as much as four. Indeed not many were getting over thirty shillings.

PROMOTING YOUR OWN PEOPLE

27. The superior positions, such as Buyerships, were almost always filled by promotion from the Rank and File. The weakness of their bargaining-position made that far the cheapest way. On the side of the employee the

terms of appointment were almost always a contract for five years with power to the employer to terminate at three months' notice. For the first of these five years the salary was generally one hundred pounds a year with lunch and tea and the contract provided for three yearly increases of ten pounds and for one of twenty pounds to one hundred and fifty pounds in the fifth year. There was never any commission or other addition to the fixed salary. (The Selling Staff received "premiums" for selling particular articles but no commission upon their other sales).

If the man (no Buyership was ever given to a woman) thus promoted made a good impression, he would be offered at or somewhat before the end of his first five years a fresh engagement for a further five. This might begin at one hundred and sixty pounds or, if the impression had been very good, at two hundred pounds but the jump from one set of terms to the next would hardly ever be higher than this and the step from year to year would be again about ten or twenty pounds.

These men had the spending of large sums and, when they had had some years of experience in buying and had become known in their particular market, they must obviously have had some inclination to seek better-paid employment.

RESTRICTIVE AGREEMENTS

28. But the terms of the original appointment included a provision that they must not take to any competitor within a radius of three miles their knowledge of the firm's sources of supply, rates of profit and other business secrets.

I am nearly sure that I am right in saying that my father got the idea of these radius agreements from the Baker firm in Bristol and it is interesting to remember that both my father, who was for some years in the employ of Mr. Peter Robinson, and the founder of Baker, Baker and Baker had set up for themselves very near to the business in which they were last employed and in which they had got all the most important part of their technical knowledge.

From the standpoint of the interest of the general community such arrangements for the protection of business secrets are not altogether indefensible. Even from the standpoint of the individual worker there is something to be said for them. Some business secrets are the result of years of work, much taking of risk and perhaps the incurring of considerable losses. If any worker, who is admitted to knowledge of them, is to be free to sell them to any competitor of his late employer, then employers will presumably tend to be correspondingly chary of admitting to such knowledge anyone whom they do not feel that they know very well. Moreover they will do all, that they can, to split posts up so that the amount of knowledge, that can be got by the holder of any one post, is as small as possible. Such arrangements may tend to inefficiency disadvantageous to the general community and they may also tend to keep pay rates down and to make promotion slow. On the other hand, as this last war has shown so abundantly, restrictive regulations tend to give the cunning and the unscrupulous a very great advantage over the dull and the scrupulous. Contracts of this kind are apt to be a much more serious matter for workers with a strong sense of honour than for those who either never intended to keep the promise, to which they were signing their name, or who having got the information persuade themselves that in the particular case they are entitled to break the promise.

29. The Partnership makes no radius agreements and I feel pretty sure that for the remainder of my own time we shall see our way to do without them. But it seems to me quite conceivable that some future development may require something of the kind. If so, I would urge that it should be restricted most carefully to whatever is thought to be absolutely necessary and that there should be the very greatest pains to make it impossible for any reasonable person to feel that this or any other form of contract, that makes it difficult for the worker to leave the Partnership, results in his being paid less than he probably might be if that difficulty did not exist. On the other hand, any contracts, that are made, should be maintained quite sufficiently firmly.

I think there is no doubt at all that the radius-agreements, that at the time of which I am speaking my father made with all his Buyers, affected strongly their willingness to accept new contracts on terms that otherwise they would have declined.

The validity of these agreements was tested in a law-suit between my father and Mr. Whiteley. Mr. Whiteley lost it. The Buyer, whom he had enticed away, returned to my father. He never tried to leave again and in the end he became far the most important member of my father's staff. The silk trade, for which my father's business was chiefly famous and that was his chief source of profit, was in great measure that Buyer's creation. He died in his early fifties. He was then getting one thousand pounds a year and he once said to me that he "reckoned he was the worst-paid man in the trade".

A BARE LIVING

30. This extreme thriftiness extended, of course, to all expenses. In this last war the records were bombed and I am speaking from memory, but most of these figures are exactly and all of them are approximately correct. The pay-rates for the Buyerships were exactly those that I have mentioned. Few, if any, of the superintendents (shop-walkers, as they were called in those days) got as much as one hundred pounds a year and all other pay-rates were of course proportionate. In fact, as a whole

the staff were getting just a bare living, with very little margin beyond absolute necessaries and correspondingly little chance to get much fun out of life and at the same time feel that they were saving adequately for their retirement.

The value of money and the cost of living were of course in those days very different. But these pay-rates seemed somewhat modest in comparison with the incomes of the three owner-managers.

Moreover, the pay-rates were not supplemented in any way. Absence for illness almost always meant stoppage of pay. Only in very special cases was there any help in that or in, any other trouble. The business was forty years old but there was not a single pensioner or any prospect of a pension for anybody and not a penny was spent on playing-fields or on any other amenity for the staff. In all such ways the management could hardly have been more ruthlessly close-fisted.

Obviously such a state of affairs could not have existed unless the general conditions at that time had been more or less similar and, though in money matters the management was so close-fisted, it must not be forgotten that a good many workers of quite good capacity chose to stay year after year. There was no petty trickery and the atmosphere was completely free from anything disreputable or otherwise unpleasant. To me, however, whose experience of life had been limited to school and my father's home, all this seemed shocking.

TIMES HAVE CHANGED

31.   Moreover, ideas were beginning to change. For a long time the drapery trade's pay-rates and the board and lodging provided for those, who "lived in," had been screwed down as shops became larger and the contact between employer and employee diminished.

By the time, of which we are speaking, it had become a general saying in the trade that the drapers used to get the farmer's son and that now they only got the farmer's labourer's son. This state of affairs was not peculiar to the retail drapery trade. It was part of the general perversion of the proper working of capitalism, a perversion that was starving British industry of its proper share of the brains of the nation and that was thereby lowering the national income.

From the policy, that had produced this state of affairs, of screwing expenses down and down, there was beginning to be some reaction. The growing scarcity of good workers produced some increases of pay-rates and, even more, I think, was there a tendency to provide better board and lodging for those who lived in.

The housekeeping in the hostel we had at 42 Weymouth Street and the catering in the staff dining-room at Oxford Street were the first thing in the way of executive power that came into my own hands. It was really not at all a bad way to get some practical experience of actual management and it enabled me to do quite a lot for the staff.

The catering had been so inefficient that I was able to save a really important amount of money. Every penny of it was cheerfully embezzled for unauthorised mitigations of the prescribed austerity.

A SMOOTH BEGINNING   1904-8

32. During most of these first few years I was in very high favour. I had taken to the business as a duckling to the water and my father had never in his life worked with anyone who had spent his first nineteen years in learning to learn. He told me once that he was amazed at the way in which my brother and I had learned, as he said, in a day to do things that he would not have expected us to grasp in less than six months. But, apart from the advantage of our education and of the pains that everyone naturally took to explain things to us and to help us, there is the history of Peter Jones and of my father's business since his death to show that, whereas my father had achieved a great but not a really first-class success by the exertion of great gifts in an occupation that was really far from being his natural field, my mother had transmitted to me qualities that had come out in her brothers who had been very successful in business of this sort and that, combined, as I suppose they must have been, with a sufficiency of my father's own qualities, made shop-keeping an occupation less unsuitable to me than it really was to him.

A LESS SMOOTH CONTINUANCE

33. Magnificently liberal though my father had been in giving such partnerships to two boys of twenty-one, the perversity of some of his notions and the arbitrariness of his temper made the strain of working with him considerable. His senior men, one after another, had found it unbearable. Their employer did not mean thus to make his business too hot to hold them. They had come to him as youngsters. He had had real pleasure in promoting them from the ranks and step by step to more and more important posts. They were now middle-aged and after very full thought he had decided that, rather than lose them, he had better give them their present rate of pay. They had been able to make him feel that he could not afford to refuse it to them but, when he had made the concession, he literally could not bear the thought that somebody's rate of pay had risen so far and with those people he became so irritable that, though in a sense he desired to keep them, he did, in fact, drive them out of his team.

THE FEAR OF POVERTY.

34. The conditions of his early life had so over-developed in him a passion for accumulating money and a dread of losing it that, where money was concerned, he was like a man driven by a demon.

He had real sympathy with the poor. He was delighted to see thrift and modest success. His temperament was strongly towards equality and freedom. (In politics he was a fierce radical and a republican—though a saucy member of his family suggested now and again that these equalitarian notions were tempered by a firm belief in the Divine Right of Employers.) In his seventieth year he defied the Courts of Law and went to prison for three weeks sooner than submit to what he felt to be an abuse of the legal rights of his landlord.

In that and other litigation he spent money like water. Yet, with this strong sense of the real values in human life and with this capacity for spending on an almost heroic scale when his temper was roused, his mind was in general hopelessly dominated and warped by an over-developed impulse to make money and by fear of losing it.

35. Looking back I am inclined to think that, though on various occasions my father showed great courage, the governing impulse of his long, hard-working and in many ways self-denying life was fear. I think that upon his particular temperament the poverty of his early years had made such an impression that the real governing impulse of his whole life was to achieve for himself in that respect the greatest possible margin of safety and to do the same thing for his children.

I think that to his subconscious mind the fortune, to the making and enlargement of which he devoted himself so utterly, represented not spending power but safety, safety from poverty, and that his intense desire to have two children, both sons (and his resolve to have no more than two) was really his way of giving value after his own life-time to his life-work of creating for himself and his household extreme safety from poverty. The second son was simply an insurance against the possibility that he might lose one.

PROVIDING FOR THE NEXT GENERATION

36. Obviously, if this idea is sound, it may mean that some sufficient freedom thus to "provide for" the next generation may be a very important—even an indispensable—part of the incentive that the general community, however much they may dislike the idea of such privilege, may for their own sakes have to give to possessors of exceptional ability.

It is, I think, relevant and noteworthy that my father constantly showed entire willingness that my brother and I should go to a university and enter some profession instead of succeeding him in the business that he had spent forty years in creating and in which he showed a natural and real pride. He was of course very conscious of the potentialities of the business as a source of income and he used to speak strongly of the advantage of the scope that it afforded for safe investment at a good rate of interest. But it seemed very clear that what he really cared for was the capital, the fortune, the ample independent means, the safety from poverty.

37.   I have been told that, when I was twenty minutes old, he asked me if I was going to take Silk (i.e., become a King's Counsel) and I think that he would not have been much, if at all, displeased if instead of entering the business I had gone to Oxford and the Bar.

1908

As I have mentioned in the Preface, after I had made in the business a start, with which he was well pleased, he seemed entirely willing that I should give it up for a career in public life. His desire for an heir was in fact not for the sake of the business as a thing in itself but for the sake of the fortune.

My father had "started for himself" at twenty-eight. For the next twenty years he had lived a very lonely bachelor life and he told me once that much of that time had been so hard and so dreary that he doubted if he could bring himself to go through it again.

It is, I think, significant that to someone, who had paid such a price for the creation of a business and who was quite genuinely and justifiably proud of it, the business meant nevertheless no more than it seems to have done to my father.

The thing was indeed never put to an absolute test and it is a fact that right up to the end of his life he continued to spend in the business as much time as his health would allow but he certainly seemed quite genuinely willing that it should "go out of the family" and, so far as that really was so, it does perhaps strengthen the argument for the view that among the necessary incentives to the development and exertion of uncommon ability may be the power to bequeath to the next generation economic security, financial independence—just that in itself quite separately from any other considerations, such as the continuance of a family business.

SIMPLE HUMANITY ON A GREAT SCALE

38.   To me my father always seems to have been an example of simple human nature highly magnified. In studying his mind I felt that I was looking through a microscope at ordinary human nature. His aims in life, his ideas and his methods were really quite ordinary but the ideas were held with a vigour and the methods were applied with an energy that was very far indeed from being ordinary. With very little education and no friends he found himself in an occupation to which he was in many ways ill suited. Nevertheless, in our fiercely competitive world he

achieved great success and he did it by methods that according to his lights were scrupulously clean.

He was a hard employer and, moreover, very arbitrary. In the end his methods provoked a great strike. Nevertheless, his staff often showed in one way and another a real respect and I think it would not be too strong to say an affectionate regard for him. Britons are said to be apt to develop a liking for anyone who is what is sometimes called "a character," especially if the vitality and unusualness, that win that name, are combined, as they were in my father, with conspicuous pluck.

A USEFUL LIFE

39.   If my father's health or custom or such a law, as may perhaps be made some day, had constrained him to retire even at seventy-five, his career would have been on the whole a quite genuine piece of substantial public service. Certainly the good fortune, that he had in so many ways, enabled him to create for himself an opportunity much greater than he was able to use. Like a man, who builds a boat so heavy that he cannot handle it properly, he added to his earlier smaller business, of which his management was brilliantly successful, a great deal of further space and capital. To do justice to this, he needed to be able to share profit and power to an extent that his temperament did not allow. The team, that he built up, was utterly inadequate to the possibilities of his business. But, until the whole thing got to that scale, it was a first-rate piece of work. Thousands of people got from it things that they wanted and that they could not have found elsewhere and the reputation of that business for value and general trustworthiness was no less strong than its reputation for providing a quite exceptionally wide choice in such things as my father understood and that were in reality the whole of his business.

From first to last throughout the whole of his long career my father held steadily to a simple policy of genuine solid service. He took immense pains to have constantly in stock the greatest possible choice in goods of certain kinds. He took equal pains to give really good value and to win in all other ways a first-rate reputation for general trustworthiness.

THE NAME OF THE PARTNERSHIP

It was his success, as it seemed to me, in those aims that made me feel that it would be good for the Partnership to bear his name.

CHAPTER 2

THE PLANNING OF THE PARTNERSHIP

40. WHEN I declined the invitation, of which I have just spoken, from the Government Whips the idea of the Partnership was not already clear in my head but I had begun to feel I was on the way to something that would justify the notion that had led me to come into the business, the notion that the business-world was the still liquid core of things in which possibilities of creative work were more various and perhaps in a sense larger than in any other field except art and science.

MISUSE OF POWER

My father, my brother and I had been drawing from the business ten thousand pounds a year in interest upon its capital and a further sixteen thousand pounds or more in profit. This latter amount was about as much as the whole of the staff except only certain factory workers were getting between them. Hardly any of the staff had ever had more than a meagre living. For years my father, while living, as it seemed to me very comfortably, and giving both of his sons a first-class education, had been saving money at a great rate. As all this dawned upon me, I asked myself what had become of those savings. Most of them had financed the growth of the business but I saw that quite a lot of them had gone into rather wrong-headed (at all events it was generally unsuccessful) litigation and a large remainder had gone into investments of which the making and the management were really nothing but a nuisance to their possessor.

41. As I turned these things over in my mind, it occurred to me that, if a very much larger proportion of the income from the business had gone to the other people who were likewise giving their own working-lives to it, the business itself would have been vastly more efficient and my father's life would have been really far happier. To get the work of a fairly large business done for about the very lowest pay-sheet, that is practicable, means constant fret and bother of one sort and another and, however contented may be the particular people, who choose to accept that employment and to continue in it, they cannot be either in quantity or in quality as good a team as the business really requires.

It became gradually clear to me that, for my father's business to be really healthy, one of two things ought to have been happening. Either the owner ought to have been taking a great deal less, so as to leave the staff a great deal more of such profit as the business was making, or else the business ought to have been managed very much more efficiently, so that the same result would have been achieved in a different way.

The charge of five per cent. upon the whole of the capital, wastefully though much of that capital was used, would have left a good living for a really adequate staff but the profit, that the three partners were taking for themselves over and above the five per cent. on the whole of the capital meant that the business was starved of competent workers.

THINGS, AS WELL AS PEOPLE, HAVE IN A WAY RIGHTS OF THEIR OWN

42.   As all this became clearer and clearer to me and I thought about it, I came to see that an enterprise, a business, is a living thing with rights of its own. Its earnings ought to be used with real care for its own efficiency, exactly as a good farmer feels a duty to maintain and develop the fertility of the land that he farms and to leave it in better, rather than in worse, "heart" than when it came into his hands.

ENOUGH FOR ALL

As I began to think along these lines, I saw that my father could actually have dealt in this way with the earnings of his business without reducing at all his own standard of living. He had not consumed the profits, that, as it seemed to me, ought to have been ploughed back into the business through the pay-sheet and that had not been. So far as they had not been wasted in unsuccessful litigation, they had gone to form a mass of savings that had been no good to anybody at all. The real truth was that for many years my father had had literally more money than he had known what to do with.

43.   Now it was very plain that, if this great total of outside investments had never been accumulated at all and the money had been ploughed back into the business through the pay-sheet with tolerably competent care to get a fair return in greater efficiency, the staff would have been very much better off and the business very much more solid and secure. If that had been so, my father would have been less rich in the sense of possessing capital but the real money-making machine, that was the supremely important consideration, would have been much sounder and stronger. My father's actual expenditure need not have been a penny less and he could still have been making substantial savings.

In any case the business itself would have been a more than ample fortune to possess while he lived and to leave behind him. It seemed to me absolutely impossible to argue reasonably that my father's real work at this time or for a good many years past had been worth eight thousand pounds a year or anything like that. But, even if he himself had taken out of the business every penny that he did, and had merely allowed the staff to have so much of my brother's income and of my own, as we were not in any real sense earning, they would still have been vastly better off, their rates of pay would in fact have been about fifty per cent. higher.

A QUITE UNREASONABLE STATE OF AFFAIRS

44. The more I considered all this, the more utterly unreasonable did it seem to me. There on the one side was my father and on the other side his staff—my father with over a hundred separate pieces of property that he never saw and that were nothing but a bother to him, and with an income so far larger than the cost of his very comfortable way of living that the surplus was constantly obliging him to make more and more of those investments: the staff with an employment that was extremely insecure and that gave them a living so meagre that they were very far less happy than they perfectly well could have been, a happiness that would have increased very greatly both the soundness of the business and the real happiness of my father's own life.

WHAT THEN WOULD BE REASONABLE?

45. All this led me to the notion that people, who control businesses, should not take for their own work more than they would think it reasonable to pay someone else to do that same work or, if their abilities are in their own view so exceptional that they cannot be said to have a definite market-value, then to their personal revenues they should set merely arbitrarily a limit that has some relation to a reasonable standard of living. They should not take beyond that limit a margin that will accumulate into a great mass of capital that will be no real good to them and that their heirs, if their own earning-power is good, will not need and, unless their own earning-power is good, ought not to have at their disposal.

To leave your sons and daughters a comfortable independence is all very well. Much of the world's most valuable work has been done by people so placed. To leave them great wealth is another and a quite different thing.

Some high authorities on such matters have declared that it is a very great misfortune for a young man to have no need to earn his living. No doubt that is often true. But it was not a misfortune for Charles Darwin or for William Ewart Gladstone and it has not been a misfortune for a great many other men whose possession of independent means has enabled them to shape their course in life without regard to financial gain. At all events, if the general community have to choose between either enduring the annoyance of seeing useless lives lived by the sons and daughters of hardworking possessors of great ability or else of losing the benefit of that exertion of those abilities, then for my part I believe that the general community will make a blunder that will cost them very dear, if their dislike of the first causes them to choose the second.

MODERATION OF INHERITANCE WOULD BE BETTER FOR EVERYBODY

46.   I felt myself that, if my father had made a much larger and stronger business, he would really have been doing more for his own sons if they had been able and willing to follow his occupation and, if they were not, he would still have been able to leave them a comfortable independence, amply enough for real happiness. The happiness, that depends upon having still larger spending-power without any need to make it, is happiness of a kind that possessors of great ability should not spend their lives upon trying to leave to the next generation.

My father himself, as really able men so commonly do, had always lived soberly and modestly. Why should he wish his children to have, otherwise than by making it for themselves, greater means than that?

47.   On his own real feelings in this respect there is an interesting little sidelight in the fact that in my own schooldays on one of our family visits to the Opera I remarked to my father that I enjoyed it so much that, when I was grown up, I should go once a week. I had no idea that he would disapprove of that at all but in fact the substance and even more the tone of his answer were a really painful shock to me. I cannot remember his words even approximately but the sense of them showed that it would be horrible to him to feel that the fortune, that he had worked so hard to make, was being misused so grossly. No doubt at that time his fortune was a good deal smaller than it was even a very few years later, for in the latter years of my boyhood its growth from year to year must have been pretty large and he may not have been confident that things would go so well. But, even so, I have always felt that this little incident showed that his own mind was set absolutely firmly upon the idea, that has just been suggested, that people, whose earning-power is large, should set a quite modest limit upon their personal expenditure. Up to this point our minds, his and my own, were really at one but, whereas I conceived that provision for the next generation should be limited to a comfortable independence, safety from illness or accident and freedom to work at things that are not ways of making money, my father conceived that the whole of any surplus, however large, should be accumulated into the very widest possible margin of safety for that particular family from poverty. The fear-motive.

MISERABLE REMUNERATION FOR CARKING CARES

48.   When some years after the time, of which we are now talking, the main plan was well settled in my mind, I tried to get my father to consider it. I did not think it safe to indicate that I took it seriously, much

less that I had any thought of trying it out. I merely asked him what in his view would happen if the profits of a business were to be thus ploughed back through its pay-sheet and the consequent additional paying-power were to be used to increase as much as possible its efficiency. As has been mentioned, my father had a certain liking for colourful phrases. "Who", he now asked, "do you suppose would bear the carking cares of business for such a miserable remuneration as this would mean?" Against this attitude of mind I mistrusted my own capacity to carry the conversation further without revealing too much of my own feelings. So I let the subject drop and I never returned to it.

A PROBLEM OF FINANCE

49. When I had got as far as these simple and obvious notions, that, if you control a business, you should take from it no more than you would think it reasonable to pay someone else or alternatively limit your personal income to the requirements of what you feel to be a reasonable standard of living and of the provision of comfortable independence for the next generation of your family, I found myself puzzled by the problem how business was to be self-financing if so much of its profits were to go not to the controllers but to the controlled.

I cannot be sure how fast or by what steps the plan, as a whole, developed in my mind between April of 1908, when my brother was admitted to partnership, and October of 1910. But in that month the plan was completed by a very obvious notion for securing that such a division of ownership would not prevent a business from being just as self-financing as if it were the property of owners content to leave their profits to finance its growth and to draw upon that capital no more than a moderate rate of interest.

CAPITALISATION OF PARTNERS' PROFITS: AN OBVIOUS IDEA

50. The notion was so obvious that I am puzzled that it did not occur to me sooner. But my father's business was not a company. It was a private firm. He never meddled with stocks and shares. I had gone straight from school into his business and I likewise had never meddled with stocks and shares. It may sound odd but it is a fact that, after I had got as far as conceiving the idea of treating a business as a partnership of all of its workers, it was quite a while, a good many months, before I saw how such a business could be self-financing. My ability to date, as it happens that I can, the completion of my plan depends upon the chance that, when the solution suddenly flashed upon me, I was in a nursing-home recovering from the second of the two operations that followed upon a riding-accident. That fixes the date as somewhere in the early days of

October of 1910, two or three weeks after my twenty-fifth birthday. The idea of course was to distribute shares (or "stock") in place of cash.

WORKER-PARTNERS' STOCK SALEABLE BUT NON-VOTING

51.   It seemed to me extremely desirable that the recipients of the shares should be free to sell them, for the capital might be of much more use to people than the income. Moreover, such freedom would get rid of a whole lot of awkward problems—what, for example, was to happen when they left the business?

If, however, the shares were to be freely saleable, they must not have votes. Otherwise outsiders might buy up control of the business. Such shares could be created. That being so, the plan of the organisation, that years afterwards was to be called a partnership, was now in 1910 complete. Ten years more, however, were to pass before the first actual distribution and ten further years before the "share-promises," as they were called, in which that distribution and its early successes were made, could be redeemed by an issue of a security saleable upon the London Stock Exchange. By that time their total face value was seventy-six thousand pounds.

"UNTIL I AM THIRTY"

52.   At some time in my early twenties I said to my mother that from what I had heard and seen it seemed to me that my father had not really intended to drive out of his business, as in fact he had, the men who had successively risen to the general managership and I said also to my mother, "If it (by which I meant the worry and vexation) kills me, I will stick it until I am thirty but, if by that time Father has not retired and his retirement does not seem to be quite certainly near, then, the next time that he turns me out, I will not come back. He may" (he did) "live to see me forty and, though I think I can stand it until I am thirty, another ten years of it would be too much for anybody. By the end of it there would be nothing left of them." There was such a break about once a year. After two or three days my mother would be sent to make peace. I would return without comment and things would go on as before. Between whiles all went happily enough. The business flourished. I enjoyed the work and for all the difficulties of our temperaments, there was a great deal of sympathy between us. We were well matched. I was very much a chip of the old block. Though my sense of values was different, not only because of the immense difference of the circumstances of my early life but for reasons of natural temperament, I was not, I think, much softer than my father in the matter of taking my own way in things for which I really cared. At all events, the fact, that things came again and again to a break and that again and again I was invited to come back, seems to show that,

resolved though I was to continue, if I possibly could, in the firm until I was thirty, there were some things on which matters got to the length of a show-down. Of course for my sake and for the sake of everybody else I tried to avoid trouble and for quite long periods together things went well. But it was not a very easy life.

53. Everyone else in the business was so much afraid of my father and so apt to make trouble by mere blunders in dealing with him that I practically never took a Saturday morning or any holiday except three weeks in the summer and I remember well that year after year the bother of tackling, when I got back, the things that had gone wrong while I had been away, made me consider quite seriously whether it would not be better to take no holiday at all. I could not, I think, have stood such a life if it had not been in many ways extremely congenial and rewarding but in many ways it was.

INVENTION OF COMMITTEES FOR COMMUNICATIONS AND THE ESSENCE OF THE GENERAL PLAN

So far as I can remember now, the general plan did not develop much between October of 1910 and January of 1914 when at last I found myself with a business of my own.

54. During those years at Oxford Street I was not in a position to try out the plan of the Partnership except in one respect alone, the Committees, that will be described in due course, for Communications between the Rank and File and the Principal Management. Apart from them, I was simply getting technical knowledge of the management of business and, more particularly, of course, of the management of business of that particular kind. Since my twenty-third year we had had magnificent playing-fields. The purchase of those sixty-three acres at Sudbury for £7,100 was the first important use I ever made of my own money. It was in fact made by a Bank loan for my father had never had a chance to play games and disapproved of them as a waste of time and would neither have financed such a venture nor allowed me to draw out for it enough of the money that he had given me. But the provision of these and such other things, as I could see my way to do, were not in their nature essentially different from what was done in some other businesses.

The Committees for Communications are thus just about thirty-five years old and possibly a little more. In all that time their nature has never changed at all and to my mind that nature makes it plain that the essential character of the Partnership, so far as that has arisen from my own mind, was completely settled before I was thirty.

All the ideas, that were going to occur to me later—the idea, for example, of maintaining a newspaper that would publish anonymous communications and the idea that elected representatives of the whole of the workers should have really substantial power to make gifts, including leaving-gifts, that in some cases may be of the nature of compensation for disturbance—these and other ideas, that seem to me to be really important to the technique of the Partnership, were to my mind merely ways of giving effect to an aim, a kind of democracy, that, however unconsciously, was completely implied in the institution of such Committees as these really were.

PETER JONES

55. My father had always hankered after branch trading. In his early years, at a time when his small shop was packed with trade and he had not yet any hope of getting any of the adjoining property, he had tried a branch some way up Oxford Street. He had soon felt that he must give it up again and he had been similarly disappointed in efforts, that he made from time to time, to establish relations with various small concerns in the provinces.

Finally upon the death of Mr. Peter Jones he bought in 1906 the control of that business in Chelsea. The results of the venture were very disappointing and to keep it going my father had to put in from time to time a good deal of additional capital.

At some time before 1914 he resigned the Chairmanship and turned that over to me. I cannot remember when he transferred to me his controlling holding of the ordinary shares but it was in January of 1914 that he suddenly invited me to take over the real day to day direction that previously he had kept in his own hands. To a question whether he meant that I could do what I liked, he replied that he did adding, however: "But you must not neglect this place. You must not go down there before five o'clock". I agreed to that.

56. Up to that time much of the loss, that was really being made in Peter Jones, had been unrecognised. The staff dared not press upon my father's notice the need of repairs to buildings or anything else or for stale stock to be forced off at a loss. There was plenty of dust to be cleared away and under the new broom it flew. Moreover, the business was dying of starvation. Before it could work, it had got to be fed. Had the war not begun in the middle of that same year, the immediate increase of sales would have gone much further towards balancing the increase of the expenses. But the war did begin and to some people the figures of Peter Jones were frightening. I thought I knew what I was doing. I thought the growth of the sales (twelve per cent. in the first six months against a previous steady fall) was sufficiently encouraging. But the elderly senior partner in the small firm of accountants, who had always had the audit, supposed himself to be a good judge of such matters and felt it his duty to write to my father that the course, that I was taking, would merely

increase gravely the heavy losses that would be suffered by all concerned in the winding up of the business, a thing that in the writer's view was bound to come sooner or later.

Long before my father had invited me to do what I could with it, he had declared repeatedly in public his conviction that the figures, by which he had been induced to buy the controlling interest, had been in some way fictitious. I suspect that he had never had much real hope that I should succeed where he had failed and I think that, when he got this letter, he became afraid that the loss, that would be in any case serious, would be increased really importantly by whatever it was that I was doing. At all events, he insisted that I should return to him the controlling shares that he had put into my name. I declined.

TAKING A RISK

57. I quite expected that this would mean a fresh break and, if it did, I intended not to come back. I had never given way on any of the previous occasions on which I had been turned out. They had all been things upon which I felt that I could not give way but, when I had been invited each time to come back, I had always done so. Upon my particular temperament the strains of that life were considerable. Only a very strong constitution could have survived the illnesses and the very severe chest-operations that had followed upon my riding-accident. I had been told that I was only the sixth case in which the operation had been attempted and I was uncertain what might be its long-term effects.

Quite apart, however, from the fact that in the view of the Army I was now C3 whereas previously I had, I imagine, been very much A1, I thought that nobody, however physically tough, could safely continue far beyond thirty in a life of such strains and vexations. To anyone, who was sufficiently dull, even perhaps to anyone, to whom the business was merely a means of making money, they might have meant little but to me they mattered too much.

58. Now it is one thing to stand such strains when you feel that by enduring them you are getting knowledge that you need for your general aims in life and of which the need will not tie you for an intolerably long time to that endurance. It is quite another thing to stand those same strains when you feel that you have knowledge enough and that every year ought now to be going into creative work, not into waiting for freedom to do it.

Years earlier—I am nearly but not quite sure that it was in 1908 soon after my brother's withdrawal from the firm—I had said that I would continue at Oxford Street until I was thirty. That time was come. It seemed quite likely that my father would not retire for many years yet and in fact he lived to see me forty-two.

For more than twelve months I had put into Peter Jones almost all of my leisure. Night after night I had got home to Harrow about nine o'clock so tired that my voice was nearly gone. The business was going uphill, not in disconnected patches but as a whole and in my own opinion the growth was satisfactory.

In the very worst event the amount, that was at issue, was not very serious in relation to my father's position and to my own and rightly or wrongly I was quite solidly convinced that much of the great growth of the Oxford Street business in the last ten years had been my own doing. 59. I declined as unprovocatively as I could to return the Peter Jones shares. I was told that, if I did not return them, my partnership at Oxford Street would be ended. I answered that, if that were my father's wish, I would accept in exchange for it the remainder of his interest in Peter Jones (the debentures and, I think, some preference shares) with such cash balance as might remain. That was an exchange of a quarter-partnership in one of the soundest businesses in England and the prospect of being my father's sole heir for a controlling interest in about as forlorn a derelict as could easily have been found in the whole of the drapery trade.

DERELICTS

60. My mother warned me that my father was saying to her that I had no conception of the difficulty of regenerating a business that had gone wrong. From having come into his own very strong and prosperous business I had got, he said, an utterly false notion of the difference between merely keeping such a business healthy and starting a new one and he went on to express his own strong agreement with what he told my mother was a general doctrine of experts in such matters that, though the great majority of efforts to start a new business end in failure, the regeneration of an existing business, that has gone wrong (and he implied that the business of Peter Jones was most certainly a case in point—as indeed it was) is much more difficult than the creation of a new one. A few years later, when Peter Jones was amply and solidly prosperous, I reminded my mother of this and said to her, "We (by which I meant the Partnership) have got a gold mine. If we can regenerate such a Valley of Hinnom as this place was, we can safely buy derelicts and the competition will be small". In due course that actually happened. When the Partnership started to experiment with trading in the provinces, it deliberately bought forlorn derelicts and it deliberately retained their names and disregarded the "bad will" that they might have acquired and one after the other they prospered until the day came when in the early months of this most alarming of all wars the Partnership ventured to buy at a stroke fifteen businesses that as a whole had long been doing

very badly indeed. As a whole these likewise prospered. This, however, is looking almost twenty years ahead.

A CALCULATED RISK

61. The auditors, who had watched the accounts of Peter Jones for the last twenty years or more and who had some other drapery audits, urged me not to make what they felt quite sure would prove the ruinous mistake of giving up my position and prospects in my father's business. They were very far from being the only people who thought that the good figures of that of Mr. Peter Jones in the few years before he had turned it into a public company had either been due to conditions that had passed or to some very special personal ability and exertion—possibly something that by its nature could be only temporary.

Few, if any, of the Buyers either in Peter Jones or at Oxford Street thought otherwise. The Midland Bank, who had a branch adjoining Peter Jones, could have been the Partnership's bankers but declined the account because, it was understood, Sir Edward Holden had happened to use for some months during my father's régime a flat over that branch and from what he had then seen had concluded that so large a business of that kind could not succeed on that site.

But I reckoned that all my training had been in my father's business. I had no experience or business-acquaintances outside it. If I were to set up for myself, it was extremely important to me to have something in the same part of London and moreover something sufficiently near to being on the scale to which I was used. Peter Jones seemed the only possibility.

I was a bachelor, with no present idea of marrying. I was still quite uncertain what would be the long-run effects of the tremendous operations that had followed upon my accident. My life might be comparatively short or I might find myself an invalid. I reckoned that, if the worst came to the worst, I should get out of the liquidation the amount of the debentures, thirty-five thousand pounds. I was prepared to risk the rest.

CHAPTER 3

BEGINNING OF THE PARTNERSHIP
WITH PETER JONES

A FREE HAND

62. As soon as my father was convinced that I meant what I said, he amazed my mother by asking her whether she thought that my brother, with whom he had rigidly refused to hold any communication since the breach six years before, would care to return to the partnership at Oxford Street. That was arranged.

In the previous year I had refrained from making in the Peter Jones business changes that were too likely to catch my father's eye and to exasperate him. For example, the shop front was of brass. My father thought that to keep this clean was a waste of money. A dull front might have been quite satisfactory but a front, that looked dirty, neglected, bankrupt, was in my view hopelessly bad policy for a business that, as I said, was on Belgravia's back-door step and should be its village shop.

Nevertheless, during that first year I had refrained from having that metal cleaned. There must have been, I suppose, a good many things of the same kind and, so far as capital expenditure went, I could not without a break get my own money out of Oxford Street, so there could be no question of any considerable alterations to the buildings. But now, that the break had occurred, so that the Peter Jones venture had become for me a matter of sink or swim, I had to do quite whole-heartedly whatever might seem to me to be best. My ideas for that were fairly definite and they were extremely different both from those that my father had been trying and from those of Mr. Peter Jones.

LOOKING AHEAD AND PLANNING FOR SIZE AND PERMANENCE

63. Although I had liked buying and had had some success in buying for the type of customer at whom I thought Peter Jones should aim, I refrained there from doing any of the buying myself. At Oxford Street I had bought with some success many thousands of pounds' worth of various things the value of which depended mainly, if not wholly, upon aesthetic considerations. But I thought that, if I started buying for Peter Jones, I might easily spend too much time that way and that, the more successful I was (I was by no means certain that that success would ever amount to very much), the more limited would be the potentialities of the business.

I was not seeking merely to make an income, small or large, for myself or merely to make a business, however interestingly large or complex or choice in its particular nature. I was seeking to start a community that by this time I was, I think, already conscious would resemble in some respects the Religious Orders of the Middle Ages. My heart was not set on hugeness but I reckoned that the thing might become huge (it seems in fact to be doing so) and I was quite definitely bent on giving it every chance to grow as far as might be really possible for any such venture. It was correspondingly important that there should be no such bottlenecks as might have arisen if any important part of the buying had depended upon myself. In just the same way, as fast as I could, I gave up engaging and withdrew from all functions that required my personal presence.

DEVOLUTION

64.   At first at Oxford Street I had had no office, only a desk in the Counting House and I had devised for myself various means of having a great deal of information written so small that I could have it in my pockets so that, if I had to give some decision, I could do it wherever I might happen to be at the moment.

At Peter Jones I tended from, I think, the beginning to be an office worker and after the first few years I worked as much as I could from my home. That is very much less efficient than working on the spot but it is very much more favourable to genuine devolution. From the outset I was always planning a partnership that would be a set of institutions so definite, a system so coherent and strong, that the continuance of the whole thing would be quite independent of my own availability or of that of anybody else.

LEAVING THE BRIDGE TO OTHERS

This obviously required that other people should not be more or less over-shadowed and hindered and inhibited by my own personal presence. It has always seemed likely that this would lessen greatly the growth of the whole thing within my own lifetime. The contrary might be true but in the former case the loss of growth would, it seemed to me, be a price that had got to be paid to secure what was much more important, solidity, security, permanence, the safety of the livelihood of the partners who would be the real owners.

A NEW DEPARTURE IN RECRUITING   1921

65.   Though it was hardly a definite policy before 1921, it was, I believe, pretty early in the days of which we are now talking, that is to say it was in the quite early days of Peter Jones, that the Partnership began to recruit itself a little from fields upon which up to that time business of our kind,

retail distribution, had drawn hardly at all, except here and there a son or other relative of the owner of a business.

Shop-keeping, unless just possibly in enterprises of their own, had not been reckoned a possible occupation for those whose upbringing and natural abilities would make them normal recruits for the public services or the learned professions.

My own experience had convinced me that business on the lines of our partnership would be a perfectly congenial occupation for people qualified to do really well in the learned professions and it seemed to me that, until the business-world got a much greater proportion of possessors of those qualifications, natural and acquired, business of all kinds, of which the efficiency is so vitally important to the national income and happiness, could never be in fact properly efficient.

Attempts to recruit on these lines were assisted enormously by the 1914 war. It became "the thing" to go into a shop—a shop, of course, of a certain status and Peter Jones came within that line. Thenceforward the Partnership went in wholeheartedly for supplementing in this way the very inadequate supply, that the rank and file of the trade provided, of really suitable candidates for positions giving important scope and of corresponding intellectual interest and income-yielding power.

The far wider range of other opportunity for men and the fact that the retail drapery and house-furnishing trades cater in the main for women and children, caused this new element in our team-building to be, especially at first, mainly feminine but it was by no means exclusively so.

A GENEROUS RECEPTION

66. It might have been expected that the "old guard", as they might perhaps be called, would resent the introduction—and the pretty copious introduction—of a new element in the filling of the more coveted posts in their own field of work. There was, however, no real difficulty. Presumably there was a general consciousness that those posts were comparatively few and that therefore most people would not in any case get one of them.

But there was in fact prompt and frank recognition that the newcomers really had some important qualifications of their own.

Now and then anonymous letters to have expressed bitter resentment of this policy. But such protests have been in fact few and the newcomers have constantly expressed warm appreciation of the generous kindliness and courtesy with which they have been made welcome and helped. At all events the results (in five years the turnover of Mr. Peter Jones' best year—itself half as large again as the level at which my father passed the control over to me—was more than doubled and a yearly loss of about eight thousand a year was converted into a profit of twenty thousand) showed that on the whole we got what we wanted.

GETTING GOOD TEAM-WORK

67. But to provide suitable occupants for Buyerships and other key-posts was only a part of the problem. The staff as a whole and especially, of course, the Selling Staff had to be able and eager to do the type of business at which we were aiming. This meant that, so far as the existing team was too small or not of the right kind, suitable newcomers had to be attracted and after the first six months they had to be attracted under the tremendous handicap of war conditions. To achieve this and to get such work, as the new policy required, there had to be created and maintained throughout the House a quite new spirit.

1914-18

This would depend partly upon material means, the spending of money, and partly upon immaterial. I cannot remember how soon there was held out to the team the prospect that they would find that they were working for themselves and getting the profits of ownership. I may have waited until there began to be a sufficiently general feeling that success really was coming but the prospect was certainly held out long before THE GAZETTE began in March of 1918. In the early days, however, of which I am now speaking, it was obvious that there would have to be some years of uphill work before there would be any profit for anybody and in the meantime sufficient effort would not be secured merely by talk, however lively and interesting, or merely by promises, however rosy.

PAY AND AMENITIES

68. Pay, of course, would do a good deal but pay would hit the profit-and-loss account. If from this standpoint the results of the early years were too staggeringly discouraging, the more desirable of our suppliers might be unwilling to serve us and our recruiting likewise might suffer badly. It was correspondingly desirable that the material means of creating and maintaining a new spirit should take as far as possible the form of capital expenditure.

One of the very first steps was to make the dining-room really pleasant and to provide a really good kitchen. At the same time there was a radical reconstruction of the bedroom floors above the shop. They were wretchedly uncomfortable and the fire-risk was shocking. The shop had been formed by throwing together a large number of tall old dwelling-houses. On the ground and first floors their internal walls had been removed to form large showrooms but the upper floors had been left intact. No passages had been driven through the original party walls by which the houses were divided. In each there was a single wooden staircase. It looked horribly dangerous and I think it really was.

All this was now put right. Passages were driven through. Hot and cold water was laid on to each bedroom. Plenty of new bathrooms were made and in the matter of coming in at night all restrictions upon personal freedom were swept away.

A doctor, who knew the house very well, said, I was told, that he would not have believed that from being so very bad it could be made so very good and in the great influenza epidemic, that followed the war, he said that the residents had been quite remarkably immune for such a community and that in his opinion it was due to the very hygienic conditions and the very good living.

FREEDOM NOT ABUSED

A night watchman was provided and all residents over the age of twenty-one were given the same freedom to come and go as have the guests of any expensive hotel. They were told that no behaviour, however innocent, that was foolishly dangerous to the common good name, could be tolerated. There were in fact never any ill-consequences.

All this was combined with as rapid an increase of the pay-sheet as seemed just safe enough from the standpoint of getting the company's accounts to look as if the business were going the right way.

HIGHER REQUIREMENTS AND SOME INITIAL DIFFICULTIES

69.   But these material means to get the right spirit might by themselves have failed. They might have seemed merely Utopian, an unpractical lavishness that was hopelessly unsound business and that must come in due course to grief, so that in the end it would be of no real benefit to anybody. Such a notion might have been very bad both for getting and keeping a strong team and for their zeal. It was essential that, as the inducements rose, the standard of requirement should rise with them. It did and of course we had not merely to balance the greater strain but also to maintain sufficiently lively hopefulness in face of the financial losses that were to be expected for the first few years.

A little business, that is getting on to its feet, may, as did my father's after the first six months, yield a profit. But a big business, that has gone a long way wrong, may have to make in the process of recovery considerable losses for some time.

Of course I am not saying that our own results could not have been much better. There is no reason to suppose that the natural impulses, the intuitions, upon which we worked, were very near to being perfectly correct but, even if they had been, our mere lack of experience must have handicapped us heavily. For my own part I do not feel able to guess with any confidence how far our initial losses would have been less if we had not had the special and very great extra difficulties that were created by the war.

1914

Subsequent events showed that the growth of our trade would have been rapid and, since in the very first six months up to the outbreak of war it was six thousand pounds, that is to say about twelve per cent. beyond the previous turnover, whereas thenceforward for many months it stood nearly still, it seems reasonable to reckon that the war not only forced upon us many extra expenses but deprived us for some time of substantial revenue.

On the other hand, in the latter part of the war trade was extremely good and these conditions may have caused our results from first to last to be better than otherwise they would have been.

PSYCHOLOGICAL FACTORS

At all events, at the stage of which we are now talking, the time when we were changing the policy of the business and endeavouring to build up such a team and create such a spirit as the new policy required, it was extremely desirable that whatever could be done in the way of better conditions and better pay, material means of producing a new spirit, should be supplemented to the utmost extent by other means that were immaterial. The air had got to be filled with lively interest and a spirit of hope, a feeling that we were pioneering, entering a new country, and that it was real, not a mere delusion, a mere mirage.

BEGINNINGS OF SOME OF THE PARTNERSHIP'S PRINCIPAL INSTITUTIONS

70.   Committees for Communications between the Rank and File and the Principal Management were the one really new idea, the one real step towards partnership for all, that it had been possible to try out at Oxford Street and because of that experience I started them, so far as I can now remember, immediately upon my taking over Peter Jones.

1912 OR THEREABOUTS

When they began, I supposed them to be genuine new ground, something that probably existed nowhere else in the business-world. But in view of all, that I have read and heard since, I should not be at all surprised to learn that in those days there were already in our country and elsewhere some other businesses where the holder of the position of chief individual responsibility or of one of those positions met regularly representatives of the Rank and File elected for that purpose by secret ballot of all their fellow-workers. I reckon these Committees the oldest of the actual institutions of the Partnership. They have never changed in any important way since first they were started more than thirty years ago.

THE GULF BETWEEN MANAGERS AND MANAGED

71. The idea was and is to bridge the gulf that in large-scale business develops between, on one side, the workers, the Rank and File, as the Partnership calls them, the people who have little or no authority over others, and, on the other side, the Principal Management, the people who have on the contrary the ultimate authority, the real control of the whole business.

For the election of these committees the whole of the Rank and File, the people who have no official responsibility for anyone's work but their own, are divided into constituencies mainly according to the nature of the work but with sufficient regard to the need that the committee-member shall be within easy reach of his constituents. No one constituency can be larger than thirty-six members and no one committee can have more than fifteen seats. The settlement of the constituencies, in accordance with the last two sentences, is to be a function of the Trustees of the Constitution. Only members of the Rank and File can serve on these committees or vote in their elections. A sufficient representative of the Principal Management (for years I always did it myself) must meet each of these committees at least once in each of at least eight calendar months of the year. Everything said in the committee in good faith is absolutely privileged. They can talk about whatever they like. The proceedings are published as far as possible but always without any avoidable indication of the identity of any particular speaker. The report merely says:

"The Committee said this: the Committee asked that". Prompt publication of the discussions and of any decisions in respect of them is highly desirable.

72. The members of the Committees told me on many occasions that, if the publication was not prompt, they found themselves in trouble with their constituents who wanted to be assured that the member had raised some question that the constituents had asked him to raise.

The members being elected by secret ballot cannot be regarded as in some improper league with the Management and speaking, as they do, in each other's presence cannot be suspected of using that contact with the Management to grind their own axes or the axes of their friends.

Intermediate officials unused to the system are apt to try to bring pressure upon members of the Committee or to interfere otherwise in the proper working of the system. It is necessary to be vigilant and firm about that. But in practice trouble has been infrequent and slight.

73. In the early days the members quite often seemed to have nothing to talk about. I did not think it was wise to let them feel that their work had been interrupted and that they had all gathered together to no purpose, so I used hastily to start a discussion upon something or other and keep it going for twenty minutes or so. There is some tendency

for small matters, that could be put right without waiting for a meeting of the Committee and that had better be done thus more promptly, to be saved up as something to talk about at a meeting of the Committee. But on the whole in my own view the system has been an unqualified success.

THE VALUE OF LIGHT

74.   When it was a few years old, I one day suddenly asked a committee, that represented some of the workrooms, if they thought the whole thing was a waste of their working-time. I still remember the promptitude of the chorus of protest against the idea that the system should be abandoned.

When I asked what it had done, I was answered at once: "Well, for one thing it has made the distribution of 'short time' much fairer". That is of course one of the supreme arguments for abundance of contact between Managers and Managed and of publicity in general.

Experience has shown that the inhabitants of a town behave far better if at night the streets are well lit. The mere light by itself is a powerful supplement to the influence of the police.

Just the same thing is true in large-scale team-work. The fact, that there are no grievances to report, does not mean that there would be no grievances if there were no such means for their being reported.

NEED OF ENQUIRY

75.   In team-work it is extremely important to do enough questioning. Quite serious grievances may otherwise remain unspoken and do great harm and, on the other hand, to leave all the initiative to the other side is to create too much temptation to self-advertisement and mischief-making.

Broadly speaking people not merely like to be asked. They feel that they have a right to that amount of help. It protects them from seeming to be self-important or ill-disposed.

Certainly there should be no atmosphere of "wait till you're asked". But the quantity and kind of asking should be ample for those who upon some points at all events will either be silent if the question is not raised from the side of the Management or will feel some discomfort in raising it themselves and may rather resent being left to do so.

Even if there is no sense of resentment, there is some discomfort, some loss of happiness.

GENERAL GOOD HUMOUR NEEDS CEASELESS CARE

76.   Really first-rate team-work absolutely requires ceaseless extreme pains to prevent discomfort and to create, maintain and increase happiness of every sort and kind. The cumulative effect is so important that the tiniest trifles should have ample care. Phraseology, little matters

of method, everything whatsoever that is in any way whatever fretting, should be so far as possible discovered and eliminated. Everything, on the contrary, that will give pleasure and produce general good temper, should have attention as carefully as the avoidance of sparks in a powder-magazine.

If it takes more than one to make a quarrel, so also does it take more than one to make real good fellowship. People, who are cantankerous or mischief-makers, should be eliminated but the feelings of those, who are not in some way definitely ill-tempered or too dangerous to the good temper of others, should be studied with ceaseless care, accepted quite objectively as if they were the feelings of the highest potentates and gratified as far as is humanly possible.

Bad engine-drivers knock engines about. Good engine-drivers treat the engine with the utmost possible kindness. In their hands the engine's total performance is far greater. A physician, who is careless of the mental reactions of his patient, or a surgeon, whose treatment involves needless strain upon the patient's physique, fails in his duty. So do managers who treat their clients, the managed, in a way that involves needless wear and tear and needless loss of the nervous energy that results from needless discomfort or other friction of any kind. It is just the same thing as a car-driver's mishandling his gears or the bad hands that spoil a horse or the lack of tact that by upsetting needlessly the mind of a sick man does him perhaps immense harm. Adequate communications, adequate mutual awareness, are one indispensable condition of good team-work and in team-work of our particular kind committees of this sort are a great help in that way.

UNWELCOME TO HOLDERS OF AUTHORITY

77. The Committees for Communications were, as I have said, the only major institution of the Partnership that I was able to start before I had independent control of a business of my own. That is to say before I took over in 1914 the control of Peter Jones.

How sensational an innovation that was in those days is shown in the fact that the Buyers of that business, who at that time were still Managers of the Selling Departments for which they bought (our subsequent separation of buying from management has been one of the rather numerous things that the Partnership has invented for itself, although we have often discovered later that the same idea had been in use for years somewhere else—commonly somewhere in America), promptly took the very unusual step of sending me a "round robin" to ask that I would hold a Buyers' Meeting and at that meeting expressed extreme dislike of the idea and showed, I thought, some inclination to commit themselves to flat opposition. The Committees were, however, started and led to no trouble.

DISCLOSURE OF FIGURES OF TRADING

78. Another innovation, that made the House gasp and that came, I think, very early indeed, was the admission of the whole of the staff to knowledge of figures normally reckoned to be highly confidential. My father had carried secrecy even to the length of not merely not giving to his Buyers figures of their own Buyerships but strenuously discouraging their attempting to keep any figures for themselves, as they might in a very rough way by noting the amounts of their purchases and ascertaining day by day from their Selling Staff the amounts of their sales.

It had seemed to me that at Oxford Street my taking the formidable risks of giving to each Buyer the figures of his own Buyership (and trusting him never to reveal his knowledge of them) had had an extremely tonic effect upon the minds of the recipients and at Peter Jones I published to the whole House every week the amounts by which the sales and stock of each department were up or down, and, moreover, a commentary upon those figures. In the years before we had a weekly newspaper of our own, that is to say before THE GAZETTE was started, this was done by a method that must have been, I suppose, much the same thing as the wall newspapers of which we hear in Russia. The figures were written on to a large card and down the side of the card there was a commentary that was intended to have some dynamic value.

79. The publication of these and similar figures has always been a marked feature of our GAZETTE and from time to time I have been told that people in our part of the business-world have said that they thought that this was very unwise. I was told that one critic declared that in doing so we "loaded the dice against ourselves". My own view has always been that to know somebody else's achievement may have a tonic effect upon your own energy but as a general rule it will not increase very greatly your real ability.

Such publicity may perhaps stimulate competition in particular respects in which that is unfortunate but really dangerous competitors will be very apt to get much the same information in other ways. Knowledge of your figures may make them more wisely exacting of efficiency from their own team but the circumstances are very likely to be in important ways different. Efficient competitors will probably be pretty adequately exacting anyhow and, if they are provoked into pressing their own people too hard, the broad result may be positively hurtful to themselves.

A PRINCIPAL ADVANTAGE OF PARTNERSHIP FOR ALL

80. On the other hand, to you the advantages of such publicity are great. Whether the figures are at first sight highly creditable to those responsible for them, or whether at first sight the contrary is true, disclosure to all the world and a prospect of continuance of that disclosure may be

a very powerful stimulant. Some said that, when the figures seemed discreditable, though perhaps they might be perfectly excusable or even in reality very good, the worker responsible would be apt to be too gravely discouraged or antagonised. I have never myself seen signs that this was really happening. On the other hand such publicity is a strong guarantee that good work will be recognised and properly remunerated. No such figures would be published avoidably by any management desiring to be ungenerous in their pay-rates and of course, to be quite certain that such disclosures will have no ill effect, you must give the workers all there really is for them to have.

It is in fact one way of exploiting the Partnership system—of getting out of it the advantages that it ought to have for efficiency. For here is a thing that could hardly be done unless you were prepared to let the workers get, if not, as we do, the whole of the profit, at all events a very large share of it. The limited publicity, that the "public" company system has forced upon the controllers of industry, has been enough by itself to produce from the controlled much pressure for higher pay. Many in consequence are the devices by which profit is disguised if the circumstances of the particular case do not require that it shall be paid out in dividends.

INTELLECTUAL INTEREST

81.   All disclosures, that are not too helpful to competitors, tend to be very welcome to the workers. Quite apart from the question of their own incomes, the mere intellectual satisfaction of knowing what is happening is in itself a really great pleasure. To be kept in the dark tends to be humiliating and is certainly dull.

It might not be wise to let competitors know where certain goods were bought, still less at what price. It might not be wise to disclose certain figures of expense and profit but in a partnership of this new type the members should be given in every possible way the advantages of ownership.

It is an advantage of ownership that you have the intellectual and moral satisfactions of knowing what is going on behind the scenes, of knowing what are the actual results of all that happens in your own business.

LIMITATIONS OF PUBLICITY

82.   Owners in the old sense could, however, keep their secrets. Owners in the new cannot. They are too many and they come and go too much. Therefore the really secret things cannot be disclosed to more than just a few of them. But a partnership should be very reluctant to reckon that any particular thing must be thus secret. It should disclose to its members

as much as ever it can. We have done it steadily for about thirty years and for my own part I am convinced that the results have been very good.

PAPER-WORK AND STATISTICS

83.   Although almost, so far as I can remember, from the outset at Peter Jones I kept as much as I could away from the actual field of battle and limited my own work first to what could be done in an office on the spot and then after some years to what could be done from my own home, it was of course necessary to play sufficiently the part that still remained to me.

Conscious as I was that inattention to figures had affected to the extent of many thousands of pounds the general course of my father's business, I developed from the outset an elaborate technique of half-yearly reviews of each Buyership. Very full notes were dictated in the Buyer's presence. He was given a copy and at the next review those notes were used to supplement memory. Sir Metford Watkins, some time after he took this work over, told me he had come to feel it was almost the most valuable of all the Partnership's regular practices.

The system tended to the production of much analysis and of many statistics and, as years passed, I came to feel that it is very easy to devise work of that kind that in theory seems certain to be well worth having but very difficult to secure that, when produced, it gets proper attention and is used rightly.

It may be no easy matter to decide whether such use is in fact occurring. But, even if it is not, the mere obtaining of the information may be extremely enlightening and stimulating to those who have to supply it.

Nevertheless, in the light of my own experience, I would advise the Partnership to be constantly mindful how very easily time, trouble and money can be wasted on the production of statistics that are not sufficiently useful and how easily statistics, that are very highly desirable, can be wasted if they do not get proper attention.

CHAPTER 4

ABSORPTION OF JOHN LEWIS AND COMPANY

84. At all events, through those six years Peter Jones Ltd., as its sales increased, showed a diminishing loss, then no loss at all and finally, in 1919, a profit so large that in the early spring of 1920 we were at last in a position to request the consent of the other Shareholders to such an alteration of the Articles of Association of that Company as would allow a beginning of the profit-sharing that was part of our general plan. The £35,000 of Debentures and almost all of the £60,000 (nominal) of Ordinary Shares belonged to me but few of the £60,000 (nominal) of Preference Shares were mine and by now their cumulative dividend of 5½ per cent. was far in arrear. As we were desperately short of working capital, we proposed that these arrears should be forgone in consideration of a permanent increase of two per cent. in the rate of the Preference dividend and of a reduction of the rights of the Ordinary Shares so that the real profit should go to the workers.

The details are upon record in the Partnership's GAZETTE.

The account there of the proceedings at the meeting of the Shareholders ended as follows:

(Conclusion of the Chairman's opening address to the meeting)

' "I understand that some of you have come here feeling absolutely convinced that the scheme is a bad one and unfair to yourselves and that you ought therefore not merely to send Proxies against it but to come here to express your opinion and, to bring over other Shareholders, if you can, to your way of thinking. You are obviously perfectly entitled to do this and I am quite sure that, if in such a case I myself were of that mind, I should take the same course.

' "I understand also that some at all events of those Shareholders, who have come to take up that position, have been led to do so partly, if not wholly, by their annoyance at what has seemed to them the unwarrantably uncompromising tone of the circulars in which the scheme has been announced.

' "So far as my advocacy of these proposals may have seemed to have been lacking in proper consideration for your own position and point of view, I hope that you will accept my apologies and that you will make some allowance for the extreme difficulty of putting things clearly and strongly enough to prevent misunderstandings and to secure attention in some cases, while on the other hand avoiding giving in other cases such offence as I understand that I have been unfortunate enough to do.

' "Negotiations of this sort are really very delicate and difficult to handle and I have unluckily had no previous experience to guide me.

' "I fear that sad experience of a wicked world may make it extremely difficult for you to believe that a programme so unusual and financially so disinterested can really be honest and have no catch in it. But, as I have pointed out to you already, I could sell my interest immediately without bothering to put through any scheme at all, for a vastly larger sum than I could possibly get for it when once the scheme is through.

' "I hope to reap to-day the harvest of a policy pursued for nearly eight and a half years and for a great part of that time ,under such a strain as I marvel that my health, which is not good, could stand.

' "Let me repeat that I am perfectly willing to answer all the questions that you care to put and that all, that I do ask, is that you will not vote against me without making quite sure that the particular objection or objections, on which your decision is based, are true objections and are not simply a misapprehension which would have been removed if you had stated those objections before you voted."

'There was a prolonged debate of various points. The Scheme was then adopted on a show of hands without any need of a poll.

'Assuming that the Confirmatory Meetings go off all right, which is as certain as anything well can be, and that the Scheme receives the sanction of the Court, and, that it will, Sir Henry Paget-Cooke says there is no reason to doubt, the Profit-Sharing Scheme will be part of the Articles of the Company and we shall have obtained the sanction of the Law for our own particular method of industrial organisation—a method which may have considerable results.

'We shall then have nothing to do but to set to work steadily to get from it whatever benefit it may prove to be capable of yielding.

'J.S.L.'

PARTNERSHIP AND PARTNERS

85. In the following GAZETTE notice on the 10th April, 1920, the words "Partnership" and "Partner" were used for the first time. The promptitude and completeness, with which they were adopted by all and sundry, seemed to me highly significant. Within a few days everybody, no matter what his or her general position and level of education, seemed to have "got the idea" and to make a point of using the new terms and no others.

"I think we had better drop the term 'Profit-Sharing' in favour of 'Partnership Benefit'. 'Profit-Sharing' has come to bear a special meaning namely a system of business in which profit is shared between workers and owners of capital.

"Now in our case the workers get the whole profit and the sharing is entirely among themselves. We are in fact putting every worker into the position of a partner and thus giving him exactly the benefit a partner does derive from partnership.

"In the same way I think it would be well if we were to cease to speak of 'the Company', or 'the Firm', or 'the Business', or 'the House', when what we really mean is 'the Partnership'.

"Of course we do not want to bother ourselves with needless or pedantic exactitude of terminology but on the other hand we must not lose sight of the fact that a carefully-formed habit of giving a thing its right name has great education-value and that, if you can get a lot of people, who really are members of a partnership, to call themselves partners and to refer to the business in which they work as 'the Partnership' you will probably cause them to think like partners and to act like partners more quickly and completely than otherwise they would.

"There is no doubt that at present few of the House do truly realise that our system of business abolishes the employer and the employee.

"Five hundred or five thousand people working on our system are just as truly partners as five solicitors or five stock-brokers who agree to work together and to divide in agreed proportions the proceeds of their combined work.

"Of course the very fact, that our partnership is so very much bigger than an ordinary partnership, will give us a vast deal to do in the way of fixing by a special code of rules the conditions under which any particular partner can be asked to withdraw from the partnership. But with patience and goodwill all those special difficulties of our particular case will rapidly be solved.

"It is undoubtedly a great part of our problem to create a sufficient sense of partnership in all the members of a partnership that is so large and that includes people of widely different age, intelligence and education and in which there must always be a good deal of coming and going, and it will undoubtedly help towards the creation of that sense of partnership if we all form the habit of speaking of ourselves and of each other as partners and of our business as what it is, namely, a partnership.

"Directors and other Officials specially concerned should be particularly careful to form as quickly as they can in themselves and their assistants the habit of substituting 'partnership' and 'partnership benefit' for 'profit-sharing', 'Company', 'Firm', 'House', 'Business', etc., particularly for 'profit-sharing'.

"J.S.L."

THE PLAN IN FULL OPERATION AT LAST

86. So by the spring of 1920 the plan, that had been in all essentials completed by the end of October of 1910, was in full operation with the sole exception of the form in which the Partnership Benefit was distributed.

The plan was that the profit of the worker-partners should go to them year by year in cash if that was necessary to prevent over-capitalisation of their business. But, if the business could use the capital, then the profit was to go to the Partners, not in cash but in the form of a security that they could sell on the Stock Exchange.

SHARE PROMISES

87. In 1920, however, and up to 1928, that is to say for so long as my father lived, it seemed undesirable to issue the Partnership Benefit in the form of a security that could be sold upon the London Stock Exchange. It was thought that this would bring the whole experiment to his notice and that it would be a ceaseless puzzle and vexation to him. In the spring of 1920 he was already eighty-four and, though his general health was quite good, he was not so young mentally as are some of those who attain this age.

To get over this difficulty, the Partnership Benefit was issued not in actual shares or stock but in printed documents with a handsome orange stamp. These documents were called "Share-Promises". They told the holder that in due course he would receive in exchange for the document the number of shares it mentioned together with a cumulative yearly dividend of 7½ per cent. so far as that dividend should not have been paid punctually, as in fact it always was, on the 1st June and the 1st December.

The Share Promise was to be binding upon my heirs and, if such shares or stock, as it contemplated, could not in the end be made available, the Promise was to be redeemed for cash. At first there was no limit to the extent to which these documents might be sold back to me for cash. (Obviously they were unlikely to be saleable for the full price to anybody else.) But the scale of selling was so great that I had to say that the recipients must keep these gifts unless their reason for wanting the capital seemed to me good enough.

FANCY ME WORTH THIRTY POUNDS!

88. During the years, for which the restriction was in force, there was one happening that threw a poignant light upon what a system of real partnership for all might mean for some. Among my letters one morning there was a report that an unmarried girl in one of the staff-kitchens was expecting a child and was leaving and wanted to encash her holding of sixteen pounds' worth of Share-Promises that she had received as Partnership Benefit. I marked the paper "Sanctioned" and passed it out. A few days later the Matron in charge of that kitchen told me that she thought I might be interested to hear what had followed. She had been going through it one morning and had noticed a lot of girls talking together and had asked them why they were not getting on with their work. One of them had left the gathering and had come up to her and said: "Oh, Matron, Florrie's got her share-money!" When the Matron answered: "Well, what about it?" the girl had continued: "But are these things really money?" The Matron said: "Of course they are really money, as I keep on telling you silly girls and now perhaps you'll believe it", whereupon the questioner said "But I have got thirty of them! Fancy me worth thirty pounds!"—and she burst into tears.

The Matron added that Florrie's young man, who was believed to be quite a decent sort, decided that, if she had a dowry of sixteen pounds, he could see his way to venture upon matrimony. But I have always felt that the really impressive thing in this little story was the words: "Fancy me worth thirty pounds" and the happy excitement that had been produced by an amount so far inside what the system will tend to mean to any girl whose earning-power is quite small and who works under it for no more than a few years.

A HELP TO SAVING

89. In our own country at all events with the temperamental difficulty, that British or at all events English human nature has, in putting by small amounts from a weekly or monthly income there may be great virtue in a system that causes a part of that income to come in substantial sums and that nevertheless is not felt to be an unnecessary and therefore an objectionable withholding of that income so as to enforce such saving. Everybody can understand that profits cannot be divided until they have been ascertained and that in business-operations of any complexity they cannot be ascertained every week or month.

EXPERIMENTS IN FREQUENCY OF DISTRIBUTION OF PROFIT

If I remember, the Partnership did actually experiment with distributions "on account", so that people might not have to wait until the end of the year for the whole of their Partnership Benefit. Obviously these anticipatory distributions had to be kept on the safe side but it was commonly possible to be sure that the distribution for the year would not be less than a certain rate and up to that extent an earlier issue was possible.

I cannot now remember whether this was definitely disliked or whether its advantages were merely felt in the light of experience to be insufficient to justify the considerable trouble and cost. Certainly the practice, that before this war had become established, of yearly distributions seems to be quite acceptable and it undoubtedly does mean that many people find—and are very glad to find—themselves once a year in possession of an amount that they would not have succeeded in refraining from frittering away if it had come to them in weekly or monthly instalments.

Furthermore, the issue of Stock with freedom to sell is probably itself some help to begin to save. Probably a good many people manage to refrain from deciding to sell Stock who might not succeed in resisting the temptation to nibble away a bit of ready money.

90.   Upon the formation in 1929 of John Lewis Partnership Limited, the Share-Promises, of which the total nominal value was by then £76,632, were redeemed by an issue of shares saleable on the Stock Exchange. These were Preferred Ordinary shares (now converted into stock) of John Lewis Partnership Limited, a holding company formed to control the whole of whatever might be eventually the Partnership's business.

In accordance with the plan those shares were entitled to a fixed (cumulative) dividend of 7½ per cent. and no more. Since the recipients were to be quite free to sell this security or to give it away, it was to have no vote as long as the dividend was not in arrear. Otherwise outsiders by buying up these Shares or this Stock might get control of the Partnership and spoil it or bring it to an end. That actually happened in the case of Filene Bros. Inc. of Boston when the workers having acquired in course of time a controlling-holding of the Common Stock let themselves be tempted into selling it.

HOLDING THE HELM AND TAKING THE RISK

91.   As an additional safeguard my own property in the equity of the company was placed below this new security both for capital upon a liquidation and also for dividend, so that I should have to lose all of that property before anybody else could lose a single penny. That seemed plainly right if I was to have as would, I thought, be necessary, during the early experimental years, a controlling-interest in the management of the business.

I arranged in fact that, until an enormous quantity (many millions) of the new security should have been issued to worker-partners, the voting-control should still remain with me, even if there were to be, as nineteen years later because of the war there was, a temporary failure in the punctuality in the payment of their dividends. In the first nineteen years between 1920, when the security was first issued, and 1939 the dividend was paid punctually every half-year upon the 1st June and the 1st December—dates that had been chosen because a bit of extra income might be specially welcome at Christmas time and when the summer holidays were drawing near.

DIVIDEND FLOW SUSPENDED AFTER NINETEEN YEARS

92. Except that a single half-year was paid on the first June 1940, the war stopped the dividend from December 1939 until the 1st June 1944. Thenceforward the flow has been again continuous. The last of the arrears were paid off on the 1st December 1945 but for the six years from December 1939 to December 1945 the voting-powers of the Stock were in force.

By that time its total amount was £492,911 but against those 492,911 votes I had still an overwhelming majority by the arrangement that was made in 1929 and that will be described in due course.

IT IS PLEASANT TO BE PROUD OF YOUR BUSINESS

93. So by the spring of 1920 the plan, that had been in all essentials complete by October of 1910, was in full operation. The tremendous growth of the trade had been, of course, exhilarating for everybody, all the more so since in its nature it was pleasant to do.

It matters a great deal to most workers and certainly to such as the Partnership was intended to gather together, to feel that the work, that they are doing, is intrinsically worth while, that *their* business, as they naturally call it—and as it ought really to be—is a credit to them. The workers in Peter Jones constantly heard the choiceness of the stock, the moderation of the prices and the extreme absence of any sort of trickery praised warmly by customers who were obviously familiar with the "best" shops and at the same time, along with the exhilaration of the rapid growth of the business and of its development along such lines as these, there was the separate interest and pleasant excitement of the successive innovations that were steadily bringing the real institutions of the Partnership into being.

From the standpoint of making a business useful to its customers, pleasant in its nature for its workers and capable of yielding them steadily a really good living the policy, that had been followed through the previous six years, might, I thought, fairly be said to have been an unqualified success.

FINANCE BY TRIAL AND ERROR

94. But profit is one thing. Finance is another. In this I had had a terrible time. Such training, as I had had, had been wholly outside the Counting House. My father had never shown me any accounts or discussed them with me. My knowledge of the figures I have mentioned came from my brother who in my father's plan was to have been "the Counting House Partner" and who accordingly started there. All my notions of management had been formed in a business in which there was constantly a great superfluity of ready money and in which a good half of the turnover was in sales for cash and most of the credit-customers paid their accounts every month.

The cost of setting right the Peter Jones buildings, dilapidated and full of fire-risks as they were, and in particular of making the staff quarters as good as they had been had absorbed pretty well all of my spare funds and as the business grew, I began to discover that to be making a profit is not necessarily to be paying your way.

A CREDIT-TRADE

The type of business, that Peter Jones was now developing, tends to be a credit trade and in fact, whereas a full fifty per cent. of the sales of John Lewis and Company had been for immediate cash, the new policy in Peter Jones resulted in sales of which a full eighty per cent. were on credit. As I look back I still marvel that we got through.

A SAD MISFORTUNE: THE SALE OF GROVE FARM, GREENFORD

95. At the end of the 1914 war there was an atmosphere of great uncertainty and in any case the immense growth of the turnover of Peter Jones and the great extent, to which that turnover was not for ready money but with account-customers, gave us extreme need of additional working capital. Just then I got an opportunity to sell the sixty-three acres at Sudbury that carried our playing-fields and incidentally my own home. I dared not let that chance slip. The amount at issue was over £20,000 and at that time that amount of additional working capital would make a very great difference to the efficiency of our buying of merchandise. The purchase of those sixty-three acres had been the first important decision that I had ever taken. A good deal of my leisure during eighteen months had been spent on looking for such a place, very hard to find even in those days. It was ideal. While the purchase was in process, I had in Regent's Park on a sunny May morning the riding-accident that was to mean two terrible illnesses (empyema), two very heavy operations and a permanent loss of much of my physical strength. The contract came when I was too nearly dead to be able to close my fingers on the pen. My mother thought that, if the purchase came to light, there would be a tremendous

family row and she urged me to break it off but I answered that, if I lived I should want it and, if I died, it would not matter. I knew they dared not excite me and, as I was too weak to grip the pen, somebody held my hand and guided it. In those days such sports-grounds were few and in our part of the business-world there was none that approached our own either in technical quality or in beauty.

It had been meant for a fairyland and it had become one. For years after I lost it, I used to dream now and again that I had got it back and that I was walking about it looking at new buildings and considering how they could be cleared away or altered to the old standards. Shortly before his death my father suddenly spoke of this property and said how sorry he was that I had parted with it and how gladly he would have lent me the money to hold it if he had known that I could not afford to keep the capital locked up.

He had obviously forgotten utterly and I did not try to recall to his mind that I had almost gone down on my knees to him to do that very thing. At this time, in 1920, he did not yet realise that the Chelsea venture was not going to end in failure. The period of some years after 1914, during which he had refused to have any communication at all with me, was already ended but Peter Jones had only just begun to make twenty thousand a year and the facts, that is to say the solidity of this spectacular success, that led my father to invite me to return to partnership at Oxford Street, were not yet clear to him.

The Partnership has now some hundreds of acres of very lovely country club on the Thames at Cookham and is starting others in Liverpool and Sheffield and in Hampshire, but nothing will make up for the loss of those sixty acres adjoining, as they did, two railway-stations (South Harrow and Sudbury Hill) by which the ground could be reached in twenty minutes from Marylebone on the Great Central Railway and forty-five minutes from Sloane Square on the Metropolitan and District. So far as I was concerned, the loss of those playing-fields was in some ways the most painful of all the many sorrows that my father's temperament, aggravated and warped as it had been by the hard conditions of his early life, made for us both.

A BREAKDOWN IN MANAGEMENT   1922

96. The release of this money eased of course enormously the financial difficulties of the business but soon afterwards fresh troubles came upon us. The Partnership and I had one of those pieces of bad luck against which it is peculiarly difficult to guard because they do not consist of a single happening but of an unfortunate coincidence. At a time when, as it turned out, ill health was going to keep me away for nearly a year, the Government pressed me as a matter of patriotism to let them have

back for specially important work for which in the event he was made a Companion of the Bath a colleague who had just left the Treasury to become the Partnership's financial adviser. With him gone and myself away the Partnership had to go through a year of passage from boom to slump. Things went terribly wrong but that particular experience did us an immense good turn. It gave me the idea of setting up a system of budgetary control. An eminent banker ridiculed the idea as quite inapplicable, upon such lines as I was contemplating, to a business of our kind but it has in fact turned out well. Without it we could hardly have escaped being swamped by the subsequent enormous growth of our operations with a team so light as for various reasons, chiefly my father's long continuance and this war, ours has been so far.

FEASIBILITY AND VALUE OF BUDGETARY CONTROL

97.   In my view every business, whatever its nature and size, should calculate in advance of the event, its accounts and any other statistics important to the management, and, as the period covered by the budget passes, the results should be compared frequently and closely with the budget figures.

If my father had had such a system or if I had got in any other way the idea before in my absence my fingers had been burned so terribly as now they were, a very great deal of my worries and troubles in the years between 1914 and 1926 would have been avoided and I suppose, though that idea is so painful that I am reluctant to face it, that the broad difference, that would have been made to the general efficiency of our operations and especially to our perception of the real problems of our finance, might have enabled us to keep the Sudbury playing-fields.

ORGANISATION OF BUYING, SELLING AND FINANCIAL CRITICISM

98.   For some years the Partnership's system of budgetary control was a function of a post that was called the Directorship of Estimates. The system was brought to a very high pitch of accuracy. In normal times of peace the difference between a forecast and the actual results was generally astonishingly small—at least it seemed so to me. The figures were obtained in two ways. By this time buying had been separated from management, as it must be if Buyers are to have proper peace of mind when they are out of their departments. A Buyer, who has to depend on himself to "lead the sales and push the trade" and to get the stock kept properly, must, whenever he is out of "his" department, be worrying about getting back to it. I had noticed this in my early days when I went abroad sometimes with one and sometimes with another of the more important of my father's Buyers. Furthermore, first-rate managers of departments are apt to be by no means first-rate buyers. The converse is also true. In

either case you have a difficult problem. Will you take the great risk of finding that a newcomer is so much worse in the respect in which the present occupant is good that you will be on balance no better off and possibly worse off, even though you may get substantial improvement in the respect in which the present occupant is bad?

For a good many years now it has seemed to me very clear that selling should be organised from the standpoint of the customer. He or she wants to find certain things conveniently near together. On the other hand, buying should be organised from the standpoint of the supplier. One Selling Department may need stock from several different Buyerships and one Buyership may sell its goods through several different Selling Departments.

Separation of buying from selling requires great care that Buyers shall be sufficiently in touch with public demand. But the separation, that a good many people thought to be impracticable, has on the whole worked well.

In this matter of budgetary control the separation of Buying from Sales Management has the considerable incidental advantage that you can ask your Selling Staff what trade they hope to do in the coming half-year and you can put the same question separately to your Buying Staff. If their results differ, discussion of that difference is likely to be highly illuminating. If they agree closely, your position is stronger if, as the season advances, one side or the other asks for the budget to be amended in a way that to your own mind does not seem to be warranted.

RETURN TO PARTNERSHIP IN JOHN LEWIS AND COMPANY

99. By this time the breach, that for some years had been complete between my father and myself, had been healed.

After some years the published figures of the recovery of the Peter Jones business led my father to pay it a visit. As often happened, he was very well able to see the merits of the results of doing things to which he would never have consented beforehand. In his own control of Peter Jones he had insisted on trying to get a profit by saving the cost of keeping the shop even clean, much less bright and cheerful. But, when he saw the results of the contrary policy (with of course, it must be remembered, the knowledge that what he was seeing had resulted in enormous growth of turnover and a satisfactory net profit), he was warmly appreciative. So far as I can recollect, he made little comment at the time but my mother told me that when he got home, he said very emphatically to her "That place is a great credit to the boy—a very great credit!"

I cannot now remember how long this was before I was invited to return to partnership at Oxford Street but that happened in 1923. There was a tacit understanding that Peter Jones was to remain my own affair.

A STRIKE

100. By this time there were at Oxford Street few of the staff whom I had known. Many had left in 1920 when, as a consequence of the war-conditions there had been a great strike from the 26th April until the 2nd June of that year. My own knowledge of it was limited to what I heard from my brother and read in the newspapers. It seemed to have two main causes. Many of the staff were acutely dissatisfied with the proportion, that had come their way, of the profits that it was obvious to them that the firm must have been making in the war-time boom with no such regulation of prices as there has been in this second war, and on top of this they were exasperated with the frequency of what seemed to them to be merely arbitrary dismissals.

To my own mind some of those dismissals were quite indefensible and were evidence that my father had passed the latest age at which he ought to have retained such responsibility and power, —as was his persistent mismanagement of Peter Jones from 1906 to 1914 in the teeth of the grave losses that it was causing.

FOIBLES OF AGE

We must not blame people for failing when they are old to realise that they ought to relinquish power that the Law permits them to retain. My father was struggling to achieve what he vaguely felt to be vitally necessary standards of efficiency in a business that had far outgrown such remainder, as advancing age had left to him, of what had once been very high managerial ability.

For the first thirty or forty years of his management he must have avoided in the main any such mistakes as these. Otherwise he could neither have achieved the success that he did nor would his staff have felt for him the respect and regard that they undoubtedly did.

Fairly early in the 1914 war he appeared before the Marylebone Tribunal to ask for exemption for the holders of some of his posts. With his fondness for a picturesque phrase, he told the Tribunal that he really could not spare any more, for "his staff now consisted almost entirely of waifs and strays." Some newspaper gave publicity to this pronouncement. Far from resenting this appraisal of their general quality the staff cut out the account in the newspaper, surrounded it with a decoration of little flags, and posted it up on the wall of their cloakroom, a pretty example of British sense of humour and consequent good temper. This must have been three or four years before the strike. Perhaps I ought to mention that in the early part of the war-period the atmosphere of the business was sweetened by my succeeding in persuading my father to subsidise the pay of those of the staff who joined the Armed Forces.

101. The strike, if it had not been mismanaged—so at least it seemed to me—almost unbelievably, might have done the firm tremendous harm.

In the actual event, however, the strikers were defeated completely. At the end a newspaper reporter inquired of the head of the firm whether any of them would be taken back. "Not," was the answer, "if they come to me crawling on their hands and knees."

Let those, who disapprove of this answer, remember the utter ruthlessness with which Left Wing politicians, if they get the chance, are apt to treat those who do not appear to them to share sufficiently their own opinions. Their use of the power they get by years of toil at vote-catching and at the other arts of politics, is apt to be no less harsh than my father's use of the power that he had got by his own years of toil at serving the community in other ways. To each it is clear that he has a right—indeed an imperative duty—to act upon certain impulses that happen to be strong in him and that involve on the one hand in some ways much self-denial and in other ways much personal advantage. In each case there is an acquisition of power and in each case the power is used in a manner that seems right to its holder but not to everybody.

It seems reasonable to hope that the Partnership will never have to deal with a strike.

On the other hand, we must remember that a great deal of labour-trouble arises not between managers and managed but between different groups of workers each seeking to assert a property-right in respect of work of some particular kind.

102. In the General Strike of 1926 Peter Jones sent out immediately to all of their account-customers a notice that, so long as funds were available, the pay of the staff would be continued and that this would be possible for longer if any of our account-customers, who could do so without inconvenience, would pay whatever they were owing to us. That circular was a great success. So many customers called to make these payments that there was a queue at the receiving-desk.

Policy in such matters has to be decided in relation to the circumstances of each occasion, but, if the Partnership ever finds itself again in any such emergency, I for my part should urge that, unless there seemed to be some very strong reasons to the contrary, it should proceed upon the idea that it is a family and that in emergencies a family should keep all of its members going as long as it can.

If it is thought desirable to reduce some rates of pay, there should be great care to avoid grave hardship. If possible, the reductions should be regarded merely as loans, so that the Partners, who happen to be members of the Partnership at that particular time, will not have to bear the cost of the extraordinary happening, whatever it is. Of course this will not be necessary so far as there is available a reserve-fund accumulated in past good times. But the workers naturally want in such times to have as much as possible of immediate advantage. Some of them would presumably have left before the occasion for distribution of the reserve. Alternatively the cost of continuing through a bad time incomes that are not being really made may be spread over the future. Earnings, that otherwise would then have been Partnership Benefit, may be used to give additional pay for the past bad time. The idea, however, that contractual income must under no circumstances suffer any diminution, and that, if it cannot be continued immediately, any temporary lessening must be regarded merely as a loan, must tend to produce rather excessive caution in raising pay when times are good. For my own part I am inclined to favour a policy of distinguishing between bad times of which the badness is due to mere fluctuation of trade when pay-rates may be simply lowered with no prospect of eventual subsidy, and badness due to quite abnormal interferences from outside, war for example or a general strike. As will be mentioned later, this idea was applied twice in the 1939 war and all of the money in question was eventually made good to those who for a time had gone without it. A community must, however, be careful how far, in order to make gifts to individuals who have been unlucky in the past, it sacrifices its collective interest in the present or for the future.

SETTLEMENT WITH MY BROTHER

103. The renewal of my partnership in my father's business raised a difficult problem for my brother and myself. The ideas, that are the subject of this book, did not attract him and his own first suggestion was that at the end of my father's life he should retain the business and my own interest in it should be paid out. I could have accepted that. My experience with Peter Jones had confirmed the belief, with which I had ventured upon that formidable undertaking, that upon the lines, that I contemplated, I could count upon swift success in any business that would be a reasonable choice and for which sufficient capital was available.

This reckoning has been further confirmed (conclusively, I think) by the Partnership's success with many businesses that, before they came into our hands, had long been doing badly.

But my brother's idea of the value, that should be set upon the share of the outgoing partner, proved to be too far different from my own. The turnover of the business at that time was about ten per cent. less than in its most successful year during the war. My brother expressed confidence that that level would never be reached again unless perhaps in conditions similarly abnormal. To my mind that was, as in due course it quickly proved to be, an extreme misjudgment.

Since I could not agree that the same partner should thus value the share to be taken by whoever was to go out and should also decide that he himself would retain the business, I proposed that one of us should do the valuing and the other should make the choice. My brother could not see his way to agree to that. The deadlock continued for some time and it seemed to me likely that in the end neither of us would retain the business. It would be simply sold up and the proceeds divided.

I was very anxious to avoid that if I possibly could and eventually there flashed across my mind the idea that my brother's desire for personal freedom might enable us to come to terms, if I could acquire his interest during my father's lifetime so that he could leave the firm without financial disadvantage to himself.

The transaction involved a very large sum, for it had to include an acquisition of the whole of my brother's prospects under my father's will and it was not easy to effect. It took in fact about four months. I arranged with my brother that for that summer of 1926 he should continue in charge of the general management at Oxford Street, so that I, who during all this time had Peter Jones on my hands, could at Oxford Street devote myself wholly to what the Partnership now calls the Buying Side. Then my brother was to go away as usual for a summer holiday and to write to his father that he felt that he needed a long rest and that now, that I was back at Oxford Street, he was proposing to take, as he had always greatly desired to do, a trip round the world.

All this duly happened. As my brother and I had foreseen, my father promptly terminated my brother's partnership with no sign of serious concern then or afterwards and for the remainder of his life (a little more than two years) he and I continued together quite smoothly until his death in June of 1928.

CHAPTER 5

LEGAL ESTABLISHMENT OF THE PARTNERSHIP
AND A FIRST GREAT EXPANSION

104. In this summer of 1928 I found myself the sole owner of the whole of the business of John Lewis and Company and of almost the whole of the business of Peter Jones Ltd., and of certain securities that had been purchased with the proceeds of the sale during the war of pretty well all of my father's investments in house and shop property.

The time was now come to redeem the "Share Promises" that had been issued year by year to the Partners in Peter Jones Ltd. and in John Lewis and Company. In the case of John Lewis and Company, the amount available for distribution had been confined of course to my own share in the profits and that share had been subject to taxation as the income of one person.

It was now necessary to do two things. In the first place the Share Promises, that were now outstanding to a nominal total of £76,632, had either to be redeemed for cash or else to be exchanged for a security that would be saleable upon the Stock Exchange.

AN IRREVOCABLE SETTLEMENT IN TRUST

In the second place future profits available for distribution as Partnership Benefit must not be taxable henceforward as the income of one person but only as the many separate incomes of those to whom the Benefit would go.

This would mean that the total amount of taxation would be very much less, so that the Partnership Benefit would be correspondingly greater both for its individual recipients, whatever its form, and as additional capital for the Partnership if the distribution was not in cash.

For this purpose it was necessary to make what lawyers call an irrevocable settlement in trust. For years all this had been under consideration with professional advisers.

ACQUISITION OF T. J. HARRIES AND CO. LTD.

105. The plan could have been carried out without any raising of fresh capital from the investing public but fresh capital was needed for another reason.

There happened to be just at this time an opportunity to buy in Oxford Street a business that was very near to that of John Lewis and,

Company. Between the two there was only the width of Holles Street, a corner building occupied by a bank and beyond the bank two small shops.

Except for one very small break, the Harries business stretched all the way along the remainder of the space between Holles Street on the west and Princes Street on the east. Roughly speaking the ground-floor of this business was just about the same size and shape as that which my father had made, an oblong of a good comfortable width but very far longer than wide. Whereas, however, my father's business had its short frontage to Oxford Street and its long frontage to Holles Street, the Harries business had its short frontage to Princes Street and its long frontage to Oxford Street.

This was, of course, immensely advantageous for those departments to which window-display is especially important. The business of John Lewis and Company, as it stood, seemed to me decidedly precarious. From years of persuading Buyers to be content with windows in Holles Street I knew very well how great was the superiority of Oxford Street frontage. The fact, that my father's business had so little of Oxford Street frontage, had very powerfully increased the extent to which his temperament had led him to let the development of his business become extremely ill-balanced. The Departments, of which his own knowledge was greatest, those that sold piece-goods, were given all the best of the floor-space and a great part of the Oxford Street frontage. Other features of my father's policy or consequences of his very extensive and persistent inadvertence, his tendency, for example, to carry at all times of year stocks that were rather extravagantly large, had fostered the growth of this side of the business and so had the dwindling of competition because the general tendency of retail trading had been away from the sale of materials by the yard and towards the sale of garments ready made.

His famous Silk Buyer, Mr. Yearsley, once astonished me by saying that, if ever he set up for himself, he would confine his business to those new Departments. He would leave other people to cater for what he felt to be the dwindling public demand for piece goods.

For my own part I did not foresee it at all at this time of which we are speaking, the later half of 1928, but in fact the piece goods trade, that had been so extremely important all through my father's long life, was now near to a sudden and very great contraction. Had we foreseen that happening, we must have jumped at the chance to get the Harries business with its incomparably better frontage for the Fashion Departments to which abundance of window-space is so extremely important.

SIZE, IF SUFFICIENTLY SOUND, IS STRENGTH

106.   Our decision, however, was based upon a very much broader and simpler notion. We simply looked at the fact that the Partnership had already competitors whose scale of operations was far larger.

The Harries acquisition would lift us more or less to that level. This alone seemed sufficient argument. Other things being equal, size must mean strength and security: a large lump of sugar, as I said at this time and have often said since, takes more melting than a small.

The fact, that the business would be divided by Holles Street, would be regrettable but that disadvantage did not seem too great.

ALL THE NEW SPACE TO THE OLD DEPARTMENTS

The Partnership decided accordingly to take the chance and buy the Harries business and, moreover, we decided that we would not start any new Department. We would transfer to the new shop with its abundance of window display, all those Departments of my father's business that had been comparatively ill-developed. The whole of the space, thus made vacant, should be used to give more scope to those Departments in which my father had been strong, the Departments that supply trade as well as retail customers, the Departments that sell dress materials of all kinds and the small things that dressmakers need.

Furthermore, we would retain in that shop what may be called "the house-keeper's Departments", the linens and carpets and so forth.

A SOUND MOVE REWARDED

107.   Had we foreseen that within a few years the piece good trade would suddenly contract so greatly as it did, this decision would have been an admirable stroke of policy. In fact it was in that respect a lucky fluke. Such ample new scope for the Fashion Departments permitted us to give to the piece goods trade not merely as much, as they had always had, of my father's frontage but a great deal more and the policy of enlarging all of those Departments instead of starting new ones to occupy the places of those, that were transferred to the other side of Holies Street, led to a very great strengthening of the former piece goods trade that had been already very strong.

GREAT SCOPE NEEDS GREAT ABILITIES: INTAKE OF NEW BUYERS

108.   In this part of the retail drapery trade the Partnership's strength was now incomparably greater than my father's had ever been. This was not only because of our ability to go much further than he had done in giving to these Departments window-display and floor-space but even—indeed much—more because, the moment my hands were free, I took extreme steps to make the buying-team not merely stronger but

as strong as it possibly could be. The results of combining the personal knowledge, skill and energy of the newcomers (Mr. R. J. Ledbrook, Mr. J. W. Murray and later Mr. J. R. Thomas and finally Mr. A. I. Hughes) with the enlargement of the floor-space and window-space available for their group of Departments were dazzling. The figures shot up to heights of which neither my father nor my brother had ever dreamed and, since we held steadily to my father's absolutely sound ideas of assortment and value and to his sound, though, perhaps, largely unintentional practice in the matter of holding ample stocks throughout the year and since we kept our stocks constantly clean whereas his practice in that respect had been very far from sound, (though in his own Department the ablest of his piece-goods Buyers, Mr. Yearsley, had, as I knew, deliberately and systematically disregarded in that respect the regulations he was supposed to be following), our hold upon this part of our business became every year firmer and firmer.

If, when the sudden sharp contraction of demand began to show itself, we had had only the former business of John Lewis and Company, we should have had to decide whether to persist in trying to keep up the piece goods figures at the risk of finding that that trade nevertheless withered away. In that case we should have made correspondingly little progress with a compensatory developing of the Fashion Departments. On the other hand, if in order to achieve that compensatory development we had reduced more or less drastically the former advantages of the Piece-goods Departments, they would have suffered terribly and first-class Buyers might not have been willing to persevere against the double tremendous handicap of the contraction of public demand and of the reduction of their own window-space and floor-space.

Placed, however, as we actually were, we were able simply to persevere with the piece goods trade. The tendency, that had been previously pretty strong, of our competitors to leave it more and more to us, was increased greatly by the contraction of public demand and, since so much of the total business was left to us, we found it still worth doing.

CHESS AND GENERAL STRATEGY IN MATTERS OF BUSINESS

109. The whole thing was a very interesting example of the completely unforeseen ways in which a move, that is intrinsically sound, can be fruitful of advantage. Though the playing of chess can easily absorb far too much time, it has in my view some important educational advantages. Success depends very much upon comprehension of general principles and upon making moves that in that sense appear to be sound, though you cannot see at all in what particular ways you will reap advantages or, on the other hand, suffer eventually if you proceed otherwise. The beginner is apt to yield to temptations to believe mistakenly that in the

particular game there is sufficient reason for making a move that appears to be contrary to general doctrine. Bitter experience makes him try harder and harder to resist such temptations and he is apt to see that resistance has been rewarded.

Such elementary ideas as that, if its financial resources, its personnel and the other factors are adequate, a larger business must be safer than a smaller, have always seemed to me very comparable to the general doctrines that have arisen in chess and here was a signal example of a completely unexpected reward.

A NARROW SHAVE

A few years later the same move, that is to say the acquisition of the Harries business, was to prove in another utterly unexpected way immensely advantageous. A bomb destroyed the whole of the Partnership's property upon the west side of Holles Street, the whole of my father's old business and all the buildings that by that time the Partnership had acquired upon the remainder of that great island site.

Without the Harries business the name of John Lewis and Company would have disappeared for years from that part of Oxford Street in which for seventy-six years up to that time it had been building up an immensely valuable goodwill.

For my own part I feel quite uncertain how far that goodwill would have survived a complete break of such a length but I am very sure that in this respect the possession of the Harries business has had for the Partnership a value that it would be difficult to exaggerate.

This, however, is looking ahead. At present we are in the autumn of 1928. We decided that into the great new shop, that we should be getting from the Harries management and of which the name would, of course, be changed to our own, we would put all the things that are ready to wear and such accessories of dress as handbags.

These decisions turned out well and upon the long view the case for making them was to my mind very plainly ample.

SAFETY FIRST: RUNNING A WAITING RACE

110. But they certainly had one great drawback. The new acquisition would mean a great sudden increase of the Partnership's working-expenses including the pay-sheet and there would be no immediate proportionate increase of the profit available for distribution as Partnership Benefit. This would diminish greatly the delightful excitement, that otherwise there might have been, in beginning immediately to distribute year after year a spectacular rate of Partnership Benefit. It might have given everybody year after year upwards of two months of extra pay on the year's work. But for resisting this temptation there was an argument that

to my mind was sufficient. Our business was as yet not on the scale of the more formidable of its competitors and—a larger lump of sugar takes longer to melt.

THE PRIVATE FIRM BECOMES A PUBLIC COMPANY 1928

111. The first consequence of the decision was that the private firm of John Lewis and Company had to be turned into a public company that could raise fresh capital from the investing public. If my father had lived a very little longer, this capital could, as things turned out, have been raised considerably more cheaply. In actual fact the amount of the issue was £750,000 and the rate of dividend was 7%, the last issue of this kind, for which the conditions, that arose in the 1914 war, made it necessary to offer this "dear money" rate.

ENOUGH IS ENOUGH

I was advised at this time that my own interest in the two businesses, John Lewis and Company and Peter Jones Ltd., could be sold instantly, that is to say at no more than two or three hours' notice, for more than a million pounds in immediate cash. The late Mr. H. Clifford-Turner, a first-rate authority upon such a matter, told me one morning that he would gladly undertake to bring me by three o'clock that same afternoon a contract for that amount signed by a financial house of unquestionable strength.

My wife and I (we had married in 1923) had made up our minds that for the rest of our lives we would limit our private expenditure to a certain rate. If we held to that programme, then this money, that we had already, would cover the whole of that expenditure, no matter how long we should live, and would indeed leave a large remainder (that should, we intended, go to the Partnership) beyond such provision, as we intended to make, for each of any children we might have, a comfortable independence, if ill health or accident or a vocation for some occupation ill-paid or quite unremunerative should prevent their making money for themselves.

We held—and hold still—that it is not a bad thing for society that some of its members shall thus have what used to be called independent means, freedom to choose their occupation without regard to the making of money. On my own twenty-first birthday my father gave me fifty thousand pounds. Almost ever since the doctors have been telling me that I really must not work so hard.

For my own part I sometimes wonder whether we may not see a very great deal more provision of unearned income. Might not a great many of society's misfits, if they were allowed to draw unemployment pay, just as if in their small way they were junior members of a wealthy family, have reasonably happy lives as small holders and rear valuable families?

With a small secure money-income might they not keep themselves and their families in fair comfort and health by what would be in the main "subsistence farming"?

LIQUIDITY: ANOTHER MOVE ON GENERAL PRINCIPLES

112. Even on extreme assumptions of the ages, to which my wife and I might live, and of the possible number of our children, the capital, of which we were already possessed, would exceed by a very wide margin our total prospective requirements.

For various reasons I hesitated whether to retain in my own possession a capital much larger than this but I have always urged the Partnership to aim in everything at what I call liquidity—freedom from ties, elbow-room, elasticity—and, just as we bought the Harries business upon the mere broad idea that in view of the size present and prospective of some of its competitors the Partnership might not be safe unless its business became much larger than as yet it was, so my wife and I based our financial arrangements upon the mere broad idea of not depriving ourselves needlessly of a surplus that might conceivably prove a valuable buffer against developments that, if they occurred at all, would be quite unforeseen. The deprivation would have been needless for we intended to let the Partnership have the use of the capital free of any interest and in the position of greatest risk.

Such developments have in fact occurred, partly in other ways but chiefly in this last war. In this winter of 1947/48 the Partnership has still in its hands a large remainder of the interest-free loan, that I made to it in 1929, and by reason of the war the value of the pounds, in which that remainder will be paid out, will be reduced below their value in 1929 to an extent that might have raised some rather awkward problems if nineteen years ago I had not merely restricted the capital claim, as I did, to an amount that was presumably a good deal, perhaps upwards of six figures, less than the most that I might have hoped to get by an actual sale but had further written off, as I considered doing, nearly half of the valuation that was in fact adopted.

CAPITALISATION OF MY OWN INTERESTS

113. The arrangement, that was now made in 1929, amounted to a sale of the whole of my property in the businesses of John Lewis and Company and of Peter Jones Ltd. to the workers, present and prospective, in the John Lewis Partnership. I took the price not in cash but in securities, that is to say in charges that the workers would pay off with profits that I could have kept for myself and taken as dividends upon those securities but that by means of an irrevocable settlement were given up to the workers. The nominal value of those securities was only the amount for which Mr.

Clifford-Turner had advised me that that property could be sold very easily, in fact instantly, for immediate cash. But the securities were to bear no interest or dividend and I intended to take no fees or salary.

To carry out these ideas the private firm of John Lewis and Company, which was now wholly my own, was converted into a public company with the same name and there was created at the same time a second public company, John Lewis Partnership Limited. I wished that the securities, that I was to take in exchange for my property in the John Lewis and Peter Jones businesses, should carry no interest or dividend and should nevertheless rank last in the theoretically possible event of a liquidation. I felt that, until the Partnership should be much more mature, the conduct of its affairs must be very much a one-man business and, if that were to be so, I must be able to answer criticisms by pointing out that no one else could lose anything at all until I should have lost all of the great fortune that these securities would represent.

Accordingly my property in the two businesses was converted almost wholly into what were called Deferred Bonds. They were to bear no interest so long as they were paid off at the rate of twenty-five each year, so that the total payment would be spread over more than thirty years. If any Bonds became overdue, I was to be entitled to charge interest at the rate of ten per cent. but this right was never exercised. I had, however, and exercised for the purpose of acquiring and developing the Leckford Estate a power to call in approximately one-fifth of the capital represented by these Bonds.

For some reason, that I have now forgotten, a small part of the securities was in Preference Shares of John Lewis and Company Ltd. As long as I held those Shares, I renounced the dividend on them, so that the money should go into the Partnership Benefit and, as soon as I could, I sold them.

Besides the Deferred Bonds and these Preference Shares, I took twelve thousand £1 Deferred Ordinary Shares of John Lewis Partnership Ltd. Of these Shares there were created only twelve thousand. They were expressly designed to carry the control of the Partnership without an important lock-up of capital. Each individual Share was to have a thousand votes. They were entitled to a non-cumulative yearly dividend that must never exceed ten per cent. That dividend also I have always renounced.

THE EXPERIMENT NOT VITIATED

114.   Thus the Partnership was getting my interest for the exact amount for which I was advised that I could sell it at a few hours' notice for immediate cash but the Partnership was being allowed to spread the

payment over more than thirty years, so that it was really getting the property for a small fraction of its immediate cash value.

This arrangement did not vitiate the experiment. As is explained elsewhere in this book, such a partnership could be started perfectly well by two persons whose enterprise consisted of a costermonger's barrow and who had no capital at all, only credit. The real effect of giving the Partnership an interest-free loan of all this capital was to give its members some of the advantage they would have had if the whole system had been started a generation earlier. In that case my private estate would have been limited to a capital giving a modest independence—say about one twentieth of the amount at which my actual interests had just been valued. To live, as I wished to do, I should have had to take not only some interest upon that smaller capital but also some pay for my work. There is no means of valuing at all closely such qualifications as are not fairly readily available if a position falls vacant. No number of short-sighted men standing at any one viewpoint can be equal to one far-sighted man. Ability to navigate a boat may mean for everyone in it the difference between life and death. If in the boat there is only one person who has that skill, how are you to value his services?

Napoleon, whose opinion in such matters is respectable, said "In war men are nothing. A man is everything." War is merely business of a peculiarly exacting kind.

So long as human nature requires that some of the needs of the general community shall be met by means of competitive private enterprise, the income scale, by which such efforts are induced, must, it seems to me, depend not only at its lower but also at its upper end not upon comparative valuation of performance but upon consumption, that is to say upon need.

As for my own case, I have always thought that all of my private expenditure, that has been really important to my own personal happiness and to that of my family, could have been covered easily by such pay as the Partnership could well—and quite reasonably—have attached to its position of chief individual responsibility. Rightly or wrongly I think I should probably have made about as much at the Bar or indeed in any of several professions in which I could have been, I believe, happy enough.

EFFECT OF THE INTEREST-FREE LOAN

115.   If I had drawn from the Partnership such an income as that, there would have remained a good pay-sheet with a good minimum wage, a good pension fund, a good margin for various collective amenities and besides all these a good rate of what we call Partnership Benefit.

The arrangement, that I actually made, saved the Partnership from having to pay that interest upon whatever portion I might still have owned of the capital of the business and from having to give any pay for the position of chief individual responsibility. If the Partnership had been started a generation earlier, I should have had to take from it an income but the whole Partnership would on the other hand have been vastly larger. For many years past the business would have been far more productive and far less of the earnings of those years would have been drawn off by taxation.

For both reasons the Partnership would have had a great deal of capital upon which it would have had to pay no more than five per cent. and that it would have been entitled to use as the base of a financial pyramid of securities to be issued to the investing public.

If all that had been happening for twenty years or more before the Partnership was actually established in 1929, the Partners would, I believe, have been very substantially better off than they actually were with this interest-free loan of my own capital and with my unpaid services for these last nineteen years.

Nevertheless, these special arrangements have saved the Partnership a good deal and to that extent they have mitigated the ill effects upon the fruitfulness and potentialities of the plan of the fact that it was not adopted a generation earlier.

116. The plan, as thus actually adopted, with the special features of the interest-free loan of most of my own capital and with my unpaid continuance in the position of chief individual responsibility, worked quite well. Until this last war the Partnership kept ahead of its obligations in the repayment of Bonds.

RENUNCIATION OF RIGHT TO DEMAND REPAYMENT OF BONDS

By that time I had given up without any compensation my right to demand (except in certain circumstances) repayment of Bonds up to £25,000 each year and my right to claim interest up to ten per cent. on any Bonds of which the payment so demanded was overdue. I had been advised that it would help the Partnership considerably in a large financial operation.

I have been told since that the advice was bad, that the renunciation of this right was quite unnecessary and that the advantage to the Partnership was not enough to justify the disadvantage to myself. I feel pretty sure that view is correct. I had never had occasion to claim the interest and I do not think that I would have done so now, that this recent war has thrown the repayment of the Bonds into arrear, but I think it has been by mere good luck that the uncompensated surrender of this right has been so harmless as now seems likely.

That Mr. Clifford-Turner's valuation of my interest was not excessive has been shown beyond dispute by the subsequent history of the two businesses.

A DIFFICULT CHOICE

117.   If my wife and I had chosen to sell out, we should have had a seven-figure fortune that invested in sound securities would have produced an income of upwards of £40,000 a year. We should have had none of the frets and worries and anxieties of exercising a controlling interest in a large business. We should have had the whole of our time to use as we might be inclined. I was still under forty-five. My wife was younger. The worries and stresses of our lives up to then had not been small. A life of leisure with resources so large was attractive.

On the other hand, the course, that we took, had for us, our temperaments being what they are, attractions still stronger.

A MIDDLE COURSE

Rather over twenty years earlier I had had a sudden glimpse of the extreme happiness that for those, who are of the right metal, there may be in a complete renunciation of great wealth. I still remember it very clearly. I was sitting at the time on the top of an omnibus that was just turning out from the Haymarket towards Trafalgar Square and that was caught in a traffic jam. I can remember very vividly the warm glow that ran through me as for a moment I saw something of the satisfaction of those who, as some have done, renounce—and do not afterwards regret renouncing—great wealth and choose a life of extreme material simplicity, such a life as in the world of those days, about 1907, would have cost three or four pounds a week.

But almost at once I felt that for me such a choice would be too dangerous. Many an inexperienced climber gets into a position to which his nerve and muscular strength are unequal. In seeking the mental satisfactions and the physical benefits of climbing he destroys himself and the world loses such services as he might have rendered.

Thrilling though that feeling had been, it seemed to me almost at once that in our modern world it was too likely that to take such a course and not to regret it too much would be beyond my own capacity. On the other hand it seemed to me that to start life with a modest independence must give in a general way as good and perhaps on the whole a better chance of real happiness than to inherit great wealth. The really intelligent commonly do not want wealth. If they do, they can always get it for themselves. At least I thought so then and I think so still. Certainly they can always get it if they start with the immense advantage of the ability, that a secure independence gives, to take a long view and bide their time. Without such intelligence is the possession of great wealth really expedient even for the heir himself?

LEGAL RESTRICTION OF INHERITANCE

118.   In any case at the time, of which we are now talking, that is rather before I was twenty, I already doubted very much whether, if my own life should be fairly long, it would be possible by that time to bequeath much more than a modest independence. I felt that in our own country capitalism was near to great modifications. In my early twenties I said to my mother that money is nothing but crystallised power and that I thought that I might live to see a day in which large capital could no longer be bequeathed and that the possibilities of giving one's own children "a good position in life" would be limited to power in other forms than the possession of capital and would depend upon their ability and will to take over that power and to keep hold of it.

There may be for example very important advantage in a chance to become well established in politics or in some other profession in which your father or some other kinsman has made a valuable position that he can to some extent pass on to you if your own gifts, though not extraordinary, will suffice to allow you to profit by such an opportunity.

No efforts to secure by laws, written or unwritten, equality of opportunity can, it seems to me, prevent those, who are successful in some field of work, from giving, if they choose, a specially good early training and a specially favourable start to anyone in whom they are interested. Certainly the possible beneficiary must be able and willing to profit by the training and by the special opportunity. But private capital likewise, however great, can be lost by folly or misfortune. A specially good training for some career and a specially favourable start in it may not be very gross privilege but it is by no means unimportant and, so far as I could, or can see, it cannot be prevented. Already in the British Labour Party there are examples of the fact that the children of successful fathers have a flying start, a specially good chance to show their fitness for membership of the House of Commons or high public office. If the management of business becomes, as in my own view it should and will, a profession, yielding no more than a good professional income I cannot for my own part see why those, who practise that profession successfully, should not have power to decide who shall succeed them in the position that they have devoted their own lives to creating or maintaining.

The tenure of each successive occupant of the position should certainly depend to a proper extent upon satisfactory results, but with that condition I suspect that the general community will be wise to let principal managers name their successors.

119.   At all events it seemed to me forty years ago or thereabouts that I might live to see a time when, even if you wished to do so, it would be no longer possible to bequeath great wealth but it might be possible to bequeath a position that carried most, if not all, of the advantages

that the ownership of the controlling interest in a business has for those who have no wish to abuse power or to consume excessively and whose confidence in their own capacity is sufficient to prevent their being too much worried by the thought that their position could be lost by a degree of mismanagement or misfortune very much smaller than would have had the same result if the same business had belonged to them in the old way. My inclination to spend my life, as I have, would have been just as strong if I had known that I should never have children or that they would not stay in the Partnership if they joined it at all.

It was obviously possible that, if I had any children, none of them might wish to succeed to my own position, whatever that might be, in the business world or be able to maintain himself or herself in it if he or she tried. But it seemed to me that, if I should live to be old, private business enterprise might be still one of the best ways of ensuring the material well-being of your children if the bequeathing of large capital became impossible. The likelihood, as it seemed to me, that such bequeathing would in fact become impossible, made it of course a good deal easier to follow a plan that would set pretty narrow limits to power of bequest.

MODEST INDEPENDENCE

On the other hand, it seemed to me likely that the law would still permit such bequests as would give moderate independence. I knew already that financial independence was said to be one of the worst misfortunes that can befall a young man. I had no doubt that that was true of many men and that in their cases such bequests must from the standpoint of the general community mean a serious waste of capital. But it seemed to me that the hope of placing one's own children in safety from ill consequence from lack of earning-power or from the loss of it and in freedom to follow some occupation, that is not "a way to make money", was an incentive that the general community could not afford to withhold from the possessors of uncommon ability, including, as in my own view that term must, the ability to work really hard, even though that particular ability be not combined with very much of what is commonly called cleverness.

AN IMMENSE INDUCEMENT TO EXERTION OF UNCOMMON ABILITY

120. I imagine that, to many, especially perhaps to the unconsciously greedy or envious, this reduction, great though it is, of the possibilities of bequest and inheritance will seem to be plainly and grossly inadequate. Perhaps they are right. But to me human nature seems to be not yet developed beyond the need of those incentives to the exertion of certain important abilities by that very small minority of each generation who possess them at the present early stage of the evolution of mankind.

Rightly or wrongly I believe that for some time yet men and women will desire to "do something for their children" and that no efforts of legislators will permanently succeed in preventing that desire from having substantial effects. Let those, who take upon themselves the responsibility of fostering such legislation, consider what have been the consequences in France of the laws that deprived men of the power to please themselves whether at their deaths their property should be divided more or less equally among all their children or transmitted in the main in one whole. My own knowledge of these matters is only vague but I am under the impression that those laws are generally agreed to be the main, if not the whole, cause why France, once so populous and so strong, has come to be called "the country of the only child".

EGOISM AND THE FAMILY IMPULSE

The human heart is a very queer thing. How many of the men, who toil strenuously to accumulate wealth, are really working as they believe, for the happiness of a child or children and how far do they desire the child or children as a means of retaining in a way after their own deaths the possession of that wealth and the opportunities that it gives? How far do they desire the wealth for the sake of the children and how far the children for the sake of wealth? In such matters politicians mistakenly confident of their own ability to foresee the effects of legislation may perhaps do fearful harm.

I have believed all my life that in our modern society great changes towards equality were due and indeed very far overdue. They are happening too late to prevent the ruin of Europe by the blundering of electorates deprived by poverty of education proportionate to their present political power and misled by incompetent demagogues. Let us hope that these changes will not go now disastrously too far.

FORMATION OF JOHN LEWIS PARTNERSHIP LTD. AND
OF JOHN LEWIS AND CO., LTD.

121. The arrangement of April 1929 brought, as has been said, into existence two new companies, John Lewis and Company Limited and John Lewis Partnership Limited and an irrevocable settlement in trust. So long as all prior dividends were paid punctually, the control of the whole organisation was in the twelve million votes of the Deferred Ordinary Shares in John Lewis Partnership Ltd. The purpose of this arrangement was, as has been explained already, to safeguard the control of the Partnership until the experiment should seem to me, as now at last it does, to have gone far enough to justify another Settlement that would be supplementary to the first and that would complete the founding of the Partnership.

Messrs. Filene Brothers of Boston, U.S.A., set up a profit-sharing scheme under which they issued to their staff "common stock". Though the business was large, the staff held in the end a controlling interest. At a time, when there was a great boom in such securities, they were offered very attractive prices for their holdings. Years after our own arrangements had been made, I heard Mr. Edward Filene, the member of the firm who had been chiefly responsible for the whole plan of sharing the profit in that way, say that he had entreated the staff not to part with their controlling interest but to bear in mind that, if they sold it, the whole profit-sharing plan would come to an end. Nevertheless the temptation was too great. I cannot see what else was to be expected. We should have a completely different world if people, whose general qualifications are such that their general position in life is that of the rank and file of a retail drapery business, had such wisdom and self-control as the Filene scheme required of them. The recent war itself would have been avoided, for the British electorate would in that case have had too much sense to allow preparations aimed so plainly at themselves to be carried too far.

SAFETY FIRST: ONE STEP AT A TIME

122. As far back as 1910 I had always intended that in due course there should be some arrangement that would safeguard the members of the Partnership from the possibility that the controlling interest might be sold or the Partnership wound up and its assets distributed. But in 1929 I still did not feel that as yet I could see any plan that looked good enough.

Absolute safety, either in investments or in anything else, is not within human capacity. In a thing so novel and so difficult I was not hoping to hit upon any plan that would seem to be virtually certain to turn out well. But I felt that I ought to wait until I should be able to feel that some particular plan was much more promising than any that had occurred to me as yet. Any man's life may end any day. I had to reckon with the possibility that my life-work might be left with this supremely important part of it still to do. But that seemed to me to be a risk that had got to be taken.

TEMPORARY PRECAUTIONS

I arranged that in the event of my premature death the controlling interest should pass to my wife, who would, I hoped and believed, endeavour to complete the thing and who was, I thought, as likely as anyone else, whom I knew, to do it well and I hoped that, if in her turn she had to leave it unfinished, the opportunity would pass to someone else who would wish to use it properly and who would succeed in doing so.

At the time, of which we are speaking, in 1929 and for more than ten years thereafter I could see no way ahead. I was quite uncertain what definite organisation would arise from such experience as I had still to get and from such reading and discussing and thinking as I had still to do.

The 1929 Settlement merely ensured that, so long as it remained in force, the profits of the Partnership's business must go to its workers. It gave them certain powers to recommend who should and who should not be admitted to participation in the successive distributions of that profit. But that is all that the 1929 Settlement really did.

It simply gave the workers, so long as it was left in force, a legal right to receive the profits to which the Settlement applied, so that those profits would be taxable only comparatively lightly as a mass of separate small incomes instead of much more heavily as the income of one person.

CHAPTER 6

FARMING

123. In the winter of 1928 I bought for a permanent home a property in Hampshire that included a length of the River Test and the village of Leckford.

The condition of the village was dreadful and the only way to provide good employment was to farm the land directly. That locked up a lot of money.

Most of it went into getting the land back into good heart, providing fencing and water-supply, tractors, combine-harvesters, corndriers and so on. The whole motive of all this was to provide good employment. No interest was charged, any more than to the Partnership. It was intended that, if the farming became profitable, the profit should go to the workers, either in a new little partnership or, if the prospect of profit became sufficiently promising, in the John Lewis Partnership as has now happened. In the meantime all the cottage-rents were discontinued, pay-rates were raised as far as seemed possible without making too much trouble in that countryside and a good many thousands of pounds were spent upon putting the cottages into good condition and giving them a piped supply of clean water, a bath-house and so on. Of this outlay a good deal has been written off as irrecoverable and a good deal more may turn out in the end to have been likewise lost. But the villages (Leckford and a good part that was acquired later of Longstock) have been made prosperous and the yield of the land has been increased enormously (the corn-yield has been raised from just over three sacks an acre to just under nine), a thing that has been, of course, valuable to the nation.

Under the Managing Director, the late Mr. W. D. Hollis, the Leckford farming has produced a quantity and quality of crops and milk that have attracted a steady stream of expert visitors wishing to study his methods. When we kept pigs, the Estate won the Herd Cup for the breed (Large Black) and all the farming has been on those lines. The Estate was among the first in England to mechanise corn-farming and to use driers. Mr. Hollis wished me to add that, unless abundant capital had been available, these things could, of course, not have been done. That is plainly true but capital is as helpless without skill and diligence as are they without sufficient capital.

The war, of course, with its effect upon prices, helped substantially but this help was sadly offset by the fact that five hundred and twenty-eight acres of the best of the land, that we had spent so much upon getting back into good heart, were taken by the Air Ministry for a rent that was not within sight of what the land would have been earning. I am told that a reasonable calculation of our loss of net revenue from this land during these many years would be upwards of £10,000.

THE POST-WAR OUTLOOK FOR THE COUNTRY-CLUB IDEA

124. War must have such consequences and we are assured that the land will be returned to us in two or three years' time, so that we shall be able to plant out the disfiguring buildings and the screaming of the aeroplanes will no longer be the plague that it has been to my own home and to all the others round about. But it was a sore disappointment that the land, instead of being returned to us after the war was retained by the Ministry at the same ridiculous rent and sublet to Messrs. Vickers for experimental purposes.

The war-needs of the Forces have inevitably brought to many places damage far worse than the Leckford Estate has suffered and, if the land is in fact returned to us, the ultimate hope, with which I have persevered, may yet be fulfilled. That hope was that in the end the Leckford Estate might turn out to be a really desirable possession for the Partnership, a place in which there could be a country club on the American lines, with communal fishing, shooting, golf and stables for the occupants of a whole colony of country homes with some dormy-houses for occasional visitors.

Perhaps this idea might be developed so that Partners, who like this kind of country life and who either cannot afford to maintain a house or a cottage or at all events do not wish to do so, can have a room or two of their own that would be permanently and entirely theirs and in respect of which they would have no worries for securing service and for insurance and upkeep and so on.

Many farms find that the proceeds of their farming can be supplemented usefully by taking lodgers. The Leckford land being as it is a very shallow, light loam over chalk and on the other hand a very good district for holiday-making, might well cultivate earnings of that kind in addition to the farming and it seems conceivable that it may be good for the general community that urban communities like the John Lewis Partnership shall develop in this way substantial country interests, so that there will be an organised permanent relation of mutual advantage to country and town.

Before the war there was an encouraging beginning of such developments. There was a very successful summer-holiday camp and an appreciable number of Partners showed an inclination to come at all times of the year to Leckford for short country holidays.

CHAPTER 7

NEW TECHNIQUES IN DEALING WITH SHAREHOLDERS

COMPLETE CANDOUR TO SHAREHOLDERS SIXTEEN YEARS BEFORE THE COHEN REPORT

125. Much of this chapter might well be held to belong to the next Part of this book rather than to this one that is to say to the ideas that have arisen from my experience rather than to that experience itself but the chapter could hardly be taken as a whole from its present place and it seemed impossible to divide satisfactorily. At all events it contains very important experience of the need to be cautious in accepting expert advice. Another equally striking case was the settlement with my brother. The plan was ridiculed as manifestly impossible first by a very eminent solicitor and then by a similarly eminent Junior Counsel but, as they could not produce authority for their extremely firm assurances, I went on to Leading Counsel and the thing went through.

In 1929 the Partnership found itself issuing for the first time a report to a large body of shareholders. My previous experience of that kind had been confined to Peter Jones Ltd., and did not amount to much, since in that little company I had held all the debentures and almost all the ordinary shares. But one of our new companies, John Lewis and Company Ltd., had issued to the investing public debentures for a million pounds and another three-quarters of a million in preference shares and was likely to become, as it has, much larger.

Moreover, the other of our new companies, John Lewis Partnership Ltd. ("The" John Lewis Partnership Ltd. as it was called in those days but the title proved awkward and the "The" was dropped) though at present small, was intended to be eventually very large indeed. It was correspondingly desirable that our accounts and reports should be in full accordance with whatever might be our permanent policy in such matters.

A BAD CUSTOM

126. Those, who on this first occasion drafted them, did so according to their ideas of normal practice in such matters and in due course the drafts came to me.

They were my first experience of such documents and to my mind they were not nearly sufficiently informative. I thought that the accounts and report of a public company ought to get very much nearer and in fact as near as they well could to anticipating and answering every question that an intelligent shareholder, who did not wish to be needlessly troublesome, might feel a serious inclination to ask.

The figures were accordingly broken up into far greater detail and upon those figures there was drafted a very full report designed to take the place of the speech usually made from the Chair at the meeting itself.

In my view at that time (1929)—a view that sixteen years later was adopted in effect by the Cohen Commission upon Company Law— that speech should be confined to any matters too recent to have been mentioned in the report and except for such matters the Chairman, instead of making a speech, should invite questions and answer them. How else, as we said in some of these reports, could shareholders judge properly whether it would be worth their while to take the trouble to attend the meeting and how else could they have a proper opportunity to make up their minds what questions they would like to ask?

The ordinary practice poured over the assembled shareholders a stream of sudden information in a speech that might or might not be consciously or unconsciously so composed and phrased as to avoid arousing certain ideas but that at all events would require that its hearers should have the presence of mind and the technical knowledge to see instantly in that speech all that they would see in it if they could read it at leisure and consult other people upon it. To me that practice seemed as contrary to commonsense as the normal division of the profits of large scale industry and, just as our partnership broke right away from general custom in that respect, so it should, I thought, break right away from general custom in this other respect of dealings with investors.

The Partnership should treat every one of them as if they were intimate personal friends of the directors of the company and it should give to every one of them every scrap of information that a director could properly give to a shareholder who was one of his personal friends and who had asked any reasonable question.

FALLIBILITY OF EXPERTS

127. When the figures and the report had been thus redrafted, they were sent to the Partnership's solicitors for technical criticism. The head of that firm, Mr. Clifford-Turner, saw me upon the draft and assured me that this innovation would be exceedingly unwise. I answered that it seemed to me to be indisputable commonsense. Mr. Clifford-Turner replied very reasonably that he had very great experience of dealing with shareholders and that I had practically none and that I should make a grievous mistake if I did not accept his advice that reports of this kind would make the Partnership's company meetings a sort of bear-garden. The meetings, said he, of any company, that issued such reports as this, would be a happy hunting-ground for the type of shareholder who has nothing much to do

and loves to hear his own voice and to pose as a shrewd man of business keeping the Board of Directors in order. Our companies would get a reputation for chronic friction between the shareholders and the Board and that would be gravely bad for our future finance.

A SUCCESSFUL INNOVATION

Mr. Clifford-Turner's opinion was plainly entitled to very great respect. He was still in the prime of life. He had had a long experience of matters of this kind and his ability had enabled him to create in the intense competition of the City of London a new firm with a large practice and very considerable standing.

But I answered that I was never willing to believe without trial that what seemed to me to be plain commonsense was in fact unworkable. If this technique, that we were proposing to adopt, had to an extent, that was too serious, such results as Mr. Clifford-Turner was so confident that it would, then we should have to give it up but we should try it first of all.

It was an unqualified success. Never once in all these years has any shareholder justified Mr. Clifford-Turner's forebodings. Far from being a bear-garden, our meetings after the first year or two never took as long as five minutes. Hardly any shareholders ever came at all. There was nothing to come for. Their interests were limited to a moderate fixed dividend. The business was always doing reasonably well. The results were always set out in extreme detail with a commentary of extreme candour. There were never any questions and year after year the proceedings literally took less than five minutes.

The most signal example of the effect of such candour upon relations between shareholders and directors was after the great bombing in the autumn of 1940. Even then, the shareholders were so content with the accounts and reports that practically none of them thought it worth while to come to the meeting.

NEWSPAPER APPROVAL: THE PRACTICE SPREADS: FORCE OF EXAMPLE?

128. The new technique was praised a good deal in the financial columns of the newspapers and within a few weeks of the appearance of the first of these voluminous reports we received from the Partnership's bankers a request to be supplied with a copy to be sent by them to a bank in Belfast who had written that one of their important customers had told them that he had heard that John Lewis and Company Limited had issued to their shareholders a report of quite a new kind and that it was "an absolute model" of what such communications should be and that he would like to see a copy.

Apart from those original Press notices the Partnership, so far as I know, has had very little credit for the example that it has been setting all these years. But from year to year the practice has spread. The times were ripe for such a development and it may be of course that the same idea occurred quite separately to the directors of some other large companies.

"THE POWER", SAID LORD NORTHCLIFFE, "OF THE PRESS IS TO SUPPRESS"

It may be that it was merely an accident that those companies, which regularly purchased advertisement space for reports of their meetings, received in the editorial columns of leading financial newspapers much praise for the completeness and clarity of their accounts and reports but there was never or hardly ever any mention that the Partnership, that was not making such purchases of advertisement space, was doing the same thing and was at first entirely alone in setting that example.

I have always wondered whether we were really wise to refrain from buying space for that purpose.

At first we did so. It cost about £2,000 a year and my colleagues urged that it was not a good use of money. Somewhat doubtfully I acquiesced. There is no getting away from the fact that by now we should have spent in that way upwards of £30,000 and that is a lot of money. On the other hand, newspapers, we are told, have to choose between living by the sale of advertisement-space and living upon subsidies and newspapers supported, as they are in this country, in the former manner are far better for the general community than newspapers supported in the latter manner, as they are in some other countries.

NEWSPAPERS MUST LIVE

Some journalists tell us that there is a good deal of cant in the assertion that editorial policy is never influenced at all by good will to advertisers and ill will to non-advertisers. Newspaper-owners and their principal employees are human and it is presumably permissible to doubt whether as a whole they attain at all times complete carelessness of any selfish interests of their own.

Now the power of newspapers is very great and their friendliness or unfriendliness, even to a very moderate degree, may upon occasion be far more important than quite a lot of money. Moreover, there is the question of social obligation. Is it truly fair that individuals or organisations well able to spend some money upon advertising and working in a field from which the Newspaper-Press does as a whole need to draw substantial support of that kind, should accept the very important advantages to the whole community of the existence of such a Newspaper-Press as we have in this country but should decline to contribute to the support of that Press by the purchase of advertisement-space?

130.   Upon the feasibility of candour to shareholders it will be interesting to see what light is thrown by the results of the new legislation.

But the Partnership's twenty-seven years of experience has confirmed our own expectation that in business of our kind, conducted upon our own principles, though it is certainly true that some matters of business are important secrets, many things, that in business are commonly kept secret, can be disclosed with impunity. Up to that line the owners of the capital of a business ought, it seems to us, to be given ungrudgingly the advantages of ownership, not merely the essentially important advantage of knowing what is really happening in their business, so that they can judge whether to leave their capital in it or whether to sell out on any terms that may be obtainable and not merely the peace of mind of feeling that in that respect they are informed adequately but also the gratification of mere curiosity, mere inquisitiveness.

Nobody says "Don't be inquisitive" to the owner of a business who happens to feel curious on some question of fact and who proceeds to inform himself on that point. A security-holder is a part owner and, though the fact, that he is only a part-owner, makes it impossible that he should be given information that must not be available to competitors who otherwise for the purpose of getting that information, might acquire such part-ownership, he ought to be given all the information that he desires up to that point.

Accounts, that are to be published at all, should be informative to this extent and not merely to the minimum extent that legislators may succeed in enforcing. The Accounts by themselves will not be intelligible without an explanatory commentary. If the manager of your business tells you that its profit is larger than last year, you, if you are wise, will not feel that there is nothing more to hear. You will want to know whether, it is the result of doing more business or of merely getting more profit upon the same amount of business as before and whether it is due to temporary accident or likely to continue.

CHAPTER 8

PHTHONOS

(This Greek word is used here because the idea cannot be expressed shortly in English).

131.   SOON after I left Westminster, Dr. James. Gow, who had been Headmaster during most of my time there, suddenly lost his sight. I was told that he liked to have visitors and I called upon him. He reminded me that among the ancient Greeks there was a belief that their gods were not willing that any man should be, as we sometimes say, divinely happy. Very great good fortune in a human life aroused, the Greeks thought, in the minds of the Gods, a jealous ill-will. They called it phthonos. "I," said Dr. Gow, "was too happy."

He had had much to make him so. He was a scholar of considerable eminence. He had loved his work and his position. His health was good. His marriage was happy. His children were doing well. He had a prospect of a good many years of full enjoyment of all that. And suddenly he lost his sight, lost it entirely: nobody could say how or why.

132.   In the early days of December of 1932 my wife and I might well have been reckoned to be on the whole among the most fortunate people of our time of life. We had three children and were expecting a fourth. The eldest was just into his ninth year. He seemed a child of great promise. After three days of meningitis he died. The shock to his mother killed the unborn child and eventually all hope of any other.

It is difficult to speak of this, and much more so to let it be put into this book but among the chief of the purposes, that the Partnership professes, is to make it easy for people to marry young and to have such families, as there must be, if our nation is not to wither and to fail to do for the world all that we yet might.

The use, that my wife and I have chosen to make of our lives, requires, I think, that we shall not let it be supposed that we have set an example of limiting our own family to two children, a number obviously insufficient, since some people will be childless and some children will be lost.

CHAPTER 9

BUILDING

133. IN 1933 the Partnership set to work upon its first important building. For this we devised and used a new technique. It had the hearty benediction of the late Sir Charles Reilly, famous for his development of the School of Architecture in the University of Liverpool. He said that our idea seemed to be a reversion to the methods of the cathedral-builders of the Middle Ages. Sir Charles' help for the fifteen years from 1933 until the end of his life was of very great value to the Partnership, all the more so since it was combined with warm sympathy with our broad aims and very encouragingly generous appreciation of our results so far.

TEAM WORK IN BUILDING

134. Mr. Selfridge had once casually remarked to me that the efficiency of building in Great Britain suffers badly because our architects do not work to the extent, that is customary in America, with steel engineers. There the designing of the steel is an integral part of the designing of the building. Suppliers of steel can therefore be asked to tender in a truly competitive way upon a precise design instead of being invited to supply designs and to tender a price for carrying them out.

Mr. Selfridge explained to me that the reason for this difference is that in this country there is not enough big building. My father had done much building and I had often heard him lament that he had had to come to a conclusion that, if an architect is an artist, he is not a man of business and conversely.

135. Meditation upon all this led me to the notion that, whenever the Partnership should begin to build upon an important scale, we would abandon the customary method of dealing with related professions only indirectly through some firm of architects. Instead of this we would form a committee of one or more architects, a steel engineer, a drainage engineer, a heating and lighting engineer and other specialists, such as decorators. To this committee the Partnership would provide a lay chairman, as the Government provides a layman to be the Secretary of State for War or for the Navy or to deal as Minister of Health with the medical profession. We have found the technique very costly in professional fees but the resultant value seems to be good and my own impression is that the method is sound. After all in things of this nature high expenditure upon

technical knowledge and brainwork in its application is plainly likely to turn out well.

After one of the earlier meetings of the Committee our very eminent steel engineer, the late Mr. B. L. Hurst, remarked to me that, if I had had his experience and had seen so many and such serious cases, as he had, of buildings being spoiled because the minds of the clients and the architects were too far settled before the engineers had a chance to play a part, I should realise how very good was this idea that the Partnership was trying.

Certainly the results have seemed to be satisfactory. The new Peter Jones was the Partnership's first big operation and it did not seem to have cost too much and it has been much praised by critics.

PRINCIPLES OF EXTERNAL DESIGN OF BUILDINGS FOR BUSINESS PURPOSES

136. Views upon the problem of civic obligations in private building and upon another question of broad policy in building design were expressed as follows in our GAZETTE of the 13th April 1935:

"I suppose we should all agree that a building should have outside and inside as much beauty as can be achieved without too great sacrifice of the purpose that the building has to serve.

"If the purpose is that of a dwelling-house or of many kinds of private business, such as a bank, or of most kinds of public business or of a palace, which is really a combination of a dwelling-house and of a place of public business, or of a place of religious worship, there is scope for an enormous variety of architectural design without any, or at all events without too great, sacrifice of the purpose that the building has to serve.

"But this is not true of all buildings for all purposes. For example it is not true of a factory that must have tall chimneys or of a shop that needs to display its goods to people outside and to have as much daylight as possible inside.

"Shops began as converted dwelling-houses and for some purposes that style is used still. For example, such booksellers; as have a very high-class clientèle, commonly give to the outside of their shops the appearance of a private house with no more than a very small shop-window, if any.

"As shops began to be larger and to cater for customers from a wider and wider area, the design of their buildings got further and further away from the converted dwelling-house and became more and more pretentious until nowadays some of them might well be taken for a great government office or a palace.

"Such designs are not the result of making the building as good for its own particular purpose, as ever you can, and of trying to give it as much beauty as such a building can have. They are the result of the contrary process of giving to the building the sort of appearance, that you vaguely feel that any building of that size and in that position ought to have, and then of trying to make it as little unfit, as possible, for its own particular purpose.

"People, who go to Regent Street in order to examine the contents of shop windows, waste their journey to a considerable extent because to such an extent they find, instead of shop windows, enormous piers of sham masonry, which is not what they have come to see.

"One of the great drapery stores in London, not in Regent Street, has a total frontage of five hundred feet. In this total frontage there are twenty-four piers of masonry. They are not nearly so broad as those in Regent Street, but they occupy altogether one hundred and ten feet, that is to say twenty-two per cent. of that frontage that has to earn by its windows an enormous yearly charge for rent and rates.

"It is perfectly possible, of course, to argue that the advantages to the world in general of those masses of masonry are such as to justify giving up to them so large a proportion of the space in which the community has chosen to put shop-windows.

"For all, that I know, there may be people who feel that every room within their houses ought to have just about the same appearance and that a bathroom or a kitchen should be very seriously unfitted for its purpose in order to give it a good deal of the appearance of a drawing-room or library. That is how we deal with our streets and it may be that some people deal similarly with their rooms.

137. "But in the rebuilding of Peter Jones the Partnership is venturing to take another line. We have worked out to the best of our ability the sort of building that would be used by the community for its shops if nobody had ever seen a shop before and everybody wanted the shop to be as efficient as possible for its purpose.

"What does that mean? It means these things—

"You must get into the building the very utmost amount of daylight that you possibly can.

"It must be very airy.

"It must be cool in summer and warm in winter.

"It must be very easy to get from one floor to another.

"You must not lose a single inch of window-space against the street.

"The inside of the building must allow to the utmost extent of complete re-arrangement if it should come at some future time to be used for selling things quite different from those that had been sold in it previously.

"All of these things must be achieved as cheaply as possible. Otherwise you will be forced either to let your goods be bad value or else to deprive your customers of the supremely important convenience of the right quality and quantity of staff.

"We set to work deliberately to design a building that should answer to this specification. We endeavoured not to ask ourselves at all whether it would be exactly like some other shop or utterly different from any shop anywhere.

A NEW DEPARTURE

138. "But for a good many weeks we failed to get in one important respect away from the subtle influence of common custom. The respect, in which we went, as we came afterwards to feel, wrong, was that, though we got clear, or thought that we did, of all other customary notions, we still followed the general notion of the present day that a shop should be designed to serve the greatest number of people that can be crowded on to the amount of land that the shop occupies.

"When we had been at work for some weeks, we said to ourselves: 'This notion is wrong. It arises from excessive greed, that is to say that it arises from a desire to serve upon one piece of land more people than that piece of land really ought to serve in that way.

"'So far as the thing can be done, it is more profitable, but one of the supreme problems of business is to know where to stop in the matter of going for profit.

"'What has been the result of this policy of trying to make your possession of a shop-site profitable by crowding on to it the very utmost amount of floor-space that you possibly can? The result has been, of course, that shops have become very short of daylight and otherwise less pleasant than they could and should be'.

"And we said to ourselves: 'Has it not been one of the secrets of the success of Peter Jones that it was exceptionally light, exceptionally airy and exceptionally uncrowded?'

139. "We meditated upon these things and thereafter we said to ourselves: 'The dark, depressing overcrowded shops of to-day are destined to be superseded.

"'Undesirable degrees of inequality of spending-power and of culture are destined to disappear. Therefore the public will become more and more exacting. Already they have screwed up the music-hall or picture-palace or tea-shop to a degree of grace and comfort that would have been absolutely incredible to those who were designing such buildings a hundred years ago and indeed much more recently. So will they treat themselves in the future to shops that will specialise far more closely upon serving a particular clientèle and that will be far pleasanter in the way of light and air and crowding and so on.

"'In fact the public will increase greatly their total provision of shops because that will be the only way of making shopping really efficient and pleasant'.

"We said to ourselves that, if these notions were false, to follow them would be nevertheless to err in the direction of safety. If they were sound, our building would be in the long run much more valuable. If they were not sound, we should still have floor-space enough to be a very fairly profitable use of our site. We should merely have sacrificed a margin of profit that we could afford to sacrifice.

"Indeed, so far as our own ideas would merely mean abnormally numerous and large light-wells that could be covered, if necessary, at some future time with floor-space, we should always be able to undo in that way the decision that we were now contemplating.

"Accordingly we went right back and altered our whole design so that it should give nothing like the greatest possible amount of floor-space upon the site.

"On the contrary, we aimed at having the least amount of floor-space that the cost of the site would permit us to carry and we aimed at giving to the shop the utmost gain of light and general pleasantness that would be made possible by such a sacrifice of floor-space.

"Those were the general ideas upon which the new building was planned.

"They resulted in a building extremely different from any other shop, so far as I know, in London and, I believe, somewhat different from any other shop in the world."

140.　It is a very difficult problem to decide how far an organisation like the Partnership can properly spend money upon the appearance of its buildings. Those, by whom the power is really exercised, ought plainly to be anxious lest they shall get the fun and perhaps glory for themselves at the cost of all the thousands of workers in respect of whom they are really in the position of trustees.

All capital, that is locked up unproductively in a building, must increase the cost to the general community of the use of that building. If it exists to sell goods, the price of those goods may have to be higher or the workers, who use the building, may have to be content with smaller incomes or both of these things may happen. On the other hand, an attractive building may be good for the vitality of the business or contribute to good relations between the business and the Public Authorities or it may be a constant pleasure to the workers. In such problems it is impossible to find any precise course that can be shown by definite arguments to be clearly the best. You must be content to be guided by vague intuitions and to follow a middle course that seems to be not too gravely objectionable upon any of the conflicting considerations of which you must take account.

DIFFICULTY OF COSTING

141.   Peter Jones was built by our own Building Company, John Lewis Building Ltd., and we believe that those, who were well-placed to judge, felt that the Partnership had had a great advantage in being thus able to build for itself when the work had to be done piece-meal because a valuable business had to be kept going at the same time. But there was a general impression that, if we had been dealing with an empty site, we might have got about equally good value from contractors.

We found proper costing a real difficulty. In England workers have not become used, as they have in America, to such methods. Obviously they must do so if their work is to become properly productive for themselves and for everybody else. But it is not easy to get that idea across to them.

In this particular building there was a disappearance of about twenty thousand pounds. It sounds a great deal and of course it was but the job was large and the conditions very difficult and the Partnership was still green in such matters. It was thought that much of the loss was due to unsuccessful efforts to push the work on quickly. It was thought that the workers became overcrowded so that production suffered seriously. But, even so, and in spite of the fact that the professional charges were very heavy, the building seemed as a whole to be quite good value.

CHAPTER 10

FURTHER EXPANSIONS: PROVIDING FOR WAR

1934—FURTHER EXPANSION

142. If my father had retired, as all members of the Partnership will have to do, not later than seventy-five, the Oxford Street business would have been at my disposal from 1911.

DEVELOPMENT DELAYED

In that case the war-time (1914-8) earnings of that business, large as they were, would have been far larger—at least I think so—and their wastage by taxation would have been far smaller because they would have been going to the staff. Peter Jones instead of being terribly harmed by inability to pay its accounts promptly would have had the immense advantage of adequate capital and incidentally the playing-fields at Sudbury would never have been lost.

143. But much more important than all these things would have been the fact that the Partnership could have begun all those years earlier to build up such a team of leaders as it was going to require. To do that, you must have suitable posts to fill. It is not merely a matter of being able to offer attractive incomes. It is a matter of being able to give people scope to learn and to show their quality. With good fortune a specially lucky find in the way of a principal leader may be pulling a really effective oar within two years. But broadly speaking I should say myself that you ought to allow the better part of five years to get any position of first-class importance filled really well. You have got to find your man. You have got to get to know each other and he has got not merely to learn the job that he is going to undertake but he has got to do some quite real constructive work before he will be able to pull his full weight in it.

Until 1928 the Partnership's possibilities in that way were limited to Peter Jones and in 1929 it found itself not only with the business of John Lewis and Company suddenly added to Peter Jones but with all the great window- and floor-space of the Harries business on top of that.

The loss of those eighteen years was a terrific handicap and the next few years had to be spent by a partnership, that until 1925 or later had really consisted simply of Peter Jones, in absorbing and adjusting itself to not merely one but two additional businesses each twice as big as Peter Jones.

EXPERIMENT WITH BRANCH-TRADING

144. But, although our development of a team of Central Managers, whom we could not see our way to get ready-made, was so far behind our development of a team of Buyers, for which work first-rate experts were available from outside, we nevertheless decided that we ought not to delay to try whether the Partnership could make a success of trading through branches outside London.

DISPERSAL AS SAFEGUARD AGAINST WAR

145. In 1940, when far the most important of our three great shops in London had been completely destroyed, three different members of the Partnership wrote to our GAZETTE to recall something that for my own part I had forgotten entirely, namely that in 1934 I had told a General Meeting of Partners that one of the reasons for which the Partnership was beginning to experiment with trading through branches outside London was the possibility that there might be another war and that in that case our business in London might be destroyed or so crippled that unless we had sufficient other means of keeping alive the relations of which a business really consists, between a set of suppliers, a set of workers and a set of customers, we should find at the end of the war that the business had in fact ceased to exist. It would be hardly more than a name and a memory. To a very great extent the thing, that had been built up in the course of seventy years or more, would have to be built up all over again. One or more of the writers of these letters to THE GAZETTE mentioned very frankly that he well remembered saying and hearing others saying all round him that this forecast was a lot of nonsense and that, if the decision to experiment with branch-trading was sound, it was not so for any of such reasons as these.

EXPERIMENTS MUST BE ADEQUATE

146. This first venture was pushed as quickly as possible to the length of four different branches. It was felt that, if it were limited to a single branch or to two, they might get a kind of help that could not be given on an indefinite scale and that the results of a test so limited might be quite misleading. But it was thought that as many as four would be a genuine test and we proceeded accordingly.

In April of 1933 we bought a business in Nottingham: in November another in Weston-super-Mare: in January of next year one in Southsea and in February one in Southampton: four new businesses in less than twelve months.

ARE DERELICTS GOOD BUSINESS?

These ventures turned out reasonably well. But I was told later that, my colleagues, after some years of experience, had come to doubt whether there was much economic advantage in the ability, that the Partnership showed again in these cases, to regenerate businesses that had been doing badly. The ability certainly widens your field of opportunity because it allows you to expand by taking businesses in that condition as well as by taking those that are prospering or by starting upon an entirely new site. But it was in fact suggested that the time and trouble of living down "bad will" and of doing the other things, that have to be done to set right a business that has been going more or less seriously wrong, mean that financially you can get about as good value by paying a higher price for a business that is already healthier.

POLICY SHOULD BE BROAD

147.   For my own part I am entirely in favour of trying out quite thoroughly any idea that seems reasonable and to my mind this certainly is such an idea. But I shall not be surprised if the results of the trial are somewhat disappointing. If the good will of a business is to be really valuable, its policy and methods must, I think, be extremely closely akin to your own and the people, whose personal work has been of high importance to this good will, must continue for a pretty long time if the maintenance of the former figures is to be truly a repetition of the previous business and not a replacement of it by new business rather different in kind.

148.   It is, I think, difficult to exaggerate the extent to which it is broadly true that, when intelligent people, who know what they are talking about, differ tenaciously, either of the courses, that are thus favoured, will turn out very fairly well. I hope that Partners will try to bear this in mind if in some matter on which they feel strongly, they find themselves obliged to defer to opposition.

I should be surprised if the Partnership were to burn its fingers badly, by paying for a business, that was already making a satisfactory profit, a price that would be thought, pretty full but not excessive by those of my colleagues who are inclined to favour such acquisitions.

For my own part, however, I suspect that, if the regeneration of derelicts, bought about equally well, is done really efficiently, they will tend to be somewhat the better business of the two. But the art of regenerating derelicts is perhaps rather more special than I realise.

149.   The Partnership's achieving tolerable success in its venture with these four branches so widely scattered and so far from London was of no more than minor importance in relation to the concurrent figures of our businesses in Oxford Street and Sloane Square but in the long run

its importance was very great indeed, in fact almost crucial. Had we not tested in this way the Partnership's capacity to trade in this manner, we could hardly have ventured to take, as we did in 1940, a chance to acquire at a stroke no less than fifteen new businesses, six in London and nine in the Provinces, that as a whole had been doing for years so badly that we were able to buy the controlling interest of the whole lot for a mere thirty thousand pounds and thereby to get a priceless insurance against the possibility that our business in London might be so badly bombed that at the end of the war it would be pretty well withered and dead.

SIMPLY A SET OF RELATIONS

150.   A business is simply a set of relations between a set of suppliers and a set of customers, relations in which the business acts as a broker. Some of the suppliers supply merchandise, others supply work. But there are really two parties, on the one hand the customers wishing to exchange their money for merchandise and for certain services, and on the other hand the manufacturers and the workers, the staff of the business, wishing to exchange their merchandise or their work for the customers' money.

To build up a business to the point, at which the total volume of this exchange is really large, is apt to take many years—very many unless the start is pretty dangerously venturesome.

The Partnership, when this war began, had in Oxford Street a business that was the result of steady following of a very definite policy for seventy-five years. Five years, three years, even one year of complete or almost complete closing down of those activities might have killed a very great part of the living organism that had grown gradually up in those seventy-five years. How could you ever have got together again the staff who knew your customers and whom your customers knew?

Supposing that you could, how many of your customers would have become so far attached elsewhere that they would return only slowly, if at all? Quite conceivably the war might have caused some potentially formidable competitors of the Partnership to adopt to a serious extent the Partnership's own policy. If, while that was happening, the Partnership had been in vigorous action, it might probably have found ways to maintain its former hold upon its own particular clientèle but, if instead of such gradual adaptation from day to day it had been for some serious while paralysed and thereafter had had to gather itself together and to start more or less afresh, the difficulties might have been terrible.

Safety from that risk was what the Partnership really got by venturing in 1934 to add to the heavy load, that its business in London was already upon its small and inexperienced team of central managers, the considerable further load of this not very large but sufficient venture into branch trading.

THE D. H. EVANS SITE

151.   In 1935 there came yet another occasion for a very great sudden expansion. On each side of my father's old business there had been another with far greater frontage to Oxford Street. To the east, on the far side of Holles Street, there had been the business of T. J. Harries and Company, to the west, from the east side of Old Cavendish Street right up to my father's own buildings the business of Messrs. D. H. Evans and Company.

Both of those businesses might easily have been held so strongly that no opportunity to get either of them would have occurred even once in a lifetime. Yet, as it happened, within seven or eight years of the end of my father's life the Partnership had and took a chance to get first the former and then the latter.

A controlling interest in Messrs. D. H. Evans and Company had been acquired some years earlier by Messrs. Harrods.

If my father had retired earlier, that controlling interest would presumably have come into the hands of the Partnership instead of passing into those of the Harrods group but in fact that had happened and the controllers of that group now decided that the D. H. Evans business should be withdrawn from the east side of Old Cavendish Street, and should be concentrated upon the west side.

152.   If the site thus vacated with its large frontage upon Oxford Street, had happened to be available at the same time as was the similar site occupied by the Harries Company on the east side of Holles Street, the Partnership might have contented itself with acquiring the Evans buildings which formed one block with the business that my father had made. But the fact, that the Partnership was now in successful occupation of the Harries buildings, did not seem a sufficient reason for letting slip this opportunity to acquire the Evans buildings.

If the total holding in Oxford Street should seem eventually to be undesirably large, it would be better to dispose of the Harries buildings and keep the Evans, than to have the John Lewis business permanently divided by Holles Street, especially in view of the fact that the business, that my father had created, was so very deep in proportion to its window-frontage upon Oxford Street. Accordingly the Evans building was acquired.

A WEEK-END JOB: THE PARTNERSHIP AT ITS BEST

153.   It was decided to transfer into that building all of the Departments that were in the Harries building. This would bring under one roof all of the clothing departments, both those that sold materials and those that sold garments and what are commonly called "dress accessories".

The Harries building, that would be thus left vacant, was to be used experimentally for the house-furnishing trade.

It was plainly desirable that the transference should be made in a single stroke and not piecemeal and it was decided that, if the operation were planned sufficiently thoroughly and the Partnership brought to bear all of its resources of man-power and vehicles, the whole of the contents of the Harries building could be transferred in a single Saturday and Sunday to the Evans building, so that, if the departments in the Harries building were closed for one Saturday morning, they might be completely available in their new position on the following Monday morning.

154.   The operation went through satisfactorily. In the course of the work on Sunday morning someone remarked to the holder of one of the Partnership's principal managerial positions, of which the functions were so general that they had no special connection with any such operation as the shifting of these departments, that it was very good of him to give up his weekend in his country home in order to do, as he was doing, a day of portering work. The substance of the answer was "It is not good of me at all: I am enjoying it. This is the Partnership at its best". They were only hearsay but the last words are exactly those that were quoted to me and I have no doubt that they are true. They are mentioned here as a small but significant example of the real psychological importance of the substitution of a spirit of partnership for employment that, however humanely liberal, has some element of exploitation, some feeling, however subtle and however unconscious, of a status inferior to partnership.

If I am not mistaken, what was really "enjoyed" was the feeling that partnership, that wholly eliminates exploitation, can be actually more efficient in a material economic sense than ordinary employment. Innovations, that savour of idealism, are sadly apt to fail because they are too far incompatible with the hard facts of the Nature of Things, the weaknesses of human nature and so forth. To anyone, who has some of the quite common tendency towards idealism, it is correspondingly exhilarating to feel that an experiment, in which he is taking part, is proving itself to be not merely feasible but so much in harmony with the Nature of Things that it has some prospect of spreading by its own mere technical efficiency, quite apart from any ethical appeal or political support.

BOMBING

155.   This acquisition again served as an insurance. Had the East House, the former Harries site, with considerable extensions that the Partnership had achieved, been destroyed by bombing or by an ordinary fire, this West Island would have remained to keep our Oxford Street business going upon a really substantial scale.

On the other hand, if the West Island were, as in the event happened, destroyed and the East House survived, as in the main it did, the same thing would happen there. It was mere accident that the sixty feet of Holies Street divided thus fairly equally the Partnership's total business in Oxford Street. But in the actual event the results were to my mind at all events a most impressive demonstration of the importance of dividing your risks.

156. On such a night of gale, had there fallen upon any of the great buildings of our competitors, none of which were thus divided, the oil bomb that fell upon our own West House, the result must, I suppose, have been a total loss.

We may hope that oil bombs will never fall again on London and with modern buildings I imagine that even in such extraordinarily unfavourable weather no fire could be nearly so formidable without the help of that oil, which within, I was told, three or four minutes was burning in the gutters of the street outside.

But this thing did actually happen and the accidental division of our risk proved to be immensely valuable. Let the Partnership be ceaselessly wary that none of its individual risks is ever allowed to be unduly large. Keep on aiming at a good balance. Remember that, whatever now is highly prosperous will have its day and cease to be. Keep on splitting your risks. Keep on building new sources of strength.

In this terrific calamity the Partnership showed, I think, a good deal more toughness, more resilience, than there would probably have been in a similar thing organised in the ordinary way. A chorus of testimony made it very clear that a great deal of this vitally important stout-heartedness was due to the leadership of those on the spot and very notably to that of the Director of Trading, now Sir Metford Watkins, but years of steady operation of our system made his leadership and that of his colleagues more effective than otherwise it could have been. Not only was there a very special spirit in many of the Partners of all grades but, thanks to my father's policy and to the Partnership's continuance of it, our relations with our customers and with our suppliers were both especially good.

At all events the very great efforts, that were necessary, were made with admirable resourcefulness and energy. One month remained in which to scrape together fresh merchandise in place of the £840,000 worth that had been destroyed in those few hours. The Partnership's suppliers were wholeheartedly helpful and in the afternoon after the fire one of the two managing directors of the National Provincial Bank, that great bank that had always had the Partnership's account, came up to Cavendish Square to meet the Partnership's leaders and began the talk by telling us his directors had asked him to say he was there to give us whatever help we wanted.

It is inevitable that in team-work of great numbers many first-rate contributions shall be unseen except perhaps by a few and meet no general recognition. Of the way, in which the Partnership as a whole met this call upon its competence and courage, the results speak sufficiently and I had better not, I think, attempt to mention here any individual names except, as I have, one only. The principal weight fell necessarily upon the head of the whole of the Partnership's executive operations, the Director of Trading of whom I shall have occasion to speak again (§702). From all, that I heard, I felt no doubt at all that there was general profound admiration of the way in which he kept everybody's heart up and of the clear-headed comprehension and brilliantly swift resourcefulness with which he tackled the endless problems and led the Partnership to the recovery that it achieved.

THE PROBLEM OF MAINTAINING UNITY

157. About 1935 I took my first important step towards decentralisation, devolution of power that until then I had exercised personally. In the years that followed I found my own contacts with the community, the Partnership, were withering much more than I had expected. I had expected that there would be some deadlocks, some conflicts of opinion, in which I should be asked to give a casting vote. I had expected that their frequency would serve to keep me in sufficient contact with the Partnership, sufficiently in touch with the development and current state of its affairs and with its leading personalities and the collective mind of its several parts and of the thing as a whole.

But such deadlocks were not thus frequent. On the contrary, there were virtually none at all and accordingly I came to feel that, if the holder of my own position was to be in such touch, as I felt to be necessary to the Partnership's safety, some sufficient special means must be found to give much more contact than I found myself getting from seeing the weekly GAZETTE, meeting the same very small ring of principal officials, holding once a year a general meeting in each of the Partnership's separate branches (or Houses, as we called them in those days) and getting a thin trickle of letters chiefly from people who felt themselves aggrieved.

158. This contact was by no means negligible. My practice of commonly gazetting such letters and my replies to them and of gazetting also many other papers arising from my personal work amounted to a quite considerable participation in and influence upon the Partnership's corporate life. But the value of that participation depended a good deal upon knowledge that I had got in the past and I felt that the functions of the Chairmanship were dwindling into excessive isolation and impotence, as did at one time those of the Crown in France and in Japan.

DEVELOPMENT DELAYED IN WAR

These ideas began to arise in my mind within three or four years of that first important step towards democratisation or at all events towards devolution and division of power. The dwindling was not then far advanced but it was beginning. At that time, however, the likelihood of war made me feel that I must refrain from any considerable changes in the Partnership's existing structure and practices.

159.   If war was coming, the members of our team must have as far as possible functions to which they were used and familiar associates. So far as they might find themselves short-handed or working with newcomers, they must not have to tackle at the same time the troubles of adjustment to new arrangements.

Our existing arrangements had served us well. No one, so far as I knew, was anxious to see any early change in them. I had deliberately provided the Partnership with alternative leaders much younger than myself and I was myself still on the right side of fifty-five. It seemed better to wait.

During these years the Partnership made in 1937 a first substantial experiment in trading in food. In April of this year Mr. J. N. Webster, who had been in the Cooperative Movement since his fourteenth year, accepted an invitation from the Partnership and resigned his General Managership of the largest of the retail Societies, the London Co-operative Society. Under Mr. Webster that part of its business has grown to the scale necessary to solid permanence. It is no longer experimental.

CHAPTER 11

WAR AND ANOTHER EXPANSION

159a. On the 1st October 1938 there was gazetted the following notice: "At a meeting of the Board of Directors of John Lewis Partnership Limited, held at 242, Oxford Street, London, W.1 on Wednesday, the 28th September 1938, it was unanimously agreed that the following notice should be published in due course to the Partnership:

"IF THERE IS WAR

"1.   If there is war, the Partnership will not wish any regard for its own interests to weigh at all with any of its members who feel that they ought to volunteer for service in the Fighting Forces or for other Public Service that involves personal risk.

"2.   In respect of Public Service of other kinds, the Board hopes that Partners will consider carefully whether it will not be as much to the public interest in the long run that they shall help to keep going a disinterested experiment in social reform, such as the Partnership is.

"3.   Obviously there may be some forms of Public Service that a Partner may undertake for reasons that are purely selfish. Partners must reckon that in any cases, that seem to be of that kind, the Partnership will proceed just as it would when its members leave it in time of peace. Within the Law, all Partners are always free to treat the Partnership as selfishly as they may choose, but they must not expect that the Partnership will feel that they have thereafter some claim upon itself.

"4.   A new war seems likely to be very different from the last. Therefore the Partnership cannot now say simply to its members that in the last war such and such things happened to the business of the private firm of John Lewis and Company and to the business, then completely separate, of Peter Jones Limited, and that, if such and such things happen again, the Partnership will be able and willing to do for its members so and so.

"5.   Because of this uncertainty the Board do not see at present how the Partnership can say much more than that it will hold, of course, to its main principle of trying to behave always to all of its members as a decent family behaves to its own.

"6. The Partnership must keep going if it can. But, short of running too great a risk of destroying itself, it will give to its members in time of war every sort of help, that it can, and will try to divide its total efforts in that way quite fairly among them all and to be guided therein, as much as possible, by the Council.

"7. It seems certain that, in its first phase, a war must hit very severely any such business as the Partnership's. If that happens, it may have to encourage its members to make for a time a living in any other way that they can.

"8. Of course it will aim at taking them all back as fast as it is able and they wish.

"9. If some of them cannot get other employment, the Partnership, even if it has no work for them, will keep them going to the greatest extent that may not seem to involve too great risk of its own ruin.

"10. In any case some will join the Army or undertake some other form of Public Service that in the opinion of the Board ought not to exclude them by reason of such considerations as are indicated in paragraph 3. So far as their incomes from that may be less than they were getting from itself, the Partnership will make up as much of the difference as in the opinion of the Board its financial strength will allow. The Board will desire, of course, to give full weight to any views that may be expressed by the Council. This making-up will be continuous if conditions allow and retrospective if fluctuation of profit makes that seem right.

"11. In some cases this Service subsidy may perhaps be given like other Partnership -Benefit in shares, so that the recipients will be in the position of having saved money and having invested it in the Partnership at the rate of interest that the dividend upon the shares will represent. Any such shares will presumably be the same in all respects as those that are issued for other Partnership Benefit.

"12. If the war changes greatly the value of money, the Partnership will wish to make proper adjustments for that. Its allowances to Partners on Public Service will not be limited as a matter of course to the rate that the Partner was drawing before he went on that Service.

"13. Apart from providing its members with continuous incomes the Partnership may be able to give to a good many of them important help in other ways, as, for example, by its power to buy things that have become scarce or very costly or getting the ear of influential people.

"14. As has been said, it will do whatever it can, exactly as does in such times a decent family for its own members.

"15. It seems to the Board. that if war comes and lasts for any long time, the Partnership is likely to find ways to make up for any temporary disappearance of its present trade in London. In that case it may find itself making large profits.

"16.   If that happens, these profits may not be capitalised completely or nearly completely and distributed as shares to those who happen to be members of the Partnership at that particular time.

"17.   To do that might be to turn them into war profiteers at the expense of all the Partnership's future members.

"18.   If it makes such profits, the Partnership will try to cause all its members to feel that they have fared as well as they would have done in any other employment that they might probably have obtained, had they tried."

160.   The War Service subsidy contemplated in this notice was controlled entirely by the Central Council, and it must be remembered that most of this money was provided at a time when the war was obliging the Partnership to spoil its cherished record for invariable punctuality in the payment of all of its interest-charges and dividends to its various Shareholders.

This suspension of the flow of the dividend on some of the Partnership's securities necessarily meant that the Partnership had to be as thrifty as possible in the extent of its financial help to members whose income suffered from the war and of course the fact, that such help was being given at all, had to be made quite plain to the Shareholders. There was never the slightest objection from their side and, on the other hand, as is mentioned below, the Partners showed no disposition to give to their claims a certain priority, so far as the stockholders should be willing, over the claims of punctual dividend-payment.

161.   Up to the beginning of the war we hardly dreamed that our record in that respect would ever be blemished and, though by the 1st December 1945 we had paid off the last of such arrears as did accumulate, it is perhaps worth recording that during the war itself these subsidies were given at the expense of shareholders whose total claims were limited absolutely to a moderate fixed rate and that there was never any suggestion that maintenance of the flow of those dividends ought to have had precedence over these subsidies to workers whose private circumstances and Service pay would otherwise have meant for them grave hardship.

The special committee of the Council, who dealt with these matters, expressed on more than one occasion very strong appreciation of the candour of Partners with whom they had to deal and of the absence of any signs of inclination to draw upon the Partnership more heavily than was necessary to prevent real hardship.

162.   On the 8th September 1939, the Partnership issued to its members the following letter. The portion that begins "I, the undersigned, hereby agree . . ." formed the lower half of the second page and was perforated for tearing off.

*   *   *

8th September, 1939.

DEAR —,

1.   At first an outbreak of war depresses trade extremely. Nobody can say how far this will go or how long sales will take to rise again to the normal level.

2.   The last war brought, after a slump at first, very great prosperity both to John Lewis and Company and to Peter Jones. There seems no reason whatever to doubt that in the end this war will do the same for the Partnership. But in the meantime, during the slump at first, something must be done to meet the facts that trade is very bad indeed and that the normal pay-sheet is upwards of £17,000 a week and that the Partnership cannot pay out money that it has not got.

3.   There are at present among the 6,000 Partners about 300 whose engagements, it is felt, should be simply closed forthwith. That will have been done by the time that this letter goes out. It is felt that anything further in the way of dismissals and subsequent engagements of strangers would be bad both for the Partnership and for the present Partners.

4.   If that is to be avoided, every present Partner must be asked to agree to as great a temporary reduction of his or her pay as he feels that he can possibly manage. In the case of Partners on the weekly pay-sheet such reduction will be from the date of this letter and in the case of Partners on the monthly pay-sheet from the 1st September, 1939.

5.   Each Partner will be quite welcome to put some time limit, such as twelve months, to the continuance of the particular reduction that he may offer to accept. At the end of that time his position and rights will be exactly the same as they are now. If trade recovers sufficiently, the reduction will be stopped before then. It will be stopped at the very first possible moment and by the most rapid possible stages if recovery is only gradual.

6.   Furthermore, it is not intended that any Partner shall lose in the long run anything at all by his accepting now a temporary reduction of his pay.

7.   Each Partner will have from the Partnership a written acknowledgment that he has given up in this way such and such an

amount of pay and a written promise that, if and when it can, the Partnership will refund to him the whole of that amount together with interest at the rate of five per cent. yearly.

8. It is intended that there shall be applied to these repayments the whole of any profit that otherwise could be distributed to the then Partners in Partnership Benefit at a higher rate than three shares on every hundred pounds of the then pay-sheet.

9. Some Partners may wonder whether cash-pay thus given up temporarily could not be made up before there is any future distribution at all of Partnership Benefit.

10. The answer is that Partnership Benefit is taken in shares, so that the cash, that it represents, is available for the financing of the Partnership's business and for the gradual repayment of its debt to the Chairman. There must be some provision for both of these needs.

11. This year the Partnership has repaid none of its remaining debt to the Chairman. It will certainly not be able to repay any next year and probably not the year after either. All of that is money that the Chairman could have had in cash in 1928, if he had sold his controlling-interest instead of using it to create the Partnership. Of all this money the Partnership has already had the use for ten years without paying a penny of interest.

12. In agreeing that all profits beyond Benefit at the rate of three shares shall be applied to making up these arrears of the pay-sheet, the Chairman is taking the risk that the conditions of business at that time may be such that the Partnership will be unable to use any of that Benefit-cash for the repayment of its debt to him. He has been advised and feels that this is as far as he can go.

13. But, even if the whole of the Partnership's debt to the Chairman had been already cleared off by this present time, it would still be wrong that the Partnership should commit itself to accumulating no fresh capital at all until it shall have made up this cash-pay for work that, however hard and risky and valuable it may have been, has not been self-financing.

14. It may be that in the later stages of the war or in the early days of the peace fresh capital will be available to the Partnership on such moderate terms that it will seem quite sound policy to use it in a way that will make the whole of the Partnership's own earnings available for the immediate redemption of these Promises. If so, that will be done.

15. It is to be understood quite clearly that these Deferred Pay-Promises are to be redeemed at the very first possible moment. If the last war is a guide they will all be cleared off before the war itself is finished.

16.   If a Partner has died or has sold to somebody else his hope of receiving this repayment, it will be made to his heirs or to the person who has bought the right to receive it, just as if it were being made to the Partner himself.

17.   It is hoped that few, if any, Partners will sell this right instead of keeping it for themselves but it is thought that they ought to be free to do that if they choose.

18.   It is hoped that with this prospect of recovering eventually with interest the whole of the money that they will be thus foregoing for the present, almost all Partners, whose pay exceeds the present Living Wage limits, will see their way to make some response to this appeal. Even a very little will be better than nothing.

19.   But it is hoped that all, who possibly can, will forego for the present one-quarter at least of their present drawings and that some will see their way to go further still.

20.   The better the response to this appeal, the more will it be possible to avoid dismissals.

21.   Present Partners, for whom the Partnership has no work and seems unlikely to have any so soon that it ought to ask them to stand by, will be encouraged to find outside the Partnership any other work that they can.

22.   Whenever the Partnership has work for them, it will invite them to come back. It will give them reasonable time to do that.

23.   If they then return and can show that the amount, that they have earned from first to last outside the Partnership, is less than they would have received if they had continued in the Partnership without any reduction of pay, the difference will be treated just as if they had continued in the Partnership and had given up temporarily a part of their pay.

24.   Partners, who may wish to discuss special difficulties, such as their need of money for income-tax, school fees and other occasional heavy payments, will be welcome to do that with their Manager or Registrar or with the Director of Accountancy or with any other member of the Holding Board or with anyone whom any member of the Holding Board may appoint to represent him for that purpose.

25.   Some Partners may feel that it would have been better if in these last ten years instead of distributing, as it has, more than £300,000 in Partnership Benefit the Partnership had accumulated a reserve for the maintenance of the pay-sheet in time of war or similar circumstances.

26.   In the past such emergencies have been extremely rare and the creation of such a reserve would have had the very serious disadvantage that the profit used in that way would have been subject to much

greater taxation than if it was distributed immediately to Partners as Partnership Benefit.

27. Nevertheless, if in the light of this present experience the Council are inclined, in spite of this great drawback of extra taxation, to recommend that such a reserve shall be created, the Management will certainly consider that recommendation very carefully.

28. Obviously the repayment of amounts, that the Partnership saves for the present by means of this appeal, must precede the building up of any such fund for the future. But, when that has been done, it would certainly be possible to place to such a reserve, say, the whole or some part of any money that could be distributed otherwise in Partnership Benefit above six shares and that could continue until the reserve had reached a certain proportion of the total pay-sheet.

29. It is hoped that all Partners will feel that the arrangements for this appeal are a well-considered and whole-hearted application of the principle that those, who for the time being are the Members of the Partnership, must be given as far as possible all the advantages of owning that business.

30. Owners cannot have from their business any more than it is producing but they have the hope that their business will make up to them in the end any normal income of which they are disappointed for the time being.

31. There is plainly a world of difference between such an arrangement, as is proposed in this letter, and the ordinary business-practice of cutting down a staff to the utmost extent that will not be plainly disastrous to the business itself.

32. By this arrangement the Partnership will be enabled to keep very many people whom it could quite safely dismiss and reckon upon replacing well enough with strangers.

33. Some Partners may, perhaps, fear that, if in response to this appeal they accept voluntarily some reduction from a trade-union rate, their acceptance may weaken that rate for the future. It seems quite impossible that voluntary response to such an appeal, as this, should have any such effect. At all events this is an absolutely definite written assurance that it will not.

34. Answers to this appeal should be as prompt as possible, please, and should be in writing and posted or conveyed otherwise to your Manager or Registrar or to the Director of Accountancy, John Lewis and Co. Ltd., 35, Cavendish Square, W.1. If any Partner makes no answer within seven days, he will be assumed to be making none.

35. It is realised, of course, that, though an outbreak of war inevitably depresses extremely the Partnership's business as a whole, some bits of it are kept going and are even specially profitable. Partners, whose work happens to lie in one of those, must judge for themselves how

far they will respond to this appeal. No doubt they will bear in mind the possibility that in some other emergency the position might be reversed. Their bits of the business might be specially hard hit and other bits might be specially prosperous.

For the Holding Board,
JOHN HUNTER,
Secretary.

....

I, the undersigned, hereby agree that payment of

*..................*shillings weekly*

or

..................*pounds yearly*

of my present remuneration from the JOHN LEWIS PARTNERSHIP *between the* 8th September *and the*......................*or such earlier date as may be sufficient for the Partnership may be deferred on the terms and conditions of the Holding Board's appeal dated* 8th September, 1939, *to Partners to make this special arrangement to meet the temporary depression of trade by the outbreak of the present war.*

Name...

House and Department...

* * *

163. In response to this invitation many members of the Partnership particularly the holders of some of its most important positions set an admirable example of helping our vessel through this appalling storm by lightening their own demands.

Some of those, who were carrying a tremendous load of work and worry, cut down their own incomes and therewith their standard of living to a degree of hardship that made me seriously afraid of the possible effects upon their ability to stand such strains as were and would be falling upon them.

The broad result of this notice was a saving of about £40,000 a year, well worth having but very far less than it would have been if the response of all Partners of fairly long standing had been in about the same proportion to their real ability.

After a while it was felt that these deferments, as they were called, could cease. When in September of 1940 the Partnership was tremendously bombed, the appeal was repeated and the total amount of their response was much the same as before. Before the end of the war all of the money thus deferred was paid off.

164.   In my view, the inference that the Partnership should draw from this experience is that in such matters the voluntary principle does not work well enough. There are too many who for no-sufficient reason do very much less than others. The next Part of this book contains some ideas upon this problem.

The Partnership's ability to give War Service subsidy would have been greater if its luck had not been so very bad in the extent to which it was bombed. But it did in fact spend upon subsidising the Government pay of Partners away on War Service a total amount of £125,000.

What this subsidy may have meant in some cases may be judged from the following extract from a letter that was written to me in January of 1947:

"Can I, in my elementary way convey to you what my reactions have been towards the Partnership.

"I left Civvy Street a Selfridge employee and was taken under the Partnership's wing whilst in the Royal Air Force.

"My pay at that time was 2s. per day, my wife's allowance very small and this to me was a great worry. I knew that it was imperative that I earn promotion so that I could get the money needed to meet my wife's requirements.

"Can you imagine my feelings when the Partnership, whom I had yet to serve, began to subsidise my service pay and so begin to ease my worries? Then and there I decided that some day I would show my appreciation."

HELP FOR THE DISABLED

165.   Subsequent Government action made more or less unnecessary the Partnership's plan for doing its share in providing employment after the war for those whose earning-power had been reduced by injuries or illness on Service. The question was raised at a meeting on the 26th November 1943 of the Controlling Board and the Board agreed to inform the Central Council "that the Partnership would, if the Council so wished, subsidise the employment of disabled men up to a sum not exceeding £1,000 a year."

The intention was that this should continue as long as beneficiaries should be available. It was not to be limited to those who before the war had been members of the Partnership. The idea was to offer positions to those who in the war had lost part of their earning-power and to spend a thousand a year upon additions to whatever they might seem to be really earning.

166.   For some reason the Board's proposal did not reach the Council until the following February. The Council approved it unanimously.

The action of the Government in requiring employers irrespective of the nature of their business, irrespective, for example, of the question whether the nature of the work produces a high or low average rate of pay and of whether the business has a large or a low labour-requirement to employ a number of persons who, whether by war service or otherwise are physically handicapped, will not, of course, affect this decision of the Partnership unless the real result is to require the Partnership to spend still more than a thousand a year upon carrying a charge that might more logically and decently be borne by the whole community, that is to say the Government.

The Board's original proposal was upon the assumption that the Government would take no sufficient action and, if the Government's requirement would allow the Partnership to spend in this way less than a thousand a year, the Partnership will, of course, be bound by the vote of the Council and to that extent will do more than would be necessary to satisfy the requirements of the Government.

167. In the early quiet months of the war the Partnership had what proved later to be an immense piece of good fortune, a chance to buy for no more than £30,000 the controlling-interest in a company into which the investing public had put three million pounds and that was then called Selfridge Provincial Stores Limited. This would give the Partnership six new businesses in London and nine in the Provinces and would increase our total turnover by about sixty per cent.

HAVE RULES OF POLICY AND HOLD TO THEM

In this operation there was occasion for the Partnership to practise that faithfulness to whatever may be from time to time your rules of policy that is, in the long run, one of the chief secrets of success in affairs, just as soundness of style is of success in games of skill.

One of the Partnership's rules of policy has always been and is still to keep our risks sufficiently divided. We have aimed at steadily increasing the separate elements in our business, so that, if a change in public demand or some other adverse development diminished the value to us of one or more of them, the others might suffice to keep our business going and our established position in those others might enable us to achieve in them compensatory growth.

168. Now this principle of division of risk applies not only to the kind of business, that you undertake, but to the means by which you do that business. Your units of whatever kind must be amply large enough for first-rate efficiency but within that line they should be so numerous and so separate that you have not too many eggs in any one basket.

Our business should, we said, be a fleet of moderate sized vessels rather than one or two huge ships destructible by, for example, a single fire. If moderate sized vessels are in any way tied together, they may be no safer than if they formed a single whole.

When accordingly we had this opportunity, that we were very anxious not to let slip, we said that we must not undertake it unless the finance could be arranged upon the separate security of the new venture.

There must be no giving of any guarantee by any of our existing companies.

We were told by the representatives of the institution, whose cooperation we invited, that such a guarantee would normally have been more or less expected and certainly welcome. We answered that, if the business, as it stood, were not considered to be sound enough for the finance that was necessary, then we must take that to be sufficient evidence that the venture was not sound enough to be desirable for ourselves and we must renounce it.

ANNOUNCEMENT OF THE ACQUISITION

169. The control came into the hands of the Partnership on the 1st February of 1940. Two days later there was gazetted a notice of which some parts were as follows:

"FIFTEEN NEW BRANCHES

"1. The Partnership has just acquired the controlling interest in each of the following fifteen businesses. The figures of turnover are for the year that ended on the 31st January 1939. It must be remembered that they probably include a good deal of trade that we should not consider sound business and that our policy will sacrifice. It is obviously impossible to put into the first notice everything, that seems likely to interest some Partners, about these new branches. Further notices will appear in due course including probably a general account of each separate branch.

In London

1. Bon Marché Ltd. of Brixton ...
2. Quin & Axtens of Brixton ... ...
3. Pratt's of Streatham ... ...

These three are all one company. For the year mentioned their combined turnover was 969,644

4. H. Holdron Ltd. of Peckham... 357,490
5. John Barnes & Co. Ltd., Finchley Rd. ... 282,712
6. Jones Brothers (Holloway) Ltd. of Holloway ... 248,531

Outside London

7. George Henry Lee & Co. Ltd. of Liverpool 519,892
8. Cole Brothers Ltd. of Sheffield ... 346,819
9. A. H. Bull Ltd. of Reading ... 191,708

10. Robert Sayle & Co. Ltd. of Cambridge ... 105,011
11. Blinkhorn Ltd. of Gloucester ... 79,480
12. W. J. Buckley & Co. Ltd. of Harrogate 77,552
13. Caleys Ltd. of Windsor 45,950
14. Trewin Brothers Ltd. of Watford ... 42,983
15. Thompsons (Peterborough) Ltd. of Peterborough 33.443
£3,301,215"
170. "3. This is our third great expansion. The others were the acquisition in 1928 of the business of T. J. Harries and Co. Ltd., now the East House of John Lewis and Company, and in 1937 of the D. H. Evans buildings on the other side of my father's.

"TEMPORARY DISADVANTAGES OF SOME EXPANSIONS

"4. Each of those two great enlargements of the Partnership's business was expected, of course, to prove in the long run good news for its members and each seems pretty certain to justify those hopes.
"5. But on the short view both of them were bad news. Each was bound to mean an increase of expenses without an immediate corresponding increase of earnings. That is to say a decrease of Partnership Benefit. Moreover, each was bound to mean an increase in the number of Partners among whom that decreased Partnership Benefit was to be divided.

"NO TEMPORARY DISADVANTAGE IN THIS CASE

"6. To this new expansion there is no such temporary drawback. It will carry its own expenses and, as all the fifteen new Houses are quite separate from the Partnership's existing business, it seems unlikely that there will be any difficulty in delaying the admission of each of them to Partnership Benefit until in that respect that House is pulling its own weight."

"IN BAD TIMES WHERE SHOULD THE LINE BE DRAWN AGAINST EATING UP CAPITAL?

171. "11. I imagine that, if the whole Partnership had been asked to vote by secret ballot whether this capital should be invested in this new venture or should be used to maintain pay-rates, especially the lower of those rates that had been affected (by the war), a good many people would have voted for letting it be consumed in that way.
"12. In that case they would really have been saying that they were so hungry that they must eat this goose, however many eggs she might lay if they stuck it out and kept her alive and however golden those eggs might be.

"13. No doubt some, who voted in that way, would have done so because they felt that, however well the venture might turn out, they themselves would not or might not stay in the Partnership long enough to gain by it.

"14. If such a question, as this, is not to be decided by such mass voting, by what rule is it to be decided? The answer is this. In bad times the Partnership must consume its capital by using it to maintain or increase pay-rates when—but only when—it cannot get otherwise the services necessary to carry it through those bad times. Until then it must keep its expenses, including the pay-sheet, down to its income, except so far as it may have accumulated reserves. As I have said lately in THE GAZETTE, if we had thought that our Governments would be so crazy as to let the Germans do what they have, it would have been perfectly easy to distribute less Benefit. The distributions would have covered the present Voluntary Deferment of pay for more than seven years.

"15. When it comes to putting into practice the rule in this last paragraph, those, who in the chances of things find themselves in charge of the management of a nation or of a partnership or of any other community, must do their best to decide what a really clear-headed, far-sighted, plucky individual would do and they must cause that community to follow that course. So far as they fail to do that, they will be failing in their job. If they succeed, they will be for a time unpopular with some but in the long run popular with all. If they lead their people along a course that is soft and easy, they will be for that time more or less popular with all. But they will be leading them to ruin or to great disaster and in the end they will be popular with none.

"EXCEPT TEMPORARILY FOR PARTNERSHIP BENEFIT, ALL MUST BE TREATED ALIKE

172. "16. Apart from Partnership Benefit, in which, as I have said, we must wait until the new Houses are pulling their own weight, all the other advantages of belonging to the John Lewis Partnership will be extended to them as rapidly as possible.

"17. As rapidly as possible they will be brought within our regulations for paid holidays, sick-absence and so on, if ours are more liberal than theirs. It seems unlikely that there will be any cases of the contrary. If there are, no change will be made without some fully compensating advantage.

"18. Committees for Claims, Communications and so forth, exactly like those that we have already, will be set up at once and the new Houses will be represented in exactly the same way on the Council.

"19. THE GAZETTE will be enlarged and will go to them, just as it does to our present branches.

"20. All of the new Partners, who may be able to get there, will have just the same freedom to use Odney. For the others, so far as their Houses have not already in that way, that is to say in sports grounds and other things, such amenities as it is the policy of the Partnership to provide for its members, corresponding arrangements will be made in due course as has been done already in Southampton for Tyrrell and Green.

"21. But, as was mentioned in paragraph 6 all of the cost of all of these things will be borne, so far as they have them, wholly by the new branches, so long at all events as they are not pulling their weight in the way of Partnership Benefit."

"NO SEPARATION OF THE NEW HOUSES FROM THE PARTNERSHIP'S PRESENT ORGANISATION

173. "33. I want to make it quite clear that the Partnership will be managed as a single whole, just as it was before.

"34. None of the new Houses will be admitted to Partnership Benefit without the consent of the Council and the Council will not be asked to give that consent until the House is earning its own Benefit or nearly enough. But except in this temporary respect, which we shall end as soon as ever we possibly can, the whole Partnership will be one, just as it is now, and more so, if that can be contrived."

"NO AVOIDABLE DISPLACEMENTS

174. "37. We shall be very anxious indeed that, if it possibly can, the Partnership shall retain anyone in the new team who is definitely anxious to continue. If there seems to be a fair hope that there will be room for him in a little while, we shall do our best to carry him until then and, if there are some people who cannot be carried but who would like to come back later, we shall do our best to arrange that. The combined team must not be needlessly large or needlessly costly for its job. We cannot carry passengers. But we shall do our utmost to avoid any terminations that are not really unavoidable and to make as considerately as possible any that have got to be made. We are very anxious that in all this sort of thing the Partnership shall get such a reputation that the staff of a business are glad to hear that it is taking over their House. We hope that in from three to five years' time we may be ready for some other big expansion and perhaps for some small ones sooner than that.

"38. We shall not think it right to displace anyone in any of these fifteen new Houses or in their central organisation simply because some present member of our Partnership is now suspended and is anxious to get back. Anyone in the new team, who would be retained if at present there were no Partners suspended, will be retained just the same.

"NO FAVOURITISM: RETENTION STRICTLY BY MERIT

175. "39. Furthermore, if there are in the new team some people who seem particularly likely to be very good Partners but for whose present services there will no longer be scope in their present posts, the Partnership will ask itself very carefully whether the newcomer ought not to be brought into one of its present Houses in place of somebody who is there already and who has not done, either in response to the recent Appeal for Voluntary Deferment of Pay or otherwise anything to show that he is himself a *really good* Partner."

"GAIN TO EACH AT NO COST TO THE OTHER

176. "77. The important advantages, that the Partnership's existing business will gain in buying-power and in some other ways, will be gained at *no cost whatever* to these fifteen new Houses and they on their side will gain from co-operating with us advantages much greater than those and that likewise will *cost us nothing at all.*

"78. This great increase of our buying-power will take us a good step along the path, that I have always sought to follow, towards getting our Buyerships *very* highly paid but at the same time *very* highly specialised.

"79. If the Management is competent, high pay means that in the end the Business develops a Buying-team of great ability and great technical knowledge who work really hard and *keep their hands clean.*

"80. If a Buyer of that type is enabled to specialise upon a comparatively small market and in that market is given *really great* buying-power, he will obviously be able to do a better job than if he had to spend half his time in the stocking-market and half his time in the glove-market or half his time in the skin-glove market and half his time in the fabric-glove market.

"81. In addition to advantages, that each side will be able to give to the other at no cost at all to itself, there will be other help that will cost the givers a good deal in the way of time and trouble of important members of their staff and perhaps in other ways.

"82. But the new Houses will certainly be able to give to us some great advantages and we shall certainly be able to give to them much greater advantages of which the giving will cost neither side anything at all.

"ADVANTAGE OF SECURITY AGAINST POSSIBLE DECLINE OF THE WEST END AS A SHOPPING-CENTRE

177. "83. The Partnership's acquisition of all these businesses outside the West End of London will be a substantial safeguard against the risk that there may be important significance in recent symptoms that traffic-difficulties and other modern developments are diminishing the advantages of the West End for business of our kind and are increasing the desirability for a large distributing organisation of owning shops in other parts of London and outside.

"ADVANTAGE OF SECURITY AGAINST SOCIAL CHANGES

178. "84. Still another possibly very important permanent consideration will be the substantial extent to which this new expansion will extend the services of the Partnership to new classes of customers. We have found that we can make a success of undertaking to serve groups of customers so different as those of Peter Jones on the one hand and of Oxford Street and of one or two of our present branches on the other.

"85. Those differences are very considerable but they stop far short of coming fairly near to covering all the principal classes of modern demands in this country.

"86. Now it is conceivable that, partly because of this war and partly because of political developments, that have been in process for more than a hundred years, there may be a very great shift of spending-power.

"87. Some of the new branches will give us an excellent opportunity of discovering how far we can make a success of undertaking to serve people whose individual spending-power is very small.

"88. To serve those customers really well should be more truly satisfactory than to serve the comparatively well-to-do, for they would be served pretty well in any case and they can afford much better to be charged needlessly high prices for what they buy.

"ADVANTAGE AGAINST AIR RAIDS

179. "89. Besides the reasons, that I have mentioned already, for the Partnership's deciding to take this chance, there is another that may turn out very important."

"93. We shall have now twenty-two separate Houses. That seems to make the continuity of our business very safe indeed against air-raids.

"ADVANTAGE OF WIDER FIELD FROM WHICH TO PROMOTE

"94. The Partnership should gain an important permanent advantage from having so much wider a field from which to draw people who really have the abilities necessary for important promotion and who have had some time to get the hang of our particular system and for us and them to become acquainted in the way that is necessary to really good team-work.

"ADVANTAGE OF WIDER FIELD IN WHICH TO PROMOTE

"95. Of course the opposite will be likewise true. That is to say that the Partnership will gain an important permanent advantage from having so much wider a field within which to give important promotion to people who really have abilities necessary for it.

"96. The smaller an organisation, the less is it likely to have just the right person at the right time for some important vacancy and, conversely, the less is it likely to have the right vacancy for someone who is just about ripe for important promotion."

"PROFIT NOT THE WHOLE MOTIVE OF BUSINESS

180. "102. In most of this paper I have been talking about this new move from the standpoint of the Partners' own material interests. I have been answering the question 'What shall we get out of it?'

"103. Besides that there is another question. 'Will this move make our Partnership more useful to the general community?'

"104. In that way we have achieved already a pretty fair level. I think there is no doubt that, when we open a branch in a new district, it is a real boon to a good many of the people who live there. They are offered goods that are nearer to being just what they want and they get better value for their money.

"105. It is, I hope, a real pleasure to very many of the Partnership to feel that they are putting their working lives into a business of which that is true and to feel that we shall be doing it now in another fifteen districts, and to feel that, if this venture turns out well, we shall be doing it better than we could before. In many things we shall be able now to give better value and a better choice.

J. S. L."

OUR SYSTEM'S PSYCHOLOGICAL APPEAL TO WORKERS THUS TAKEN OVER EN BLOC

181. One pleasing consequence of this acquisition was the encouraging evidence it afforded of the real potentialities of our system.

Although the flow of Partnership Benefit was stopped by the war and for a time the flow of dividend upon stock, that in the past had been issued in that way, was likewise stopped and though there was not much that could be done in those days to bring conditions in the new branches up to the Partnership's practice where that was in fact higher, it was nevertheless remarkable how fast the general ideas of the Partnership were appreciated in the new branches and how much intelligent cooperation they induced.

Much of the credit for this must, I think, have been due to THE GAZETTE. In such a case there is great value in a weekly newspaper that deals candidly and freely with all the affairs of the business, especially those that are matters of immediate concern to the majority of its workers and that moreover invites them to make use of it for anonymous communications that will be published to all the world.

The existence of such a book as this should be in the future a great further help and, of course, as a general rule Partnership Benefit will be flowing year by year so that a new set of Partners will get within twelve months at farthest the very enlightening experience of "receiving something for nothing".

182. In the same GAZETTE with the announcement, that has just been reprinted, of the fifteen new branches, there was another headed "The Partnership and the Partner: (A note that may, it is hoped, be welcome to the Directors and Staff of S.P.S. Ltd. and of its associated companies.)" This described the general plan of the Partnership, its policy and methods and included the following paragraphs:

"I always say that the right thing to do with a fool is to give him rope and every chance to hang himself. Regulations, that sensible people do not need, must be to them more or less of a nuisance and a fret and therefore bad business. As for the fool, they may prevent him from *showing* that he is a fool. They will not prevent his *being* a fool and in a host of ways the business will suffer by his folly. Give him rope.

"Another thing, that may be worth mentioning here, is the effort that the Partnership constantly makes to discuss with an individual Partner the quality of his own work or some other matter of business as candidly as ever it can. It tries to talk to him as if the talk was about some third party in whom both sides were interested and about whom both sides desired to get at the truth but to whom both sides desired to be as friendly and helpful as possible.

"Another very important general rule of the Partnership is to keep all matters of business in writing. Very great pains are taken to make everybody realise that he must take care to get in writing any promise that is made to him or any expectation that is held out to him and that he will be entirely welcome to produce that paper whenever the time comes to claim the fulfilment of that promise. But he must not come along and claim that two years ago he 'understood' somebody or other to say that, if he stayed, as now he has, another two years, he would get this, that or the other."

183. "As I said at the beginning of this paper, I want to avoid repeating in it things that can be found in the printed 'Short

Description' of the Partnership. I will therefore say nothing here of the Partnership's arrangements for securing as much as possible in the way of freedom of speech."

"For many years I have been trying to make the Partnership as completely independent as possible of my own personal availability. With that object I work as far as possible on paper and from a distance and interfere as little as I can in matters of detail.

"People tell me that I have overdone it. That may be true. It is difficult to know just where to draw the line in that sort of thing. But I should feel that I had wasted my life if I was not able to believe that the Partnership would be thoroughly solid after that.

"Social and political changes may leave no scope for such a thing as this. Apart from that possibility, I hope and believe that the Partnership will last for some generations.

"Because of this policy of withdrawing as much as possible I have dropped into the habit of visiting branches only once a year and of hinting frequently to my colleagues that I should be delighted to hear that they thought that that was unnecessary. But, if any of the new Houses want to have such a meeting as I have mentioned, I will, as I say, arrange it as soon as I can.

"I hope that you will like the Partnership. Developments on these lines are, so at least it seems to me, the natural next step beyond the Family in the evolution of human society. The Family has had its day. We are entering the Age of Corporations. In business of all kinds saving and investing is becoming a function of the Many Small instead of the Few Great. Management is ceasing to be combined with ownership. It is becoming, what it ought always to have been, a profession yielding a professional income. For hundreds of years in many different ways for many different purposes the Corporation has been arising alongside of the Family. Now it is beginning to supersede the Family as the unit of which society is built, as a house is built of bricks and pieces of wood and stone and metal. In this field there is still to be done a great deal of invention and experiment. It is important work and urgent, a principal need of this present time. We are doing a bit of it."

THE PLEASURE OF DOING A GOOD JOB

185.   Naturally there were some particular people who were especially appreciative and responsive and to a remarkable extent they of their own initiative set themselves to spread their feelings among their fellow-workers. I think, however, that it would be difficult to exaggerate the extent to which the general helpfulness, that developed quite fast between the new Partners and their new Management, was due simply to the

pleasure of the new Partners in finding themselves giving much better service to their customers.

They found themselves offering a greater variety of such goods as their customers wanted and they were able to be proud not only of that efficiency but also of the better value that to their expert eyes was very obvious. British workers are not cynically indifferent to the question whether the organisation, to which they belong, is in their own view serving the general community well. Some are cynical. Some positively enjoy taking part in knavery. They think it clever. But the general mass have too much good sense to think that bad service can be in the long run good business for themselves and, moreover, their sense of decency makes them like to feel that what they are doing is socially useful.

The war upset, of course, extremely all normal comparisons and the bombing of John Lewis and Company made available for these new branches goods that were very scarce and in great demand.

For these reasons, it would not, I think, be useful to set out here figures in support of this general suggestion that the workers in these fifteen businesses now found themselves giving to their customers better service to an extent that was strongly satisfactory to their own minds. It will be enough, I think, to say that the acquisition was a great success, though at the time more than one of our Buyers reported that some of their business acquaintance had asked them whether the Management of the Partnership had gone mad.

TEAM-WORK

186. The workers in the S.P. (Suburban and Provincial, formerly Selfridge's Provincial Stores) businesses are now full members of the Partnership. The Partnership's acquisition of these businesses will only make the John Lewis Partners better off if those businesses contribute more to the Partnership Pension Fund and Partnership Benefit pool than they take out and if that margin is not in any way balanced or outweighed. The contrary would obviously be likewise true. But it will never be possible to be very closely certain of what really happens in that way. Team-work is team-work, and the better it is, the more is it impossible to say precisely who does what. The Partnership will not look at its businesses in groups. It will try to give each individual business all the help it can and it will carry no passengers. Three things are however certain. The Partnership's acquisition of the S.P. Stores gave us during the war a safeguard that might have been almost priceless and, apart from that, it has about doubled the number of our partners, the people within the benefits, whatever they may prove to be, of our system, and it has given to the Partnership certain important advantages that size alone can give.

CHAPTER 12

PENSIONS

187.   FROM the end of 1940 the Partnership made a very great alteration in its method of distributing its profits to its members. Up to the end of 1940 those profits had been distributed in three ways. Some had been used to give help in exceptional need, that is to say as a system of free insurance against calamity. Some had provided certain collective amenities such as the Odney Club (the country-club at Cookham) and the financing of concerts and dances and so on. All of the remainder had been capitalised as Preferred Ordinary Stock of John Lewis Partnership Ltd. and distributed to the Partners in proportion to their individual pay as the best available measure of their individual contributions to the work by which that profit had been made.

COMPULSORY SAVING SEEMED UNDEMOCRATIC

188.   Now and again letters in THE GAZETTE had advocated a pension-system. I had always replied that this would be incompatible with the degree of democracy at which the Partnership aimed. Why should the Partnership dictate to its members what arrangements they should make for their own retirement? Some might prefer to take risks in order to have more to spend in their earlier years. Some might reckon with virtual certainty upon inheriting an amount that would make this last course quite prudent. Those, who wished to put money by for their old age, could use their Partnership Benefit for that purpose.

No one ever pointed out something that I now feel that I ought to have seen for myself but that I had not, namely, that a partnership, that distributes thus all of its earnings year by year, will find that some of those, who have stayed in it for many years and who are now past work, will declare that it has been quite impossible for them to save and will protest that after such and such a number of years of faithful service the Partnership is turning or has turned them out of doors penniless. They will not mention that they would have left the Partnership if they had thought that to stay in it would not be advantageous for themselves. They will not mention that during all those years they have had continuous employment at a full market rate of pay and on top of that probably some help from the free insurance and certainly such and such an amount of Partnership Benefit.

All, that they will say, is that they served the Partnership with exemplary zeal for such and such a number of years and now they are being—or have been—turned out without a penny.

A CONCLUSIVE ARGUMENT

189. To my mind this is in itself a conclusive argument in favour of putting into a pension-fund some of the money that otherwise would be available for distribution as Partnership Benefit and this argument was much stronger at the time of which we are now speaking, when the State pensions, for which the Partnership helps to pay, were much smaller than now they are.

But this argument was far from being the whole of the case in favour of pensions. Savings are not at all easy to keep. Quite reasonable investments may go sadly wrong.

There is also the tendency of good-hearted people, especially women, to lose their savings or at all events a gravely large part of them in helping relatives or other friends. In some cases provision, that has cost them years of hard work and some self-denial, is depleted by absolute gifts. In other cases they may part with the money as a loan that they feel more or less sure will be duly repaid but that in fact is not.

A minor but, perhaps, a real consideration is that people with long tenure are apt, as the saying is, "to presume upon it". They are apt to feel that a termination of their engagement would meet with such general disapproval that they can safely indulge in obstinacy, bad temper or other foibles. Of course that is not true of nearly all of those who hold a post for life but it is true often enough to be rather serious for the welfare of the general community and for the members of the teams to which those veterans belong.

The possibility of losing a pension might not be in all of these cases a good influence. In some it might be rather the contrary but on the whole it must, I think, tend to prevent people from letting themselves slip bit by bit into pretty gravely bad habits of obstinacy or cantankerousness or other such things.

IMMEDIATE ADVANTAGE FOR THE NEW PARTNERS

190. Yet another consideration was that, although in 1941 it was not feasible to get the general system of the Partnership applied to the profits of the Suburban and Provincial Stores, it was perfectly feasible, provided that the Shareholders would consent, to set up a pension-fund and thereby to give to the new Partners a share and, moreover, an impressively large share of the profits of their business.

The Shareholders agreed very readily and in that portion of the Partnership's business the pension-system came into operation from the

1st February. In the John Lewis group the bombing had thrown some of the dividends into arrear and, until those arrears could be paid off, it would have been quite inconsistent with the Partnership's conception of proper treatment of its investors to divert from their dividend-claim anything beyond the money that was being paid out to prevent excessive hardship to Partners who were on some form of war service and whose pay was much less than their ordinary earnings. Furthermore, there were the Partners who had deferred some of their pay. These deferments likewise had to be made good before there could be any use of Partnership Benefit or any appropriations to a pension-fund.

DEMOCRATIC PROCESS

191. The system, upon which the pensions were to be provided, was settled very elaborately with much ventilation in THE GAZETTE and discussion by the Council. By the 1st December 1945 the last of the arrears of dividend in the John Lewis group had been paid off and so had all the deferments of pay and in respect of that same year the John Lewis group were able to put into the pension-fund their proper contribution both for that year and also for the previous year.

Already there have begun to be efforts to re-open all the questions that were considered when the scheme was set up and perhaps to raise some that could have been raised then but for some reason were not.

The object of these efforts is to ensure that people, who continue in the Partnership for fifteen years or more, but who leave before the qualifying age (fifty-five for women and sixty for men), shall nevertheless get pension whether the Council, whom they have helped to elect, think that they ought to have a pension or not. In other words the aim, howsoever unconscious, is in fact to make the obtaining of a pension over and above the Partnership Benefit, that the Partner will have had in any case, depend not upon his retaining the good opinion of the Council, whom he has helped to elect, but upon his success in keeping what is sometimes called the Eleventh Commandment—"Thou shalt not be found out" in the Law Courts' sense that inevitably gives impunity to so much obvious guilt.

192. The effect of the changes, that are advocated, would be to secure that a Partner, who had not reached qualifying-age, could still extract pension from the Partnership unless his disqualification was of the sort that can be proved in a Court of Law.

Under the present constitution of our particular partnership such a change would require the Central Board's concurrence and, so far as I can judge at present, there is not the faintest chance that in my time that concurrence will ever be given, if I can prevent it. The system, as it stands, means that, if the Management consider that someone ought not to be retained in the Partnership, his membership can be terminated and in that event his getting a leaving-gift will depend as a general rule upon the judgment not of the Management but of the Council, a judgment that must be given by secret ballot if any member of the Council or anyone concerned in the particular case so requests.

193.   There may be cases in which it may seem to the Management that the business-interest of the Partnership requires some leaving-gift that the Council are not able and willing to provide from their own funds but such cases seem likely to be very rare. It is theoretically possible that upon a particular occasion the fund at the disposal of the Council might not suffice for some expenditure that they wished to make but in this respect the broad policy of the Partnership is to make the appropriation to the Council so large that as a general rule there will be at the end of the year an unspent surplus.

If the fund were in fact insufficient, the Council would be quite free to recommend the Management to supplement it.

The Council are similarly free to recommend the Management to commit the Partnership to giving some particular pension but the Council themselves cannot do so because they cannot bind their successors. They can only leave to those successors a recommendation that a payment made by way of pension in the. expiring Council-year shall be repeated in the next and that a similar recommendation shall be made from year to year. There is no restriction upon the number of consecutive years for which the same Partner can serve upon the Council. Up to now membership has changed little from year to year and that state of affairs seems quite certain to be permanent. So far, as this is so, recommendations by an outgoing Council will obviously be effective.

194.   In my view this arrangement gives to the elected representatives of all the Partnership a degree of control that they ought to have over each Partner. Title to pension ought to be all or nothing in the sense that, if the Partner loses his membership before he has reached pension-age, the question, whether he will get any pension at all, must be a matter for the discretion of the Council that he has helped to elect. A Partner ought not to be able to say to the Partnership: "It has suited me to stay in this team for many years. I have never previously yielded to a temptation to behave in a way that might cost me my membership or, if I have yielded, I have not been found out. Therefore I expect to receive in respect of all those years pension on top of the full pay that I have had already and also on top of all the Partnership Benefit, that I have had over and above that full pay".

Obviously, if the Partnership made a rule of this kind, it would be far more defenceless against disloyalty.

If other partnerships think fit to try in this respect some other idea and the results seem in due course to be good, I hope that our own partnership will learn of that and will follow that example. But for my own part I am convinced that it is only too true that for the governed a well-meaning but weak government is apt to be a worse misfortune than almost any that is strong.

195.   It is intended that every Partner shall have received during his membership all the pay he would probably have got by doing the same work in any ordinary business. It is intended that on top of that he shall have received year by year substantial Partnership Benefit and perhaps other substantial advantages that he would not have got in the ordinary way. But it is definitely not intended that on top of all these things he shall have any absolute right to pension before he has actually reached pension-age.

It is vitally important to the interest of the workers themselves that there shall be sufficient discipline and the value for that purpose of the possibility of losing pension is too great to be sacrificed. If someone has already a good many years of accumulated pension-prospect, a temptation will need to be very exceptional if it is to induce him to behave in some way really badly to his Partners or ex-Partners and, if the granting of premature pension is entirely a matter for the discretion of the Partnership, the Partnership will be a very great deal safer against being victimised in one way or another.

As years pass, there will obviously arise a more and more complete set of precedents that will tend to enable prospective pensioners to judge with a good deal of confidence what course the Council would take in such and such a case. It will be the duty of the Partners' Counsellor to take care that those precedents are known to anyone whom they concern and are urged on his behalf. Eventually it may be possible to build up gradually a set of hard and fast rules but in all this the Partnership ought in my view to move very cautiously. The existing pension-system cannot be altered without the consent both of the Council and of the Central Board and, so far as I can see, there is no likelihood that, if I can prevent it, there will be any alteration in my time.

SCALE OF THE SYSTEM

The pension is one-sixtieth of each year's pay with a maximum of thirty years. If the membership is longer, the calculation is upon those years in which the Partner's pay was highest. By the end of January 1948 the amount of the fund was £726,474. It will grow fast. The Rules require that it shall be always actuarially sound. They will be an Article of the Constitution of the Partnership that the Chairman will have to maintain or be liable to displacement by the Council.

We had hoped to combine with this provision for retirement a substantial provision for dowries. We felt this was required by the Partnership's professed principle of fostering early marriage and reasonably long families. The authorities, however, could not see their way to give to a provision for dowries the same advantage in respect of taxation as to a provision for retirement, so we gave up the idea. Perhaps in the future it may be revived.

CHAPTER 13

TROUBLE WITH THE STOCK EXCHANGE

197. The Partnership is intended to try out a certain idea for setting right a perversion, a distortion, of capitalism. Its system seems to be the same as that of the "Producer-Cooperatives" that the Russians call Incops and that are apparently a very great and rapidly increasing element in the present life of that country. But, after all, the Russians themselves have had to maintain capitalism. They have merely gathered all the capital into the hands of the State, so that those, who contrive to get and to keep control of the government, are virtually the owners of the whole of that capital.

But the system of the Partnership, however compatible it may be with such state capitalism as has arisen in Russia, is no less compatible with private capitalism, provided that private capitalism is no longer so perverted and distorted as to produce the disastrously excessive inequalities that in our modern world are so gravely endangering the stability of society.

198. In private capitalism the system of the Partnership makes only two changes. In the first place it abolishes unlimited dividends to those who take financial risks. A gambler, however venturesome, never expects that his reward for winning a bet shall be unlimited and those, who "take a gamble" in financing industry, should likewise reckon that, when they have had a reasonable, definite reward for having taken that particular risk, their loan has become riskless and their claim to further interest should be no more than is appropriate to a riskless loan.

In the second place the system of the Partnership requires that possessors of exceptional ability shall not take an unlimited reward but shall be satisfied with a handsome professional income.

Those are the only changes, that the experiment involves in private capitalism. If therefore the system were to become universal, there would be no reason whatever why Stock Exchanges should not be just as busy as they are to-day. Indeed, they might well be busier, for any system, that secures a much more reasonable division of the proceeds of large-scale industry among all who work in that industry, can hardly fail to produce a great increase of production.

199. There is, therefore, no reason whatever why there should be any friction between the Partnership and Stock Exchanges. On the contrary, the Partnership is and always has been anxious to cultivate thoroughly good relations with Stock Exchanges. In our view Stock Exchanges are

a very valuable part of the machinery of a modern civilised community. They enable losses and gains to be shared among many successive buyers and sellers of any particular security and they make available to everybody an almost infinite variety of choice of investment.

200. From the outset it has been an essential part of the plan of the Partnership that the profits of its workers might be received by them in the form of a security that they could sell on Stock Exchanges. The system allows profits to be distributed in cash if a particular enterprise would be otherwise over-capitalised, but one of the principal merits of the whole scheme is that it allows profit to be shared among all workers in a way that enables the business to be self-financing and yet gives each individual worker freedom to liquidate his investment if he wishes.

Profit-sharing schemes commonly involve some "fancy" arrangement to prevent the worker from getting hold of the capital itself, so that he is obliged to let that part of his savings as well as his prospect of employment depend upon the continuance of the same enterprise. The Partnership takes the view that he should be free to do that if he chooses but that he should also be free to sell out if he likes and either to use up the money or to put it into some quite separate investment.

All this plainly involves recourse to Stock Exchanges and, as I say, the Partnership did in fact from the very beginning aim at cordial cooperation with the Money Market as a whole and with Stock Exchanges in particular.

201. Nevertheless in 1945 there arose between the Partnership and certain members of the London Stock Exchange friction that led for a short time to a total suspension of all dealings in all of the Partnership's ten million pounds' worth of securities. The total amount involved in the friction was trivial, a matter of a few hundred pounds' worth of what are called fractional rights.

The action against the Partnership was not taken by the committee of the London Stock Exchange but by certain jobbers who were specially interested in that particular very small matter. Some newspapers criticised their action as improper. The newspapers said that the matter at issue did not justify a step so serious as a refusal to deal in any of the Partnership's other securities. Those, however, who took that course, presumably felt that it could be justified as a matter of principle and, when at last I understood what the point really was, I felt for my own part that their view was by no means unreasonable, though I was surprised that the jobbers thought proper to take such extreme action without giving us beforehand a friendly warning that in their own view the matter was so grave.

SUICIDE IS NOT REALLY CLEVER

202.   Believing, as I do, that capitalism has the choice between reforming itself pretty importantly or coming to grief altogether, it does not seem to me very clever of people, who live by Stock Exchanges, to use such power, as they have, to make things difficult for such experiments as ours. To my mind it is silly to think that you can teach everybody to read and write, give them cheap travel, illustrated newspapers and the cinema and expect them to be still content with such excessive inequalities as have arisen not from the real nature of capitalism but from its perversion— abuse of power by those possessed of exceptional ability or lucky in some other way. There is nothing whatever in our own experiment to make Stock Exchanges unnecessary or to prevent their yielding a good living to those who work in them and for my own part I suspect that before very long capitalism will either have reformed itself on the general lines of our own ideas or else it will have turned, as in Russia it has, into State Capitalism and in Russia there is not, I imagine, very much in the way of Stock Exchanges. The Partnership had acted under a genuine misapprehension. It had accepted as trustworthy an assurance that turned out to be mistaken but to my mind it had quite clearly put itself in the wrong. The whole story is too long to be set out here. It was brought in due course to a satisfactory end.

RESUMPTION OF DEALINGS

As soon as this had been put right, the jobbers resumed dealings in all of the Partnership's other securities but they refused to act upon the permission of the Stock Exchange for dealings in the two-shilling Ordinary Shares in respect of which this trouble had arisen. They refused on the ground that the value, that they wished to set upon these Shares, differed so much from the Partnership's opinion. They might have added that it was likewise obviously utterly inconsistent with the value that they themselves were setting at the same time upon the One pound Preference Shares of this same company.

The Partnership had always wanted to put an end to the gambling, out of which in the course of the nineteen years, for which these two-shilling Ordinary Shares had existed, some people had made very fat profits while others had made corresponding losses. The shares themselves from first to last had never received any dividend. In the opinion of the Partnership, they had likewise never from first to last had any prospect of receiving any repayment of capital if the company had been liquidated. They had never been anything but intrinsically worthless gambling-counters. In the company's early days they had been sold for over twelve shillings. By the time that the control of the company passed into our own hands they were being sold for one penny. If such a decision of the jobbers to leave the Shares alone had come much sooner, the Partnership would have had a great deal less difficulty in coming to terms with the Shareholders. The position, therefore, that had now been reached, was quite satisfactory so far as the Partnership was concerned for the process of complete settlement with the Shareholders went forward smoothly.

CHAPTER 14

EDUCATION

Since this chapter was passed to the printers, the experiment described in paragraphs 204 to 215 has been suspended, in the first place because the Warden's health made him unavailable for the second three-year term for which there was provision in the Partnership's original agreement with him and in the second place because post-war conditions made it convenient to save for a time the formidable cost of the experiment and in the third place because it was thought that, satisfactory though the results were considered to have been on the whole, there might be some advantage in a complete discontinuance and a completely fresh start. The fresh start seems quite certain and will not, it is hoped, be delayed beyond the spring of 1950.

SHOULD THE PARTNERSHIP HAVE ITS OWN SCHOOLS?

203.   Soon after I moved my home into Hampshire, I began very seriously to consider whether the Partnership would do well to establish there for the children of its members a school with the advantages of being in a very healthy district and of supplies from the Estate farm and of the use of the cricket fields and golf course and so on. The school would be either completely free or would charge fees in proportion to the parents' earnings. The essential aim would be to bring within the reach of Partners one of the things they steadily desire. It is common knowledge that the best and most intelligent workers, as soon as they begin to make money beyond what is required for basic needs, aim at giving their children a better education than they had themselves, if in that respect they were not fortunate, while those, who have received the best this country provides, desire fervently that their children shall have it likewise. In spite of liberal State aid the cost is apt to be so formidable that free schooling of really first-rate quality might be a very great boon even for Partners whose earning-power was much above the average. The Partnership explicitly aims at fostering early marriage and reasonably large families and the provision of free education of first-rate quality seemed very proper to that aim.

   Moreover such a school, recruiting its pupils from homes of all levels of income and culture, would give to the more as well as to the less fortunate something that at present each misses, something that is said to have been formerly a very good feature of education in Scotland and to be so to-day in the United States. To children from well-to-do homes it would give knowledge of and sympathy with the less fortunate and respect for their often great ability, a knowledge at present too apt to be confined to those few who chance to grow up in small village communities.

That school was to have been upon the land that the Air Ministry have requisitioned but that we still hope to get back. Action upon the plan was delayed by uncertainty whether the Leckford venture would be permanent and in the meantime there have been in national education developments that may prevent any such private ventures.

ADULT EDUCATION

204. In Education there is, however, another field, a field that seems increasingly to be reckoned immensely important—the field of Adult Education. To the possibilities, that there may be in this direction, our attention was drawn in October 1941 by a review in "The Economist" of Sir Richard Livingstone's book "The Future in Education". It has already led the Partnership into an experiment involving a capital outlay of about £50,000 and a yearly expenditure of upwards of £10,000.

The first general mention to the Partnership of Sir Richard Livingstone's book was in 1941 in the Christmas Message that for some years I have been asked to send to our GAZETTE.

A GENERAL NEED OF MANKIND

In the course of it I said (after mentioning my hope that some day the Partnership will have its own Glyndebourne, as but for the war it might have done by this time):

"In a postscript to his book, Sir Richard contends that some great improvement in our education is needed to set right our civilization's alarming loss of its perception of certain things that include Freedom, but of which 'the most important are Justice, Mercy and Truth.'

"Any Partners who are interested in this paper should read Sir Richard's book for themselves. Our own library has fifty copies.

MINOR POSSIBILITIES

205. "When we have, as we think we almost certainly shall before long, even if the opera-house has to wait a while, a thoroughly well provided college of our own, we can try with it many experiments. It might offer courses in particular subjects for which people could come in their leisure without ceasing for a time to earn an income. It might advise people on courses of private study. It might arrange occasional debates and give occasional lectures. It might also, we think, be very desirable that people who went for a residential course of some few months should be able, if they wished, to get physical as well as mental accomplishments. In that sort of time anyone could get a really thorough grounding in swimming or tennis or golf or dancing or in playing some musical instrument, an

accomplishment that might be a very great pleasure for all the rest of his or her life.

"People would have to take care not to overdo it, not to try to do too much learning all at once, but I think that experiments on these lines would be well worth making.

"I often wish that at some time or other I had treated myself to two or three weeks of methodical instruction from a competent teacher of chess. I suspect that I should have got far more pleasure out of the very considerable amount of time that for some few years I spent on that exasperating occupation."

CONFERENCE AT ALL SOULS COLLEGE

206. The general suggestions in these notices seemed to me to be welcomed warmly and the idea was explored accordingly. The Partnership was greatly helped by the kindness of Mr. Lionel Curtis, the Sub-Warden of All Souls College, Oxford, who in June of 1942 gave me there an opportunity of hearing the views of Sir Richard Livingstone himself, the Master of Balliol, the Warden of All Souls, the Dean of Durham, who happened to be staying with the Warden, and Professor Reginald Jones, the Editor of "The Law Quarterly" who had been one of the Partnership's advisers upon the first edition of its Constitution.

PROSPECTIVE COST

In the light of that conference the scheme was developed to a definite programme that seemed likely to cost about fifteen thousand pounds (£15,000) a year.

In relation to a yearly pay-sheet of upwards of three million pounds £15,000 may not be excessive expenditure upon the double objective of giving a certain benefit to a few scores of Partners by whom it seems likely to be very specially valued and of leavening through its effects upon them the Partnership as a whole.

THE COLLEGE OPENS

207. The college was actually started in March of 1946 in "The Grange", Cookham on Thames. The Partnership had acquired that house for a dormy-house for the future golf-course and in the course of the following summer took an opportunity to purchase in the same district "Dial Close" on Winter Hill, a property that seemed really ideal for such a purpose.

On the advice of the Master of Balliol the general direction of the initial curriculum then was study of the History of Western Civilisation. The Partnership had been furthermore advised on very high authority that in the Universities the general capacity of students to profit from their work tends to be somewhat less after the first six weeks of each new term. It was decided accordingly that in the Partnership's College the term should be no more than six weeks.

LENGTH OF TERMS

208. It was intended originally that the full course should consist of four such terms within two years but, when the cost was found to be so very heavy, it was thought better to begin by giving each student two terms in one year. After all, the Danish course appears to be generally five months for men and three for women and it seems reasonable to hope that such provision, as the Partnership is proposing to make, will give the students more than a Danish Folk School can give in the same space of time. For women the course will be of the Danish length with the advantage of the break and, though for men it will be shorter, there will be again the advantage of the break and it seems reasonable to hope that the effect may not be much less than in Denmark.

POST-COLLEGIATE STUDY

Moreover, it must be remembered that the College is not intended to give its students a certain equipment and thereafter rarely, if ever, to see any more of them. It is intended to give them a taste for intellectual interests and to break for them the ice of the difficulties of making an effective start upon such matters. It is intended to aim at continuous subsequent relations with such of its students as may be so inclined. In this direction the possibilities may perhaps turn out to be important.

Educational institutions have not generally any appreciable subsequent contact with their students except in the case of those, who after graduating devote themselves to an academic career. In the Partnership the students will be able for as many years as they may choose to make use of the advice of the tutorial staff upon reading and to join in discussion-circles, attend occasional lectures, take short refresher-courses and so on. The College is beginning already to experiment with short courses for students who may feel they cannot leave their work for as much as six weeks or who may wish to come to the College for some very limited purpose, a few days' study of some particular matter.

COLLEGE CHARGES

209. The question of charges was found far from easy to settle at all firmly, all the more so since the actual cost of the conduct of the College remained to be discovered and its start was in conditions very abnormal and unsettled. This general atmosphere of uncertainty and experiment did not diminish the difficulties of deciding how the first set of students should be collected and how to deal with the problems of their absence from their places in the Partnership's business. But on the whole all has gone well.

At the end of each term first at "The Grange" and afterwards at "Dial Close" I met the students to get their impressions at first hand. They seemed quite satisfactorily encouraging and those meetings have raised in my own mind a growing hope that from the standpoint of the Partnership, as distinct from that of the individual student, the College may be really self-supporting.

On various strong grounds, including the Danish experience, there seems to be a high prospect that it will affect really importantly the subsequent relations of many students with the Partnership, their understanding of its real nature and aims and their will and ability to help in those.

HELP OF COLLEGE IN PERSONNEL ADMINISTRATION

210.   In addition and apart from this, it seems possible that in the course of years the College may supplement importantly the Management's other means of becoming adequately acquainted with the real aptitudes of individual Partners.

In large-scale team-work this is a most difficult and serious problem. Among those best qualified to judge of such matters the war has produced much recognition that selection for really difficult functions requires something more than a brief interview, whatever the qualifications of the interviewer, and something more than reports from those ordinarily associated with the person upon whom they are reporting. It requires in the selectors fresh eyes and a certain special skill but their opportunity must be essentially different from a single interview.

Unless it is found practicable eventually to provide adequate college courses for many more students, this incidental use of the Partnership's arrangements for giving to some of its members an opportunity of adult education can be only supplementary in a pretty small way to such arrangements as would exist otherwise for the achievement of acquaintance.

But in the course of any considerable number of years the total usefulness in this way of the College may perhaps prove really important even if the experiment does not go beyond its present scale on which it is frankly no more than that of a pilot plant.

EXPERIMENTAL

211.   Some years must pass before it will be possible to judge with any confidence what are for the individual Partners and for the Partnership the real consequences of the existence of the College, how far it will seem to have affected really importantly for its individual students the subsequent course of their lives: how far it will seem to have affected their value

to the Partnership as trustworthy, intelligent, energetic, public-spirited members of the community and how far it will seem to have brought to the knowledge of the Management particular aptitudes that might otherwise have gone undiscovered and of which even their possessors might in some cases have remained more or less unconscious—aptitudes of which the discovery may be very highly valuable both to their possessors and to the Partnership. On the whole I have a growing hope that in one way and another the College will seem to be a justifiable use of the money that the Partnership will be spending upon it. It is plainly extremely desirable that the broad result shall be provision of similar opportunities for a far greater number of students and at present I have, as I have said, a growing hope that in the long run that will happen. It seems to be happening in the corresponding cases in Russia. There the colleges provided by some of the "Incops" are said to be much better than the Government's.

COST

212.   At present the cost of the twelve-week course is upwards of £200 for each student and the continuance of the students' normal earnings is additional to this formidable figure. In Denmark the students expect to be paid nothing and on the contrary make an appreciable payment.

The Partnership is continuing the student's full normal pay and charging only three shillings a day, that is to say a modest estimate of the amount by which the student would actually gain financially if he got from the College free residence and merely continued to pay the rent of his home or lodgings elsewhere.

It may well seem unreasonable that, if admission to the College is going to increase importantly the happiness of the student's subsequent life and very possibly to increase incidentally his earning-power, he should pay for it nothing except a rather modest estimate of the cost of his food. Nevertheless it has been thought on the whole expedient to ease the starting of this experiment by making it thus costly for the Partnership and costless for the student and at present I am inclined to think that, even so, the Partnership will in one way and another get its money back. But that is, of course, purely a matter of opinion.

DIFFICULTY OF APPRAISING RESULTS—A PILOT-PLANT

213.   The real consequences must be largely such as cannot be measured or demonstrated. As years pass, competent opinion may come to be very confident upon one side or upon the other but at present the whole thing is inevitably the merest guess-work.

It does seem, however, reasonable to reckon that, if by providing so extremely attractive a house and grounds and giving the whole enterprise such lavish advantages, the Partnership does succeed in discovering really important possibilities of adult education in the best sense of that phrase, then, as those possibilities become clear to all concerned, it will be practicable to extend operations so as to secure considerably more cheaply results that will be really of just the same value.

After all pilot-plants are not expected to run thriftily. Their function is to demonstrate what can be done, not to discover what will be the ultimate cost of doing it.

HOPES: A LONG VIEW

214. For my own part, however, I have, as I say, a quite strong hope that even on the rather ultra-magnificent lines of "Dial Close" the whole thing may, as years pass, seem to be well worth doing. After all, if the average length of a student's subsequent continuance in the Partnership will be somewhere between ten and twenty years and the College makes for that time a real difference to his general character and intelligence, it does not take very much imagination to believe that from the standpoint of the Partnership the College may be quite truly self-supporting without taking any account at all of what may be the very great value of such discoveries of special aptitude as may occur in the course of dealing with, say, three hundred students, the intake of no more than five years.

OTHER EDUCATIONAL WORK

215. Though the subject of this chapter is education in general, we have been speaking hitherto solely of two particular ideas, the long-cherished vague idea that some day the Partnership may have schools of its own and this particular college experiment with adult education. It is, in fact, hoped that the tutorial staff of the College will help the Partnership a good deal in other educational activities—the arrangement, for example, of evening classes, lectures, discussion-circles, advice upon reading and so on. But it is much too soon to attempt any appraisal of the probable importance of any such incidental consequences of the College's existence and of course the existence of a College would not be indispensable to things of this kind. They might be achieved quite separately.

This chapter has been concerned mainly with the College because of the far-reaching nature and apparent possible importance of that particular experiment and because it seems desirable that in this book there shall be a fairly full answer to those who, in view of the cost of the College, may wish to know how the Partnership came to start that experiment and with what ideas it is being continued. But, quite apart from any residential College, the Partnership seeks to make in the way of continuation-classes adequate provision for its junior members and to provide first-rate vocational training for the development of the earning-power not only of the juniors but of all others also.

Of course all of these activities have been grievously hindered by the war and there is correspondingly little to be said here except that the principles of the Partnership are held to require that both for the sake of its own efficiency and for the welfare of its members it shall grudge no trouble or money to achieve in such things first-rate efficiency.

AN ADDRESS BY THE PARTNERSHIP'S DEPUTY CHAIRMAN TO THE BRITISH ASSOCIATION FOR COMMERCIAL AND INDUSTRIAL EDUCATION

216. Here follow some portions of an account of this side of the Partnership's educational activities. This was given by the Chairman of its Education Committee (Mrs. Spedan Lewis, the Partnership's Deputy Chairman) to the British Association for Commercial and Industrial Education in January 1946.

"This particular experiment seemed to us a case for beginning on a very small scale and deciding in the light of experience how much further to go, if at all. In the field of education, as distinct from strictly vocational training, we have one very small experiment in junior education actually in being, a more complete one in contemplation and are just about to launch a substantial one in adult education in a residential college.

"The little continuation classes that we have been running now for three years arose, however, spontaneously from two purely practical and utilitarian motives. In 1943 we were, in common with all other traders, suffering from an acute shortage of staff of any kind, let alone of staff whom we should normally consider up to our requirements. By that time almost all of our people between 18 and 45 were in H.M. Forces or some form of national service, and the under-18's we could get had mostly suffered a badly interrupted education.

"Our recruiting officials in London found that the London County Council would be willing to arrange some teaching for these ill-equipped youngsters, and in September of that year we opened five classes in three different shops, frankly as "equipment" classes and to assist recruiting. By a pure coincidence a reading of Sir Richard Livingstone's "The Future in Education" had led the Partnership to consider starting after the war a residential college for our own adults, somewhat on the lines of the Danish Folk Schools. A committee was formed to investigate this proposition and at the same time to survey the whole field of possible educational activities. Finding those Continuation Classes already just started, we naturally invited their organiser to join us and set to work to learn all we could about the possibilities of that form of education.

"The first consequence of this adoption of the existing scheme was a complete change in its policy. The classes had arisen from the needs of the moment, but we set to work to adapt them to a more permanent and wider use.

SELECTION OF JUNIOR STUDENTS

217. "We took the view that even at that time, if education could not be given to all, it should be given to the best, to those most likely to profit permanently and to become a potent leaven for others. Very few juniors could be spared, even for four hours a week, from the pressing necessities of trade. Obviously those to be spared ought to be those we should be most likely to retain after the war and those with the best natural abilities, without too much regard for the precise educational standard they had reached before they came to us. As we often say, we are concerned with the quality of the jam in the pot, not with the label on the pot.

"Harassed though they have been, especially in London, through the war, the Department Managers have throughout shown a keen interest in the welfare of their juniors, and they played up extremely well. Once the policy was understood it has been well supported, and I recollect hardly any cases of reluctance, still less of opposition, from Managers whose most useful youngsters we withdrew from them for four hours a week.

"We ran the classes in groups of about 20 pupils—beginning with five groups in 1943 and in the next two years extending it to eighteen— that is to say there is at least one group in every Partnership shop with a personnel of over 200. For the present we have felt unable to provide them in smaller units than that.

"In almost every case the teaching is given by the Local Education Authority, sometimes in our premises, sometimes in theirs. In a few cases we find and pay our own teachers. In some we co-operate with the L.E.A. both in selection and salary. And I must take the opportunity to acknowledge the admirable help and support we have met all along from the Education Authorities in all districts, both from the Directors of Education and their staffs and from individual teachers and particularly from the officials of the L.C.C., who have been most generous of time, service and valuable advice.

DIFFICULTY OF SETTLING CURRICULUM FOR JUNIOR CLASSES

218. "I have stressed the small scale of this venture. It concerns about 200 juniors in London and the suburbs and about 160 in the Provinces. It gives them three 12-week terms of four hours a week in a year, and that is very little time in which to accomplish anything, and I think that is the teachers' one complaint.

"Even with the full provision of eight hours' attendance a week and that attendance continued till the 18th birthday, the time at the teachers' disposal is short. And in our case at present, four hours a week for one year, it is so small as to be rather daunting. What can you usefully teach in that amount of time? It has not been an easy question to decide.

"The thing began with a strongly utilitarian bias and included in some shops a class on Textiles and in others a class rather vaguely termed 'Commodities' or 'Commercial Geography'. The titles never seemed very apt, but the intention in all cases was the same—to awaken interest and impart knowledge about the things with which the pupils dealt in their trade. In spite of what I now think about the desirability of a vocational bias in continued education, I am bound to admit that these classes were less successful than those in such an ordinary school-subject as arithmetic. One difficulty I think is that Retail Drapery is so varied an occupation that you cannot find a commodity to study which has practical relevance for pupils chosen from different departments, as you might perhaps (I don't know) in a factory or a Wholesale House.

ADJUSTMENTS TO EXPERIENCE

219. "With the early re-casting of our whole scheme of which I have spoken and the re-orientation of its aims, we also changed our curriculum, giving it this time a much more 'cultural' and less vocational bias. The chief subjects then became Written and Spoken English (including play-reading), Arithmetic, Current Affairs and a class called 'Form and Colour' which was in effect a class in applied art. Nominally most of this has survived, but the content has been continually revised and is now very different from its first shape.

"Our first move towards pure culture wasn't an unqualified success. Here I think the difficulty was in hitting on the right methods. I remember being astonished to be told by the Organiser that neither play-reading nor arithmetic could hold the pupils' attention long enough. Elementary arithmetic was soon exhausted and more advanced work could not be attempted in the time. Play-reading interested only those with some talent in that direction. Discussion methods too easily lapsed into a duet between two bright-witted or assertive people with the rest mildly bored. Clearly we must revise both the content and the methods.

TENTATIVE CONCLUSIONS: PREFERENCE OF THE YOUNG FOR VOCATIONAL TRAINING

220. "I think the main conclusion we have reached so far is that the teaching does need to have a definite vocational colour without being narrowly vocational or attempting to teach any technical skill.

"I think we started with an idea that with so little time to do anything at all, the best we could hope would be to open some doors, to awaken the pupils' minds to new interests which would enrich their leisure time. I certainly myself thought of these classes as providing for the pupils an avenue of escape from the work-a-day world, giving them at least a tiny foothold in that larger and more varied world in which more fortunate youngsters browse until 18 or even 21 and 22.

"I have come to think at present (I am still busily learning) that the youngster, fresh from school, and with his or her mind set on becoming self-supporting and independent, is naturally bent specially upon vocational work, whereas the adult, even the young adult, to whom wage-earning has ceased to have the glamour of novelty and of uncertainty of his own particular gifts and hopes in that field, tends just the other way—has a reaction from vocational subjects and a very great gain in appetite and therefore in capacity for general culture.

"I think, too, I overlooked the fact that, while you are as young as 15 or 16, you are not much in need of 'outside interests'. Life itself is absorbing, all roads, even the daily road to work are roads to adventure. It is when it has all settled down into the daily routine that there comes the hunger for something outside it and for mental adventure. I think we shall be wise to wait for the fruit to ripen and to offer general culture in the early days of man- and womanhood when the appetite has grown.

"The teaching that we now offer to our juniors is not vocational, but we do endeavour throughout to relate it to their daily work, to make it the sort of instruction of which they can at once 'see the use' and turn to immediate practical ends.

CRITICISMS FROM JUNIOR STUDENTS

221. "I said that we met from the first excellent support from the Department Managers. But we did not get it at first from all the pupils. We did, however, extract from the discontented some very useful and pertinent criticisms. One dissatisfied group on being interviewed said that they all wanted to give up the classes because they were no use to them; they would be better employed working in their departments. Some of them had apparently expected to receive some kind of special training in selling, book-keeping, stenography and such skills. But the gist of their accusation was that whatever the subject the classes were not sufficiently serious and 'meaty'. On another dissatisfied group we tried a questionnaire asking them to vote for the most and least useful subjects. English and Arithmetic got the most votes—subjects at once useful in daily work—Commodities, our misfire vocational subject, the least, and there was a steady demand for general information about the modern world, variously described as Current Affairs, General Knowledge and other disguises, but all amounting to the same thing.

MODIFIED CURRICULUM AND METHOD: RUTHLESS REALISM OF THE YOUNG

222. "On the question of method, I think some of our first teachers had been over-anxious to break away from school methods. They felt that the pupils must not be made to feel they were being sent back to school, must be met on equal terms as grown-up wage-earners, and they had tried, with the best possible intentions, to establish an informal, discussion-group atmosphere rather on the note of 'Isn't this fun?' Here they came up against the ruthless realism of the young. They didn't think it was fun, nor were they looking for fun. If they were to have fun they knew better ways of getting it. If they were not to be really set free, they would rather get on with their jobs.

"None of this took long to correct. More substance in the syllabus and a more formal atmosphere in the classroom were soon provided. But the criticism is interesting and valuable. It is, I think, another point of cardinal importance in framing such a curriculum to bear in mind the urgent demand of the young for certainties and definite answers. They have an insatiable appetite for facts. They still think of knowledge as something that can be acquired in its entirety, and like to pigeon-hole away bits as something definitely and certainly added to their growing store. It is when one first begins to perceive the number of questions to which there is no definite answer that one feels the first chill touch of middle-age, and our pupils were years away from any such discovery.

"So now we wear our rue with a difference—the same topics but differently handled.

RESULTS

223. "Finally a word as to results. I know of none that are very startling, but I don't think any could be expected. There is general agreement that the children who attend the classes benefit and that it shows in generally improved alertness in their daily work. There has also been from the pupils some demand for evening lectures and classes when they cease to attend the day ones. Five per cent. of each year's intake are allowed a second year if they wish, and each class this year has its full quota of second years, and more would have taken a second year if they had been allowed. This year we are laying plans to offer as a prize for the two best pupils in each class, attendance for a week at a Summer School in the Residential College which is housed in our country-club on the Thames at Cookham. There they will meet their fellow-students from all the branches, an experience that will in itself, I think, be very valuable in giving them the sense of forming part of a large community and there, I hope, we may have a chance both to give them a delightful time and to widen and broaden their horizons.

"And one of the benefits I anticipate from this visit to the College is to raise, in some at least of them, a desire later to attend the College courses, thus giving them a motive to keep up some intellectual work as a preparation for a fuller education after the age of 18. For I am of Sir Richard Livingstone's opinion, that most of the subjects of pure culture—history, philosophy, literature—can only be fruitfully studied when the student himself has had a little experience of life, and it is for the young adult that such education is best provided. I hope our present Continuation School pupils are the adult students of tomorrow."

MUSIC

224. This may be a proper place to mention an idea that seems to be turning out well. For some years before the war the Partnership bought each year about two hundred seats in the Glyndebourne Opera Festival. No price-concession was requested or offered. The Partnership took the view that the Glyndebourne enterprise was a valuable public service that Mr. John Christie had financed with great liberality and that, if the Partnership, being a specially large family, wished to make for its members proportionate use of the results of that liberality, it should not attempt to do so on specially favourable terms.

On the other hand, being, as in fact it was, the most substantial individual supporter of Mr. Christie's enterprise and taking the seats, as it did, at the earliest possible moment, the Partnership felt justified in asking that those seats should be in the best part of that opera-house in which the disinterested nature of the whole enterprise has meant that all places are good.

The Partners therefore and their friends (for in many cases the Partnership gave its members a second ticket that might not be sold or given away but that might be used for a non-Partner) heard the Glyndebourne opera to the very best advantage.

The results appeared to be so good that they have now been extended to a good deal of purchasing of first-class seats for other productions in London and elsewhere of high artistic or intellectual value. In those cases more or less substantial price-concessions are sometimes available and, if so, are taken but, even so, the tickets, if not absolutely given away to Partners as in the case of Glyndebourne, are at all events heavily subsidised.

Care is, of course, taken that such tickets are issued so far as possible only to Partners who are thought likely to get really important benefit from an entertainment of that particular kind and quality. It would be useless to provide music for the tone-deaf or pictures for the blind and the Partnership endeavours to concentrate its expenditure in this way upon those who are thought to be sufficiently qualified to appreciate what they hear or see and to get from it really important benefit such as must tend to promote the Partnership's own general efficiency.

225.   The practice arose from a notion that some people, who would be really wise to spend that much money in that way, might not do so without more or less serious uneasiness lest they were being wrongly self-indulgent, an uneasiness that might gravely impair their pleasure and so probably their real benefit.

It was thought this might happen even if the money itself were frankly a bonus, an addition to such income as otherwise they would expect from their work for the Partnership and from the normal operation of its system of sharing profits.

It was thought, on the other hand, that the gift of an actual ticket with in appropriate cases travelling-expenses and so on would prevent any such uneasiness. Obviously practices of this kind may be reckoned excessively "patriarchal". In this direction there is obviously a difficult question of degree but all of us have to accept a good deal of what in effect is patriarchal guidance from those who have devoted themselves to acquiring expertise that we ourselves do not possess, our lawyers, for example, and our doctors and dentists and others by whose advice or, as they are often frankly called, orders our lives are largely governed.

Opinions will differ whether this particular practice is on the whole desirable but its apparent results so far have been thought to justify the Partnership's persevering with this particular experiment.

CHAPTER 15

RESULTS UP TO 1948

226. AT this date (January 1948) this experiment with education is, I think, the latest of the happenings that have been important fresh experience for the Partnership and for myself. Unless perhaps it is worth mentioning that on the whole our results through the war and in the post-war period, that is to say in these last two years 1946 and '47, have seemed to me to be very fairly encouraging as an indication of general strength.

That strength has been tested by the fall of a combination of mishaps, chiefly in the way of death and illness, upon a business already badly deranged by, on the one hand, a very large sudden intake of new branches, needing separate study and, on the other hand, tremendous bomb-damage.

That large mass of new Partners had not been recruited upon the Partnership's policy and as a whole the businesses, in which they were working, had been doing very badly. The war prevented the Partnership's bringing to bear on them the most powerful of all its influences, the yearly distribution of Partnership Benefit. Nevertheless their immediate appreciation of and reaction to our ideas and practices seemed to me importantly encouraging. The ill-effects of the war and especially of the bombing suspended the flow of dividend upon the most junior of our securities, the Ordinary Stock of John Lewis Partnership, and it obliged us on two occasions to invite voluntary reductions of pay and to accept such responses as there were, amounting in each case to about £40,000 a year.

226a. Yet within a few months of the end of the war all of those arrears of dividend had been paid off and all of those voluntary reductions of pay had been refunded, while at the same time the Partnership had been paying out to members upon Service approximately £125,000 to prevent their suffering hardship that in the judgment of the Partnership's Central Council would have been excessive, from the difference between their Service pay and their previous income from the Partnership.

Along with all this, the Partnership has been accumulating a Pension Fund that now by the 31st January 1948, has reached £726,474. After an interval of eight years Partnership Benefit flowed again. This was in respect of 1946/7. On this occasion, when the Pension Fund was taking so much that before the war would have been Partnership Benefit, the flow of Benefit itself was only enough to increase a full year's earnings by between two and three weeks' pay with of course a proportionate increase to newcomers whose claim was not in respect of the full year.

Until almost the end of the next year (1947/8) the Partnership Benefit for that year seemed likely to be at the rate of four weeks' additional pay upon a full year's earnings although in this year also the Pension Fund was taking (for the last time) a double contribution from the John Lewis group and was thereby diminishing by the equivalent of about one week's pay the Partnership Benefit for all participants.

226b. Towards the end of that year, however, certain sudden adverse happenings (the November Budget and the twist of fashion to the New Look) worsened the outlook a good deal. Before the war the results of the Partnership's operations tended to agree very closely indeed with a budget settled twelve months ahead and, as the year advanced, the profit and loss account and balance-sheet, that are produced each month, rarely required any sudden important amendment of that original budget. The war created of course extreme uncertainty and since the war a return of the pre-war calculability of the course of the Partnership's affairs has been prevented so far partly by the general state of the world and partly by the present initial phase of efforts in our own country to substitute "planning" for certain pre-war processes.

To this very great extent any present forecast of the fruitfulness of our system for the members of our partnership must be mere guesswork. But at present it seems reasonable to hope that the Partnership will be able in the fairly near future and thenceforward to give, in the first place, to all of its members, as much as it is doing already and indeed rather more pay than on the whole they would be really likely to get for equivalent work in any comparable business and, in the second place, as it is likewise doing already, the pension-prospect that is described in this book and, in the third place, rather liberal help in individual cases of exceptional need and rather liberal collective amenities in the way of sports clubs, music, adult education and so on and, in the fourth place, yearly Partnership Benefit that will probably not be less than about eight per cent. upon the total pay-sheet of the recipients, that is to say about four weeks' additional pay upon a full year's work and proportionately for newcomers.

THE LINE BETWEEN PAY AND PARTNERSHIP BENEFIT

226c. There seems to be a real possibility that in the most profitable years the rate of Benefit may be about twice as high as this. But however much pay-rates may tend to be regulated by the state or by collective bargaining, there will always be some uncertainty how much is being really earned by particular workers, especially those who are outstandingly capable and energetic.

If the Partnership found itself with a prospect, that seemed to be sufficiently assured, of a steadily high rate of Partnership Benefit, it would be correspondingly able to take a higher view, than it quite defensibly might, of the dues of particular Partners in the way of pay-rate. To receive Partnership Benefit is pleasant but a margin of weekly or monthly pay is naturally what most people like best of all and therefore it seems probable that from every point of view the Partnership will be wise to let pay-rates rise to the highest rates that seem sufficiently likely to be steadily maintainable and to let the Partnership Benefit be limited to those marginal earnings that must vary with good times and bad.

THE NEED TO GROW AND THE POSSIBLE NEED TO BE SELF-FINANCING

226d. There is a separate question that may be very important. It remains to be seen how far the Partnership will need to be self-financing. Profits distributed in cash through the pay-sheet are lost. Profits capitalised and distributed in stock as Partnership Benefit are saved for financing the Partnership's own growth. Fairly substantial growth will obviously be necessary if all those of the younger Partners, who are qualified for important responsibility, are not to have to wait for dead men's shoes and apart from this substantial growth may be necessary to the general healthiness of the Partnership's business.

Perhaps a day may come when individual pay above a certain rate may have to be taken in stock. But that is as may be. The Partnership already stipulates that non-contractual bonuses, that are considered to have been earned by particular individuals, shall be in cash up to £10 but that larger amounts shall be in stock and already there is strenuous pressure to raise this limit to £25. Time will show how this particular partnership develops in this particular respect. It seems to be one of those things in which different partnerships will cater for worker-members of different requirements.

COMPARISONS ARE DIFFICULT

227. It is never possible to be very sure what is happening in comparable businesses but, so far as can be judged from such figures as are available, I think that during this war-period there has been some falling-off in the extent, never very sensational, to which the Partnership was doing better than its competitors.

Such a falling-off was to be expected not only because of our bad luck in being so heavily bombed but also for technical reasons. War-conditions were specially unfavourable to the piece-goods trade, that is particularly important to us, and the combination of regulation of rates of profit with restriction of supplies diminished a good deal what is normally one of our chief advantages, the efficiency of our buying. If there was some falling off, it certainly was not great enough to be unmistakable but my own impression is that there was in fact some.

It is likewise my own impression that in recent months there has been some recovery but, as I have just said, the Partnership has never achieved spectacular growth against its competitors except in two limited periods. In some of its early years the growth of Peter Jones might, I think, fairly be called phenomenal and for a short time the same thing happened to the Oxford Street business after my father's death.

Perhaps also it would be fair to say that the success of some of the Provincial Branches has been similarly noteworthy. Except however in the solitary case of the early days of Peter Jones, the results could, I think, be attributed in the main to mere technical efficiency such as could have been achieved quite well by a competent management of the ordinary kind, that is to say a management carrying what in theory should be the great handicap of having to let a substantial part of the profits be diverted year by year from the workers. Obviously absence of that diversion should increase efficiency really greatly by the sheer economic weight of the money, quite apart from the psychological consequences, and these also might be expected to be important. There was, I think, one really clear consequence of that kind in the steady stream of praise that the Partners in the Selling Staff won from customers for cordial courtesy all through these years when there has been such general complaint of ill manners in shops.

228.   For a good many reasons, of which this is one, it would be going, I think, much too far to say that the system of the Partnership has shown no signs of achieving success comparable to that of the Cooperative System of Consumers, as it plainly must do if the system is to spread by its own economic efficiency.

For my own part I am inclined to think that in this supremely important respect the results have been sufficiently encouraging but, I think, this involves taking the view that there was sufficient significance in the extent to which the Partnership has been really handicapped and has nevertheless achieved prosperity that would not seem remarkable otherwise. In the same way trials of racehorses are not really significant to anyone who does not know what weight each horse was carrying.

In some of the early years of Peter Jones the Partnership was carrying no weight at all except deficiency of working-capital. The rate of Benefit was spectacular and the proportion of the managerial element to the total size of the team was very high.

The next major happening was the absorption of John Lewis and Company but, so far as those workers were concerned, the effect of our system was weakened drastically by the accident that we happened to get just then a chance to buy the neighbouring business of T. J. Harries, an operation that meant a great increase of the pay-sheet upon which Partnership Benefit had to be distributed but by no means an equivalent immediate increase of the amount available for distribution.

Before we could get back to a normal equilibrium, it seemed to be time to experiment with branch trading in the Provinces and it seemed desirable to begin that upon the scale of at least four separate ventures. In the aggregate they had an appreciable effect of the same kind as the absorption of T. J. Harries and quickly upon these there followed the chance to get the great D.H. Evans buildings on the other side of my father's original business.

Both the T. J. Harries chance and the D. H. Evans chance might easily never have occurred in the whole of a long lifetime. The one, however, occurred immediately upon my father's death and the other very soon afterwards. At the same time we had the general effect of the 1930 world depression of trade.

229.   Towards 1940 the Partnership was getting into a position of having dealt reasonably successfully with these great expansions and it had made some progress towards building up at all levels an appropriate team of leaders. The system was beginning to be normally fruitful for our workers as a whole and there was a corresponding prospect that we should begin to get such an advantage in efficiency as it should in theory have. We were getting some. Obviously nobody was working worse than he would have done in an ordinary business and many were working quite a lot better. Moreover, there had been already some quite considerable effect in the very important way of attracting and retaining recruits of a kind hardly available to ordinary profit-seeking enterprises in our part of the business-world. All this, however, though it was beginning to happen, was not yet happening enough for the results to be spectacular.

Towards 1940 there were, I think, some signs that the real harvest for which we had been hoping so long was nearly ripe and of course, when it came, it would be all the more important and impressive because from motives of long-range prudence the Partnership had accepted those successive opportunities of expansion at the cost of delaying the achievement of such a proportion of profit as would bring into operation the real dynamic possibility of the system upon recruitment, training and zeal and therefore upon general efficiency and economic success.

The war put all that off yet again and the bombing deepened and very greatly prolonged the ill effects of the war.

230.   In my own view the Partnership's actual achievement up to now has not been unmistakably greater because of its special system. I feel very sure that a really intelligent profit-seeking management could have taken out of our business quite £50,000 a year and probably a lot more

and have had to-day as good a name for value and as sound a business in all other respects as the Partnership has actually got.

I do not think this would have happened if we had not taken those extraordinary opportunities to absorb first T. J. Harries and then the D. H. Evans buildings. If those chances had not arisen or we had chosen not to take them, I think the fruitfulness of the system for the workers would have had economic consequences of which the importance would have been quite unmistakable.

But in that case the business would have been standing upon a much narrower base. Both its buying- and its employing-power would have been much smaller. In quality its team might have been first-rate but the smaller quantity of its major key posts must have made it much less stable and secure.

If such losses, as in these last few years the Partnership's team has chanced to suffer by death and illness, had fallen upon a much smaller organisation, the consequences would have been far more serious unless in the filling of those gaps the Partnership had had such luck as would, I think, have been hardly possible. It needs really fantastic luck to replace almost immediately the loss from any very important post of someone whom you have been training for fifteen years and who has been making himself steadily more and more important by his knowledge of other members of the team and of their business-associates and their corresponding knowledge of him and whose age led you to count upon him for many years to come.

231. But, however all this may be, I think it is certainly true that in many ways the Partnership has made heavy weather of getting out of its system the economic advantages that in theory that system must have. It is no easy matter simultaneously to undertake a succession of very great sudden expansions and to build up a really adequate managerial team and a really sound technique in the way of customs and practices, definite rules and so forth. To an extent, that may or may not have been on the whole expedient, the Partnership has been exceptionally ready to give experimental engagements to people without previous training in business of our kind but it has certainly fallen a long way short of perfectly feasible efficiency in the way of watching such engagements and being properly prompt to close such as did not promise sufficiently well.

232. Looking back, I feel that in the event we have suffered quite as much as in theory we were likely to do from the fact that my father, instead of retiring as all members of the Partnership will have to do, at seventy-five, continued for another seventeen years and during that time blocked very completely a full two-thirds of what would have been otherwise our scope for building up a principal managerial team.

Such people take some time to find and then they take a good many years to be fully effective. It was, I think, to be expected that in this vitally important respect the Partnership would hardly reach much before 1940 the stage that it would have reached about ten years earlier if my father had retired at eighty. In the development of a business ten years matter a very great deal. Moreover, by then it was beginning to be time to do something quite different and likewise vitally important, namely, discover what arrangements ought to be made for the management after my own time.

These operations ought to have been successive, not simultaneous. A management ample not only in quantity but in quality should have been well established before I began to withdraw, before, as I used to say in THE GAZETTE, I died experimentally. It did not seem to me safe to delay that experiment. I was by no means sure how long it would take me to reach conclusions that rightly or wrongly I should feel to be trustworthy and I reckoned that, if that position were reached about as quickly as there seemed to be any hope that it would be, I should need the better part of another ten years before I could rightly feel that I really was quite free to retire.

If the war had not occurred, that last ten-year period would have begun a little before 1940. The war produced a virtually total suspension of the building up of our managerial team and the special losses, that I have mentioned, have meant an actual setback.

233.   When I try to see these things clearly and dispassionately, I find myself feeling that in them there may be much stronger evidence, than would be perceptible to a merely superficial view, that the system of the Partnership really has important potentialities of sheer economic strength.

I used to say of my father's success in making a fortune that was only about half or indeed a third of some similar achievements by others of his generation but that was nevertheless very ample, that he was like a racer who insists upon hopping on one leg and who amazingly succeeds in keeping quite near to the winners.

I suspect that something of the same sort is true of the Partnership. I suspect—it is no more than a mere suspicion—that a really competent judge, accurately informed of the handicaps that have befallen us and of what we have attempted, might perhaps hold that our achievement on those rather ambitious lines of such unspectacular but pretty solid and adequate success was a strong indication that our armament must include some weapon not ordinary but exceptional, something of a special kind, that had supplemented really importantly the technique that would have been available to us if we had been an ordinary profit-seeking enterprise. By "ambitious lines" I mean with such expense as we have carried partly upon very long-term views of our future needs and partly for the immediate happiness of people who were already working so well that they could not be expected to give much more in return.

234.   In drafting this part of this book I have tried in vain to see some line that seemed clear and satisfactory in the matter of deciding how far to mention technical matters of business-management, our ideas in those respects and their apparent results.

I hope that I have not drawn that line much too narrowly.

At all event in this book I propose to say no more of the facts that underlie the Partnership's present broad figures.

In this year, with five of its businesses, including far the most important of all, completely destroyed by bombing, it is affording whole-time occupation to almost exactly twelve thousand people. In proportion to the business, that it is doing, its pay-sheet is, I believe, decidedly high rather than low. Certainly that total contains a substantial element of people who are being tried and trained for the future but that does not alter the fact that in proportion to our present operations the pay-sheet is decidedly high for business of our kind.

On top of this the Partnership is spending approximately £53,000 a year in sick-pay and help in special misfortune. An appreciable part of this money would, I believe, certainly not be provided in an ordinary business. On top of this it is spending about £55,000 a year upon sports-clubs, the fostering of music, adult education and other things that we call amenities.

A good deal of this money likewise is the result of our special system. In an ordinary business it would certainly not, I believe, go to the workers.

On top of this the Partnership has just put into its Pension Fund £210,038. Until a few weeks ago we were hoping, as was mentioned a few pages back, that on top of this again the Partnership would distribute in respect of this last year Partnership Benefit to the extent of about four weeks' pay on a full year's earnings and proportionately to newcomers. The exact results of the year's trading are still unknown but this hope has been substantially weakened by the effect of the November Budget upon the Partnership's earnings in the very important month of December.

In 1946/7 the proportion of the pay-sheet, that carried Partnership Benefit, was eighty-five per cent. The pay of those, who for one reason or another were excluded from participation in the distribution, was only fifteen per cent. of the whole.

Before the war the Partnership never failed in absolute punctuality in all payments of interest and dividend to the owners of its capital. During the war the failure was only in respect of certain junior securities and that failure was made good almost as soon as the war ended.

At present the total dividend-requirement is already in hand for approximately three years ahead.

235.   Because of the hindrances that our experiment has encountered, its results are not yet conclusive. We have still to see whether the dynamic potentialities of our system, its capacity to spread itself by sheer economic efficiency, will be really important but there are the parallel development in Russia and the history of the Consumer-Cooperative.

Thirty-seven years ago, when the scheme was complete in my mind and I was resolved to put it into operation as soon as I could, I thought that position would have been reached long before this and I think it might have been if we had escaped the great hindrances that I have mentioned.

But I have always tried to make safety, solidity, permanence, the Partnership's supreme aim. It is much more important that those, who are really happy in it, shall get from it permanently incomes on which they are just comfortable, than it is that for some years they shall have a pleasantly exciting margin but only at the cost of a real risk that the whole thing may collapse or wither.

If the dynamic possibilities are really there, they will in due course show themselves and all the more effectively so far as by reason of patience the scale of the whole thing is then greater.

PART TWO

THE GENERAL IDEAS THAT HAVE ARISEN FROM
THOSE FORTY-FOUR YEARS OF EXPERIENCE

CHAPTER 16

AN OUTLINE OF THE PLAN

236. I HOPE that, so far as there is not elsewhere in this book a sufficient answer to any questions, that may be asked in future years, of the Partnership's fundamental principles, the real essence of its nature, that answer will be found in this second Part.

With matters of business in the ordinary sense of those words I have not tried to deal. The Partnership will always be able to get easily from other sources a multitude of ideas for the maintenance and expansion of a business. There seems little need to say such things as that the Partnership should confine itself to undertakings in which it believes it has a good enough prospect of attaining sufficiently soon really first-rate efficiency and that among those it should prefer such as should stand alone if some related portions of the undertaking wither away but that, on the other hand, while all survive, should draw strength from them and they from it.

Neither the sudden great increase from 1906 onward in the previous yearly rate of growth of my father's business from under seventeen thousand to over sixty nor the regeneration of Peter Jones depended essentially upon any radical breakaway from the customary methods of profit-seeking enterprise. The real causes of those successes were merely technical. They were merely my father's own methods amended importantly but not in any way that would have been essentially unacceptable to a management ruthlessly selfish but intelligently so. Certainly there were concurrent efforts to give those workers not merely what such a management would have given but as much more as possible.

Because, however, of my father's views in his own business and because of those of the outside shareholders in Peter Jones before the amendment in 1920 of the Articles of Association, an amendment only secured by spectacular previous success, the immediate possibilities were too small for the real innovations, the giving of "something for nothing", the true sharing of the advantages of ownership, to affect importantly the conduct of the business.

THE GREATER THE SCALE, THE GREATER THE NEED OF COMMUNITY OF INTEREST

237. As the years have passed, this has been less and less true. After 1920 the special character of the Partnership began bit by bit to affect importantly its recruitment and its strength in other ways.

There is no means of knowing whether that factor has been really indispensable to our considerable but by no means phenomenal achievements between, say, 1926 and this present day. But its importance has certainly been very substantial and for my own part I suspect that, even if as yet it has not been really indispensable, it will become so as the whole thing grows in size and complexity. I suspect that the possibility of getting to more than a certain extent the advantages of size and of variety without too much disadvantage in other ways will be found to depend absolutely upon a genuine and sufficient sharing of all the advantages, material, intellectual and moral, of ownership.

238. With no other inducements than are used by the ordinary good employer genius could presumably keep healthy for a time a manufacturing and trading enterprise of almost any conceivable size and complexity or alternatively in a smaller and correspondingly more intense operation build up, retain and get the best efforts of an absolutely first-rate team.

But genius is available only very rarely and never in any particular case for very long, hardly ever, indeed, for more than a single generation. In the absence of genius the possibilities of really efficient team-work in a political democracy (I am not talking, of course, of the possibilities under a strong and ruthless tyranny) may well be limited to a small scale so long as any important part of the team have not a sufficient general sense of ownership as well as sufficient contentment with their own particular conditions.

The supreme problem, as I see it, of large-scale team-work is to give that sense about as fully as is really possible, the human nature of the potential members of the team being what in fact in the particular case it will be. But the provision of this psychological factor is only a part of what may be at the present very early stage of the development of human nature the sole means of achieving really satisfactory efficiency in team-work on a really large scale.

FINANCING OF EFFICIENCY IN THE PRINCIPAL MANAGEMENT

239. The other factor; no less indispensable, is not psychological at all but purely economic. It is to make available for a greater quantity and better quality of subordinate management revenue that is now diverted wastefully to the over-remuneration of controllers, whether they be a great body of shareholders insisting upon a larger dividend than they ought really to be drawing or a handful of principal managers or even a single individual, whether capitalist or manager.

The facts of the human mind restrict to no more at most than a dozen the real principal managers of any human organisation, however large and however complex.

If the controllers themselves are not able and willing to do that principal managing, they can, if their enterprise be really large, afford very well to offer for those few posts inducements sufficient to attract first-rate ability, retain it and secure its utmost efforts, though its possessors may be ruthlessly selfish. They will, of course, tend to drop off after a time to take chances to do still better for themselves but they can always be replaced.

Mr. Marshall Field of Chicago, whose business was, I believe, in his own day the largest of its kind in the world, is said to have made it a rule that as soon as any of the most important of his team had drawn from his enterprise a million dollars they must go out of it.

It is, in fact, not in the few supremely important posts that genuine partnership may be indispensable to first-rate efficiency either by its moral and intellectual or, if the word be preferred, its psychological effects or by its purely economic effects, its making available for the nourishment of the business money that would otherwise be drawn off.

FINANCING OF EFFICIENCY IN THE RANK AND FILE

240. Upon the economic side I question whether the system is really indispensable to the efficiency of the rank and file, those who have no official authority over and responsibility for the work of others.

The psychological effect alone might perhaps make them sufficiently zealous and good-humoured, that is to say manageable. At their level the recruitment and retention of first-rate workers depends, I suspect, upon the reputation of the organisation for security of employment and general humanity very much more than upon a margin of pay.

In this connection it is interesting to remember that Mr. Henry Ford's extraordinarily high rates of pay resulted in very strong competition to enter his factory but did not prevent an exceedingly high rate of labour-turnover—so high that it would have been a tremendous and, I imagine, almost certainly a fatal handicap if the nature of the work had not allowed newcomers to be fully efficient almost as soon as they started.

If the rank and file are to have a sufficient sense of ownership, they must, of course, be satisfied with their incomes and that will probably mean that their incomes must be somewhat above what they reckon to be the current market-rates for such work. But I feel pretty sure that the feelings expressed by the experienced salesman, whom I have quoted in paragraph three are typical. At that level the importance of a margin of income is psychological rather than economic and its psychological potency does not depend at all closely upon its amount.

Of course I am not saying that a greater margin of actual income will have no effect at all. All, that I am saying, is that, so long as the margin, real or supposed, is enough to have a certain psychological effect, full efficiency in team-work of no matter what size may be attainable so far as the rank and file are concerned.

FINANCING OF EFFICIENCY IN THE SUBORDINATE MANAGEMENT: THE SUPREME NEED

241. It is, I believe, in the subordinate management, at all grades, of which there may be very many, that the purely economic, as distinct from the psychological, consequences of genuine partnership will be found to be indispensable to real efficiency in such a case as we are considering.

Industrial team-work to-day, as it becomes larger and larger, tends universally or nearly so to develop an organisation that may have at the top an excellent brain and that may have also excellent muscles but that is disastrously handicapped by inadequacy both of quantity and of quality in all those nerves of various sizes and importance that have to link the brain to the muscles and the muscles to the brain.

Here there is, I believe, immense scope for expenditure to increase efficiency and that expenditure will require a stoppage of the present diversion of revenue to the over-remuneration of the ultimate control.

THE RANK AND FILE AGAIN

242. If the controllers of a business gave up to the subordinate management all that would accrue to them in a genuine partnership but the controllers kept for themselves much that in a genuine partnership would go to the rank and file, the efficiency of that business might perhaps not suffer seriously so long as its controllers contrived to prevent the rank and file from knowing what was happening or from having more than a faint suspicion of it. In that case the controllers might perhaps find that the better payment of the subordinate management was actually self-financing and that their own gains were as great or greater than before.

But, if in some special cases this state of affairs could be created, I doubt if it could be maintained for very long. Obviously any such possibility would depend upon a sufficient absence of competition from genuine partnerships working in the same field but, even if there were no such competition, consciousness of what was happening would, I suspect, develop to an extent that would weaken too seriously the psychological factor and even quite conceivably reverse it.

A combination of exploitation with a pretence of genuine partnership might well produce much more discontent and much more care to do as little as possible in return for the pay than would the mere sense not thus aggravated of exploitation itself.

Education is spreading fast. Bodies of workers of all kinds will tend to be more and more perceptive and vigorous in their reactions—in fact better and better subjects for genuine partnership and worse and worse for a continuance of the general present conditions of modern industry.

KINDNESS MUST BE INTELLIGENT

243. If in this part of this book there is something of real importance, it is, I believe, in the combination of really strenuous effort for what I sometimes call the Higher Decency, the unselfish impulses of human kindness, with a really cold realism, real hard-headedness, the mind, as I shall suggest presently, not of a Utopian doctrinaire but of a naturalist.

Selfishness, except so far as it is intelligent, is self-defeating but so also is kindness. The problem is to keep a good enough balance, to be sufficiently realist without being less than fully strenuous in the effort to perceive possibilities of happiness and to work for them. That is the idea that I am trying to leave behind me in this book, the idea of a community that will deliberately pursue happiness as diligently as plenty of communities pursue material wealth, but that will do so with enough of cold realism not to lose a possible good in trying for something that would be better but that is not possible.

Happiness, as I am conceiving it here, requires a sense of all-round fairness, a sense of all-pervading justice. But, if that be achieved, the workings of the whole thing will still abound in trouble and discomforts. That is part of the Nature of Things.

If you want the joys of cricket or of climbing or of any other exhilarating physical effort, you must pay the price of many knocks and strains and bruises and perhaps some risk of serious, even fatal, accident. And only at the risk of loss can you have anyone or anything to love.

If a partnership, large or small, is to be capable of sufficient permanence, there must be in its conduct a good deal that is grim. With experience the troubles should become fewer. Some of the worst kinds may perhaps be eliminated completely or very nearly so. But the partnership will always have to be very much on the alert to prevent itself from developing flabbiness, to say nothing of real corruption, and not only alert for symptoms but sufficiently resolute and vigorous in action, howsoever reluctant.

ONLY A MATTER OF DEGREE

244. The ideas, that arose from the experience recorded in the first part of this book and that are the subject of this second part, arose haphazardly, some long ago and some quite lately, some at a stroke, and some piecemeal. The conception of partnership for all the workers in a large business is very obvious and in various ways has been tried, I believe, many times.

The most ruthlessly selfish exploiting employment, short of absolute slavery, differs only in degree from the contrary extreme, the utmost development of the idea of partnership.

Partners employ in a sense each other. Each owes the other effort of certain kinds and is in return owed, as his remuneration, a certain part of the results of the team-work.

It might be fair enough that one partner should be guaranteed a fixed remuneration and in return for the advantages of that degree of certainty should let the other have now and again, when the team-work was sufficiently fruitful, a share that would be larger but not in unfair proportion to the other. This is in kind but not in degree the ordinary relation of employer and employee. The employee is guaranteed a certain remuneration, whatever the results of the enterprise. The whole of any remainder goes to the employer unless indeed, as happens quite often, he thinks it right or expedient or both to let the income of the employee benefit somewhat when results are good.

THE HONEST BROKER

245.   It is interesting to notice that this state of affairs is the exact opposite of that which has arisen in respect of capital. If you have some capital to invest, you will find that the members of certain professions, who do their utmost to be expert in such matters, will give you full benefit of their knowledge and judgment. They will take due account of your particular wishes, your conscientious objections to investing your capital in any enterprise of certain kinds, your willingness to run a certain degree of risk for the chance of a better income, your willingness to run very great risk for what seems to be a possibility of proportionate gain. Your professional adviser will do his utmost to help you to invest your capital successfully according to your wishes as he understands them.

For that service he will charge you no more than a fixed fee, broker's commission or whatever it may be called. If your investment is fantastically lucky, the adviser, but for whom you would never have heard of that particular gold mine or new invention or theatrical enterprise or whatever your gamble was, will make no claim to any of your prodigious gain.

In a sense you will owe it entirely to him but the money, that you risked, was yours and the results of the taking of the risk will belong to you.

LESS HONEST BROKING

246.   Suppose, however, that, instead of wanting to invest some capital, you want to invest your life or a bit of it. In that case you will go to a possible employer. He may answer that he has no vacancy that he can offer to you. Equally, if you went to a professional adviser upon investments

in mining and said that you wished to invest your capital in rubber, he might answer that he could not undertake to advise you: you must go to somebody else.

But suppose the employer says to you in effect; "I have a position in which I advise you to invest your life or some bit of it." If you do so, you will be taking the risk that it may not be by any means the best use that, if you knew more or looked further, you could make of that part of your life. You will be taking a risk that your tenure of the post will be cut short unjustifiably or that the post itself will come to an end by a collapse or contraction of the whole enterprise. If, however, all goes well, you will get in return for your time and exertion and for taking those risks little, if any, more than a certain fixed amount.

GROSS PROFITEERING

247.   If the enterprise has in some way tremendous luck, luck that, perhaps, whether you realise it or not, may be due partly or even wholly to yourself, the employer will take all or most of that margin. To himself and to you and to all the world he will justify this by the argument that he was risking capital and perhaps that the results were due to some extent to his personal work in the past and, it may be, in the present also.

This is plainly a complete reversal of the behaviour of the professional advisers upon the investment of capital.

If the enterprise has been established long, the risk, that was taken by the person or persons who provided its capital, may have been written off not merely once but several times over, but that will not affect the nature of the bargain.

The controllers of the enterprise, the employing side, will still give you, the worker, the same fixed or nearly fixed amount. They will still keep for themselves not merely a reasonable interest upon what now, so far as their original capital is concerned, is really a riskless loan and not merely such remuneration for their personal work as they would expect to have to give someone else to take their place—they will also keep for themselves whatever more the enterprise may produce.

TOO RARE TO HAVE A MARKET-PRICE: BUT RARITY IS RARE

248.   In very exceptional cases it may be contended reasonably that the skill and energy upon the employing side are so great that they cannot be said to have a market-value. The fortunate possessor of those very exceptional qualifications could not retire from the enterprise without great disadvantage to it. Only by a very improbable chance could he get his place filled well enough.

Such rare special cases raise the question whether those, who have the luck to possess such ability, should not regard it as in some degree a trust and set for themselves some limit to the profiteering that its possession makes possible. That, however, is a special question.

The very great majority of controllers of prosperous businesses could get their place filled quite as well and often much better for an income far less than the business is yielding to them beyond a reasonable interest upon their investment.

ALL BROKING SHOULD BE HONEST

249. The experiment, that this book describes, is merely one more effort to find a practical way of improving upon this state of affairs. The experiment is in fact aimed at bringing the employer, whose function it is to enable the worker to invest his working-life to the best advantage for himself, into line with the broker or other professional adviser whose function it is to enable the capitalist to invest his capital to the best advantage for himself, so that true profit, the thing that some economists call "windfall profit", that as a matter of natural justice does not clearly belong to anybody, shall go to those, who being less lucky in the possession of ability or of opportunity or of both have more need of windfalls, instead of going to those whose luck in these other ways is greater and whose need of windfalls is correspondingly less.

The ideas, that are the subject of this Part of the book, are put forward as amounting to such a practical way.

In the main the book says nothing here or elsewhere upon the mere technique of business-management, ideas that might be held and things that might be done by an ordinary profit-seeking entrepreneur. The book likewise does not go far into detail even in the practical matters of action upon the essence of its main plan.

If anyone qualified to manage a business with the ordinary aim is trying sincerely to give effect to this different aim, the essence of this main plan, he will necessarily see for himself good enough answers to the multitude of practical questions that arise in the conduct of any business, answers, I mean, that will be sufficiently appropriate to the difference of aim.

The purpose of this book is merely to give the members of this particular partnership, especially, of course, those who from time to time will be in some degree its leaders, so thorough an understanding of its essential character, its fundamental aims, that its policy will be steadily consistent and will be applied with the vigour that comes of having clear enough ideas of what you are really trying to do.

CHAPTER 17

A CLASSLESS SOCIETY

250. THIRTY-EIGHT years ago in October of 1910 the main plan of the Partnership was completed. At that stage it had not got beyond a set of broad notions. Capital was to take no more than a fixed interest, the lowest for which it could be got, but within that limit there was to be scrupulous good faith from borrower to lender. Management was to take no more than a good professional income. All the remainder of the revenues of the business was to go in one way or another to the Managed but always with extreme care to get for the service of the customers the utmost efficiency available for that inducement without overstrain of body or mind for workers of the best ability obtainable. Within that limit the Managed were to have to the utmost extent, that was really possible, all of the advantages of ownership—income, sense of security, sense of status, intellectual interest and everything else.

AN UPWARD LIMIT TO INCOME

251. Upward the pay-sheet was to have a ceiling, a limit to the income of those luckiest in the possession of energy and of other ability that in our modern world affects earning-power and luckiest in the very important matter of scope to show and use whatever ability they have.

AS IN PUBLIC SERVICE

252. It may be objected that any such upward limit to the possibilities of individual gain will deprive industry of qualities it cannot afford to lose of initiative and drive.

But will not such a development in private enterprise be a mere repetition of a process that has already actually occurred in public affairs? In the days of the first Duke of Marlborough a very much poorer Great Britain made that illustrious ancestor of Mr. Winston Churchill a millionaire, which meant then far more than it does now. In those days it was still thought necessary to allow such fortunes to be made by those who brought into public affairs ability and energy that were really great. Nowadays a quite modest financial reward is considered a sufficient addition to the other attractions of public service.

MANAGEMENT A PROFESSION

253. The function of creating and managing private profit-making enterprise is indeed plainly becoming a profession. The functions of risking capital and of managing are becoming more and more separate. And why should the profession of management yield to the luckiest of its practitioners much more than that which induces possessors of abilities, that surely must be reckoned at least as great, to enter other professions and to work their hardest all their lives? Why should efficiency in creating or conducting a large business be rewarded by an income so far beyond any genuine consuming-power that it is in fact either accumulated until its recipient's death or squandered or given away?

VOLUNTARY SUPPLEMENTARY TAX-GATHERERS

254. In the last case its recipient is really taking upon himself to be a supplementary tax-gatherer, raising perhaps millions by levying upon his workers an income-tax, so far as he pays them less than he could afford to do, and by levying upon his customers a purchase-tax, so far as he charges them more. In some cases the proceeds of such volunteer supplementary tax-gathering may be put to very good use but on the whole is it really better than—is it not indeed very far inferior to—the advantages of letting wages be higher or prices lower?

255. Along this road we should get in time to middle-class standards for all.

Absolute equality is plainly unattainable. You cannot force everyone to spend his money in exactly the same way or make all persons equally efficient in their spendings for the same purpose. What is attainable is not absolute equality but such a degree of equality that differences of spending-power would not be great enough to produce class-barriers— distinctions that are the result of differences not of natural qualities but simply of spending-power.

CAPITALISM DISTORTED

256. The enlargement, to what we call big business, of the scale of private enterprise is an inevitable consequence of the advance of science and of all technique and, like most things human, it is a mixture of good and bad.

At present it distorts quite unnecessarily and indeed very injuriously for its own efficiency the natural proper working of capitalism to the excessive advantage of a merely sectional interest, that of the real controllers, who as a matter of fact tend more and more to be not true captains of industry but financiers employing professional managers.

This over-nourishment of the controllers of a business-organism, who may be only one or few, lightly worked or completely absentee and of very ordinary ability, means as a general rule such undernourishment of all or some of the other parts as diminishes seriously the efficiency of the organism as a whole.

As will be remarked later, it is a development notably similar to the disease that we call cancer.

The distortion, the excessive advantage of the controllers, so far as they thus consciously or unconsciously abuse selfishly their power to decide how the proceeds of the team-work of a particular enterprise are to be divided between themselves and all the members of that team, is of course correspondingly disadvantageous to all the other parties concerned—and those other parties include not only the controlled within the businesses but the whole of the general community.

GREAT CHANGE MUST COME

257. If we do not soon get far enough back to a sounder, more natural working of capitalism, this distortion will perhaps break our society down into revolutionary change ending, as in the present early infancy of Mankind revolution almost inevitably does, in tyranny.

Tyranny or, if the word be preferred, bureaucracy, may be, as by many it is believed to be at present in Russia, well-meaning and efficient but for nations capable of self-government (that is to say of democracy) tyranny or bureaucracy, however well-meaning and efficient, is surely a plainly inferior way of life?

If in such a breakdown our British democracy were to fall back into a form of government in which the ultimate authority was not to a sufficient extent public opinion formed freely, even if ill educated, then, before there could be any true further advance, we should, so at least it seems to me, have to struggle gradually up again to a position not essentially different from that from which we should have fallen back.

Whether or not the general ideas, upon which the John Lewis Partnership is based, might perhaps amount to a sufficient reform of present-day capitalism, it is certainly a chief purpose of the Partnership to throw light upon the problem of preventing such a breakdown.

So much for the idea of an upward limit to individual income, a ceiling to the pay-sheet, a term intended here to include all remuneration of individual workers, however important their functions and however great their achievements.

A NEW DESTINATION FOR PROFIT

258. If in private enterprise the reward of the utmost exertion of the highest ability is to be limited, as in public affairs it has already come to be, to a mere handsome professional income, what is to become of the profit that is now drawn off into excessive remuneration of the controllers?

The amount thus available will tend to be larger—possibly very much larger—if for their handsome professional income the controllers still do what in other professions a similar income induces other men of first-rate ability to do, namely their best, and if the remainder of the team of each enterprise are so improved in quantity, quality and zeal as obviously they will be if the remuneration available for them is thus raised substantially and the management do, as presumably they will, their best to get from the team in return for this better pay proportionately better work.

We have yet to see how far such a gain of efficiency in the team as a whole will add to the marginal revenue that is no longer to be diverted wrongly to excessive remuneration of the controllers. But the addition seems likely to be substantial.

What is to become of this money? In the first place it will provide a decent Minimum Wage, no matter how much more cheaply equivalent performance may happen to be available in the conditions of the modern world. A business that cannot give a decent living to every worker, whose services it really needs, should not exist at all. The Minimum may vary according to the nature of the particular work. The proper Minimum for the light work of a door-keeper may not be the same as for the heavy work of a stoker. At the top, there will be no reason for differences.

NO POVERTY: NO MONSTROUS WEALTH

259. Both the Pay-Scale's floor and its ceiling, both the Minimum Rates and the Maximum, will be based not upon economic values but upon consumption. The Minimum will be a decent standard of life for workers of such age, sex and so forth as will be right for the particular work. The Maximum will be simply whatever meaning it may be thought right to attach to the words "handsome professional income".

Years ago I hoped that by this time it would be possible either to name definite figures with some provision for adjustment to possible future changes in general conditions (the earning-power of various professions, the value of money and so forth) or at all events to fix for the Maximum a definite multiple of the Minimum for, say, an able-bodied man in the prime of life with, say, a wife and four children, a multiple that it should be the object of each partnership to reduce by raising its Minimum while leaving its Maximum unchanged.

The limitations of my own experience and of such knowledge as I have got otherwise being what they are and present conditions being in this respect so peculiarly unstable and puzzling, I cannot here undertake to be more precise. I cannot offer a definition less vague than the words "a handsome professional income".

260. It seems to me virtually certain that the national income would suffer grievously if the functions of a true entrepreneur of really high ability and even those of first-rate principal managers of large enterprises created by others did not offer a material reward well up to the best that would be concurrently regarded as a high but not an absurd hope for a really able and hardworking lawyer, physician, architect or member of professions similarly exacting in their requirements and economically important.

It may well be that for some long time and perhaps permanently the profession of managing businesses may need to be considerably better paid than any of these. There may be certain drawbacks that must be compensated financially if the business-world is not to get for its most important positions the leavings of certain other occupations, a state of affairs that might be very bad for the national income.

261. The further we get towards full equality of opportunity, the more will every really able boy or girl have a quite free choice of occupation. The really able are, I gather, pretty generally agreed to be at present not many more and quite possibly rather less than five per cent. of each generation. It must surely be immensely important to the national income that they shall be distributed to the very best advantage. It may be very necessary that a difference of material remuneration shall balance as far as possible attractions in which other occupations would have otherwise too much recruiting-advantage over the profession of managing businesses. But, even so, there might be such a reduction of the share now taken by controller-managers as would be of great advantage to all grades of the Managed and so to the efficiency of the team-work of industry and so to the national income. We must not lose sight of the fact that much of the present maldistribution of the earnings of industry does not go to any workers at all, not even to principal managers. It goes to absentee-capitalists who in any particular case may be many or few but few or many be getting in the particular case a quite excessive reward for their function of saving and lending.

We may be told that such happenings are expedient because some risks go wrong but that is nonsense. There should be in every case provision that borrowed capital can be paid out on certain definite terms. If that limitation to the dreams of avarice reduced the number of "wild-cat" ventures, so much the better.

To return to the remuneration not of the provider of risk-bearing capital but of principal management, there will obviously arise the question how far the manager, who creates or maintains a quite minor enterprise, is to be content with a personal income much smaller than even under our system he might be taking if his own performance were much greater.

But this book is not an attempt to answer all relevant problems of economics or statecraft. It is merely an account of a particular practical experiment. So far, as it suggests and discusses apparent implications of the ideas that have arisen from that particular experiment, it does so merely as part of the process of making those ideas themselves as plain as possible not to the economist or to the statesman but to the present and future members or potential members of this particular partnership.

DISPOSING OF PROFIT

262.   If in fact a partnership's pay-sheet has a floor and a ceiling and if its intermediate rates appear sufficient to secure first-rate occupants for all of its posts and if the partnership finds that, after putting to reserve whatever amount prudence seems to require, the earnings of the year or other period, that is under consideration, leave some surplus, what is to be done with that surplus?

If the business is in danger of being over-capitalised, the surplus should be distributed in cash, otherwise it should be distributed in Stock. The Stock should be in the position of equity capital, Ordinary Share capital, that is to say it should be at the base of the partnership's financial pyramid, so that these accumulated earnings of that partnership's workers, present and past, may constitute a margin of security for borrowing cheaply from the investing public.

But this last-charge capital should not have, like Ordinary Shares, an unlimited claim to dividend. It should have, on the contrary, the lowest rate at which such a security is likely to be saleable on average for its nominal value or sufficiently near to that. The dividend being thus limited should be cumulative, a thing that will, of course, help the sale-value.

When I say "sufficiently near to that", I mean that it must be rather gravely undesirable for the efficiency of a partnership that whatever its members may get, in addition to whatever they are supposed to have "earned" in the ordinary sense of that word, shall come to them neither in cash nor in the form of a security that they can, if they wish, turn into cash for its nominal value or so nearly so that the difference will not be too disagreeable to their minds.

263.   It is easy to point out that because of certain facts of human nature workers in modern industry are caught in a vicious circle or on the horns of a dilemma or whatever it should be called. All of us, when we are workers, desire that capital shall be cheap, so that as much as possible of the proceeds of industry may be available for our own pay. But, as soon as any of us has saved, inherited or otherwise acquired some capital that we do not wish to consume but to invest, we lend it to whoever offers the

highest rate of interest with at the same time such safety or appearance of safety as will satisfy us for our investment.

So far, as this technically "unearned" portion of the income of the members of a partnership becomes for the business, in which it is made, working capital on terms cheaper than the business would have to offer to the investing public, this vicious circle or dilemma or whatever it should be called is broken. But most people think very disconnectedly. They are not conscious that what they want at one time is incompatible with something else that they will want at other times.

If workers are uncomfortably puzzled or disgruntled, the fact, that that may be unreasonable, will not diminish the ill-effect upon their efficiency.

264. It happens, however, fortunately, that the Powers That Be in the Money Market, those modern equivalents of the mediaeval castle-owners, who charged all passers-by so very stiffly for the service of not letting anyone else rob them, charge nowadays so very stiffly for their go-between services, that the actual average rate the private investor can get, even for taking the risks of the Ordinary Shareholder, is not a prohibitive figure for a partnership to offer as a fixed rate with the immense attraction of cumulative rights.

265. Now let us suppose that we have to dispose either in cash or in Stock of a large surplus beyond a quite adequate pay-sheet and a quite adequate appropriation to General Reserve. What are we to do with it? This is money that, the partnership could have added to its pay-rates if at the beginning of the period it had known for certain that the results were going to be what it now knows they have been.

If it was going to need the capital for its own business purposes, it would have had to stipulate that that extra part of each pay-rate should be taken not in cash but in stock. With that limitation at all events it could have raised all of its pay-rates proportionately. But in that case it would have been doing two things. It would have been undertaking to give as contractual remuneration rates higher than seemed to be necessary to attract first-rate workers, retain them and secure their best efforts. As a whole they are not likely to be very clear in their own minds that the rates judged to be sufficient for that purpose really are sufficient.

If they find themselves getting more, even though the margin may come to them not in cash but in stock, they will tend to feel that it is in the full ordinary sense of the word "earned" and that if it is reduced, they have a grievance.

Sense, however mistaken, of grievance is, as I have just said, apt to have effects that a partnership must avoid so far as it possibly can.

266. Now, if future conditions are less favourable to the making of profit, the business may be no less efficient. It may even be more so but the rates,

that have been raised to this level, may be for that time more than the traffic will bear. They will have to come down and the partnership will be very lucky if there is no appreciable damage to its efficiency.

If, on the other hand, this marginal income, that in the ordinary sense is not really earned at all, is kept wholly separate from contractual remuneration and is distributed not week by week or month by month but at the end of the year, you will get two good results. First and more important, you will diminish greatly the risk that lean years will produce discouragement and loss of efficiency and, second, and by no means negligible, you will cause a lot of people, whose private circumstances and temperament would cause them to use up pretty well the whole of their income as fast as it came to them, to find themselves once in each year in the position of having quite a tidy lump of savings available for some purpose for which perhaps they would have saved if they had been wise. That purpose may of course include the possession of a nest egg.

It is easier to refrain from consuming a fairly substantial amount, that you get in one lump, than it is to refrain from consuming it if it comes to you in small weekly or monthly separate portions.

Upon these arguments we will assume that the partnership, while taking a fairly liberal view upon the question what money is really earned, will let any remainder be distributed once a year.

As I have said elsewhere, we experimented with more frequent distributions and came to feel that yearly was on the whole best.

AN ABSOLUTE UPWARD LIMIT TO INCOME

267. Should a Partner, whose own pay is the ceiling rate, draw Partnership Benefit on top of that? To me the answer seems to be no. There is a natural tendency to pursue rather blindly the attractive idea of share and share alike. But the ceiling rate is supposed to be all that it is really decent to take in the way of personal reward for strenuous exertion of first-rate ability.

How can it be really decent that Partnership Benefit should be accepted on top of a rate fixed in that way? On the other hand, if you fix the ceiling rate so much lower that it will rarely, if ever, happen that the Benefit will be a greater addition than can be decently accepted, then the ceiling rate will not be a true ceiling at all and what are you to do when somebody, whose work would be actually worth far more to the Partnership, says that he will be content with the ceiling rate, provided that it is a guaranteed contractual remuneration but that, if he chose, he could make for himself a much bigger income and, if the Partnership is going to ask him to depend at all upon the Partnership Benefit, he will prefer to take his services elsewhere?

IN SOME CASES THE PARTNERSHIP'S MAXIMUM RATE OF INDIVIDUAL INCOME SHOULD PERHAPS BE CONTRACTUAL

268.   Perhaps such a case would never happen. But why create needlessly a risk that it might? Why not keep the Partnership's hands free to offer the absolute ceiling rate to somebody who would be really worth more—perhaps very much more—but who is willing to work for the Partnership, provided that the ceiling rate itself is guaranteed to him?

In the same way, if somebody's drawing rate is near to the ceiling, he must not have more Partnership Benefit than will just fill the gap.

Another question, that arises here, is whether the Partnership should aim at keeping its pay-rates as low as does not seem to be plainly bad for the efficiency of its business. It may be argued that, if all the rates are in fair proportion to each other and all the profit is distributed as Partnership Benefit, it will make no real difference to the Partners how much of their incomes comes to them in cash and how much comes to them in stock that they are free to sell as fast as they get it.

But the effect of such a policy would be that the Minimum Wage would tend to be kept low and so would the rates that were near to the minimum. Those are the posts that it is easiest to fill and it is the holders of those posts who will have most difficulty in understanding the principles of the Partnership and in judging what their own dues really are.

ABILITY MUST NOT TAKE MORE THAN A FAIR SHARE

269.   As you get to higher rates, you begin to deal with such people as are comparatively scarce. You are more anxious not to let slip a chance to get any of them who happen to come along and you are more anxious not to lose them when you have got them.

They know that perfectly well and the abilities, that make them thus valuable, tend also to make them better at bargaining and better at seeing just how much they can reasonably claim.

They will tend to get their own pay-rates pushed up pretty high. They will argue quite reasonably that the pay-rate is supposed to be all that they could get elsewhere and they will not tend to under-estimate that amount or to be at all feeble in claiming it.

If the policy of the Partnership is to keep its pay-rates as a whole about as low as it can, the effect of that policy will tend to be greatest at the minimum and at the rates that are only a little above the minimum.

The rate of the Benefit will be correspondingly higher. The better paid people will get full Benefit and the result in the end will be that they will really be paid more liberally than the people on the floor of the pay-sheet or near it.

PARTNERSHIP BENEFIT MUST NOT BE TOO LARGE A PROPORTION OF THE TOTAL EARNINGS

270.   This would be plainly inconsistent with the Partnership's profession that its supreme aim is the good of those who are worst off. Therefore, it seems to me that, as the real possibilities of the system begin to be clear and the whole thing settles down into steady working, the Partnership ought to aim at keeping its rate of Benefit no higher than seems to be necessary for two purposes, first, the purpose of avoiding having to cut pay-rates down in times of bad trade. The Partnership Benefit ought to act as a buffer, so that any but very extraordinary variations in the year's earnings of the whole team will merely cause the rate of Benefit to be higher or lower. The second purpose is that the Partnership shall accumulate in this way enough working capital at the base of its financial pyramid. Subject to the achievement of those two purposes, I believe that partnerships will be wise to make their minimum rate, the floor of their pay-sheet, as high as they can and to give correspondingly liberal rates right up the whole ladder.

As I have just said, to pay in this way the people, whose qualifications are really a bit scarce, eases so greatly the work of the Management that such people are pretty sure to be paid liberally. Anyhow they are too few to make a really big difference to the Partnership's general finance. The people, who really matter in that respect and who really are in danger of being somewhat squeezed with advantage to the rate of Benefit that is drawn by the others, are the people who can be replaced very easily.

For my own part I believe that it will actually be expedient for the Partnership's business efficiency to put as much as possible of its earnings into the contractual cash pay and to keep as little as possible back for the non-contractual Partnership Benefit. The less margin people have for saving and the lower their general ability, the more are they anxious to have as much as possible of their earnings in immediate cash.

When distribution-time comes round once a year, they are naturally keen enough on getting then as much as possible. But a margin of cash-pay is what will really attract them to the Partnership and enable them to do the very best work of which they are really capable.

PROSPECTIVE SPECIALISATION

271.   This is certainly one of the many things in which separate partnerships might try between them many different ideas. Such differences might be permanent. As efficiency grows, competition will be more and more severe and that will mean more and more specialisation.

As each individual partnership becomes more and more efficient in getting for itself exactly the right customers and exactly the right workers, that is to say those whom it is best qualified to satisfy, and as it becomes better and better at achieving that satisfaction, so must it become proportionately less and less satisfactory to customers and workers outside its own true field of operation.

In the particular matter, that we are considering now, I am inclined, though not very confidently, to think that the particular partnership, that has given rise to this present book, will be wise to be content to let its average rate of distribution of Partnership Benefit be just comfortably high enough to seem to produce real contentment in those whose rates of pay are above the Minimum, rates that it must be remembered will be intended to secure and retain absolutely first-rate workers and to induce them to do their best.

It may or may not happen that over and above such an average rate of distribution of general Partnership Benefit together with the pension fund and the collective amenities, of which something will be said presently, there will be a margin that will allow of raising considerably the absolute Minimum, the floor of the pay-sheet. If there is such a possibility, I am inclined to think that this particular partnership will be wise to use that money in that way rather than to use it to increase probably not very importantly the general rate of distribution of Benefit to everybody.

POSSIBILITY OF DIFFICULTIES WITH JEALOUSY

272. If a particular partnership follows this policy of making its minimum really handsome and if that partnership's success enables it to carry that policy quite a long way, its minimum wage will obviously raise higher and higher the point above which difference of ability will mean difference of income. Human nature being what it is, those, who rightly feel that their performance is appreciably more valuable than that of someone else, will be apt to feel aggrieved if their income is no larger than his.

They will be apt to say that a humanely liberal Minimum Wage is a splendid idea but that there must be something wrong if they themselves are not getting more than somebody else whose work in fact is not so valuable as their own.

Strictly speaking the Partnership ought to answer: "Do not be silly. A Minimum Wage is not a matter of 'earning' in that sense of the word. It is a matter of need". But human nature being what it is, the Partnership will, I dare say, find that wholehearted application of that doctrine will make so much trouble that it would be actually disadvantageous to the recipients of the Minimum Wage themselves, for they would suffer along with all the rest of the Partnership if discontent, however unreasonable, in such people, as we are considering, prevented them from doing their best.

The Partnership ought simply to drop anybody who in things of this kind is exceptionally greedy or in some way a trouble-maker. But there is a limit to the extent to which that can be done without too much disadvantage to the real interest of the rest of the team and, if the Minimum becomes at all high, it may be necessary to give to some other grades pay that is plainly more than a proper market rate for what they are actually doing.

This is obviously another argument for the suggestion in paragraph 270 that partnerships may be wise to make pay-rates as high and benefit as low as possible rather than to pursue the contrary policy.

If it is possible to get for those slightly senior grades people who will do their best, even though those, whom they reckon quite reasonably to be their inferiors .as workers, are getting a rate nearer to their own than would happen in the world outside, so much the better. The Partnership may perhaps find that to an important extent this awkward meanness of human nature, this desire to feel that other people are not as well off as you are, can be satisfied sufficiently by a difference that is to some extent merely a token.

DIFFICULTY OF A GRADUATION OF RATES AS THE MINIMUM RISES

273. Obviously you are likely to have to stop somewhere. If you are going to pay the least able of your workers a really big percentage more than their opposite numbers in the world outside, you can hardly hope to be able to add that same or at all events a substantial percentage to every grade right up to the top.

This difficulty may prove serious. Class feeling and individual jealousy do not become less as you go down the scale of intelligence and culture. They become stronger and we have yet to see how far material equality can be achieved without too much loss of general energy. The desire to win House colours and School colours, something that recognises that you are to a certain extent a superior person, has a great deal to do with the keenness of a schoolboy's efforts to become good at some game.

In Russia, just as much as anywhere else, material possessions are an incentive not solely for the nourishment or the warmth that they give but as a sign of superiority, a recognition of achievement. The world has yet to discover what are the limits to which the less able many can force the more able few to work not for themselves but for the community.

In our particular country and in a partnership of this particular kind this problem may turn out to be theoretical rather than real. That is as may be.

If all goes well, we shall in due course see what we shall see. But in theory at all events there may be a need of care in this matter of incentive as the Minimum Wage rises further and further. Possibly we have here one of those things in which specialisation will develop. A particular partnership's rules on such a point might be agreeable to some but too puzzling and irritating to others.

VARIOUS METHODS OF RAISING MINIMUM INCOME

274.   Perhaps the difficulty may be met in part by letting the Minimum Wage take to some extent forms other than spending-power. For example, pension might be full pay up to a certain line. Holidays might be subsidised: so might other things. Such raisings of the standard of life for those, whose real earning-power was lower, might be to them quite as good as more pay and less dangerous to the zeal of other workers in whose efforts those of lower earning-power cannot afford to induce slackening.

But, though there may be something in this idea, it will need great care. Cash pay may be frittered away in amusements that are worthless or even harmful, yet the freedom, even if from stupidity or ignorance it is used badly, may be in itself too great a good to be rightly withheld.

For my own part I feel very strongly indeed, and my wife feels at least equally strongly, that, wherever a partnership is in doubt how far it can leave its members free in one respect or another, its decision should be upon the side of freedom.

COMMUNISM AT £10,000 A YEAR

275.   It was only quite recently, that is to say, I think, within the last ten and even perhaps within the last five years, that in our own partnership we got to the point of conceiving that the supreme aim of our own venture might upon final analysis turn out to be the advantage of those of our members who are worst off. That seems to be the true consequence of our professed aim that in income, as in authority and personal freedom and indeed everything else, there shall be no more inequality than may seem to be really necessary to the Partnership's efficiency in the business by which it has to live, that is to say necessary to giving to the general community the best possible service.

So far, as this last supreme consideration may allow, equality and the sense of equality will be cultivated in every possible way. If the earnings of some particular partnership allow its Minimum Wage to be raised so high that the pay of the least important position is brought very near to that of the most important, so much the better. "In fact," remarked the Partner of twenty-five years' standing, to whom this was dictated, "it will be communism at £10,000 a year" "I," added the lady, whose own income, though well on the way to this figure, has not yet actually reached it, "am all for that."

DEVELOPMENT NOT CHANGE

276.   This was, I suppose, implicit in the original conception but in the way of our conscious aims it was a real and, I think, perhaps an extremely important advance. I was very much impressed by the welcome that it

met from some of those whom I should reckon to be from the standpoint of business-efficiency among the ablest of the Partnership's members.

This disregard of market-rate of pay, if it does not seem to be a good enough standard of living, must, I think, be far the most important of such developments as the years have brought in the first, simplest form of our plan. That original core has stood quite firm. In it there has been no change whatever and to-day, so far as I can see, there is no prospect of any. The developments have been merely the result of greater discernment of the implications of aims that in themselves have stood firm.

Originally every member's pay was to be the current market-rate for a worker of his kind and quality. Anything more was to be either the general Partnership Benefit distributed in proportion to that pay or a special gift to balance exceptional need, in fact a free insurance against misfortune. Later this idea of the current market-rate was qualified by the more advanced idea that no member of an age to be self-supporting should get from his membership less than a certain minimum wage, a decent living for himself or herself—and a minimum wage virtually involves allowances for dependents when the worker has any.

Originally the whole amount of profit available each year for distribution as what we now call Partnership Benefit was to be distributed at once. Later this idea was qualified by the institution of a pension-system.

Originally the fundamental idea was proportionate betterment for all members without any upward limit. Later this idea was replaced by another much deeper and, we think, much sounder, the idea that the true ultimate purpose of the whole thing should be the advantage of those who were worst off, the idea that the relation of Manager to Managed ought really to be a relation of service from the stronger to the weaker and not, as usual, the other way round. It should be a relation of professional expert to client.

ABILITY IS A TRUST.

277. Everyone, whose total remuneration in no matter what form exceeds the least that the Partnership is yielding to any other of its members, is to be regarded as drawing that margin in return for rendering service to those of his partners who are thus worse off.

The purpose of his efforts of every sort and kind in the business of the Partnership is not to advance his own fortune while that of those others stands still, so that there is a widening of the gap between his standard of life and theirs.

The purpose is to advance the interests of the whole Partnership, the whole team, the whole community, so that there will be a betterment of the position of those worse off than himself and the gap will tend to grow narrower rather than wider. If he does well enough, he may reach eventually an absolute limit; a line at which the Partnership will say to him: "This is enough for anybody; statesman, scientist, artist, professional worker of no matter what kind. To this line you must limit your consumption or your accumulation of a private capital. If your services to the Partnership become still more important you must be content with the glory and the other satisfactions but you must not expect to be paid at a rate higher than this that you have now reached. If the result of this system is that the Partnership is eventually able to give this standard of living, this handsome professional income, to every one of its members no matter how limited his personal earning-power, so much the better: that is what the Partnership is for. If you think that a bad idea, work somewhere else. If the Partnership cannot get along without you, it must come to an end."

POWER OF CONSUMPTION IS NOT NEARLY EQUAL

278. Of course we never shall get anywhere near such equality of income and that need not trouble us, for, broadly speaking, capacity to consume in a genuine way, that is not merely wasteful, is proportionate to capacity to earn. What is the good of a large library to someone who will in fact spend his leisure in playing golf and bridge or working in his garden? What is the use of much of a garden to someone who will spend his open-air leisure on golf-courses? What is the use of money for travel to someone who, for all the real good that he will get out of travelling, might just as well stay at home? What is the use of stables to someone who does not want to ride? The world is certainly barbarously poor. We have a very, very long way to go before everybody will have a standard of life with which he might well be content. But that standard will be reached far short of absolute equality of spending-power. People of different degrees of intelligence and nervous energy no more need the same spending-power than those, who are small, need as much dress-material as those who are large.

A PERSISTENTLY RISING MINIMUM WAGE TENDING TO A CLASSLESS SOCIETY

279. Nevertheless this aim plainly means that the Partnership's Minimum Wage must not only give a standard of living sufficient for good physical health. It must go a long way further. It must give a standard of living that can quite reasonably be considered enough for real contentment. With a fixed top rate, every raising of the bottom rate will be, of course, a move towards equality.

As the gap narrows, the Partnership will get nearer and nearer to being a classless society.

If an idea is to matter much, it must be new, large and simple and the world must be ripe for it.

Some critics of this partnership praise it as a conception but from the standpoint of practical value condemn it as "fifty years ahead of its time". Is that, however, really so? According to the Webbs, writing in 1936 upon "Soviet Communism", this plan of ours, that was devised in and before 1910 and that was published in 1918, has since then arisen separately in Russia and has there become enormously important.

280.   As for our own country, we hear that "We declare ourselves the unsleeping opponents of all class, all official or all Party privilege".

These are not the words of a Left Wing doctrinaire or a thoughtless utterance in casual conversation. They were uttered by Mr. Churchill in October of 1946 when, as Leader of the Conservative Party, he was addressing at Blackpool a conference of that party. In a classless society the only important inequalities will be in natural gifts.

In the main it should come not by levelling down but by levelling up. It should not be a matter of universal poverty but of middle-class standards for all, middle-class standards that might range between substantial but not inordinate wealth and modest competence. Within such a range all might be very fairly happy and life sufficiently various and colourful with enough of those incentives, that the general community has got to provide somehow, to development and exertion of ability. Such a society might be quite truly classless. Even now distinguished men and women, whose personal wealth is very small, mix upon terms of equality with everyone else, no matter how wealthy, and have, indeed, often the greater prestige.

A classless society is perfectly compatible with quite wide differences of spending-power. Such differences would indeed, obviously, still exist if incomes were large and equal, for the temperament of some would allow them to consume while the temperament of others would oblige them to save and even among the spenders different uses of money would mean great inequalities in particular respects. The spenders would have a higher scale of living, the savers would prefer a different satisfaction. Such differences need not involve any difference of what is called "class".

CHAPTER 18

INTERNATIONAL CONSIDERATIONS

281. THE experiment this book describes has amounted already to more than thirty years of effort to throw useful light upon what may perhaps be a way, smooth, quiet, peaceful and yet sufficiently swift, to immense changes in our modern society, changes in the direction in which Mr. Churchill says that England is moving, changes that may perhaps be necessary to peace not merely in England but between the West and Russia.

PEACE WITH RUSSIA

282. Professor Arnold Toynbee, in a recent address upon "The International Outlook", suggested that the only hope of world peace is "a sufficient reciprocal assimilation" of "the ideas and ideologies" of Russia and those of the United States. He continued, "Neither the Capitalist nor the Communist world is immune against subversive influences radiating from the other, for neither of them is the Earthly Paradise that it claims to be".

283. Is it unreasonable to hope that development along the general lines of the suggestions in this book might be a major element in such a "sufficient reciprocal assimilation"? Is there not real hope in the fact that ideas of this, kind have arisen quite separately both in the capitalist West and also in present-day Russia? In the West there has been for much more than a hundred years past a whole succession of experiments with the idea of the Self-governing Workshop or Producer-cooperative. Perhaps they may end in the discovery of a satisfactory technique, as actually happened in 1844 to the idea of the Consumer-cooperative. In present-day Russia, according to the Webbs, ideas, that seem to be essentially the same, have come already so far into practice that the Producer-cooperative, the Incop as the Russians call it, is a major element in the structure of that society. May there not be here the beginnings of Professor Toynbee's "sufficient reciprocal assimilation"? Moreover, may not some individual organisations of this type be as international as have been and still are some that have arisen from religion? Our own partnership has just financed in South Africa the starting of a business that will be its first affiliate overseas. The broad idea is that such enterprises shall be conducted so much upon our own system that cooperation advantageous to both sides will be possible. Information and even staff may be exchanged and both sides may profit by a consequent growth of buying- and employing-power. Perhaps

such developments of business may contribute to the development and maintenance of better relations between national communities.

CHAPTER 19

A PRACTICAL PLAN FOR INCREASING
NATIONAL PROSPERITY

284.   IN England such changes may, perhaps, be indispensable to the increase we need so desperately in our national income. Perhaps it may be possible to achieve in this way—and perhaps in this way alone—the necessary change in the minds of the workers: a sufficient will to do their best instead of wasting their working-lives in doing much less than their best because they so resent their present status and what they feel to be their intolerably wrongful deprivation of their proper share of the proceeds of team-work to which they give their lives.

But by itself that change, however thorough, would not be enough. British industry, if it is to give us that increase in our national income, must achieve very great change not only in the minds of the Managed but also in the Managers.

British industry must have a far larger share of the brains of the nation. The possessors of important ability must cease to overcrowd other occupations. Many more of them must go, as they do in the United States, into business. They will hardly do so without a very high prospect of a handsome professional income but their behaviour in other occupations shows they do not need the attraction and stimulus of a prospect of inordinate wealth.

EFFECT UPON THE MANAGED

285.   In the John Lewis Partnership these things have been happening for years. Throughout the war and right up to this present time we have had from our customers a steady chorus of surprised and delighted comment that those members of our partnership, with whom as customers they come into contact and who, in the main, are the Managed, have continued on the whole to be just as polite and friendly and helpful as in the days before the war lowered so much, as we are told that it has, the general standard in these respects.

So far as this praise has been deserved, it has been the more remarkable because the war has stopped for eight years until very lately the yearly flow of Partnership Benefit, the yearly distribution of profit that, affecting as it does every single member of the Partnership, is necessarily extremely important to the Partnership's general atmosphere, the feeling in the minds of the Rank and File of its workers that the business is in a real sense their own.

I am not saying that nearly the whole of the Partnership's Rank and File are to this extent either generous or else intelligent in their selfishness. Rome was not built in a day and, moreover, a whole succession of adverse chances have hindered the Partnership's development of full fruitfulness for its members and of full efficiency in securing that it admits and retains only the best of those who are available and that it makes the most of them.

But there is much other evidence of such general effect upon the minds of the Rank and File as may quite possibly mean that upon this system the British worker will work with as good heart and as much energy as the German and as we are told that the British worker himself does when he has migrated to the United States but only, so it is said, after he has taken there about two years to lose his old habit of mind, his habit of ca'canny.

EFFECT UPON MANAGEMENT

286.   Whatever may be true of the effects of its system upon the Rank and File of its members, the Partnership has certainly succeeded in bringing into its management plenty of men and women with all the qualifications, natural and acquired, for success in the Public Services or the professions, such people as, partly for social and partly for other reasons, tend in our country, unless perhaps they have a highly advantageous family connection with some particular business, to confine themselves to the Public Services and the learned professions and to consider business hardly a possible occupation for possessors of such natural abilities and education as their own.

The Partnership has not only attracted into itself at the beginning of their careers some who otherwise would have made such a different start in life, it has also to a fairly impressive extent attracted into itself some who were already well established in one or other of those fields.

The fact, that it was from the Partnership that the Government at the beginning of this war got their Director-General of Civilian Clothing, the originator of the Utility Idea, may obviously have been a mere accident but it is certainly true that the Partnership's special character, its social and political implications, increases importantly its ability to recruit itself, as in that case it had done, from the ranks of the learned professions.

After a brilliant career at Cambridge the future Director General of Civilian Clothing was prosperously established upon the staff of a great public school with every reason to look forward confidently to a satisfactory career that would bring him in due course to a headmastership.

Already on a considerable number of occasions the Partnership has taken the responsibility of inviting someone to give up a secure position and good prospects in some field of work very different from its own. In such cases it always tries to offer an opportunity for such a visit as will give for a few days or weeks an inside view before there is any burning of boats.

It is also always willing to agree beforehand upon some substantial payment by way of compensation for disappointment if the venture ends because the Partnership is unwilling to carry it further. But no such precautionary previous visits can make such ventures riskless or even nearly so and no such arrangement for some compensation for disappointment can amount to more than a sharing of disappointment.

If the venture is not a real success, there must almost always be upon both sides grave regret that the move was attempted. If, therefore, it is, as I believe, desirable for the public interest that major business enterprises shall recruit themselves, as they seem to be tending increasingly to do, from the ranks of those who in other occupations have given already to themselves and to others proof of important capacity, the business enterprises must offer inducements of great strength. In this respect, genuine partnerships may have, I think, a really important advantage.

MONEY ALONE IS NOT ENOUGH. WORKING LIFE IN ITSELF MUST BE BETTER WORTH LIVING

287. Any large business can attach to some of its posts substantial financial inducements but money is by no means everything and for my own part I believe that it is broadly true that, the better the real ability of the worker, the greater is the importance to him of considerations other than money.

If a business wants to get many possessors of high ability, it must be able to offer a handsome professional income but at that level other considerations tend to be not merely alternative to additional income, they tend to be indispensable and the Partnership can, I think, show that, whether or not a different policy might have secured a managerial team of comparable competence and energy, its system does secure management of first-rate efficiency, management at least equal, I believe, to the best American quality.

BETTER TEAM-WORK

288. Obviously, the more efficient a business, the more complete will be the unity, the more genuine the team-work, between Managers and Managed. Here is perhaps one piece of evidence of such efficiency in the organisation that is the subject of this book. Some years ago there arose more or less simultaneously both in this country and in America a new technique in business of our kind for preventing certain wastage. It is arduous to operate. The Americans have, I am told, kept it going but on this side of the Atlantic, so I am told, only the John Lewis Partnership has done so. All of the other organisations, that took it up in this country,

have dropped it as too troublesome, too much of a strain for the general energy at their disposal, the competence of their Managers and the good will of their workers. I cannot prove that this is true but I was told it upon authority that I believe to be quite trustworthy.

Doubters, however, are entirely welcome to doubt. I am not concerned to establish this or any other point. In due course the Partnership will by its own success or failure settle such matters.

MERELY AN EXPERIMENT

289.   As I find it impossible not to keep on saying, this book does not claim that the plan it describes is good. The book is merely a statement of that plan and of its apparent results so far and of what seem to me to be its prospects.

The real question is not whether organisations on the lines of the John Lewis Partnership, "Self-Governing Workshops" or "Cooperative Societies of Producers" or "Partnerships on the Scale of Modern Industry" or whatever else they may be called, are bound to succeed but whether they are bound to fail, not certainly in the sense of total failure—for some ventures of this kind have been quite long-lasting—but in the sense of failing, as so far all those have, to play in the modern world a part really important, a part more, or less comparable to that of the Co-operative Society of Consumers.

290.   If organisations on the general lines of the John Lewis Partnership can succeed in this sense, then the experiment, that this book describes, will perhaps have done more than contribute to the happiness of the lives of some at all events of this partnership's own members and render services, that from both sides have been a good deal praised, as an honest broker between its suppliers and its customers.

THEORY FROM PRACTICE, NOT THE OTHER WAY ROUND

291.   From a tiny shop in Toad Lane, Rochdale, the Cooperative Movement, that is to say the idea of a Cooperative Society of Consumers, within a hundred years spread all over the world. Those consequences of that little experiment were merely incidental. Those "twenty-eight poor workmen", the Rochdale Pioneers, as they have come to be called, were not aiming at anything of the kind. They were merely seeking to make their own small wages go a little further. They were merely clubbing together to buy at the wholesale price oatmeal and a few other things that they all needed.

The John Lewis Partnership has arisen from a similarly practical attempt to solve a particular private problem, the problem of bringing as much reasonableness as possible into the conduct of one particular business. In both cases practice has led to theory, not the other way round.

CHAPTER 20

THE FOUR MAIN POSSIBILITIES IN THE ORGANISATION OF INDUSTRY

292. THE "Self-Governing Workshop" or "Cooperative Society of Producers" may, I think, be needed to supplement the Co-operative Society of Consumers and various forms of "nationalisation" in removing from our modern world the evils that have arisen from the gross distortion that Private Enterprise has produced in the proper working of capitalism.

The limitations of the various forms of nationalisation seem to be recognised increasingly and the Cooperative Society of Consumers shows in practice the limitations that in theory it must. For, after all, the Cooperative Society says to the worker: "Come to me and I will exploit you for the benefit of the consumer. If you get to a high position, you may be able to supplement your official earnings by illicit gains but, even if you are willing to do that, I shall prevent it as far as I can".

Private Enterprise says to the worker: "Come to me. I shall exploit the consumer as much as seems to me prudent and I shall exploit you as far as I can but, if I do well enough for myself, you may find that you can get more out of me than you could out of the Cooperative Society of Consumers".

THE IDEA OF THE PRODUCER-COOPERATIVE

293. But the Producer-cooperative, the Self-Governing Workshop, says to the worker: "Come to me and, so far as the law and your own conscience will allow, I will exploit the consumer for your benefit. To those, who save and lend, I will offer reasonable interest upon a riskless loan and in addition such inducement as in each particular case may be necessary to get them to take whatever risk they may feel that they will be taking. But that reward shall never be, as now it may be, an unlimited dividend for ever and ever. In betting, nobody, however risky the bet, asks for an unlimited reward. So, when I, the Producer-cooperative, borrow, I will always set a definite limit to what in the best event the lender is to get. It may be a permanent fixed margin above reasonable interest for a riskless loan or it may be some temporary extra payments whereby, when those payments have been made, the risk shall be deemed to have been written off, so that thenceforward the loan will be riskless and any further claim shall be proportionately small.

LUCK SHOULD BE SHARED BY ALL

294. "Whatever I, the Producer-cooperative, may earn beyond these reasonable fixed dues to those who save and lend, shall go neither in further reward to them for having taken a risk that has really been written off nor to my own Managers in excessive reward for their own contributions to the work of my team. All of this remainder, that the economists call 'wind-fall profit' and that can hardly be said to belong, as a matter of natural justice, to anybody, shall go to you, the workers, Managers and Managed alike, in the proportion of your pay as the best available measure of your individual contributions to the work of the team. Thus, no worker's reward will be absolutely fixed. The consequences of an enterprise's mere good luck will not go, as now they do, wholly or almost wholly to those who really need them least, for they already have good luck, that is to say those who possess capital or exceptional ability or both.

295. "The consequences of an enterprise's mere good luck will be shared proportionately by all of its workers and that means that far the greater part will go to those whose need is greatest, that is to say the Managed, for the Managers will always be few. Certainly in some particular enterprises, in which the Managers are getting quite reasonably a handsome professional income, this may be a large proportion of the total pay-sheet. But, as any enterprise grows, this will be less and less true and over industry as a whole it will never be true.

"In industry as a whole the Managers will always be so few in proportion to the Managed that handsome professional incomes will be no more than the Managed can well afford to let their Managers take, just as students and athletes can well afford to let good teachers and good trainers get good incomes and must do if they want really good teaching and training to be available at all."

THE PICK OF THE WORKERS

296. Human nature being what it is, it seems conceivable that the third of these forms of organisation, that is to say the Self-Governing Workshop, may get on the whole the first pick of the workers and may get on the whole better effort from any particular set of workers than except in brief periods of very special excitement, such as the early stages of a war, would be got from them by any form of nationalisation or by the Cooperative Society of Consumers. That efficiency may, as seems to be actually happening in Russia (See the Webbs' "Soviet Communism", Vol. 1, pages 220 to 233), make the Self-Governing Workshop good for the general community and, as for ethics, how is it more righteous for a set of consumers organised in a cooperative society to get out of a set of workers

as much work as they can for their money than it is for a set of workers to get out of a set of consumers as much money as they can for their work?

NOT ONLY MORE HUMANE BUT ALSO MORE PRODUCTIVE

297.   But let me make it quite clear that for my own part I doubt whether the main advantage for the general community of a proper exploitation of the potentialities of the Cooperative Society of Producers would be in the extent to which it would humanise the conditions of team-work in the business-world.

The advantages in that way should be, I think, very great. Their importance to the general community should be quite first-class in their effects upon the happiness of workers and therefore upon their characters and so upon their influence on others, the next generation above all.

Nevertheless, important as all this must be, I suspect that even more important may be the effects of the system upon sheer economic efficiency. It is very plain that at present the general community suffers terribly from the inadequacy of the brainwork of the business-world, the Management, and of the inadequacy of the good will of the Managed.

The inadequacy of the Management leaves the Managed far short of a proper chance to do their best but their actual performance is far short of what even now it could be. In all this there is appalling waste from which everybody suffers.

For the vast majority the material means for the Good Life are quite needlessly meagre and even the few, who are rich enough to be, even under these conditions, very well off, suffer the discomforts and anxieties of a general atmosphere of discontent and instability.

If they are not pretty stupid, they suffer this however selfish they may be and, so far as they are not selfish, they have other and worse discomforts from their sense of the extent to which their own good fortune is exceptional.

ATTRACTING BRAIN-POWER

298.   The Cooperative Society of. Producers is, I suspect, the only means by which it is possible at present for the brain-power of great parts of the business-world to be increased sufficiently not only in quality but in quantity and for the good will of the workers in those same parts of the business-world to be raised to what it should be for the happiness of those workers themselves, quite apart from the consequences to anybody else. If this is so, then it may be that the general community's gain from the increase of production would be even more important than the advantages from the separate matter of making the team-work of industry as humane as it might be not only for the Managed but for those Managers who, consciously or unconsciously, are destroyed and injured

by the needless inhumanity of their present functions, precisely as decent-minded doctors or nurses will be destroyed and injured by the need to do the best they can with bad drugs, bad instruments and so forth.

For my own part I suspect that the best brains in modern industry are as good as can be. But I believe that very many more are needed and that there would be immense advantage to the general community and to those workers themselves if there were to be such a shift from certain occupations that are now over-crowded with brain-workers of quite good quality.

Furthermore, I suspect that brain-workers of smaller but still valuable gifts should be likewise far more numerous and moreover much better paid. I suspect that, if they were less pinched financially, they would be much more energetic and otherwise effective.

A CANCEROUS PERVERSION OF THE PROPER WORKING OF CAPITALISM

299.   The present arrangements are the result of a distortion of the proper working of capitalism, a cancerous process by which a very small minority draw off to themselves far more than their proper share of the proceeds of the team-work. Is not that exactly what happens in the illness we call cancer? A cell takes more than its proper share of the nourishment of the organism. It starves the other cells and the pressure of its own excessive growth may produce agony, just as in the body of a human community monstrously excessive inequality in the division of the national income produces heart-breaking frustration and horrible poverty.

300.   The present paucity of brain-workers and the inadequate natural capacity and even more the inadequate culture of such, as the team-work of industry does contain, may, for all that I know, be necessary to this present state of affairs.

It may be the best way and perhaps the only way to make available for this cancerous diversion so much of the proceeds of the team-work as are at present drawn off wrongly to the immense disadvantage of the efficiency of the team-work itself.

301.   But none of us would expect that the efficiency of a warship or regiment would not suffer seriously if the captain of the one or the colonel of the other or in each case some small group of senior officers drew for themselves far too much out of the total amount that the nation provides for that ship or for that regiment as a whole.

It may be argued that this analogy is false. But is that really so? Suppose the nation provided much more money. Could not a very wide margin of additional provision be used quite effectively to increase the efficiency of the ship or the regiment?

Is not this what is really happening in our modern industrial team-work? Is not such a cancerous diversion of the revenues of our coal mines and of our cotton factories and so forth the reason why their efficiency has fallen so far behind those of other countries?

CANCER NOT A DISEASE OF YOUTH

302. If we are asked whether the same process is not at work elsewhere, we shall say: "Yes, it is. But a cancer's harmfulness depends upon its age. In other countries the process in the main began later and has not gone so far. It may or may not be destined to run there the same course. But it did not begin in time to prevent those other coal mines and those other cotton factories from getting a much more proper equipment than our own have got".

May it not be in fact true that to keep industry properly equipped to give the right service to the general community you must never allow any important development of this cancerous diversion of the earnings of enterprise?

303. What happens when a business enterprise is young and vigorous and fighting its way to a good position? The controllers are taking from it little or nothing. Its earnings are being in the main ploughed back. The controllers may be looking forward to getting presently a bigger and bigger rake off. Their motives may be very excessively selfish but for the time what matters is not their motives but their actions. They may be doing the right thing only temporarily and only with a view to eventual inordinate gain for themselves. What they are doing in the meantime is none the less right while it lasts and for that time the, enterprise is likely to be more and more efficient. May it not be true that the real interest of the general community requires that this state of affairs shall not be merely temporary, not confined to the period during which a business is being established, but shall be in a reasonable sense permanent for the whole period of the existence of that business?

A NEW LEVEL OF EFFICIENCY

304. If this is true, then the humanising effects of a successful establishment of the Cooperative Society of Producers may be less important to the general community than the effects upon production of its sheer economic efficiency in those parts of the business world for which that system may be at present importantly better than nationalisation or the Cooperative Society of Consumers.

It may be said that all but exceptionally foolish managements are careful to be moderate in their demands upon their business. It is not true. Accumulation of reserves that represent starvation of the pay-roll or of equipment is not ploughing back. It is merely bleeding the business and then storing the blood.

CHAPTER 21

FINANCE, SIZE AND NATURAL HISTORY

THE CORE OF OUR PLAN

305. IN the course of years effort to bring in one way and another as much reasonableness as possible into the practical conduct of our particular business has given rise bit by bit to a whole system of team-work devised to gather together from the general community some of the ablest of those persons who are willing to serve that community in certain ways and not only to gather them together but to hold them together and induce them to accept any necessary training and in all other ways to do their best. The process may be compared to a crystal's self-formation and self-enlargement by its attraction of appropriate molecules.

In return for such services, as its members may render to the general community, the organisation, the "partnership" or whatever it may be called, will get whatever payment may be obtainable not only lawfully but expediently for the organisation's future. It will borrow no capital on terms inconsistent with good enough service to its customers and a good enough living for its members, among whom its remaining earnings will be divided as fairly as possible.

LARGE CAPITAL NOT NEEDED

306. Critics of our experiment have sometimes said that such a scheme is only practicable if someone possessed of large capital chooses to make such arrangements as these. That is not so. Suppose that, when I formed this partnership, I had not had a penny in the world and had been following the occupation of, say, a street-hawker of bananas. Suppose I had needed an assistant. Suppose the normal market-wage for lads of that sort had been ten shillings a week. I might have said to my would-be assistant: "You are expecting to get ten shillings a week and I will give it to you. I have also got to pay so much a week for the hire of this barrow. Those are all of my trading-expenses but, if I wanted to hire somebody else to do my own job, I should have to give him about two pounds. Out of all the money, that you and I make each week, I shall pay you your ten shillings and I shall pay for the hire of the barrow. I shall take for myself the next two pounds. If there is anything left, I shall call it Partnership Benefit and you and I will share it. Out of every fivepence I shall take fourpence as my share and one penny will go to you because the world reckons that the job, that I am doing, is worth about forty shillings a

week and that the job, that you will be doing, is worth about ten shillings a week and, as far as I can see, that will be about a reasonable measure of our respective shares in the work by which this profit will have been made. If you do not want to stay with me, you will be free to go and, if I am not satisfied with your help, I shall be free to get another lad. For him I shall do just the same as for you. And, if our business grows and carries more than two of us, then we shall do the same for them. Each will get what seems to be fair pay for his particular job and any profits will be divided proportionately to pay. Illness or other exceptional need will be carried to some extent by the business. To that extent it will come out of the profits before they are divided. Thus all of us will to that extent get a sort of free insurance against serious bad luck. Perhaps also we will have now and again some sort of a treat at our common charge, that is to say at the expense of the Partnership Benefit, and we will put some of the profit into a pension fund.

307. "If our business grows and we want to make it self-financing, we shall have to let our profits accumulate in it but we will have interest on them at such and such a rate and, when the business is big enough, we will turn it into a company and you and I and any partners, whom we may have by that time and who have likewise some savings in the business, will then take stock in proportion to our claims and thenceforward this Partnership Benefit each year will come to us in the form of stock that we can sell at once, if we like, to anyone who will buy it.

"To prevent the whole thing from being captured by purchase of the stock, this must have no votes as long as its dividend is paid punctually or even perhaps is already in hand for a certain time ahead. If we are ever in danger of over-capitalisation, we will distribute cash instead of stock.

"If the enterprise grew, it could and should become as little of a one-man management as might be consistent with proper efficiency."

That is exactly and precisely the system of the John Lewis Partnership with its twelve thousand members and its eleven millions of capital and it could be applied every bit as well to a banana-hawker, whose staff consisted of one lad, as to Imperial Chemicals or Unilever or any of the other businesses that according to our present ideas, are large.

To many readers of this book I am afraid that its description of this partnership's present structure will seem bewilderingly complex. I hope they will bear in mind that this example from a banana-barrow is a perfectly genuine description of the extent to which a little partnership can be simple. We ourselves have now to deal with 12,000 members scattered from Edinburgh to Southsea and from Somerset to Cambridge and carrying on between them a vast variety of quite different occupations of which the total volume last year (1947) exceeded sixteen million pounds. Moreover, we are planning for a continuance for many years of such rapid growth as so far we have always had and seem to be getting still. There is no reason at all why partnerships much smaller and much less scattered and much less various in their occupations should not be almost as simple as the most primitive type of one-man business of the same nature and on the same scale.

FUTURE POSSIBILITIES OF SUCH ORGANISATIONS

308.   What, if any, will be the limits to the size of enterprises of this kind? Governments would presumably intervene if in any case growth aroused serious jealousy or other serious adverse feelings in public officialdom. But competition may lead to such specialisation as will itself restrict size for any but very simple functions and in those the general community may be satisfied with the results of nationalisation.

I could hardly know less than I do of the history of the great Religious Orders but I have a fairly strong recollection that I have somewhere read that in the case of the Society of Jesus there was such Government intervention. I imagine, however, that, it would be difficult to find public authorities more jealously suspicious and more ruthless in their precautions than the present rulers of Russia and in that country, according to the Webbs, enterprises of this sort have been allowed to become very prosperous and important.

309.   For my own part, however, I have no wish to concern myself with any such forecasts. To me the relevant matters seem too complex and, because of the world-wide ferments of universal education and of the advance of material science, too unstable for such appraisals to be worth attempting.

Perhaps personal relationship may be a factor. Relatives or friends of important members of an existing partnership and especially of course of the holder of its position of chief individual responsibility and therefore of real power may want to start partnerships of their own and may perhaps be helped even to the extent of a deliberate splitting of the existing partnership.

310.   Presumably, so far as such things can be controlled by the making of rules, rules will be made.

But at all events it seems quite likely that in size and permanence partnerships of this sort may vary as widely or even more so than do private enterprises of the present kind. Some may become very large indeed. In "The New Freedom" Woodrow Wilson declared that big business was not efficient but we have yet to see what will be the consequence of a system that should go very far to counteract the tendency in big business to excessive centralisation of power, the carcase outgrowing too far the brain and nervous system, as is said to have happened to the gigantic animals that died out before Man had a chance to be responsible for their extinction.

311. The particular partnership, that has given rise to this book, would have been by now, I think, at least twice as large if my father had retired at seventy-five and if this last war had not occurred or even if it had not destroyed so great a part of our own particular business.

Without these tremendous handicaps, our own partnership would certainly have been already not merely vastly larger but much more impressively spectacular in its attractions. For example, by this time it might very easily have had a Glyndebourne of its own and have done really notable things in adult education. According to the Webbs this latter has been one of the conspicuous consequences of the similar developments in Russia.

NEED OF LARGE-SCALE TEAM-WORK

312. There are of course purposes that, though they require team-work, are best achieved by small teams. But, on the other hand, it is in large-scale team-work that mankind has most claim to have made real progress within the few thousand years of which we have record. Within that short time the abilities of individuals seem not to have increased perceptibly but the ability of modern nations to gather vast multitudes into a single effort and to communicate with them and to keep them supplied and in health is far out of sight of the utmost possibilities of the past.

Obviously there are purposes—the cutting, for example, of a Panama Canal or the giving of such value, as Mr. Ford gave the world in cheap locomotion—that could not have been achieved by any organisation that was not very large.

We have yet to see what, are the possibilities of service to the general community in such team-work as will combine the abilities of thousands of first-class workers all getting fairly near to doing their best.

NEED OF MUCH EXPERIMENTING

313. There are obviously a multitude of points of really high importance upon which it will be possible for partnerships to differ and to try between them a vast variety of experiments.

The John Lewis Partnership is not concerned to claim that its own present practice is good, much less that in any respect it is the best possible. This particular partnership always was and still is merely one practical experiment: something done to discover and demonstrate what are in fact the results of doing that particular thing.

We are not concerned to convince other people that we are right or to win applause or to avoid disapproval, except so far as there may be some consequence, good or bad, to our partnership's commercial good will among its customers or potential customers or upon its recruiting-power or in some other way. From that stand-point criticisms, anonymous or otherwise, of our partnership or of anything in its conduct, have always been welcome and have generally been published in its own weekly newspaper, "The Gazette of the John Lewis Partnership", so that all of its members might know of them. If, as we hope it may, this book brings us some fresh suggestions, we shall do our best to profit by them if we can.

Our work, as we see it, is essentially pioneering, exploration, research.

NATURAL HISTORY

314.   It is, however, noteworthy that there was no spectacular novelty, no astonishing new invention in the methods by which the Rochdale Pioneers made the success, that they did, of their little shop in Toad Lane. The difference between their methods and those of their predecessors seems to have been merely that the Pioneers used rather more commonsense, sense of the Nature of Things, hard-headedness.

If the experiment, that this book describes, has much real importance, that importance is probably due in part to something of the same sort, a certain success in discerning how far things, that are desirable, are practicable, the mind in fact of a naturalist, a naturalist perhaps not wholly unemotional but a naturalist not a Utopian doctrinaire.

Forty years ago, as with an ample independence and a very uncertain prospect of future health I lay recovering from the first of two heavy chest-operations, the result of a riding-accident, I considered seriously whether I would give up business for the pleasures and peace of what nowadays is called ecology, the study of the way in which the web of Nature holds together, the unconscious team-work of soil, climate, wild plants and wild animals. Natural History had always been for me one of the supreme delights of life. Although, however, the idea of the Partnership was not yet complete in my mind, it was beginning to take shape and I thought I had better go on with it. In the end it has been all that I ever hoped. But I still suspect that, as far as real happiness goes, I should have done better to have used my life in that other way.

PURE RESEARCH

315.   At all events, if the plan, that this book describes, turns out to have some serious importance, I think that may be because the plan has grown from the mind of a naturalist, of someone who finding a strange seed washed up by the sea might try to rear from it the plant and to discover, as it grew, what were its needs and to provide for those needs, not with any design that the plant should be large or small, long-lasting or the contrary, useful to men or useless, but with no other aim than to see what

the plant would become if it were enabled to grow according to its nature and to exist for its own sake.

If from the standpoint of men it turned out to be beautiful or useful or both, so much the better. But important discoveries are apt to be made not by those who are seeking such results but by those who are merely seeking knowledge for its own sake, pure research, the satisfaction of mere curiosity.

The John Lewis Partnership has grown like that. If members of a certain type have been invited to join it, they have not been invited for their own sakes but for the Partnership's. If there has been, as in fact there has, constant extreme effort to make the Partnership as useful as possible to the general community, it has not been for the sake of the general community but because such an organism can obviously only live by service.

HINDRANCES AND PRESENT RESULTS

316.   For upwards of twenty years altogether its growth has been tremendously handicapped. My father lived to be ninety-two and never retired. In his time the building up of such a team, as the experiment was going to need, was confined to the very narrow possibilities of Peter Jones. Eleven years after his death the Partnership has had this war and, moreover, extreme bad luck in the extent to which it has been bombed.

But thirty-one years ago it consisted of Peter Jones, a small business in a desperately bad way. To-day the Partnership's yearly pay-roll is upwards of three million pounds and but for the bombing would be much larger.

CHAPTER 22

A WOOD, NOT A PYRAMID:
THE RULE OF LAW SAFETY FIRST

317. IN a sense all this has been the work of a fairly long lifetime. But very much of the growth has been quite recent. What grows quickly may wither quickly but from first to last the supreme consideration has not been size or spectacular immediate betterment of the working-life of the Partners—jam to-day as we call it. The supreme aim has been solidity, permanence—an aim that has seemed to require patience in the matter of jam.

We have striven to keep our policy simple, easy to understand, easy to apply. We have striven to keep on increasing the variety of our business, so that standing upon many legs it should be well able to endure the loss of some of them. For the same motive of solidity we have tried to limit this variety to things in which we had a sufficient prospect of serving our customers really well.

We have tried to make the work of each of our posts as simple, as nearly foolproof, as possible and at the same time to secure that they would be always filled to the very best advantage. For real efficiency you must do your utmost both ways. The work must be made as easy as can possibly be contrived and the workers must nevertheless be the very best that can be got and they must be given the utmost possible incentives. We have tried to formulate sound, clear rules that could be maintained absolutely. For example, never to let our operations outgrow our ability to make punctually every payment due from us and always to give premature payment in every case in which there was a just sufficient financial inducement: never to finance those payments by loan-capital that could be called back from us at short notice and always to conduct our affairs with the utmost publicity that would not give to competitors too much information or make too much trouble in the way of personal jealousies among our own members or in some other way hurt our business too seriously.

USE OF PUBLICITY

318. A business, that is conducted wholly and solely for the benefit of each of its workers and with a whole-hearted wish to deal quite fairly with each of them, can afford to have very few secrets. We have made it a rule to have as few as ever we could. Our idea was partly to give peace of mind to all concerned but partly to give the Partnership the

great safeguard of such criticisms as would arise in the financial Press and elsewhere if its management appeared to be becoming unsound.

We hoped thus to reduce the dangers, that otherwise there might be, in the fact that the tenure of our managers does not depend upon any separate interest, whether the House of Commons or the voters in a Cooperative Society or the shareholders or other owners of any ordinary private enterprise.

Sixteen years before the Cohen Committee made their recent recommendations to Parliament, the John Lewis Partnership in the teeth of highly authoritative expert advice, that such an innovation would be most unwise, adopted of its own accord all the substance of those same ideas. Of this something has been said already in Paragraph 125 and thereafter.

MAKING EFFICIENCY POSSIBLE

319. We have tried to develop our business so that our Buyers could offer larger and larger orders and always cash payment and so that our Engagers could offer higher and higher attractions to desirable recruits.

To that same extent, that is to say as far as ever we could, we have, while trying our hardest to get the very ablest Buyers and Managers of every kind, tried at the same time to make their work easy, so that the survival and prosperity of the Partnership should depend as little as possible upon any at all uncommon degree of ability or zeal.

THE KEYSTONE OF THE ARCH

320. Above all we have tried to make the whole organisation as independent as possible of the occupant of the position of chief individual responsibility. We have tried to limit the absolute requirement of his functions to ordinary intelligence, ordinary energy and ordinary decency, the qualities in which a right choice is relatively easy to make, and by letting the remuneration of his functions be as high as those of any post in the Partnership we have sought to secure that anyone, to whom it was offered, would be willing to take it, anxious to keep it and proportionately vigilant lest under the Constitution his tenure become terminable by the Trustees at the instance of the Council. We have sought to ask of him no more than the functions of the umpire in a game of cricket (though, it must be admitted, with at all events some of the negative functions of a selector) and we have tried to secure that he would have an ample motive for giving properly close attention to the game.

TWO PRINCIPAL IDEAS

321. For my own part I suspect that, if my own life-work turns out to have some importance, it will be largely because of two particular devices, the use of journalism to secure constant ample communication

in all directions among all members of such a team; no matter how large, and the use of constitutional monarchy to give not creative initiative or drive but prudence and stability. In these two devices above all others is my chief hope that this form of Cooperative Society of Producers may perhaps turn out to have that subtle something for lack of which the Cooperative Society of Consumers never came to much until at last it was set right by the Rochdale Pioneers.

THE KEYSTONE AGAIN

In one respect the requirements of the constitution, that the holder of the position of chief individual responsibility, the Partnership's managing director as he might be called, is to undertake to maintain, are extremely definite. The tenure of this principal post is to be terminable by the Council if the Partnership ever falls at all short of absolute punctuality in its payment of any interest or dividend due to the holders of any of its securities.

If, therefore, friction between the occupant of the position of chief individual responsibility and any of the Partnership's other members affects to this extent the financial results of its business, the Council will be thereby empowered to make a fresh appointment. Perhaps this will turn out to be in practice the means by which the members of such an organisation will be able to hold their own with its head.

"Labour-troubles" might interrupt the flow of dividend. Other alleged failures in the Chairman's undertaking to maintain the Constitution of the Partnership might perhaps be difficult to prove to the satisfaction of the Courts of Law but failure to maintain the flow of dividend would be indisputable.

THE JOHN LEWIS PARTNERSHIP IS STILL ONLY AN EMBRYO

322. To me the Partnership has always seemed—and still seems—to be no more than an embryo. What may prove to be its ultimate natural limits I have only the vaguest ideas. If the law sets no limit to the growth of such organisations, some of them—including perhaps the Partnership—may become very large indeed.

The late Mr. H. S. Wright, K.C., when at the outset of the technical work upon the details of the plan I met him in conference, said to me that a very few years earlier he would have had to advise that the plan was outside the British Constitution. From the first beginnings of Company Law until very lately it had been the policy of Parliament not to permit under that Law any plan that provided, as did this, for indefinite expansion.

Of late years, however, Parliament had been persuaded to depart from this policy.

POSSIBILITIES

323. If there were legal restrictions, partners of sufficient intelligence might perhaps secure the advantages of large-scale operation by letting their teams cooperate, as ships not tied together can yet manoeuvre as a fleet and to a certain extent combine their separate strength into a single whole.

They may, for example, by keeping just within sight of each other maintain a far-flung watch and share immediately any knowledge that is got by any one of them.

Partnerships of this kind, if they were numerous, might vary very greatly. Some might be tiny, limited, for example, to particular village-shops, firms, factories or what you will. Others might be spread over many branches and some over all the world.

Everything, that makes for internationalism, may, we imagine, help towards permanent peace and general increase of wellbeing. Organisations of this kind should have an immense advantage in their ploughing back into their own efficiency the whole of their earnings beyond a moderate fixed interest upon an unwatered capital and perhaps some partnerships would be so intelligent in their use of that advantage that they would achieve the advantages, including the sheer strength, of immense size without too much of countervailing disadvantage.

LIMITATIONS

324. It seems certain that such of the problems of a partnership, as require a certain unity of control, must be the field of no more than about a dozen minds at most for it seems to be well-established that this is about the largest number for really efficient team-work in the practical administration of human affairs.

In really severe competition there may be fairly narrow limits to the extent to which any one particular controlling board of about this size can achieve first-rate efficiency but presumably the limits must vary pretty widely according to the nature of the particular business. We shall not, it seems to us, see the thing really tested until the competition is between genuine partnerships. As we remarked in one of our Reports to our Shareholders, the partnership system operated properly should have in competition with ordinary exploiting employment advantages comparable to those of the gun over the bow and arrow.

It seems likely that such organisations will often split, so that some part or parts will become completely independent partnerships. The parts may grow again so as to become as large or larger than before. Such splitting may occur in every—or almost every—partnership that reaches a certain scale and of which the business is not in its nature too highly integrated.

ANOTHER RECAPITULATION

325.   However all this may be, I have held steadily from the beginning that in its fundamental organisation our own partnership should constantly try to allow for a real possibility that it may become many times as large as it is at any particular present time. It may find itself spread over a vast variety of occupations and perhaps over many countries. It should never forget that a true partnership, however small it may be, must in its nature be a state within a state. It is a communal enterprise conducted for the unlimited benefit of all of its members without any exploitation whatever of some by others. That must mean that, however small the particular partnership, membership will correspond quite genuinely to citizenship in our modern democracies.

Whatever may happen in practice, in theory our modern state of Great Britain is managed for the unlimited and reasonably proportionate benefit of each and all of its citizens. In theory the whole of the national income and everything else, that is at the disposal of the national power, is intended to be shared in a fair and reasonable way among all of the citizens. But in such a community there may be a very high degree of individual independence.

In that case possessors of great abilities must tend to have a great degree of freedom of initiative. Everyone on this island, who sets up for himself as a professional worker or as an entrepreneur in any kind of business, must keep within the laws of the land. But within those laws he has great freedom.

CONCLUSIONS FROM RESULTS OF DEVOLUTION

326.   That is the kind of organisation for which in the light of the results of experiments I have come to hope. To my mind there need not and should not be in a partnership so large as our own any single post of which the holder will play such a part that nobody else will ever have a chance to make any really great mistake. Such an organisation I should call pyramidal. There would be one person who had much more real freedom of initiative than anyone else. There would be in fact a commander-in-chief. I have come to hope for something quite different, something much more like a wood of living trees, joining, as the trees in a wood do, to break the gale for each other and to draw down moisture to the common advantage and to restrict by their joint canopy the invasion of the forest floor by competitive forms of vegetation but having each enough space of its own, enough light and air for vigorous growth.

INITIATIVE WITHIN TEAM-WORK

327.   This, as it has seemed to me, is in harmony with the conception of a state within a state. In a state there are many entrepreneurs or venturers

(as we are told that we ought to call them) having great freedom of initiative but all working within a common set of laws, all having recourse upon occasion to the same law-courts, the same money-market, the same learned professions and so on.

Partly consciously but largely unconsciously those separate venturers combine in various ways for their joint advantage. Nevertheless, to a really important extent they have independence of initiative. To a really important extent they are not bound, before they can act, to persuade someone else that their idea is so good that he can properly consent to the intended procedure.

Whether this conception of organisation is feasible remains to be seen. If it is not, the Partnership will be driven by experience to revert to the ordinary pyramidal form but, if what may be called the woodland conception is feasible, then its possibilities must be, I think, far greater.

DEMOCRACY

328.   Our present arrangements for putting the plan into practice are the results of a good deal of experiment. They seem likely to be pretty permanent so long as there is not too much change in circumstances, the nature and size of our business, the law and so on. What are those arrangements? The Partnership aims at democracy. In a democracy the ultimate authority is public opinion. The health of the democracy will depend upon the extent to which its public opinion is sound and able to express itself. That soundness will depend partly upon the personal quality of the members of the community, but partly upon proper information and proper discussion.

We have come to feel that all this cannot be achieved in any one way. It needs a combination of means. There must be adequate personal contact between all ranks and to an adequate extent. This contact must be in an atmosphere of sufficient friendliness and with on both sides sufficient freedom of speech. Such contact we seek to secure by meetings formal and informal in councils, committees, general meetings of branches and social gatherings large and small, indoors and out, at home and abroad.

All this costs a lot of money but to individual partners it should give much pleasure and other benefit and upon the team-work of the Partnership as a whole it should have such good effects as must increase greatly its efficiency in its business.

Personal contact needs in my view to be supplemented by much journalism and moreover by journalism that makes great use of anonymity. All this fostering of discussion must be combined with very full information. There must be constant publication of everything partners are likely to wish to know and that can be published without too much risk of too much disadvantage to the partnership. It is supremely important that any such wish shall prevail.

It is the wish of an owner and it must have corresponding attention and effect. If in fact the partnership has a general public opinion that is lively, well-informed and freely expressed, how does that opinion operate?

THE RULE OF LAW

329. What is the Partnership's Constitution? In an autocracy, a despotism, whether the despot be an individual or a clique, life is not ruled by law but by the mere will of the possessors of power, the controllers of the army or of the police.

In a really civilised country the Law of the Land sets limits to the powers of individuals, whether they be public officials or holders of some position in private enterprise, which itself may be just as much public service as any work of any public officials. The freedom, the security, the happiness of everyone else, other than those holders .of power, public or private, depends upon two things. First, the extent and of course the quality of the Law and, second, the competence and good will of those who hold such power as still exists within the Law, the power that begins where the Law stops. Apart from the possibilities of Divine Revelation, all law is made by men and, being human, is narrowly limited in its competence.

It cannot foresee every possible case. It cannot be perfectly clear in all of those cases for which it does to some extent provide. There must be some real discretion, some real power, to the umpires of cricket-matches and to the captains of the two sides and to those who hold corresponding positions in all the infinitely various team-work of human life.

But, though the Rule of Law cannot be complete, it should extend as far as may be.

UNITY

330. The supreme argument for the Rule of Law is that humanity is intended not for selfishness, not for separation, but for brotherhood, equality. So long as men are born so unequal in capacity, there must be some who decide what shall be done and others who accept those decisions. But no really sensible person will think that to have power over others is preferable to being one of a team in which there is such equality of competence and such unanimity of aim that there, is no need for any giving and taking of orders.

As yet, however, just as there must be surgeons, fishmongers and other workers whose occupation a sensible person would hardly choose for its intrinsic pleasantness, so there must be guides, coordinators and impellers of teamwork, those who supplement the perceptions, the tenacity and the energy of others and enable them to achieve purposes they desire and without that leadership would not achieve.

The function of starting and conducting industrial enterprises comes under this last head and in our primitive society it has come to be monstrously overpaid, so that from the result of the combined effort the other members of the team get far less than their proper share.

Furthermore, the Law of our land and some supplementary other agencies, chiefly Trade Unionism, have come as yet very far short of setting such bounds as are really desirable to the powers of the practitioners of this profession of management.

IRREVOCABLE SETTLEMENTS AND DIVISION OF POWER

331.   What is the Partnership's present Constitution, that thus extends the present Law of our land and such supplements to that Law as have been achieved so far by Trade Unionism, trade custom and so on? What is the machinery, the organisation? What is the Partnership's principal management? By means of what organ or set of two or more organs does the Partnership take decisions and act upon them?

First of all there are (or will be) the two Settlements in Trust: that which was made in 1929 and that which is being made now to supplement in the light of these nineteen years of experience the first, and so to complete the foundation of the Partnership. Those are decisions that are virtually irrevocable. To get rid of them, the Partnership would have to dissolve itself and start afresh. Second, next under the Settlements in Trust, there are to be the Articles of the Constitution. These are to be alterable but only by agreement between the Central Council and the Chairman of the Central Board. Both sides may be slow to agree to any change but a Chairman near to retiring-age will be apt, I think, to enquire whether the Council wish to make compulsory upon his successors practices that he had followed of his own accord. Under the Settlements and the Articles of the Constitution principal authority is to be divided into three. One part is to belong to the Central Council, another part to the Central Board and the remainder to the Chairman of that Board. These three together, the Council, the Board and its Chairman, are to form the Partnership's principal authorities in the strictest sense of the words. None of them is to be exclusively sovereign. Within the law of the land principal power in all affairs of the Partnership is to be divided between these three in an arrangement intended to be, so far as possible, self-balancing. The law of the land will include, it must be remembered, the Partnership's own constitution, for by means of the Irrevocable. Settlements in Trust that Constitution will be welded into the law of the land, so as to be really for all members of the Partnership an extension of that law, just as are ordinary deeds of partnership between ordinary partners or contracts of service between employer and employee.

THE CONSTITUTION CHANGEABLE

332. It must be remembered also that this constitution will not be rigid, static, unchangeable. It is designed to be fluid, dynamic, changeable in case of need with extreme swiftness and easily enough but not too easily. For my part, I hope all change will be devolutionary and so towards democracy. Obviously that need not mean that there shall be no experimenting. Obviously there must be some experimenting. But there should be extreme care that it is genuinely intended and clearly understood to be merely tentative, merely exploratory. It must not be intended or supposed to be a forward move of a more substantial, permanent kind. There should be the very utmost care not to give ground from any advance of this last kind, any advance that is really supposed to be established. In relation to such advances, further movement should never be backward but always either forward or sideways.

If you are too venturesome in the way of making forward moves, that you are not able to maintain, so that you find yourselves having to retreat, you may find yourselves developing too much disposition to give ground. You may find you have come to have too little tenacity and resourcefulness in clinging, when you might, to advances that you have in fact made.

AVOID REACTION: GIVE UP NO GROUND ONCE GAINED

333.   Look before you leap. Look very, very carefully. But having leaped, try your very utmost not to give up that ground again. Hold on somehow. Don't let reaction start. Building-alterations, my father was fond of saying, are like telling lies. If you start, you can never know where you will be able to stop. Partnerships of this modern sort will, I suspect, find the same is true of reaction. Once you admit the idea that it may be necessary or at all events right to give ground sometimes, once you admit the idea that it may sometimes be necessary or at all events right to diminish the degree of democracy that your particular partnership has in fact attained, you will have no good enough foothold against folly or cunning. Bit by bit you will be pushed and wangled back into unnecessary inequality, privilege, selfishness and selfishness is apt to take root quickly and deep. For certain drug-habits the price of safety is total abstinence. From this danger of insidious reaction towards the evils, that the Partnership is designed to diminish, the price of safety—so at least it seems to me—is caution, patience, modesty and thereafter firmness. Before you advance, wait to be pretty sure you can hold on. In judging of that be most carefully on your guard against over-confidence.

But, once you have taken another step towards the Partnership's professed objectives, democracy, equality and so on, hold that ground if you can, so that in the Partnership's mass mind there may grow up the strongest possible habit of never retreating: the strongest possible tradition that, if advances, that are beginning to be contemplated and desired, seem disappointingly slow in coming, that slowness is the easier to take in good part because it belongs to the Partnership's declared policy of never retreating, a policy to which the exceptions, if any, have not been such as to prevent a development of very great confidence.

CHAPTER 23

ADMISSION AND ADVANCEMENT
QUALIFICATION FOR MEMBERSHIP

334. SETTLEMENT of main aims, fundamental ideas, is one thing. It is an entirely different thing to devise ways of carrying those ideas into practice. It is the difference between strategy and tactics.

One such practical question is how are you to decide who are to be admitted to your partnership of those who would be willing to join it? To answer this is to get very near to answering a question on which feelings will on the whole run much higher: Who is to be retained of those who have been admitted?

In Part III in the chapter that deals with the position of chief individual responsibility, called at present The Chairmanship, something will be said upon the question whether the Partnership shall use the judgment and resolution of one person or of several as its means of deciding whom it will admit and whether it will somehow rid itself of those who, if they were ideally sensible and ideally unselfish, might perhaps resign of their own accord.

But, whatever the Partnership's means of deciding such matters, it is plain that the decision must be not in respect of any one quality alone but in respect of everything that affects desirability as a member of that particular team.

If a partnership is not as exacting as it could and should be in its standards of pleasantness of behaviour, not only to superiors but to equals and subordinates, it may fall really seriously short of achieving for its members as a whole as much happiness as it could and should. Particular social accomplishments do not give separately an absolute right to expect admission to the society of others and in exactly the same way excellence as a worker in some respects will not necessarily mean that someone will be a desirable new member for some particular partnership or that, if he resigns, he should be, if possible, dissuaded from doing so or even that his membership should be continued so long as he does not resign.

EMPLOYMENT OF WOMEN

335. Here it may be well to mention two vexed questions, the employment of women at all and the employment of married women. My wife believes that in the twenty-six years, for which she has known the Partnership, there has been in the minds of its abler women members

a strong and more or less justified feeling that none of the Partnership's leaders would go nearly so far as I do in giving important posts to women.

For my own part I believe that at present the world wastes a vast amount of really valuable feminine ability and that the Partnership has gained heavily from the extent to which in making important appointments it has disregarded sex. At present (February 1948) the Partnership has one hundred and fifty posts that are already carrying four-figure incomes and of these thirty-nine carry £2,000 a year or more. Of the former thirty-four are held by women and of the latter ten.

THE BUYING SIDE: DURATION OF FULL EFFICIENCY

336.   Experience, however, has seemed to me to show that the duration of a woman's availability for a really exacting post is generally much shorter than a man's. Some women are able to hold a difficult post steadily through a long lifetime and are in every way as good as a very good man. But Mrs. Lewis agrees that our own experience has been that, though women tend to live longer than men, the average length of their effective career in a difficult post is much shorter. This is by no means wholly because marriage, though it does not always prevent a woman's continuance in a business career, does so, of course, very much oftener than in the case of men. Even more serious is the fact that, even if a woman does not marry, her efficiency in middle age and later is much more likely than is a man's to be lowered by ill health. I say "even more serious" because those women have become really expert and their complete or partial disablement is proportionately serious.

Therefore men are on the whole to be preferred to women for posts in which long tenure is really important. In such business, as the Partnership has at present, this means all those of the Buyerships in which first-rate success is apt to require many years of experience and long-standing relations with suppliers.

Apart from this very important matter of duration of full efficiency, the work of many Buyerships suits, I think, men much better than women, though the much greater competition for able men will often make a woman the better choice if the Buyership is not large enough to carry a pretty big income.

Certainly a good few Buyerships, whatever their attractions, require qualifications found much more easily in women but on the Buying Side many posts, of which this is not true, should be reserved, I think, as far as possible for men. As the team-work of the Buying Side develops, there may be a good many posts in which the advantages of long experience and of long-standing relations with suppliers can be provided by a man in the Directorship of Buying or in some post very near to that in responsibility and perhaps carrying as high a rate of pay.

Below this there may be other positions requiring qualities that can carry such an income as women do not easily get and in which permanence is not so important that a woman may not be the right choice.

THE SELLING SIDE

337. On the whole, however, I think that the Partnership's more lucrative posts for women will be mainly managerial positions on the Selling Side. The qualities, that make the first-rate head of a household and hostess, are just what are needed there.

MARRIED WOMEN

338. Before the war THE GAZETTE received every now and again anonymous letters, most of which, if I remember, appeared to come from spinsters, expressing strong resentment of the complete freedom with which the Partnership employed married women and moreover gave them coveted posts. In my own time this always has been and I believe always will be the Partnership's policy. In my own view the Partnership should be very careful never to over-influence a married woman against giving up business or towards coming into it or returning to it after some absence but, if she has a real wish to earn an income, I would make all feasible adjustments to develop her full earning-power and to give her full scope.

TRAINING

339. Admissibility with a view to the newcomer's occupying in due course some position that requires special knowledge, must be limited to those already possessed of such knowledge unless the Partnership is prepared to give them a training.

If their potentialities are high, they may not be available except for a fairly substantial immediate income. If the Partnership admits them, it will have to take the risk that the choice may result in a pretty serious loss of time, trouble and money. Should that risk be taken freely? The answer must depend on the availability of newcomers ready trained and sufficiently likely to be in the long run as good on the whole as those whom the Partnership could hope to get by drawing upon a wider field of choice and taking the risk aforesaid.

In the conditions of my own time I have felt rightly or wrongly that this risk should be taken very freely. This particular partnership is designed for people of really high trustworthiness, people who watched or unwatched, thoroughly well content or with a strong feeling that their services are undervalued, will, except in passing moods of negligible frequency and intensity, put their heart into their work and, moreover, a quite separate and vitally important thing, be to a similar extent helpful and kindly to those to whom different behaviour on their part would be importantly injurious to the Partnership's team-work, even if only in the sense of making membership less pleasant and therefore less valuable for some of their fellow-workers. I would admit and retain permanently some who to a really important extent are very much less generous, much more careful to do no more than they feel to be clearly due in return for their pay but whose professional conscience up to that point is really strong and who are perfectly trustworthy to the extent of their own ideas of honesty and whose ideas in that way, though not really generous, can be considered on the whole quite acceptable for their particular functions.

UNDESIRABLES

340. The Partnership has always contained and for some years at all events to come will continue to contain a great many people who upon these standards ought never to have been admitted or, if admitted, retained beyond the shortest period within which their deficiencies could have been discerned.

It has always contained and it still contains a great many people who work little, if any, better than they would for ordinary exploiting employers and who in such employment would in return for whatever they got do as little as upon purely selfish—and by no means intelligently selfish—considerations they dared.

Before this war the commonest guess at the Partnership's success in attracting recruits of first-rate quality or at all events in producing continuously that state of mind in those, whom it did in fact admit, was that about one-fifth or one-quarter of the members of the Partnership had a more or less strong affection for it, while the remainder were "only in it for what they can get out of it". In this respect I have never heard an estimate higher than one half.

DISASTROUS CONSEQUENCES OF FALSE ECONOMY IN EDUCATION

341. That has never disappointed me in a country that from being so well off as we were has so ruined itself by the astounding folly of extending the parliamentary franchise without a proportionate development of education. How can you expect to find for work, that at best cannot offer much of an income, great numbers of people who will be either unselfish or at all events really intelligent in their selfishness? Out of the population of this island or even of London it may seem that, if the sheer business-management is reasonably efficient, an enterprise on the special lines of our own partnership should find it quite possible to collect such a team. I should agree. I believe the thing is quite possible but it takes time—quite a lot of time—and during all these years the Partnership has been growing very fast. Not only have we had to keep on adding

quite a big percentage to our previous membership, we have also had to keep on replacing the substantial proportion who leave to marry or upon retirement or for various private reasons, a moving, for example, of the family home.

The broad result is that it is still possible to hear, as I did last week, that one of the Partnership's canteens has within eight weeks lost three hundred cups over and above breakages. That is the sort of thing that has made me feel that, though people, who, either because they are sensible or because they are good-hearted, are really trustworthy, are not very rare, they are rare enough to be desirable recruits, even if they have to be carried for some time at a loss while they are getting certain qualifications.

TITLE TO LIFE-MEMBERSHIP

342. In respect of permanence my own feeling has always been that the Partnership should no more drop a really good-hearted member well able to fill in a first-rate way a position that could quite properly carry an income with which he would be quite well enough content, than a family should consider dropping from their family business one of themselves who for some reason or other was obliged against his own will to leave it for a time but who had never been willing that his place should be filled in any permanent way if he were going to be able to return to it and who had always been reasonably likely to return within a period for which the position could be kept available without too monstrous disadvantage to the family's other members and who is, in fact, returning as soon as is reasonably possible.

It has always seemed to me that general absolute confidence, that the Partnership would not merely aim invariably at achieving in each case such permanence but that it would be extremely painstaking and resourceful in its efforts to achieve that aim, would be of almost inestimable importance to the Partnership's ability to recruit first-rate workers, retain them and secure their best efforts.

In all such matters judgment, how far a Partner ought to be reckoned to have upon the Partnership the claims that a decent family recognises in the case of every decent member of itself, must be, first, ability to fill well enough a position that the Partner will be sufficiently content to fill and, second, the will to be not only as a worker but in all other ways a truly desirable Partner for the Partnership's other members.

In other words there are two touchstones, ability, that is not a matter of the will, and unselfishness.

RETAIN ONLY THE REALLY DESIRABLE

343. Those, who in the Partnership's judgment are not at least very fairly unselfish in those matters that affect not only the Partnership's

material prosperity and security but its general happiness, should not be retained for any but purely business reasons, reasons of the Partnership's own selfish interests. If they are at all seriously doubtful whether it will pay them to stay in the Partnership, they will not be prevented by any other considerations from leaving it.

The Partnership must deal correspondingly with them. If the course of events raises a serious doubt whether their retention will be expedient, they should not be retained.

People, who are not to a fairly important extent unselfish, must be rather undesirable Partners for any enterprise that is to last for long. They are not the right people to invite to take part in a tiger-hunt. Their ability may be excellent and circumstances may never arise in which their selfishness will cause them to fail in the team-work that tiger-hunting requires. But a man, whose temperament will cause him in certain possible cases to desert a companion and to save himself, is not the right person to invite to take part in a tiger-hunt if there is available somebody whose ability is just adequate and whose will is better.

If, as the hunt progresses, someone, who has somehow raised serious doubts of his trustworthiness, can be dropped from the party, they will be wise to drop him.

SOME TERMINATIONS OF MEMBERSHIP MAY BE GOOD FOR ALL CONCERNED

344.   In the case of such an organisation, as we are contemplating, any termination of membership will mean a vacancy. The successor to that vacancy may turn out to be importantly more desirable and, so far as the dues of individuals are concerned, his need of it may be much greater than was that of its previous occupant.

There must be some real chance that its previous occupant, however aggrieved he and his friends may feel at the time, may come eventually to consider that his displacement was very good luck for himself and he may be perfectly right, for a partnership properly organised and conducted will afford little scope for taking selfish advantages and those, who rightly or wrongly have made an impression of being excessively self-centred, are not likely to get any great promotion unless their ability is judged to be so high that their membership would be in fact continued.

It is plain that in such cases the Partnership has to steer a course between two conflicting considerations. As a general rule its judgment, that someone is excessively self-centred, will be correct, for, unless its judgment of such things is on the whole good, its business must necessarily come to grief.

To retain someone, who is thus judged to be not in the highest sense trustworthy, must be bad policy for, though in the particular case the judgment may be wrong or the untrustworthiness never have occasion to have any serious ill-consequence, a large partnership will be taking that risk not in one case but in the long run in so many that many of the judgments will certainly be sound and among the cases, in which it is sound, there will certainly be some in which the consequences of retention would be very seriously bad.

Furthermore, such retention will deprive the Partnership of a chance to get a new member who would be on the whole very much more desirable or perhaps it will create a chance to promote somebody whose promotion will be for all concerned a very good thing.

IMPORTANCE OF EFFICIENT PROBATION TO SENSE OF SECURITY

345.   As against all these considerations there is the fact that, except when the reasons are such as all, who know that the termination has in fact occurred, can see to be quite clearly sufficient, every termination of membership, even when it is a resignation that is not merely entirely voluntary but that is very much against the Partnership's own wish, tends quite strongly to damage sense of security, the sense that it is supremely important to make and keep very strong indeed.

I suggest that the best inferences from all this are, first, that engaging should not be entrusted to anyone who does not seem to have a very definite talent for discerning such traits of personality as can be discerned upon first contact, especially if that is assisted by some knowledge of past record. Second, a partnership should make the very best arrangements, that it can, to ensure that newcomers are studied properly and that, if the impression, that they make, is not quite sufficiently favourable, appropriate action should not be undesirably delayed, so that, as the duration of a membership increases, its prospect of permanence may rise really fast. Third, when a Partner has been in fact allowed to continue for more than a certain time, there should be very great reluctance to decide against his further retention unless there are quite definite happenings that are really substantial indications of undesirability.

PROPER STANDARDS ARE GOOD FOR HAPPINESS

346.   At the earliest stage a really sensitive and sufficiently experienced mind may quite rightly draw an unfavourable conclusion from symptoms that to very many people would seem to have no real significance at all. But, as the period of probation (and there certainly should be in effect a very definite system of probation) is allowed to expire, there should be more and more inclination to treat as insignificant, happenings that may raise doubts but that quite conceivably are not really important.

In respect of definite happenings a quite high degree of strictness may be perfectly consistent with a first-rate general sense of security. Everything of this kind must form a consistent whole.

Of course the lines, that a particular partnership draws, must be appropriate to the particular type of mind at which that partnership really aims, either generally or in that particular part of its organisation.

Equally of course, the greater the benefits of any sort or kind that a partnership can offer to its members, the more exacting can be its requirements and the two must necessarily go more or less together, for in the case of many benefits the Partnership's ability to give them must depend upon its efficiency and its efficiency must depend upon its strictness. But strictness, so long as it is reasonable, is tonic. Indeed strictness and cheerfulness seem to be quite definitely related.

It is plainly of the essence of good personnel-management to take proper account of all relevant facts and to be very liberal in giving weight to any real excuse that there may be in the particular case.

SCOPE FOR RESOURCEFULNESS IN DIMINISHING LABOUR-TURNOVER

347. Within these general lines I suspect that it is very difficult for a partnership to spend too freely upon making its membership permanent.

Long periods of leave of absence on full pay, liberal help in illness or other troubles, a bold risking of substantial sums in giving training for a change of work that may seem to be the best hope of preventing someone from making himself too hot to hold, training that in some cases may involve not merely a risky loan but an absolute gift, liberal use of the time and trouble of very highly qualified and correspondingly expensive people in efforts to find somehow a way to make possible some retention—the total cost of all such things as these must have, I think, to be very great indeed before it will be an excessive price for the avoidance of the very real wastage of substituting newcomers, who will have to pick up a lot of threads, for people who are already well settled in the team and above all for avoiding weakening of the sense of security of those who give no trouble at all.

In large-scale team-work it is, I think, extremely important to give really great weight to the idea that, though the present and prospective desirability of a particular individual may not seem to justify some perhaps very considerable expenditure of time, trouble and money, that expenditure may be very amply justified by the incidental effects upon a whole lot of other people not only inside the Partnership but outside it.

PROMOTION

348. The question of admission and promotion will always be thorny. The members of every organisation will naturally wish to turn into a piece of property for themselves any employment that that organisation may have occasion to give. They and their friends are very likely to be quite genuinely incapable of perceiving, no matter how painstaking the

explanation, reasons that may be really ample for a decision that they have selfish reasons for disliking. It is of course conceivable that for a particular partnership the disadvantages of limiting all of its appointments or some section of them to a particular source, a particular nation, for example, or section of a nation may not be an excessive price for certain good consequences of that limitation or for avoiding the probable or certain ill consequences of the contrary course.

For my own part I have always contended that our own partnership ought to recruit itself with an absolutely single eye, first, to its efficiency in the service of its actual and potential customers and, second, to the happiness of its other members, apart from those particular individuals and their friends to whom such width of recruitment might be disadvantageous.

My own impression is that in such matters the general mass mind is pretty sensible. There is general understanding that inferior choices are advantageous only to the minority who are thus chosen and that to all the rest of the Partnership there must be some disadvantage that may perhaps be serious.

Certainly the Partnership has been from the earliest days remarkably broadminded and genuinely kindly in its attitude to engagements that are still rather unusual and that in those early days were very unusual indeed and that meant that some more or less coveted post would go immediately or ultimately to someone not already engaged in business of our kind.

EFFICIENCY SHOULD NOT BE SACRIFICED APPRECIABLY

349.   Nevertheless, used as the Partnership has become to this markedly exceptional feature in the procedure of its Management, THE GAZETTE has received every now and again anonymous letters of more or less bitter protest against particular appointments of this kind. I have always answered them with the bluntest possible assertion of the Partnership's policy and of its reasons and of my own intention that, so long as the responsibility should be mine, that policy should be followed with unflinching thoroughness. But that is not to say that I would not for my own part advise a partnership to spend pretty freely upon avoiding, so far as may be possible without real loss of efficiency, any engagement of newcomers that would prevent promotion of someone already within the partnership.

I would pay quite a stiff price in trouble and money to enable an existing Partner to become qualified for promotion rather than leave him unpromoted and avoid that same expenditure by engaging a newcomer who would need no such training. But I would most rigorously limit such promotion to people expected, if all goes well, to fill the intended position at least as well as it would be filled by a newcomer.

KEEP THE STANDARDS UP: BEWARE OF MEDIOCRITY

350. That is the real point. Avoid mediocrity. Avoid it like the plague. Disregard resentment, however confident those, who feel it or who sympathise with it, may be of its justice. Spare no pains to prevent or diminish such resentment—no pains, I mean, in the way of explanation at the time or demonstration of the subsequent results, even though it may seem expedient to make in that demonstration no mention of its real motive. But let there be no appreciable sacrifice of the interests of the Partnership's customers and therefore of the interests of its members as a whole to any greedy desire of some of its members that they or their friends shall get some promotion that will be in fact against the true interest of the Partnership.

Greed may seem too harsh a word to use of a conviction that may be perfectly sincere and that may arise from inevitable ignorance of facts or incompetence of judgment. Greed would perhaps be the right word only if there were real indifference to the interest of the Partnership. But whether there be in the particular case such indifference or not, the disadvantage to efficiency will be the same and in any partnership that aims, as this one always has and I trust always will, at absolutely first-rate efficiency in its service of its customers, actual or potential, that efficiency should never be sacrificed at all to any other consideration.

SPECIAL CASES

351. Presumably some partnerships will arise in such circumstances and will develop along such lines that it would be grossly impolitic for them to disregard in such a matter the wishes of certain customers or of certain members or of both as it is for someone, who desires to serve the community as a politician, to fail to make all such concessions, as he justifiably can, to those whims and fancies and foibles of which disregard may mean a serious loss of votes.

If the John Lewis Partnership decided to create a branch in some town or countryside where some sectarian feeling is strong, I should be entirely in favour of any sacrifices of efficiency that might seem to be required by the strength of that sectarian feeling but, so far, such a case has never arisen and for my own part I should endeavour to study most carefully the relevant facts before I accepted any view of that kind.

It never has actually happened but suppose that the Partnership found that it had got in some key position someone who made some not really proper stipulation that he or she should not be required to work with subordinates or even perhaps with colleagues who were members of a particular nation .or religious community or something of the sort. For my own part I should be very slow indeed to let the Partnership submit to such dictation and of course, the more I felt that the feelings professed were not absolutely sincere but that the root cause was a desire for self-assertion, the greater would be my reluctance. But, if the concession were practicable and the result of refusal seemed likely to be a quite considerable loss of efficiency and there did not seem to be too much risk that the concession would have incidental disadvantages that would be too great a price for avoiding that loss of efficiency, then for my own part I should be inclined to give way. I should feel that that was required by the Partnership's policy of aiming at a sufficiency of cold realism.

REALISM BUT WITH GREAT CAUTION

352.   A naturalist does not say that a plant ought not to be cantankerously fussy about lime or draught or the particular quality of its water-supply. He tries to discern what the plant does in fact need to be its best self and he tries to satisfy wholly that requirement.

The question, where such a policy is to stop, is of course a matter of ethics. In a worker of much higher quality the Partnership can, I think, tolerate quite properly rather more even of unkindness or discourtesy to subordinates, colleagues or superiors than it would otherwise. In human life all of us can without loss of self-respect make to some extent such special concessions. We may have reasons, that are in every sense an ample justification, for our tolerating in one person what we should not tolerate in another but for my own part I would draw that line pretty narrowly.

It is sometimes necessary to venture upon slippery slopes but to my mind this particular slope is extremely slippery and very dangerous. If the Partnership starts to allow possessors of exceptional qualifications to demonstrate their importance and generally assert themselves by indulgence of an inclination to unkindness and discourtesy, it will need to be extremely careful that it does not slip too far down that slope and suffer in one way or another an amount of damage that is far too heavy a price for whatever good the tolerance did in fact achieve.

CHAPTER 24

PAY

353. UPON Pay I have, I am afraid, said here and there much that I ought perhaps to have contrived somehow to keep together in a single section and that I might perhaps have managed to marshal if my work upon this book had not had to be so piecemeal and disjointed. It has been one of my great difficulties that so many of the matters, that make up my total subject, are from their nature so interwoven that it is very difficult—at least I have found it so—to keep them tidily apart.

I have been thus led already into dealing with the conceptions of a Maximum and a Minimum Wage both fixed rather upon considerations of consumption, the standard of living necessary to full efficiency, than upon the current market value of the services that the Partnership will be getting in each case and I have said already that all intermediate rates should be in my view a liberal estimate of the amount necessary to get that particular position filled in a really first-rate way but no more than that amount.

In this respect I think that it may be enough if I add here that I suspect strongly that the earning-power of many positions is still much underestimated.

LATENT POSSIBILITIES

354. In my early days I attached to Buyerships rates that not only my father, whose views in that respect were quite exceptionally penny wise and pound foolish, but, I believe, almost everyone else, who would have considered himself well qualified to judge of such matters, would have felt to be quite indisputably absurd.

In fact, however, the resultant traffic bore those charges very easily.

Such are the results of that which is so very difficult to achieve — the bringing together of exceptional qualifications and an appropriate opportunity.

355. Now I am very sure indeed that there are very many posts other than Buyerships in which there is comparable scope. Put a really able man or woman into some particular opportunity that to the superficial eye looks utterly unpromising and see how very often that chance, that seems to be hardly a real chance at all, will prove to be a springboard to very great and quite often to very swift achievement.

The qualities, that make someone the "life and soul" of an enterprise, large or small, are not so rare as they are supposed to be and many and many a position, that is generally believed confidently to be incapable of carrying an income much larger than is attached to it already, has an unsuspected scope that is really important.

GET RATES UP AND KEEP THEM UP

356.   In this connection I would urge the Partnership to be very reluctant to let a post, that has once been worked up to a certain level of income, be held for long on terms much lower. It may be necessary to let a newcomer have a little time to pick up threads, gain confidence and so forth but I would keep as near as ever you can to offering the vacancy on the terms on which it has come to be held and to warning those, who are inclined to undertake it, that they must maintain the results and thereby earn the money or they must produce a quite sufficiently convincing explanation of any considerable falling off and that, failing either of these, they must make way for somebody else willing to try his own luck at that same undertaking.

UNDER-PAYMENT OF BRAIN-WORKERS A WEAKNESS OF NATIONALISATION AND OF THE CONSUMER-COOPERATIVES

356.   For enterprises, in which this policy of pushing income as high as possible is more or less indispensable to real efficiency, the Producer-Cooperative should have an important advantage over either Nationalisation or the Consumer-Cooperative. In nationalised enterprises it is at present—and seems likely to be always—too difficult to retrace in the way either of appointment to a post or of the fixing of a pay-rate a step that has once been taken and steps must therefore be, as we see that in fact they are, very cautious.

In the Consumer-Cooperative the committees of management are not likely to be very well qualified to deal with matters, that are not pretty easy, and the members of those committees are bound to have difficulty in bringing themselves to value anybody's performance at a rate that will give him an economic position far above their own. Compare the financial rewards of first-rate service to the workers as a manager or buyer for a Cooperative Society, trade-union official, or labour-politician with those of service to those same workers as a music-hall artist or a film star. The first three are paid directly by the workers and they are not paid much. If the workers had had sense enough to pay handsomely for brains, Producer-Cooperatives would have been common long ago. It is said, I believe, that the pay the miners have lost by strikes would have bought up the whole of the mines. The music-hall artist and the film star are really employed by just the same people but not directly and so their pay is not so limited. If to possessors of really good brains the professions of trade-unionism and of labour-politics had been as financially attractive as the Law, the Dictators would not have been allowed to ruin Europe.

ABLE BECAUSE HIGHLY PAID

358. This matter of remuneration is enormously important. I would urge the Partnership to take very seriously the idea, to which experience has given rise in my mind, that people may be not only highly paid because they are able but able because they are highly paid. The greater the ability, the greater the likelihood that the worker will be importantly, though perhaps only inconspicuously, "temperamental".

Managers are often warned that a really big increase of pay will "only spoil" the person to whom they are inclined to give it. That can happen. There are people who "cannot stand corn". If I had reason to believe that someone was of that kind, I would give him only functions that would afford no scope for the making of such an income as would create for him temptations, that he could not resist, to self-indulgence of one sort or another. If that would not content him, he could not be carried in our partnership.

If I could not so counteract his supposed weakness, I would either drop him or give him his corn and give him any helpful warning, that I could, and hope for the best but to my mind, quite apart from any question of ethics, it is in the long run thoroughly inexpedient to give people less than they are really earning and no less inexpedient and to my mind thoroughly anti-social to let someone, however intensely he may desire it, retain at an income, with which he is entirely content and that he is whole-heartedly anxious not to lose, a position in which he will earn no more but in which somebody else would do far better for the collective interest of the team and for himself.

THE CASE FOR PLOUGHING BACK

359. In the team-work of industry huge private fortunes are not good for efficiency. No man will be importantly more efficient because, if he is in a position to take for himself a total income far beyond ten or, if you like, twenty thousand pounds a year, he chooses to use that power selfishly instead of letting the money go to others to whom its real value would be incomparably greater.

He himself certainly will not be importantly more efficient and he is very likely indeed to be less so. Whatever use he makes of it, his vast superfluity of spending-power will tend to distract him from his proper occupation, the work upon which it would be better for the general community that he should concentrate. Even if he saves the superfluous income, the care of all that investment is quite likely to detract somewhat from the quality and quantity of the work that he will put into his proper occupation.

UNDER-PAYMENT OF MINOR KEY-POSTS

360. But, even if his own efficiency is not positively diminished by this wrong division of revenues that happen to be under his control, there will be a very great loss of efficiency in others.

Even if in the team, for which he is responsible, there are as many key-posts as there really ought to be, many of them will be filled less adequately than if they carried better incomes and many of such of the occupants, as really are quite adequate, would be much more efficient if they were much better paid.

It is quite false to imagine that ability and the will to use it are both of them what mathematicians call, I believe, constants and that all, that varies, is the income that the worker happens to get in return.

Not only your will to do your best but your actual ability depends very largely upon what you are paid. As I have just said—and here deliberately repeat—not only are people highly paid because they are able: they are also able because they are highly paid. All of us know how in any game of skill good luck tends to affect our nerve. It keys us up in every way. It affects the whole of our performance until we are either tired out or the luck changes enough to get us down.

In exactly the same way the man or woman, who feels himself or herself to be a success in life, envied, secure, free from small worries and vexations and in sure command of reasonable comfort, including the ability to help friends, will put into his or her occupation a better quality of brain-work, greater imagination, keener insight, more vigour. All that is lost, so far as the revenues of the business instead of going into its pay-rates are diverted to other purposes, good or bad, outside the business itself. A business conducted in this way will tend to have a much lower rate of profit but it will tend to be a much more efficient business. Of all occupations the most profitable, so long as it is successful, is theft but it is not commonly reckoned sound policy.

I have just been speaking of huge private fortunes but of course the efficiency of a business will suffer just the same if to an equal extent revenues, that might with advantage be ploughed back, are drawn out of it, not to form one or more huge private fortunes but to give to a number of capitalists, individually small, a reward that is really excessive for their function of saving and lending and bearing risk.

Small leeches, if there be enough of them, can weaken their victim as much as would fewer and larger.

361.   Another matter, upon which there still remains to be said something that may as well be placed here, is the Living Wage. It was not until 1924 that we got beyond the idea of giving to everybody below the top (which in those days nobody, so far as I can remember, was even within sight of reaching), whatever we supposed to be the current market-rate for such work. But at the lowest level that rate was so low that we were more and more uneasy about it and finally we began to experiment with what we called a Living Wage.

The excess of this Living Wage over what was supposed to be the current market-rate was treated as an anticipatory drawing of Partnership Benefit. Its recipients got week by week in cash an additional percentage that the Partnership Benefit for the year was confidently expected to provide for everybody. The system involved the risk that the percentage might turn out to have been too high. If the actual results of the year were in that way disappointing, the other members of the Partnership would lose some of their own Partnership Benefit because of these excessive anticipatory drawings.

The Council decided unanimously that it would be right that all, whose earning-power was above this Living Wage, should take that risk. So far, as I can remember, anticipatory drawings never did turn out to have been above the general rate of Partnership Benefit that was found at the end of the year to be available for everybody but of course there was then little or nothing to come to the recipients of these anticipatory drawings.

At their level of pay it was perhaps hardly to be expected that they would not have a vague sense of disappointment and grievance. They did and the position was the more difficult because nobody could demonstrate beyond doubt either that the market-rate was proper in any individual case or that any particular worker was really earning no more than that minimum.

In the end we decided that a Minimum Wage, based upon standard of living, should be treated as really earned and should rank accordingly for full Partnership Benefit.

362.   At the same time we tackled the problem of Family Allowances. Foolish or cunning persons urge that a married man, whose housekeeping is not within sight of being an adequate occupation for an able-bodied, childless wife, should be paid upon the idea that, though the actual work, that the husband does, is worth much less, his masculine dignity requires that he shall be paid enough to have not merely a decent standard of living for himself but the means of supporting an unoccupied wife.

Foolish or cunning persons go further. They urge that, if the man is unmarried, he should be paid so much more than he is earning that he will not only have a decent standard of living for himself but also be able "to save up to marry".

An electorate, who have used the parliamentary franchise to avoid for a time taxation and military service at the cost of failing to stop the Dictators when that could have been done cheaply and easily and who have thereby brought upon their own country such ruin as we are now suffering and upon the rest of Europe ruin much greater even than this, cannot afford thereafter to indulge any inclination, that they may feel, to keep an army of able-bodied young women doing next to nothing.

As for saving to marry, young men, who fail to make an income larger than will support themselves, may certainly be nevertheless potential husbands and fathers of good quality but, if, so long as they do not marry, they will be able to spend upon themselves the money that otherwise they will have to spend upon maintaining a wife, it is perhaps questionable whether that state of affairs will powerfully encourage them to assume the responsibilities of matrimony.

The Partnership has accordingly resisted persistent and strenuous pressure that has been put upon it by some of the more philanthropically- or politically-minded of its own members to let its bachelors repeat this ancient manoeuvre of claiming that whatever is paid to men, who are married, must be paid also to bachelors because perhaps they may save the money and perhaps they may marry. After much investigation and discussion in the Central Council a figure was adopted as sufficient to give a bachelor a decent standard of living. The Partnership then took the view that an able-bodied, childless wife could and for the sake of the nation should be at least a half-time worker and upon the words "half-time" it put the moderate interpretation—four hours a day, five days a week. It assumed a certain minimum rate of earning and it reckoned that that ought to be supplemented by a Marriage Allowance to the Partner-husband of (at that time) fifteen shillings a week.

The Partnership took further the view that in a really civilised or, to use a less ambiguous word, a really intelligent community, the children of each generation would be a charge upon the whole community. From this standpoint it judged the allowances made as yet for this purpose by the Government of our own country to be inadequate and it decided to supplement them by an allowance of (at that time) twenty shillings weekly for a first child and of seven shillings and sixpence weekly for each subsequent child.

The rate for the first child took account of the probable loss of the mother's earning-power, though the news from Russia and the increasing pressure in this country for the provision of day-nurseries in factories and similar places suggests that in a good many cases the mother's earnings will continue.

DANGER THAT MINIMA WILL BE TREATED AS MAXIMA

364. There have been some symptoms of a thoughtless tendency in some engagers or controllers of engaging to behave as if a regulation, that no bachelor may be engaged below a certain rate, was a regulation that no bachelor may be engaged above that rate. It seems likely, however, that in the long run the payment of Family Allowances may actually broaden the minds of the more efficient managers, so that they will get away from the trouble-saving practice of paying a flat rate with little attention to each worker's real performance and will give to outstandingly good workers either a specially high fixed rate or a succession of bonuses that will have the same effect of bringing into a post someone who will really earn the amount that previously was being given in respect of that same post as Family Allowance but that was not being really earned.

FAMILY ALLOWANCES A CENTRAL CHARGE

It was, of course, necessary to provide against the likelihood that if Family Allowances were charged against the expenses for which an engager or a controller of engaging was responsible, he would avoid, so far as he could, engaging or retaining men who were married and, still more, any who had several children.

The Partnership arranged accordingly that Family Allowances should be a central charge upon the business of the Partnership as a whole. They should not be charged to the expenses of the particular Department in which the recipient of the allowance was working.

At this moment (the end of January 1948) the total yearly cost of these allowances is £15,300 but the progressive inflation, that is pretty rapidly raising pay-rates for work that is no more productive than before, seems likely to suspend the whole system for some time, for in scales fixed outside the Partnership foolish or cunning persons generally contrive to secure that the pay-rates of those, who have no dependents, are fixed upon the ground that the rates must be sufficient for those who have. The result, since the possible total is limited, is that the former get too much and the latter go short.

As life becomes harder or education better, such follies will no doubt diminish. Those, who have dependents, will then be paid better than they can be so long as the need of trade-union officials and of politicians to catch votes obliges them to use those, who have dependents, as stalking-horses for getting for those, who have no dependents, a standard of living, that, though certainly modest, is higher than is really fair to those who have dependents and whose incomes must suffer because of this vote-catching drain.

PAYMENT BY RESULTS

366.   In what, if any, cases is payment by results preferable to fixed pay? This question seems to me to be upon the border-line between the true subject of this book and those problems of business-management that will be more or less the same whether the business be organised as a partnership or in some essentially different way.

The true subject of this book is first, the case for adopting the idea that work in a business should carry as much as possible of all of the advantages of ownership and second, all the questions that arise if, but only if, that idea is adopted.

Along, however, with these I am anxious not to omit sufficient mention of any ideas that are not of this special kind but that may perhaps be valuable to the Partnership and may be lost if they are not included in this record.

INNOVATIONS QUITE SEPARATE FROM THE IDEA OF PARTNERSHIP FOR ALL

367.   Our technique for dealing with shareholders, that, when we adopted it, was a radical innovation, is now a commonplace, indeed compulsory upon all companies, and is only worth mentioning, if at all, as evidence that some of our new ideas have proved sound and that others of them may perhaps be worth consideration.

Our technique for building, likewise, so far as I know, radically new, is another case in point. Neither of these innovations has anything to do with our conception of partnership, a conception that turns completely upside down the general aims of private enterprise, so that the supreme consideration becomes the advantage of those who are worst off and the managers become, as it were, their professional advisers, with the aim that the incomes of their clients, instead of being limited severely to that which their clients are quite certainly "earning" in the ordinary sense of that word, shall on the contrary be enlarged as much as possible by additions that are as frankly "unearned" as the revenues of a landowner, whose tract of nearly worthless land may become suddenly immensely valuable for some purely accidental reason, a sudden local development of manufacturing or something else. In such a partnership all workers above the lowest grade will tend to be rather in the position of the teachers of professional musicians or of any other students for a profession or the trainers or "managers" of professional boxers and of other professional athletes.

This matter of method of payment is, I think, on the far side of that border line, of which I have just spoken. It is no less a problem of enterprises essentially different from our own partnership. But, though our experience is not, I think, worth much mention, I do not feel that I can omit it altogether.

AN EFFORT TO VALUE THE WORK OF BUYERS

368.   In the course of years we have done in this direction quite a lot of experimenting. In business of our kind payment by results is important chiefly in two sections, the Buyers and the Selling Staff. In the case of the Buyers our most ambitious effort was as follows. The Department (or Departments), that was to be the Buyer's field of work, was to be charged with all expenses that would cease if that Department were to be closed down and its floor-space and so on were to be put to some quite different use.

These were to be called the Particular Charges. So far as the gross profit of the Department exceeded the amount of these Particular Charges, the difference was, if I remember, to be called the Second Profit (the Gross Profit being of course the "First"). From this Second Profit was to be deducted the Department's share of what were to be called the General Charges—all the other expenses of the business as a whole, that is to say all those that could not be satisfactorily brought into the Particular Charges.

These General Charges were to be levied as a percentage of all the Second Profits of all the Buyerships—the principle of taxation in proportion to ability to pay.

This would give a Third Profit and by the time you got as far as that you would have covered every expense whatsoever except the remuneration of the Buyer himself.

The idea was that the Buyer's own remuneration up to the Partnership's limit for any member, whatever his place in its team, should be a fixed proportion of this Third Profit. The remainder would be Partnership Benefit.

Any Buyer's success would raise his Second Profit and so would lighten the General Charges for all of his colleagues. This would tend not only to good feeling but to actual team-work in the way of sharing information and giving other help.

THE EFFORT FAILS

369.   The thing broke down because the boundaries of Buyerships were too unstable. In such business, as we had then, the ceaseless change of fashion and of manufacturing technique kept on defeating all efforts to draw between separate Buyerships lines that would be sufficiently clear and lasting. In the end we came to feel that we could find no good enough substitute for mere intuition. It was impossible to get rid of the invidious and tiresome work of fixing remuneration upon lines of merely rough justice, such justice as can be achieved by taking account of things

that seem to be relevant but of accepting the impossibility of developing that process to such a degree of sheer record and measurement that the element of mere judgment, mere intuitive appraisal, is eliminated wholly or nearly so.

EFFORTS TO VALUE THE WORK OF SELLERS

370.   In the case of the Selling Staff our experience has been much the same. When I came into my father's business, I found them paid fixed salaries with what were called premiums for selling particular articles. With efficient supervision the premium system tends to prevent a good deal of waste. Without such supervision it is liable to great abuse and may be gravely disadvantageous to customers. It was, I believe, in those years that the system of giving to each assistant commission upon the amount of his or her sales came into almost universal use either in addition to premiums or more commonly instead of them. This system of what in the Partnership we call Individual Commission is likewise open to very great abuses. It affords great scope for unfairness and it is a ceaseless source of more or less bitter friction among those who ought to be colleagues, helping each other for the good of the business and making each others' working lives pleasant.

371.   Consideration of the objections to the Premium System and to Individual Commission led us to an experiment with what we called Pool Commission. The idea was that commission upon sales should be paid not upon the amount of each individual's separate sales but upon the total amount of the sales of a Department or group of Departments of such a nature and so placed that its members ought to help each other substantially.

The commission was to be paid into a pool and all the members of that particular pool were to share the commission in proportion to their pay-rates.

The Selling Staff of Peter Jones took eighteen months to agree to try this experiment but it became so well liked that there was a good deal of opposition to its being dropped, as eventually it was.

A REACTIONARY EXPERIMENT

372.   The dropping disappointed, as I had felt very confident that it would, those who advocated it. They found that the reversion to Individual Commission did not produce, as they had felt quite sure that it would, clearly better performance for equivalent pay and, on the other hand, it had of course the obvious disadvantages that have been mentioned already.

The reason, why I acquiesced in this experimental but really reactionary reversion to a method of which I felt that I had already seen enough and the reason, why we have never returned to Pool Commission, was that the Pool System had one fatal drawback: the worker could not know, as he could under the Individual System, day by day how his own commission-claim was accumulating for next pay-day. He would be pleased enough if, though his own sales happened to have been rather low, he found his share of commission amounting to much more than he would have been getting under the Individual System but it was difficult for him to take in good part the contrary event and the keenest workers missed, I felt, too seriously the daily and indeed continuous incentive of knowing just what commission they were making.

FUTURE POSSIBILITIES

373. It is, I think, conceivable that, if the Managerships of our Departments develop as perhaps they may, the Pool System may be tried again because with really intelligent, energetic managers the necessary calculations might be made daily and conceivably twice a day, so that the members of a pool would know how their commission-claims were accumulating as the week advanced. Up to now, however, the Partnership has been coming in respect of its Selling Staff, as it has in respect of its Buying Staff, to a conclusion that the advantages and disadvantages of various systems tend to work out to much the same general result and that, if adequate supervision is possible, it is not plainly wrong and may quite possibly be actually best to be content with fixed pay-rates. This view is said to be spreading in that supreme Land of Experimental Incentives, the U.S.A. Fixed Rates, however, will have to be reconsidered sufficiently often in the light of actual results, so that, if it is then felt that, if those results could have been foreseen precisely, the fixed pay-rates could have been fixed higher for the period now just ended, the difference may then be given as a bonus with or without an alteration for the future of the fixed rate itself.

NO GOOD ENOUGH SUBSTITUTE FOR DISCRETION

374. For my own part I do not think that the giving of such bonuses could be done really well upon any hard and fast rules. I think discretion should be exercised if there seems sufficient reason to regard a particular performance as specially meritorious or, on the other hand, not so good as it looks. In that way you can take account of the fact that one particular assistant tends to dodge all work that is not selling while another is, on the contrary, very unselfish in doing work that may be important and in doing it well, though such work does not show in the Takings Record.

It is possible also to allow for the fact that the same amount of sales may represent very different skill and pains according to the particular section of the stock in which those sales were made. And in the same way the Takings Record to the credit of a particular assistant may represent sales that were really effected mainly and perhaps wholly by somebody else. A customer, who on the previous day gave a lot of time and trouble and made no purchase, may come back later and spend a lot of money. The assistant, who took the previous trouble, may be absent or engaged and someone else may get the credit or the essential part in the selling of those particular goods may be taken by the Head of the Department or by somebody else. There are a multitude of things of which it is necessary to take account if in such matters you are to get as near, as is humanly possible, to achieving real fairness. Department Managers, who could work such a system so sensibly and fairly that they won and kept the confidence of their team, might perhaps prove so helpful to efficiency that their own earnings could be really high. There will tend of course to be comparable variables in other work than buying and selling.

FORESIGHT IS TOO LIMITED

375. Broadly speaking, I think it is very undesirable to fix systems of payment by results in advance of the event. If the bargain is for some accidental reason quite extravagantly favourable to the worker, it is rarely satisfactory to attempt to secure a sufficient adjustment. On the other hand, if it proves seriously disappointing to the worker, the Management must choose between making some sufficient change in the terms of the bargain or having the worker discouraged or even losing him or her altogether.

Bargains of such a "Heads I win: tails I don't lose" type are very undesirable and, moreover, the fixing of them tends to give an improper advantage to those who are greedy or skilful at haggling and it also affords much scope for favouritism (and the converse) or the suspicion of it.

If supervision of sufficient quality and quantity can be provided, I suspect that a policy of really liberal fixed pay with retrospective adjustment in cases in which that seems to be required for proper fairness will give on the whole at least as good results as any other and for a genuine partnership is likely to be best of all.

ELECTION OF MANAGERS

376. According to Monsieur Dubreuil in his book "A Chacun Sa Chance" translated by Mr. R. J. Mackay as "A Chance for Everybody" and published by Messrs. Chatto and Windus, election of managers has been a permanent success in certain fields of work both in France, and in Britain. But for the war the Partnership would have already experimented with this idea. It might perhaps tend to a sort of pool-system, a fixing of pay collectively, a kind of gang-contract, the eventual individual shares being treated as pay ranking for Partnership Benefit. But notions

attractive by their freshness and ingenuity, their apparent reasonableness, are sadly apt to cost a good deal to operate and to have such drawbacks of their own that in the end there is no clear advantage over a simple agreement for fixed pay, reviewed sufficiently often and corrected by a special supplement in the light of the event if that seems necessary for fairness. In all such matters it is of course an immense advantage of any genuine system of partnership that all workers feel that between them they are getting all there is to have.

RETRENCHMENT

377.   In the management of business there tends naturally to be, when times are good, pressure for the creation of new posts and for the raising of existing pay-rates.

Any resistance of a management to such pressure may arise from either of two quite separate motives. They may feel that the proposed expenditure will be a needless sacrifice of profit or they may feel that, though the present level of business and even the prospective level for some time to come is high enough to carry the proposed new charge, there is too much risk that the business will contract too soon to an extent that will make the new charge so excessive that there will have to be dismissals or reductions of pay and that the ill-consequences then would probably be worse than would be in the meantime those of refusing to let the new outgoing begin at all.

BETTER PAY WELL WHEN TIMES ARE GOOD AND TAKE SOME RISK OF HAVING TO RETRENCH

378.   In matters of this kind there is fairly wide scope for managerial discretion. At one extreme there is the possibility of raising expenses very freely upon the most optimistic view, that does not seem plainly unjustifiable, of the likelihood that there will be no falling away from the present revenues and that on the contrary it will be really wise to proceed upon an assumption that the revenues will be not merely maintained but will rise in such and such a way.

At the other extreme the management will on the contrary take the most pessimistic view that does not seem to be too seriously destructive in its immediate consequences. A management of this latter type must give way to some extent, in face of tenders of resignation or of serious complaints from customers or of other indications that the business is suffering seriously from short-handedness or discontent. But, apart from perhaps occasional rather foolish panic, they certainly will not be forced to be nearly so liberal as a management of the contrary type would be of their own accord.

It has in fact been always the policy of the Partnership to take this latter course, the optimistic course, and to run the greatest risk, that upon careful consideration did not seem to be plainly excessive, of finding itself forced by disappointment of revenue, present and prospective, to make some considerable retrenchments.

DON'T BE TOO NERVOUS OF INEVITABLE UNREASONABLENESS

379.   Such a policy means of course minimum friction when things are going well and maximum when they are going badly. It means maximum exploitation of opportunity and that is a very great advantage, though against it must be set the unreasonable resentment that arises from certain awkward facts of human nature.

Someone, who wants a trial engagement or a trial promotion to be given to himself or to someone else, will commonly urge that he is only asking for a chance and that, if it ends in disappointment, he will take that disappointment in entirely good part, will feel obliged because his proposal was accepted and will have no sense of grievance.

In practice, if the venture does end disappointingly, he will be rather exceptional if he does not resent that disappointment more or less bitterly. He will be very apt to persuade himself and, so far as he can, other people that he or the person, on whose behalf he made the request, has been in some way ill-treated. The chance given was not a proper chance such as was in effect promised or the results have been grossly misjudged from incompetence or from some bad motive.

This same awkward side of human nature, this tendency to think disconnectedly and to see results affecting yourself not dispassionately but through glasses strongly coloured by some emotion does a lot to make managements nervous of making appointments, that are experimental in any at all venturesome way, or of raising pay-rates when times are good.

It is bad enough to have to give offence to somebody and his friends outside the business and inside it if his engagement has to be closed because he cannot be carried at all. But it may be much worse to have to ask someone, whom you would be sorry to lose, to accept, even temporarily, some reduction of his rate of pay.

There is a general strong tendency to feel that it cannot be really impossible to continue any rate that has once been given and that it is unwise to acquiesce at all readily upon any grounds whatever in any downward adjustment of your own pay.

DIFFERENCE OF TEMPERAMENT

380.   That is one of the arguments for payment by results. Under that system some rise and fall is automatic and within a fairly wide margin bad times, especially if they seem unlikely to last long, mean much less

discontent. The disadvantages are considered in paragraphs 366-75 and of course payment by results is in the main only possible for posts in which that system is customary and acceptable to the workers. The remuneration of a very great many posts is always fixed. A proposal to make it vary with the rise and fall of trade would be, I think, generally very unacceptable unless the broad consequence was not merely to maintain existing fixed rates but to give a new average that was quite plainly higher.

It is, I think, broadly true that posts paid by fixed rate are, sought by workers with a more or less definite temperamental preference for certainty, while on the other hand workers of the contrary temperament go for the chance of "a bit extra" at the cost of some risk.

Accordingly, whether payment by results is used in some cases or not, there will be many in which the. Partnership will have to choose between offering a starting rate or giving an increase of pay that can only be permanent if results continue to be sufficiently near to the present level or even higher. Many a starting rate may be fixed quite rightly upon an assumption that the earning-power of that part of the business is rising or perhaps will rise because of this particular new engagement.

NO CALLS FOR VOLUNTEERS

381.   I have always felt that this particular partnership's right policy is to be as optimistic as seems to be not quite plainly wrong and to make the best of occasional needs of some retrenchment. But if such downward adjustments become necessary, I would not ask for volunteers. We tried that twice in this last war. The volunteers were not asked to forgo irrevocably some part of the pay that they were then drawing. They were only asked to renounce their legal claim to it and to trust the Partnership to let them have it eventually, if it really could. The renunciation of the legal claim was necessary, for otherwise there would have been no sufficient advantage to the Partnership's published accounts.

On each occasion the response amounted to about £40,000 a year and was quite worth having but in any similar emergency in future I should advise the Partnership to make the reduction general, stepping it downward in smaller and smaller steps from the higher incomes to the lower with adjustments for dependents and other special circumstances.

The Council should be asked to appoint a committee to consider applications for such special exemptions.

VARIETY OF MOTIVE

382.   An ungenerous response to such an appeal is not, I think, always due to what is commonly called meanness. It may be due to what for my own part I should regard as a false notion of what is right and proper. Some of those, whose failure to help in this way, either at all or more than

they did, was particularly surprising, may have felt that the real Nature of Things is such that it is proper to expect the advantages—and in some cases they have been very great—of belonging to such a partnership but to take in respect of such an appeal the attitude that, if the Partnership can afford to let the response be voluntary, then they are justified in preferring to take such risks as there may be for themselves in making no response or only a meagre response rather than in taking such other risks, as there may be for themselves, in responding more liberally.

In the former case there is the obvious likelihood that, if all goes well, the Partnership may forget important differences of behaviour in such matters as these. In the latter case there is the alternative possibility that all may not go well, so that in the end those, who have made sacrifices, will have done badly for themselves in comparison with those who have not.

CHICKENS MAY COME HOME TO ROOST

383.   There is obviously a difference between taking a rather rigorous view of the meaning of the- words "business is business" (and accepting with good will the consequences) and meanness in the real sense of that word. In this particular case the consequences may conceivably be very substantial, for in 1941 the Partnership set up a pension system and there will arise in due course the question what pensions, if any, shall be given in respect of years before the pension system came into operation.

The Partners, from whom more helpfulness might have been expected, are, of course, all people of substantial earning power. They had had no reason to expect any pension and no doubt they have been saving proportionately, so there is really no reason why the Partnership's interpretation of the proper meaning of the words "business is business" should be any less rigorous than their own.

This, however, is a problem that has not yet been settled.

A SLIDING SCALE

384.   The Partnership is now in the winter of 1947-8 considering ideas for automatic adjustment of the pay-sheet if times become very bad. It is not intended that, when times are good, pay-rates shall be raised so far that they are pretty well certain to have to be lowered again from time to time but it is very definitely intended that the existence of an agreed system of automatic adjustment to bad times shall make the Management less nervous, than otherwise they would be, of raising pay-rates when times are good.

The aim will be merely to diminish this managerial tendency to be excessively grudging but in that direction the possibility of benefit to efficiency is, I think, really important.

The arrangements for lowering the pay-sheet are not intended to be ever actually used unless conditions become so very bad as we can quite reasonably hope that they never will be.

All ordinary contraction and expansion of the income of the Partners as trading conditions vary between good and bad would be met not by a lowering of pay-rates from any level, that they had once been allowed to reach, but by a rise or fall in Partnership Benefit and perhaps a rise or fall in a distribution of bonuses that would be additional to each Partner's contractual pay.

385. These ideas are still under consideration but, if they go through, the system would be available in such extraordinary emergencies as arose in the course of this war and it would no longer be possible for the selfish to get an unfair advantage over the unselfish.

In this war that did not really matter because account could be taken of such things in deciding what pension, if any, the Partner should draw in respect of years before 1941. But in the future there will be no such years in respect of which pension was not promised beforehand, so the Partnership's only means of securing fairness would be by terminating membership before pension-age had been actually reached, a step so very serious that it could hardly be used except in cases that seemed very bad indeed.

Moreover, the services of some of these Partners might be a serious loss, so that in dropping them from the team their fellow-workers might be merely exchanging one injury for another. They would be getting compensation for the original selfishness but they would only be getting it at the cost of suffering damage in another way.

Altogether the case for an automatic system of adjusting the pay-sheet to emergencies so extraordinary as arose from this war seems to be very strong.

For my own part I am inclined to think that some such certainty of automatic retrenchment, if future results are too seriously disappointing, must be virtually indispensable to getting the Management as a whole to apply sufficiently vigorously, when times are good, the Partnership's declared policy of aiming at the greatest liberality that there seems to be a just comfortably sufficient hope of maintaining permanently or at all events for so long that the good consequences in the present and nearer future of saying "yes" will outweigh the disadvantage of an ultimate need to make some reduction that would presumably be only temporary.

PUBLICATION OF RELEVANT FIGURES

386. A declared possibility of such general retrenchment would be a strong additional reason for something that in any case I think the Partnership should do and that we are now in process of starting, namely

publish its budget to all of its members, though this will incidentally mean publication to all the world. That might be too helpful to competitors if the business were small and correspondingly homogeneous but the Partnership's branches are now so many and so various in their nature and size and its total operations are so large and so various in their composition that there is now, I think, sufficient agreement that the budget can be published safely to an extent that will be very adequately informative for such purposes as these.

The publication is to be much more than a mere announcement each year of the estimates of the trading of the coming twelve months. What is intended, is a monthly publication not merely of these estimates for the coming year but of the actual results up to that time and of the view that in the light of those results is now taken of the prospect for the remainder of the year.

IMPORTANCE OF KNOWLEDGE TO STATUS AND GOOD SENSE

387. If, as I feel almost sure that we shall, we start doing this and find there is no excessive drawback, the advantage may be very great. The mere disclosure of such figures tends to be very welcome to workers of all grades. Admission to such knowledge is obviously a great step upward in real status and to many the intellectual interest of having such information will be worth a very great deal. Above all, it will enable every individual Partner to judge for himself how near the broad results of the Partnership's total operations are getting towards the point, which will be fixed quite definitely, of operating the system of general retrenchment.

The system would be set out quite clearly on each successive (presumably monthly) publication of the latest budget figures, so that the idea would be constantly in the minds of all members of the Partnership. 388. All this seems to me to be a very important step towards the development of such general understanding of what business really is and of such general awareness of the results of their own particular business as must be necessary to genuine partnership and as must make that system very desirably educative for all of its members.

RETRENCHMENT, THOUGH IT SHOULD BE RISKED, SHOULD BE RARE AND BRIEF

389. For my own part I hope and fairly confidently believe that the system never will be operated. I think the Partnership should do its utmost to be always in a position to say that this system of automatic adjustment of pay-rates to extraordinarily bad times was set up in such and such a year and has never yet come into actual use. If it ever does come into use, the period should be kept as short as can possibly be contrived, so that the Partnership may be able to say that, though on such and such occasions

the system came into use to such and such an extent, this has happened only once or whatever the number of times may have been and on that occasion or those occasions lasted for no more than such and such a time.

CHAPTER 25

TENURE

390. PAY cannot achieve full efficiency or even get near to doing so if there is too little sense of security of tenure but it is, I suspect, much easier for this sense to be too strong than it is for pay to be too high. When, however, I say that sense of security can be too strong, I mean belief that blameworthy shortcoming will have no serious consequence. It is impossible for sense of security to be too strong in the way of belief that no ill will be suffered undeservedly. The more absolute the sense of security in that respect, the better for efficiency. Here we come back to the idea of the Rule of Law. But, human nature being what it is, the law must be to a very great extent unwritten. It must be in the minds of all concerned but it cannot be written completely. Upon each separate occasion one or more men or women must decide what in that particular case the law is.

If you try to carry written law—the letter of the law, as it is well called—too far beyond mere statements of general principles, so that the letter of the law shall provide clearly for each particular case, not only will your laws become almost impossibly multitudinous but, even so, the letter will be too rigid, so that the spirit of the law can be cunningly thwarted. In the enforcement of rules there must be to a quite sufficient extent the factor of human perception, the function of the umpire.

FOR HIGH EFFICIENCY THE SUBTLETY OF THE HUMAN MIND MUST BE UPON THE SIDE OF THE LAW AS WELL AS AGAINST IT

391.   In fact the subtlety of the human mind must be used to uphold the spirit of the law against that same subtlety. This means that the letter of the law must not go too far into details. Otherwise the subtlety upon its own side will be so fettered and impeded that the subtlety upon the other side, the subtlety of the would-be law-evader, will use the law's letter to thwart its spirit.

He will be only "law-honest" but he will "get away with it". The Courts of Law will find themselves forced to give, however reluctantly, judgment in his favour. If in cases of a certain kind the Courts find themselves doing that often and seriously, they will suggest improvements in the letter of the law whereby they are thus bound. But in the meantime they will be bound. They will be helpless to prevent the cunningly law-honest from taking advantage of the law's existing weakness and, if that particular weakness is made good, it will often not be long before some wrong-doer discovers some new loophole and immediately that gap will be exploited until eventually that too is stopped by the slow and clumsy machinery of legislation.

A LIMITATION OF NATIONALISATION

392.   Here we see a principal limit of the possibilities of nationalisation. Nationalisation means monopoly. The individual worker has not the protection of competition for his services among would-be employers of the same kind. In compensation he must be given more latitude in the way of tolerance of inefficiency. But beyond this difficulty nationalisation is handicapped in its need to be administered politically. Politics is inevitably as, I believe, John Morley said, "the science of the second best" and incidentally itself a most happy hunting-ground for the law-honest, the cunning exploiters of technicalities, the skilful in such dishonesties as cannot be brought home to you, the victimisers of the fallibility of their fellow-men in the making of written rules.

THE PRICE OF EFFICIENCY

393.   The true requirement of the general community is the highest efficiency that any particular worker can achieve without overstrain of mind or body. In a genuine democracy that requirement cannot be enforced under nationalisation nearly so closely and firmly as in private enterprise, where competition to attract the best workers and desire to retain them enables the good worker to play one employer off against another. Certainly it is only too true that even by present-day standards many employers are not good and of those reckoned good many could and should be far better. But the remedy for this is not in abolishing private enterprise but in preventing the cancerous diversion of its earnings to the wrong recipients.

If in those fields of work, in which the Producer-Cooperative will be best for the general community, the worker is to have the best possible income and working-conditions in all other ways, that worker absolutely must be safeguarded quite sufficiently against his own tendency to fail to play the game, as for his own sake he should.

The Rule of Written Law should be carried to the utmost length that experience may seem to allow but it must not be carried too far. Its administrators must have sufficient discretion. And that means much more than in a genuine democracy is possible under nationalisation. It is possible to say very woundingly things that on paper seem admirably polite. You cannot put on paper the speaker's tone of voice or gesture or all the subtle attendant circumstances that made that innocent-looking utterance exasperating or cruel.

This is but one of an infinity of ways in which those cunning in exploiting the letter of the law can defeat its purpose, its spirit. If in the judgment of the umpire one cricketer has "obstructed" another, he is "out". If in the judgment of the selection committee he has in some unforgivable way let the side down he is dropped. Written law could never cover every possibility of real obstruction or force a player to do his best if his own inclination were otherwise.

As the possibilities of shortcoming with impunity came to be realised, general efficiency would suffer more and more seriously until various factors produced an equilibrium at a level that would be pretty low.

MANAGERS MUST DESERVE TRUST AND BE TRUSTED

394. To me at all events that seems to be true and, whatever ideas other partnerships may think it well to try, I hope this one, that I have spent my life in making, will take always the line of putting really great responsibility upon—that is to say of putting really great trust in—mere human discretion in the matter of appraising desirability for membership and the merits of members.

For my own part I am absolutely convinced that, unless such discretion is sufficiently great and is used with sufficient competence (of which an essential part is moral courage) the total efficiency of the team and therefore the interest of the general community must suffer. If Producer-Cooperatives become, as for my part I expect, an important element in the world of tomorrow, they will, I believe, become in various ways very highly specialised. Just as an almost infinite variety of stocks and shares have been invented to satisfy different ideas and degrees of desire for on the one hand, income and, on the other, safety, so will there arise partnerships catering with great precision for a wide variety of worker-demand for income, sense of security and all those other things in respect of which the wishes and indeed the true needs of individuals differ.

395. There would be in a team no sense of security if members were dropped for no good reason. The climber, who feels himself to be competent and fit, climbs with care but without fear. Far from being miserably nervous he gets intense pleasure from his climbing. But he is thus fearless only if he knows the rock to be sound and the mountain safe. No skill, no care, will give safety on rotten rock or where there may be a fall of stone or an avalanche.

That, neither more nor less, was the degree of security intended in this plan. In just the same way, a cricketer, who accepts with great pleasure an invitation to join some famous club, will feel that he cannot afford to take risks with his physical fitness or to play slackly. But he will also feel that, so long as he retains on the whole the level of competence that got for him that invitation and so long as he seems to be really doing his best, he will be in no danger of losing his membership from mere caprice in the representatives of his fellow-members or for some such occasional failure as will occur now and then to every cricketer.

PERSONAL INCOMPATIBILITY

396. The quality of the cricketer's play, the efficiency of a Partner's work, will not be everything. It will be absolutely indispensable that the play and the work shall be good enough but it will not be impossible for a first-rate performer to be in one way or another so disagreeable to the other members of the team that his presence in it will be too bad for the efficiency of the team as a whole.

A partnership, that aims at the happiness of its members, cannot afford to carry individuals with whom such association, as the team-work of the Partnership requires, is too seriously disagreeable.

Minor frets are bound to happen in any human society and there should be a quite sufficient tolerance. But in the case of the really thick-skinned a community may not be very well able to protect itself and, if a club gets somehow a member whose resignation is desired too strongly by too many of his fellow-members, then the committee, whether it be a "committee of one"—a host or hostess—or a committee of more than one or the whole club in general meeting, should ask for the desired resignation and, if it is not forthcoming, should proceed with sufficient firmness and vigour.

STABILITY

397. A tree throughout what may be perhaps a very long life keeps, on the one hand drawing nourishment from the air and soil and, on the other hand, returning again to the world outside itself some of that substance in the leaves, blossom, fruit and twigs that drop from it and even perhaps now and again an important bough.

In just the same way human communities, whether sovereign states or corporations, large or small, within such states, are constantly, on the one hand, recruiting themselves and, on the other hand, losing their members, some at retiring age, some very soon and some at intermediate stages.

Up to a certain point such coming and going is perfectly healthy.

VALUE OF SENSE OF SECURITY OF TENURE

398. Effort to prevent it will be wasted and perhaps gravely harmful. Yet, permanence of membership must be quite sufficient. Newcomers may bring new knowledge and may have for a time the proverbial efficiency of the new broom, seeing, as they do, with fresh eyes and working with the excitement, the stimulus, of a change of environment and a new set of hopes.

But against all those advantages must be set a good deal of wastage. In some respects newcomers must be more or less gravely inefficient until they have had all the initiation of which they are capable and until their new associates have made on their side the corresponding adjustments.

To be happy, many people need not only a sense of freedom to change their employment but also a belief or at all events a half belief that sooner or later they will use that freedom. No small number, however, of those same people, as well as all the others, need also to feel very sure that they will not have to move against their will. They need to feel very sure that in the ocean of the uncertainties of life their present source of livelihood and daily occupation is a secure island, an island that is in no danger from earthquake or tidal wave and that will neither sink under them nor shake them off.

This desire for peace of mind has got to be satisfied. It is, indeed, so important to happiness that serious failure in this respect would injure very gravely the Partnership's collective interest, its own vitality, its security, its chance of future prosperity.

BUT THIS SENSE CAN BE TOO STRONG

399.   But here again we come to one of those innumerable pairs of conflicting factors between which we have to see and hold a good enough middle course. Only a minority, exceptionally fortunate in natural energy and in training, will not be enervated somewhat, even if they are not disastrously corrupted, by a climate of complete freedom from any possibility that failure on their own part can have for them grave consequence. Subject, however, to the vital need of care in this respect, a general sense of really sufficient security is no less vitally needful.

In all these things we must of course remember those essential differences of personality that make it impossible to please everybody. The better any particular partnership suits a certain range of types of customer or of worker, the worse will it suit others.

In this matter of security our aim must be to judge rightly the range of types of worker-temperament that our particular partnership is designed to serve. In quality and quantity the sense of security, that we create, must be not what some other workers want but what these want.

By "quality", I mean here that it will not be really satisfactory to them if they feel it is the outcome of incompetence or negligence or that in some other way its real motives are not to their minds really sound and healthy.

By "quantity", I mean that a policy of creating a sense of security may arise from sound motives but may be pushed too far or not far enough.

400. These are the ideas upon which it seems to me that a partnership should make and administer its rules in respect of tenure but in such a community rules affecting tenure are not nearly all that strengthens or weakens a general sense of security. There must be sufficient confidence that business policy and method are sufficiently stable.

A partnership, that ceased to cater for customers of a certain type or for the same needs of its existing customers, would have to drop many of its members and those, who were no longer able to hold their places, would be in the main the experts, the people whose places would be most valuable to their holders.

Here is the deepest reason why it is desirable that a partnership having a business so various and so complex as our own shall be large enough to carry so many leaders of really high ability that no occasional changes at that level will alter nearly so much, as otherwise they might, the established business policy and methods.

In a more highly specialised business this consideration would be very much less important. But, on the other hand, a business so specialised is in much greater danger from possible changes of public demand or manufacturing technique. A partnership with many strings to its bow may be able to retain very many at least of those of its members whom such a change concerns. It will have other work to offer them and because of its general strength it may be able and, for the sake of its own general sense of security, if for no other reason, it may be willing to give them a lengthy and costly training and to maintain them for that time.

PERMANENCE OF OFFICIALS AS FACTOR IN SENSE OF SECURITY

401. But this stability of business policy and methods is again not nearly all that is needed for a general serene confidence, a general sense of security.

There remains the factor of personality. The holder of some desirable post must not only feel sufficiently sure that that post will continue to exist. He must also feel sufficiently sure that the individual or committee or other group, by whom his own performance will be judged, will continue to have in that respect the same ideas, the ideas that he believes himself able to satisfy.

Now far the strongest way to create confidence in that respect is to create confidence that those powers will continue to be held by the same person or persons. Certainly that confidence should be buttressed as much as possible by the Rule of Law, published written rules, published records of precedents, and by such institutions as the publication of anonymous enquiries and criticisms, the Partners' Counsellor's Department and leaving-gifts controlled by elected representatives able, if they think proper, to vote by secret ballot and bound to do so upon request.

But though all of these are very highly desirable, greater than all of them is confidence in respect of the personal factor, the highest possible likelihood that Mr. So and So or Miss Somebody Else, whom you find a sympathetic and congenial chief and with whom you feel comfortably sure that you will always get on well, will never be replaced by some successor whom you may fail to satisfy or to meet whose views you may at all events have to make in your own habitual ways of working changes pretty seriously disagreeable to yourself.

For these reasons, even if there were no others, it would be extremely desirable that such a partnership, as we are contemplating, should have a very permanent framework, a cadre, as armies call it, of holders of posts specially important to the general sense of security of tenure.

LIFE-APPOINTMENTS

402.   Directorships of Buying and the corresponding posts in all other parts of the organisation should be as far as possible life-appointments and I would most certainly carry this down to the Managerships of Departments. These people are the opposite numbers of the separate entrepreneurs at a more primitive stage of the evolution of the business world. In a not very distant past they would have been the independent heads of businesses, large or small. Their ideas of what was right and proper in the performance of the holders of subordinate posts was then the supreme guide, the thing that really mattered to all other workers.

If a worker found himself in one of those businesses and came to feel that he had thoroughly won the confidence of its owner-manager, he felt that his livelihood would be solidly safe so long as that owner-manager remained and his business did not come to grief.

No Rule of Law can eliminate entirely this personal factor, not even where efficiency is sacrificed to the extent that is possible in a monopoly and above all in a monopoly supported by the public purse.

Much more must it be important in a partnership designed to produce for its members incomes requiring a far higher standard of efficiency in the service of the general community.

The higher that standard, the less must be the Rule of Law, bound, as is all man-made law, to be abused consciously and unconsciously by the foibles of human nature, and the greater must be the discretion, the vigorously exercised discretion, of the local leader, the Man on the Spot.

403.   I would attach to these posts the highest income that the Partnership's imagination and knowledge may just allow it to feel to be wise. Having made those posts as attractive as ever it can in that and in every other way the Partnership will, I suspect, be wise to pay a

considerable price for the advantage of permanence. I mean that it should prefer a just sufficiently competent occupant, who will be willing and indeed anxious to retain the post permanently, to a succession of cleverer persons who from the standpoint of permanence would be misfits. They would be taking the post as a stepping-stone. If they were not moved on within a certain time, they would begin to be discontented: their efficiency would tend to suffer and, the better they were, the greater the likelihood that they would leave the Partnership.

In my own view the Partnership should try not to appoint anyone, who seems unlikely to be content to hold it permanently, to any position of executive power important to the happiness of some Partners and above all in respect of security of tenure.

Let those, who would not be so content, occupy in each section posts that are not at the actual head. There is no reason why subordinates intended to be only temporary should not be in some ways cleverer than the chief who is intended to be permanent. Let a subordinate wait to reach his ultimate level, his ultimate field of work, before he himself becomes a chief. If vanity, greed or mere misjudgment of the real pros and cons makes him unwilling to wait to that extent before he has powers of that particular kind, let him drop out of the Partnership.

ECONOMIC EFFICIENCY OF LIFE-APPOINTMENTS

404.   Rightly or wrongly I for my part believe that the wastage in this way might be pretty serious without being by any means too heavy a price for the advantages of such stability as might result from a proper operation of this policy, for observe that the advantages to the general sense of security, so immensely important to happiness, and the advantage of avoiding the wastage of undesirable changes of personnel are far from being the whole of the possible gain.

So far as these posts involve contact with the outside world and above all so far as they involve contact with customers, permanence will tend to be enormously advantageous. Of course it will be just the opposite if the occupant of the post was or becomes a bad choice. But such a partnership, as we are contemplating, ought to achieve very fair efficiency in its initial judgments of that kind and in its subsequent vigilance and procedure.

Given such judgment, then I believe that a really permanent framework of holders of positions, that in this particular respect are key-posts, will be so good for happiness and in some important ways for efficiency that these advantages will justify a pretty stiff price in height of pay-rates and in loss of some other efficiency that could only be achieved at the cost of appointing to the position in question someone who would not be content to hold it permanently or at all events for a good many years.

I think the Partnership should try its utmost to achieve in this matter real permanence, life tenure. If results seem too discouraging, then let the infrequency of change be the very greatest that does seem to be really practicable.

PROBATION

405. Probation is one direction, in which there may be, I think, important possibilities for the development of the Rule of Law, on the one hand, and of devolution, trust in the Man on the Spot, on the other. The franker and clearer your system of probation, the greater surely will be the sense of security of those whose membership has survived it?

This is one of the many ways in which because of the war the Partnership is still a long step short of such maturity as otherwise it would, I think, have achieved by now. I hope that, before many years have passed, we shall find that the heads of the smallest units, the Managers, as they are tending at present to be called, of Departments, will have very substantial powers in such matters as the assignment of functions within that section, the granting of leave of absence, including the fixing of holiday-times, the awarding of bonuses for performance considered to exceed a satisfactory average performance for the Partner's rate of pay and, beyond all these, very substantial power over the newcomer's retention in the particular section.

It will be for the Head of the Branch to say whether the newcomer shall be offered some other position therein and it will be for the Heads of still larger units to say the same thing in respect of any possibilities outside the particular Branch.

406. The Department of Personnel and the Partners' Counsellor will both watch all such matters and the Department of Personnel will have certain powers to decide that a Partner, to whom no Head of a less wide field makes an offer of retention, shall be nevertheless retained and the means, of course, of financing that retention.

But I am inclined to think that in the first six or possibly the first twelve months, of an ordinary membership the Head of the Section should have absolute power to prevent the newcomer's retention in that particular section and that those in charge of wider fields should think carefully before they decide to retain someone who has been thus displaced from a section in which it was intended that he or she should remain longer.

When I say here "ordinary membership", I mean that it should be possible for particular appointments to particular sections to carry a special stipulation that that arrangement is not to be rescinded without the previous knowledge and consent of some particular authority senior to the Head of that Section. But I hope that experience will show that such stipulations should be far from common. The rules in respect of newcomers to a section, who are not newcomers to the Partnership itself, may have to differ somewhat from those in the case of the latter. But consideration of space prevents more than a mere indication of such niceties of administration.

407. I conceive that, when a newcomer to a section has been allowed by its head to continue in it for more than a fairly short time, say, six or twelve months, a later decision, that the section does not suit that Partner well enough, will require the concurrence of a senior authority and, if that senior authority allows the arrangement to continue beyond a certain further period, perhaps another six or another twelve months, a later adverse decision would require the concurrence of a still senior authority.

At each step, if the authority whose power has not been used within the period of its own sufficiency asks for such concurrence from the appropriate senior authority, there will of course arise the question: why was this Partner allowed to continue until now in a field of work to which the Head says now that the Partner is too ill suited?

FIVE-YEAR MEMBERSHIP AND SEVEN-YEAR

408. From a recent enquiry into the apparent possibilities of this general idea, it was judged to be practicable that no membership of any Partner, who had been retained in the Partnership for five years, should be terminated without the written consent of the Director of Personnel himself and that, if the membership had been allowed to run to seven years, termination should require the consent of the Chairman.

As the Partnership's technique improves, it may be possible to shorten these periods drastically. I think our general aim should be that for Rank and File workers anyone who is retained in the Partnership beyond twelve months and certainly anyone, who is retained beyond two years, should be able to feel very safe against having his membership terminated on merely general grounds of inadequacy of ability or of will to satisfy the Partnership's requirements.

DEVELOPMENT OF THE RULE OF LAW

409. The membership of survivors of probation should be terminated only by very senior authority unless there is some definite happening that is capable of proof and that under the current rules of the Partnership involves either termination or at all events liability to that.

There must be, of course, always some power to terminate without cause assigned. I have seen too many cases in which mysterious persistent wastages have ceased as soon as some suspected person was dropped to let the Partnership be quite at the mercy of those who excel in keeping the alleged Eleventh Commandment— "Thou shalt not be found out".

Moreover, in any community, that varies much in individual competence and especially in any, that comprises both sexes, there must be freedom to drop without explanation anyone who in one or more highly responsible judgments is too undesirable an associate for some of the Partnership's other members.

This is the kind of way in which it seems to me that there may be really great possibilities of developing the Rule of Law without too much ill effect upon efficiency. Experience will show whether such a system results in such effort during the period of probation as the particular worker is unable or unwilling to maintain thereafter. But, if the period of probation is not too short and the various managerial positions are filled adequately, I think that any troubles in this way should not be an excessive price for the good effect that a system of this kind clearly expressed and operated properly might have upon the general sense of security.

MONEY PENALTIES

410.   In the past the Partnership experimented very carefully with the use of small money penalties, forfeiture of a percentage of Benefit. We argued that our aim was to reproduce as completely as possible in large-scale team-work the conditions of independent one-man enterprise and that in such enterprise the worker is kept up to the mark not by fear of dismissal, that is to say fear that his business will come immediately to an end, but by suffering some small loss or prospect of future disadvantage whenever he makes some mistake or fails to satisfy a customer.

We argued that such independent workers have to bear the whole of the consequences not merely of happenings for which they ought to blame themselves but also for pure ill luck and that, since the Partnership would hold its members responsible only for damaging it avoidably and without sufficient excuse, a system of small forfeitures of prospective Benefit should reproduce that spur to the efficiency of the independent worker while relieving him of all risk of pure ill luck.

Although money penalties, fining systems, are used commonly by clubs and trade unions and similar democratic organisations, the old abuses in retail distribution of the fining system make workers very suspicious of anything that looks like a return thereto. But objections of that kind were met by the facts that the Partnership Benefit is non-contractual and is frankly intended to be wholly additional to such income as the worker would ordinarily get for equivalent work in any ordinary business of the same kind.

A MARKING SYSTEM

411.   We thought also that these forfeitures might be so adjusted to the importance of shortcomings that they would serve as a marking system,

so that the Partnership would be sufficiently safe against carrying the type of worker who never does anything very wrong but whose frequent petty shortcomings are in the aggregate much too serious, while, on the other hand, the Partnership would not have to use in such cases the alternative method, that is so destructive of sense of security of tenure, of dismissing people because their services are judged to be in such a general way too unsatisfactory, though each individual happening appears to be too small to justify dismissal.

All this was my own idea and it contained a fatal oversight. I simply lost sight of the fact that only a minority of people are of such a temperament as to set up in business on their own account if they have the chance and that of that minority the vast majority fail and that the cause of their failure is very largely precisely the fact that they are not affected, as in their own interests they should be, by the immediate small consequences of their individual shortcomings of one sort and another.

WARDEN OF THE CONSTITUTION

412.   Before we gave the system up, we took great pains to make it succeed. We set up an independent judiciary called the Wardenship of the Constitution and we rather welcomed the fact that its first (and only) holder seemed to us to be very much too lax in his judgments. We were so anxious that the system should become, if possible, popular that we rather welcomed its being applied with excessive gentleness in its early days. But after, if I remember, two or three years the Head of the Executive Side felt that it really was impossible to continue to turn a completely blind eye to the persistent sacrifice of the collective interest of each offender's fellow-workers to the Warden's admirable sympathy with the human fallibility of those from whom some penalty was claimed.

Accordingly I was asked to agree that for the first time the Management should have recourse to a rule that was part of the system that, if either side was dissatisfied with a ruling by the Warden of the Constitution, the Management should name three practising barristers from whom the Partner or group of Partners concerned should make their own choice. His decision upon the appeal should be final but in any future similar case there could be appeal to some other barrister who must, however, be informed of the previous case and of its result.

The rules further provided that, if any Partner was held liable to a penalty, the Central Council, in their absolute discretion, could provide as much as they thought fit of the necessary payment, otherwise the Partner must pay or leave the Partnership. The appeal to a barrister never occurred because on the solitary occasion, on which it was intended, the Warden proposed to reverse his own decision and, as the whole system was about to be dropped, the Management acquiesced.

NO SUBSTITUTE FOR THE POSSIBILITY OF TERMINATION OF MEMBERSHIP

413. All this seemed to me a very hopeful scheme for eliminating without ill-effect on efficiency the fear of dismissal but its drawbacks were too many and too serious. One was that the less scrupulous people admitted nothing that they could hope to deny and put the Partnership to formidable expense in endeavouring to establish a sufficient case to outweigh their denial. But a much more formidable drawback was the fact that the honourable, zealous people, who admitted at once when they were in the wrong, tended to be caught by the system while the others commonly succeeded in persuading the Warden that the case against them was not sufficiently clear.

If those, whose duty it was to notice shortcomings and to make claims in respect of them, turned to any serious extent a blind eye to lapses on the part of a first-rate Partner, there began to be murmurs of favouritism and the beneficiary was apt to prefer not to be given that particular reward of his general excellence. On the other hand, conscious as he would be that he was ungrudgingly generous to the Partnership in the way of special efforts upon special occasions, he was bound to feel more or less aggrieved at finding himself required to make good some damage that he was held to have caused avoidably and without sufficient excuse or to forfeit some fragment of his Partnership Benefit for some breach of some rule.

FUTURE POSSIBILITIES

414. The system was accordingly dropped entirely. Perhaps some day we shall experiment with something in the way of a marking system in which an adverse mark will not stand on record for more than a certain time, though the time may vary according to the seriousness of the matter. It is not easy to get people to work as hard as for their own sakes they should without creating too much of an atmosphere of school-room discipline or too much harassment. The Partnership has still a long way to go before it will have settled in these things upon some system that it will feel to be on the whole probably about as good as the various alternatives that may be suggested from time to time. Of course it must be desirable that such rules shall be changed as little as possible.

DEMOCRATIC CONTROL OF COMPENSATION FOR DISTURBANCE

415. These will be, I suggest, the principles upon which such a partnership, as is contemplated in this book, will manage itself in the vitally important matter of creating and maintaining a proper sense of security of tenure, a sense that is about as strong as without too much ill effect upon efficiency can be created in the minds of such members as the particular partnership is able to get and willing to admit.

In appearance and legal freedom for both sides there will be only one change from the existing state of affairs. The Partners will have ordinary legal contracts. They will be free in the ordinary way to resign and the Partnership will be likewise free in the ordinary way to drop them from its team. But in that case elected representatives of all the members will have certain powers to give at the expense of the Partnership what in farm-tenancies is called compensation for disturbance. This is the one change.

At present a worker's chance to get such compensation is ordinarily limited to his chance of getting a Court of Law to award him damages for wrongful dismissal. Members of our own partnership at all events have and will continue to have in addition to those legal rights the chance that the Partnership's representative institutions culminating in and controlled by its Central Council may award from the Partnership's funds a leaving-gift that has amounted already in some cases to some hundreds of pounds and that may be a large pension if each successive Council sees fit to repeat for their own year of office a gift that their own predecessors made and of which those predecessors recommended continuance.

In practice the membership of the Central Council is not likely to change very much from year to year and, so far as it consists of the same members as before, it will presumably continue any pension that depends upon the Council's yearly vote.

PERHAPS ONLY A DEVICE AD INTERIM

416. For forty-three years I have been puzzling over this problem of finding the best line between the conflicting needs of efficiency in the service of the general community and therefore the safety of the livelihood of those engaged in a business that has to live by that service and, on the other hand, the natural, intense desire of most people for a sense of absolute security, a desire that is, I believe, supported wholeheartedly by general public opinion.

This device of democratic control of leaving-gifts, that can be used to compensate for disturbance, is the best that I have been able to do in the way of a solution of this problem. But I suspect that there may be important further possibilities. I suspect that, as the whole system of the Partnership is better and better understood and better and better operated, there will develop such ideas, such habits of mind and consequent behaviour and such financial strength that it will be practicable to give to Partners absolute assurance of things that now they can only have by an exercise in each separate case of the free discretion of the Central Council or of some representative body subordinate thereto.

ADVANCE OF THE RULE OF LAW

417.   After all, we have seen this actually happen in the matter of sick pay. For years sick pay beyond pretty modest limits depended upon that same discretion. In the course of those years experience showed that the successive elected representatives of the Partnership's general public opinion took steadily certain views of the way in which their discretion ought to be used. During those years they and everyone else concerned had a chance to see the consequences and in the end it seemed practicable to substitute for all that exercise of discretion hard and fast rules, so that those, whose temperament and education made them dislike the idea of getting their sick pay by an exercise of the discretion of other people instead of as a matter of absolute right secured by hard and fast rule, had that satisfaction and those, who were unable to feel sufficiently happily confident that the exercise of discretion always would be sufficiently favourable to themselves, were freed from that anxiety.

The total cost of the change was negligible. It would not involve the Partnership in any appreciable greater expense than it was carrying already. Perhaps it may be well to give here an example how far the Council went in giving sick pay.

LIBERALITY OF THE COUNCIL IN SICK PAY

418.   The Partnership once engaged a stranger unconnected with any of its members, gave him a four-figure income that was much larger than he had been getting previously, and found that after his first twelve months or thereabouts he went ill on its hands. He had a very serious internal trouble. He had a family to support. He had shown himself an ordinarily satisfactory occupant of the position that he was undertaking to fill but there had been nothing to give him any very special claim.

The Council gave him full pay for upwards of a year and thereafter some considerable further help—I cannot remember what. In fact he either never came back at all or only for a short time, for within the second year of his absence he died.

That was an extreme case but the Council and their Committees have always taken very great care to be strictly fair and consistent in their awards and I think that this is quite a fair indication of their general conception of proper liberality in such matters.

HARD AND FAST RULES BUT SOME PROVISION FOR TRIAL BY JURY

419.   What has actually happened in the case of sick pay may, I think, happen in due course in the case of compensation for disturbance. The Partnership may, as experience accumulates, see its way to make hard and fast rules that will be sufficiently safe against abuse but that will give more peace of mind to those who would be uneasy if their hopes of getting out

of the Partnership something beyond whatever they will have had already in pay, Partnership Benefit and otherwise would depend entirely upon the discretion of elected representatives of their fellow workers. Some discretion there must always be. There will always be some who will have in the public opinion of the Partnership claims greater than their dues under any hard and fast rules.

In this sort of thing we are plainly getting near to trial by jury. The problem is to safeguard the Partnership's efficiency from being victimised consciously or unconsciously. It must be safeguarded sufficiently from having the letter of its own rules twisted against it by claims that are within the letter of the rules but against its spirit.

Something amounting to trial by jury seems the right instrument and such an arrangement certainly saves the holder of the position of chief individual responsibility or the members of any particular board or committee from a duty that may be arduous and at times exceedingly invidious and painful. Standing committees or special committees appointed by a Council two-thirds of whose members are elected afresh every year must, it would seem, be about as good as any arrangement can be for giving all members of the Partnership peace of mind both for themselves and for other people.

GIVING REASONS FOR TERMINATIONS OF MEMBERSHIP

420. A worker, unless he is withdrawing his services in apparent breach of a contract, cannot be required to give his reasons, no matter how disappointing and harmful to "the other side" that withdrawal may be. But workers naturally wish to be quite free to cause that disappointment and to inflict that harm if they are so disposed. It seems to them clearly right that they should have that freedom. On the other hand, they are also very apt to feel that on their side they have a property-right-to continue for so long as they may choose in any employment to which they have somehow gained admittance. They claim in fact that they ought to be quite free to leave "their" business but the business ought to have no freedom at all, to leave them, not even if that business happens to be a coal-mine that has been nationalised and that the nation can only keep open at the cost of loss to the national purse. The longer they have been allowed to continue, the stronger becomes that feeling of property-right and the stronger the resentment if the worker is asked to let someone else have a turn of whatever may be the advantages of occupying that particular position and to let the organisation have a chance to find that it has gained importantly by that change in its team.

In my own view it is extremely desirable that both of these feelings shall be satisfied as far as possible. If the enterprise wishes to be sure of someone's continuance to a certain extent, it should stipulate for an appropriate contract and offer whatever pay or other attractions may be necessary to secure acceptance by the worker of that arrangement.

SAUCE FOR THE GANDER, SAUCE FOR THE GOOSE

421.   In my own view such contracts should be maintained very strictly. It is common to find that workers and their friends and third parties, who have nothing to lose, show astonishment and indignation if a worker, who has obtained a particular position by entering into a particular contract, is not granted release from it if he so requests. A corresponding request from the other side would be almost always thought most improper and, if it were ever to be made, would be most unlikely to be granted. In my own view a partnership should be strictly businesslike in such things. Let it make no contract that needlessly restricts the worker's freedom. If it can expect to make a satisfactory fresh engagement sufficiently quickly and without excessive cost in one way or another, then let it leave the worker free to withdraw his services at notice no longer than upon those expectations will be just sufficient for its own welfare.

Moreover, I would by no means rule out the idea that the worker should be given a legal right to longer notice or to a larger payment in lieu of notice than he himself was bound to give.

I think it highly probable that this particular partnership will, as years pass, give such assurance of leaving-gift in proportion to length of service and perhaps to record during that time and will not ask in return any surrender by the worker of his previous freedom to withdraw at no more than a certain notice.

But, whatever may be the terms of the contract, it should be enforced properly.

WHEN RELEASE MAY BE RIGHT

422.   If the worker's reason for requesting release is not a matter of his own gain or hope of gain but real *force majeure*, something that is quite outside his own will and that is in itself a really good reason, then in my view the Partnership should grant release. But in such matters people, who in the ordinary way seem very pleasant and trustworthy, are apt to differ widely in their ideas of right and wrong, their sense of honour. Acquiescence in what is really dishonourable behaviour is in my view gravely anti-social. It is profoundly corrupting. Workers, before they enter into a contract, should be given written warning, of which delivery can be always proved, that requests for release will encounter this general attitude and there should be great care not to let those warnings appear to have been mere bluff and not to make in such cases any impression of unfair discrimination, favouritism.

Obviously every Management ought to be fastidiously scrupulous in never tempting any worker to break the spirit of any written contract with any other employer. But, if an employer claims verbal promises or understandings, I for my part should be always inclined to take the view that it would presumably have cost that employer something to have got the alleged promise or the alleged understanding made a matter of written contract and I should be slow to think ill of a worker who, while honouring any written contract, refused to regard himself as bound by any verbal obligation.

SEEKING FRESH EMPLOYMENT IN WORKING HOURS

423. If someone, who has not given or received notice of termination of membership, asks for leave of absence with a view to getting other employment, I should think it was reasonable to refuse the leave or to give notice to terminate the employment. But, unless there were some very special features in the particular case, I should always give such leave pretty liberally to anyone who had given or received notice of termination.

It is impossible to put into writing the almost infinitely various shades of the requirements on both sides of what may conveniently be called sense of decency, sense of right and wrongs. Some workers appear to feel no compunction in accepting much more than their legal dues or the benefit of very liberal arrangements in that respect and then refusing on their side to make any concessions at all beyond their bare legal obligations. We have had some Partners who have received hundreds of pounds in Partnership Benefit and have been discovered eventually to have been steadily robbing the Partnership.

For my own part I see only a difference of degree between such cases and those who accept liberality but in return behave selfishly.

PENSION-PROSPECT AS A FACTOR IN DISCIPLINE

424. This is one strong reason for which in my time the Partnership will never give up its present freedom to decide by means of its Central Council whether a Partner, who leaves before pension-age, shall have any pension at all.

The pension fund exceeds already £700,000 and there will be persistent and growing efforts to claim that membership gives a moral right to some of that money. Such claims will be based upon the argument that, if there were no pension-fund, the money would have been distributed as Partnership Benefit. That is quite true but the source of that money was only partly the work of the Partnership's members in that particular year. It was partly the result of over eighty years of work by other people. Morally it might be held to belong to the general community as their reward for taking, in the classic French phrase, the trouble to be born. But, human nature being what it is, the general community makes laws under which the earnings of this particular partnership can be used according to its Constitution. In my own view membership of a partnership gives no moral right whatever to anything more than such pay as the same worker would ordinarily get for doing about the same work in an ordinary employment and in addition whatever may have been promised to him by that particular partnership's constitution. Anything more than ordinary remuneration, whether in an exceptional amount of paid holiday or of sick pay or of help in other special need or of Partnership Benefit, cannot be a matter of moral claim except upon one ground only, namely that it is a consequence of the constitution of the particular partnership into which the worker was invited to come and in which he has been invited to continue for a certain time.

In our own case the pension-prospect is set out absolutely clearly in writing. In my view no one can be justified in claiming that the fact, that he chose to accept an invitation to come into that partnership and an invitation to continue in it, gives him a title to anything beyond the written provisions of that constitution of which a knowledge was always easily accessible to him and to his advisers.

The opposition really means that the objectors want to get out of the Partnership whatever it will give to them and at the same time to be free to behave to it, if they like, as badly as ever the Law will allow them to do. Needless restriction of freedom is utterly wrong but so is excess of freedom. If in this country there had been no wrong freedom, the ignorance and folly of the mass of our people could not have ruined us all by shirking our national duty to ourselves and all the world to stand up to the Dictators before it was too late.

Discipline in proper cases is one of the greatest needs of all human life and in my own view the Partnership would be utterly wrong to let itself be coaxed, badgered or browbeaten into failing to maintain these disciplinary potentialities of its present pension-system and to use them with all proper firmness.

NOTICES OF TERMINATION OF MEMBERSHIP: A TECHNIQUE TOO DIFFICULT FOR THE AVAILABLE OPERATORS

425.   For many years I tried very hard to secure that every Partner, whose membership was to be terminated, should be given in writing a reason that was true in fact and sufficient in law. When I began to cease to write those letters, I tried to get them written by other people. I made for them the rule I had always followed myself, that in all but very rare special cases dismissals by anyone, to whom that power had been devolved, must be by such a document and must bear the signature of the person responsible for its contents.

Cases alleged to be of the very rare kind in which the law made this procedure impossible were to be referred to me. Any letter, that terminated membership without giving a reason that was true in fact and sufficient in law, was to bear my own signature.

The rule turned out to be unworkable. It was simply beyond the competence of too many of those by whom the system was to be operated. They evaded it by such contrivances as making rules that membership could be terminated for "unbusinesslike behaviour" and by giving that as the reason in the letter of termination and then declining to put into writing the actions or shortcomings that in the particular case were considered to have amounted to unbusinesslike behaviour so serious as to justify termination.

Rightly or wrongly I became convinced that the idea was unworkable by people no better able to grasp a concept and to express themselves than would be too many of those whom it would be necessary to appoint to the positions in question and to retain in them.

I was very sorry for it but it seemed to me quite inevitable that the Partnership should give up for the present its intention that none of its members should ever be dismissed without the satisfaction of such a written statement of such part at all events of the reasons as would be in itself good ground in law for the dismissal.

Officials should, I think, be free to give such reasons in cases in which they feel themselves able to do so but should not be bound to do this in one case because they have done it in another and there must be, I think, a very strict rule that nothing of this sort must be said otherwise than in writing.

People, who cannot see their way to put such reasons into writing, will certainly get themselves and the Partnership into legal difficulties if in any such matter they allow themselves to say to "the other side" something that they cannot allow themselves to dictate to a shorthand writer.

TESTIMONIALS, ETC.

426. A related matter is the giving of testimonials and answering of enquiries from intending employers whom a Partner or ex-Partner refers to the Partnership. Throughout my own career I have made it an absolute rule that such an enquiry should never be answered otherwise than by a document signed by the person responsible for its contents and containing a clear statement that it may be shown to the person concerning whom it is written or to anyone properly authorised by him to see it but that otherwise it is strictly confidential. No information may be volunteered that does not seem quite certain to be harmless and probably beneficial to the person in question but questions, that are expressed or

that are reasonably deemed to be implied, must be either left unanswered or answered with the truth, the whole truth and nothing but the truth, precisely as if they were evidence given upon oath in a court of law.

Unscrupulousness in these things is common and in my own view it is gravely anti-social. I hope very much that the Partnership will never depart from this practice except by constraint of law.

It has always been our rule to give a written testimonial upon request and to answer enquiries up to four but in every case with mention that a previous enquiry of the same kind from So and So was answered on such and such a date. I would allow answers to be given verbally in cases of sufficient urgency but for my own part I can only remember doing so once and then it was possible to stipulate that the Partner in question should be present at the interview and I insisted upon that. It was many years ago and the post was a good one, the Secretaryship of Messrs. Fortnum and Mason Limited of Piccadilly.

427.   If now and again an enquiry has to be answered verbally, a written confirmation should be dictated immediately and despatched at once. But verbal enquiries should be answered only in very special cases.

For my own part I would not retain in the Partnership an official who seemed to me at all persistently lax in any such matter as this.

Quite lately there has been pressure upon the Partnership to answer such enquiries before the expiration of a Partner's contract. That seems to me quite wrong. Until the Partner has ceased to owe any duty to the Partnership, I would never go beyond saying that he or she has been in it for such and such a time and that up to now there has been no reason why the Partnership should not act as a reference in due course.

PROSECUTIONS

428.   There will arise occasionally a question whether the Partnership should prosecute one of its own members or somebody else. In such a case I would ask myself whether there is sufficient reason to believe that the offence was committed in consequence of a temptation not ordinarily incidental to the offender's occupation and general position in life. In such a case it may, I think, be right to refrain from prosecuting but except in such a case I think myself that the very general practice of shirking the expense, trouble, worry and odium of prosecuting is thoroughly anti-social and may well be a part of the reason why the people of England, whose fathers and even more perhaps grandfathers were entitled to pride themselves on their outstanding honesty, are now so shockingly dishonest.

No doubt it is a passing trouble due mainly to the ferments of too low a quality and quantity of education. But, whatever the cause, there is no doubt about the lamentable fact. To refrain from prosecuting is to increase temptation upon all who will have that reason to think that, if they yield to it, they will probably escape detection and, if they are detected, will probably get off with a fright.

I am told that the Partnership is quite exceptional in the extent to which it does prosecute and that its policy has been praised repeatedly by those who are specially concerned with such matters.

CHAPTER 26

AMENITIES

FREE INSURANCE AGAINST EXCEPTIONAL NEED

429.   WORKERS, whose earning-power is not very high, will need special help in serious expensive illness or other exceptional need of money. So far as insurance may be available and the worker may be able and willing to bear the charge, the need can of course be met in that way. But the members of a family may meet such needs by taking the misfortune of the individual member upon the collective financial strength of the family.

Each member of such a family will have in a sense free insurance. The larger the family, the better can this be done and the Partnership has done it for many years. Ordinary employers, some as a matter of intelligent selfishness some from better motives and some from a mixture of the two, commonly do a good deal in this way. But, if this power is exercised by the management, any use of discretion is apt to savour of favouritism and, if hard and fast rules are applied with no attempt at discrimination, the deserving will be apt in some cases to get too little help while at the same time there will be some abuses, some improper exploitation.

To overcome these difficulties, the Partnership instituted many years ago a committee that came in the end to be named the Committee for Claims. Enquiring visitors, of whom we get now and again a few, commonly think well of this idea and often, if they are themselves managers of some business, express an intention to adopt it for their own.

There are now a whole set of such committees. They will be described among the Institutions that are the subject of Part III.

CONTRACTUAL SICK-PAY

430.   So long, as each Partner's right to sick pay was limited to a comparatively short period of absence, more serious illness was, of course, one of the chief uses for the funds of these committees. We found, however, that quite a lot of workers dislike the idea of getting sick pay or anything else by the decision of a Council whom they have helped to elect. Some of them speak of it as "charity". They cannot grasp the idea that the system of the Partnership turns them into owners and that such a function of such a Council is merely a way of working that system. But more, I suspect, dislike the theoretical uncertainty, the theoretical possibility that, if occasion were to arise; a committee might not see fit to let them have the sick pay. Here again there may be failure to grasp

an idea, the idea that, if the Partnership is to lose the safeguard of that possibility, it must be proportionately careful not to retain anyone who does not seem to be trustworthy to that extent.

Study of the records showed that a drastic enlargement of each Partner's absolute right to sick pay would, so long as there were no abuses that the committee-system would have prevented, cost little, if any, more than was being already spent. The work of the committees was heavy enough to make quite desirable such a lightening as this would be and, since the change would apparently be welcome to some Partners and not seriously unwelcome to any, the absolute right to sick pay was raised to a maximum of twenty-six weeks in any consecutive fifty-two weeks, the right below this maximum being one day for every two weeks' membership, whether continuous or otherwise, up to the beginning of the absence.

A MATTER OF TENURE

431. This rule raised the question whether in every case in which a Partner, whose membership would have been terminated if he had continued on duty, became absent for illness before the notice of termination had been given to him, the giving of that notice should be suspended until his return to duty, so that it might happen that, whereas representatives of the Partnership had decided that it ought not to carry him further, he might draw a large sum in sick pay and upon returning to duty draw by way of payment in lieu of notice a further sum that might itself be several months' pay.

Until the second Irrevocable Settlement in Trust, of which the making is a slow process that has been long in hand, shall have been completed, the final decision upon a matter of this kind rests with myself, though in substantial matters or indeed in any, upon which feelings seem likely to be strong, I should always ascertain and consider the views both of the Central Council and also of the holders of nearly a dozen posts that carry membership of a certain regular Conference that in the affairs of the Partnership plays a part that corresponds pretty closely to that of the Cabinet in the affairs of the Nation.

432. When this question was put to me, I said that, except in cases in which there was, as in some there obviously would be, special reason to proceed otherwise, the notice must be given as soon as might be expedient for the Partnership's collective interest.

The question, whether some payment or gift should be made to him or to her beyond his or her legal dues, would not be ordinarily a question for the Management at all. It would be a question in the first instance for the Council of the Branch, to which the Partner belonged, and finally for the Central Council if the matter were referred to them either by the Branch Council or by the Partner or ex-Partner himself.

It may be well to mention here that the functions of the Partners' Counsellor, which like those of the Committees for Claims will be described in Part III, include that of keeping upon all matters of this kind a vigilant watch that no Partner or ex-Partner gets less than full proper benefit from the Partnership's rules and .precedents.

When I say that such a matter would not be ordinarily one for the Management, I mean that in some special cases the Partnership's business-interest may require in the view of the Management that some gift shall be made beyond any that is being made by the Council out of their own funds and from their own standpoint. In such a case the Management would make from the funds under their own control such special gifts as they might think proper.

FINANCING RECREATION

433. Beyond the Partnership's aim of giving special help by loan or gift in any sufficient need, there is the question of financing sports-clubs, music and other things that in some cases may be of the nature of mere pleasure but that will commonly be considered desirable for health of body or mind, to be in fact recreation desirable for the Partnership's efficiency.

Our present total expenditure in this way is approximately £55,000 a year. A country-club with cricket-fields, tennis-courts and a large fleet of river-craft is maintained at Cookham. There is another considerable club of this kind in Liverpool and negotiations have been long pending for a third in Sheffield. The Leckford Estate in Hampshire has been mentioned already.

The Partnership spends freely upon fostering dancing and music. It is always particularly willing to spend upon giving its members a new accomplishment or a greater degree of one that they have already. Skill in dancing, tennis, swimming, chess or, indeed, the acquisition of any skill that tends to be a good exercise for body or mind and that is incidentally a pleasant social accomplishment, is an indestructible possession and in the view of the Partnership a particularly desirable form of gift.

A DIFFICULT PROBLEM OF VALUES

434. Other expenditure, that would come under the head of what are called at present "Amenities", was the regular purchase before the war of about two hundred seats a year at the Glyndebourne Festival and the expenditure at this present time of £1,500 a year upon subsidising heavily good reserved seats at good concerts and for plays that are not of the merely catchpenny sort.

The Partnership finances also "outings" of various kinds. Before the war these reached the length of fairly large winter-sports parties to Switzerland.

It is plainly very difficult to adopt for such purposes as these ideas that are satisfactorily definite and that seem likely to result in a tolerable degree of fairness among those of the Partnership's members who are regarded as really permanent or who ought for some other reason to have some benefit from this particular expenditure.

To the extent of their own funds it is, of course, always in the power of the Central Council to make directly or through any of the Branch Councils any gifts that in their own view are desirable for any such purposes as these. The expenditure has been growing gradually for many years but the development of these things, as of almost all of the Partnership's affairs, has been so distorted and hindered by the war that we are now much further, than otherwise we might perhaps have been by this time, from being able to offer much in the way of conclusions, confident or tentative, from our own actual experience.

435. The beneficiaries of such expenditure will presumably tend to be mainly young people who have not yet homes of their own or people whose temperaments or acquired tastes give them in some way an exceptional need. The idea, for example, that has arisen only lately, of a general subsidising of good seats for good concerts is considered to have proved very sound. On more than one occasion, when the results of this experiment have been under consideration with a view to its possible discontinuance, various leading members of the Partnership, who had no personal need of such a subsidy and no share in the starting of this particular experiment, have spoken warmly of their own impressions of those results. One such comment was: "It is one of the best things the Partnership has ever done". Certainly it has revealed a remarkably wide distribution through all grades of the Partnership of people to whom music in the fullest sense of the word is really important.

For such people such music would, I suppose, be pretty generally agreed to be a very desirable recreation in the best sense of that word. The boon to those Partners of a really good seat with incidentally no need to stand in queues is very great and for my own part I always felt that the Partnership's gift of tickets for Glyndebourne, including the dinner, and its practice of giving in some cases a second ticket that enabled the Partner to have, if he or she liked, the company of a non-Partner friend, though some people might consider it an improper extravagance, was a really good use of money.

436. Within a negligible margin the Partnership can, I think, be sure that such gifts are made only to Partners whose general merits are such that an occasional bonus of about £3 or £6 (the cost of one or two tickets

for Glyndebourne) could certainly not be said with any confidence to be clearly beyond their real earnings. If they had been given the money in cash, they might very probably have felt that they must not allow themselves to spend it upon an evening at Glyndebourne. Even if they had done so, their pleasure might very probably have been more or less seriously impaired by twinges of conscience. The Partnership's procedure cut all that out and for my own part I suspect that an occasional experience of that kind, a substantial taste of really intense delight, is a truly wise use of money.

But, though it is not difficult to imagine that some present-giving on these lines, some provision of very heavily subsidised lawn-tennis or days on the river or seats for a first-rate concert or a discussion weekend at Dial Close (to say nothing of the couple of six-week terms in a year, that some Partners got), may be an expenditure justifiable from the standpoint of the quality and quantity of the pleasure that it gives and of its broad effects upon individual relations to the Partnership and so upon its collective atmosphere, it is plainly very difficult indeed to see where this sort of thing is to stop or on what principles such expenditure is to be made and its results distributed.

A TEMPORARY PSYCHOLOGICAL FACTOR

437. Throughout the Partnership's history and for the remainder of my own life I have been and shall be enabled to meet any symptoms of disapproval with the answer that for nearly twenty years I have been making to the Partnership a very large loan free of interest and giving it the whole of my working-time without remuneration of any sort.

The Partnership's benefit in those respects has so outweighed the cost of all the amenities that, if the money had been completely wasted, the Partners would have had in a sense no real title to complain. But that position will not last for ever and, though certain habits of mind, certain traditions, may have developed to some extent, they may not persist so strongly that the Partnership, if it is going to continue such expenditure at all, may not need to have well-considered answers if there is not to be rather gravely undesirable friction.

My own personal inclination is towards an imaginative policy of rather liberal expenditure. I have always felt very strongly that whatever the Partnership does provide should be absolutely first-class. There should be nothing at all in the way of what I call cheap-and-nastiness. The hard tennis-courts should be standard size, each enclosed separately and first-rate both in quality and in upkeep and everything else should be of the same kind.

438.   One argument for this is that it fosters pleasant social leisure-time contact between Partners of all ranks. If the quality of the dancing-room and its music or of the tennis-courts or of the cricket-field is all that any family, that were not very grossly luxurious, would think it right to provide for themselves and their friends, then those Partners, whose earning-power in the chances of our modern world happens to be low, have much less reason to feel that more fortunate colleagues are making perhaps rather reluctantly some sacrifice in spending some time in the Partnership's Club or wherever it may be.

Furthermore, I feel very strongly that it has an excellent psychological effect, a real cultural value, to have really choice things. It seemed to me highly significant that, when the Partnership made in a provincial town a residential club that was furnished and decorated really beautifully and with obviously very great care on the part of the lady who was kind enough to undertake the designing and to supervise the carrying out of her ideas, the Partners, who used the house, showed the most extreme care not to damage its decorations and that care persisted. It did not die away as the first impression passed.

Treatment of things may throw really important light upon character. I have never forgotten seeing someone, who had graduated with first-class honours at one of our principal universities, take a new cricket-pad, that had just been issued to the Club, lay it face downwards on a patch of mud and sit on it, to save himself the trouble of walking a few yards to a seat at the side of the ground. That was incomparably worse than the frequency with which in the early days of the Harrow Club, forty years ago, the tennis-rackets provided were left out all night in the grass.

439.   Behaviour of this kind is only partly a matter of education and I suppose that no large community, whatever the early advantages of its members, can hope to be quite free from some troubles of this sort.

Intelligent conscientiousness, a real sense of decency in such matters, cannot be expected in a country that, from being one of the most honest in the world, has in, I suppose, the first ferments of general education become one of the most dishonest. We must hope that these things will pass. Ill effects of the first ferments of an education, of which the quality has suffered grievously from financial starvation, can only be cured by more and better education and of course by a sufficient satisfaction of the new claims, the new discontents, to which education was bound to give rise, and it made people more imaginative, more critical, more conscious of unreasonable inequalities.

As I have said elsewhere, capitalism seems to me to have outgrown the family, so that we are perhaps passing in a real sense from the age of the family into that of the corporation, corporations that may be largely of the general nature of this partnership and that may have great opportunities of creating and preserving beauty and of fostering appreciation of and so care for it.

QUALITY NOT QUANTITY

440.   In connection with this extremely difficult problem of dividing rightly whatever the Partnership is going to spend upon pleasures or other advantages, that cannot be given to everybody, I would say two things. In the first place, it seems to me very desirable to confine any particular expenditure to those to whom it really will be importantly welcome. The zeal, for example, of organisers of dances is apt to tempt them to over-crowd their ballroom either from a desire to boast of the number of the tickets that were sold or of the dancers that were present or from a reluctance to refuse tickets to all who want them. In the result the ball is spoilt for everybody. In. much the same way, pressure upon tennis-courts may prevent everyone from getting a reasonable amount of play.

In all such things I would for my own part enforce to the utmost of my ability such results as would be achieved if everyone were too sensible and too unselfish to spoil in any such way the pleasure of others.

To secure reasonably full satisfaction for as many as could have it, I would always pay the price of arousing a sense of grievance or jealousy and resentment in some who, if they were more sensible or less selfish or both, would of their own accord refrain from thrusting themselves where they could not come without spoiling too seriously the pleasure of others.

LEAVEN

441.   For my own part I am inclined to think that there may be really important indirect benefit to a community from something that happens directly to a minority, perhaps a very small minority. Suppose the Partnership, by spending quite handsomely upon some pleasure or benefit for a small number, sweetens their tempers and improves their minds quite importantly. Must not substantial good come from, that to all those whose own happiness depends to some considerable extent upon the behaviour of this minority? Is it not a fact that, if a small community includes a sprinkling of individuals who, in the matter of courtesy and of general consideration for others, have been what is commonly called very well brought up, that community as a whole gets really important advantage from the good fortune of those particular people in having such an upbringing as its other members had not the good fortune to share?

I believe that those, who have to consider the expediency of expenditure for the benefit of separate groups, large or small, in a community, should keep these ideas in view and be rather venturesome in imaginative appraisals of the theoretically possible good consequences.

PARTNERSHIP DISCOUNT

442.   The following matter ought perhaps to be placed under "Pay" or at all events elsewhere than under "Amenities" but I will in fact mention here the Partnership's aim, that I am very anxious to see developed with the utmost possible resourcefulness and energy, of doing all that it possibly can to increase for its members the value of their money.

As fast as merchandise becomes sufficiently freely available, we intend to give to all Partners purchasing from the Partnership provisions for themselves or their dependents a Partnership Discount of fifteen per cent. and upon all other merchandise, such as clothes and furniture, twenty-five per cent. There will be some particular things upon which discount cannot be given but we propose to do in this way all that we can.

DANGERS OF ABUSE

443.   In all this the Partnership will have to be on its guard against two things. One is the thoughtless or cynical selfishness with which some will take for themselves to the utmost extent that they can something that they can only have at the cost of loss to all of their fellow-workers. It would be unreasonable to expect people, whose earning-power is not very high, to carry unselfishness to the pitch of behaving as if they were certain to be able and willing to continue in the Partnership for life. Even if they were, many would turn consciously or unconsciously a blind eye to the fact that they would be injuring their fellow-workers if they took for themselves at a heavy discount goods that were irreplaceable and that would be otherwise sold at the full price not only with financial advantage to the Partnership's members as a whole but also with important advantage to the Partnership's good will among its customers, actual and potential.

444.   There will be also a danger of private trading. It will be human nature to tell other people that you have got something for no more than three-quarters of the price at which it would be very good value for ordinary customers and would in fact sell freely. Hearers will ask whether a similar purchase cannot be made for themselves and whether, in the alternative, they cannot be allowed to buy the new acquisition with the idea that its present owner will then get another from the Partnership.

Some people also will be quite capable of suggesting, if they think that they can do so safely, to some customer of the Partnership that, if instead of buying in the ordinary way, she will buy from the speaker, he can offer her such and such an attractive rebate.

A sufficiently sharp watch will have to be kept for this sort of thing and for my part, unless perhaps in some very special case, I should regard any ill-behaviour of this sort as absolutely unpardonable. Such things are too dangerous, at least I think so, to admit of such fostering, as might be the real result of some degree of toleration. But, so long as such abuses do not arise, there is here plainly a possibility for all the rest of the Partnership to give with hardly any disadvantage to themselves a very great advantage to any one of themselves who wants to buy something with which the Partnership can supply him for a price much lower than he would otherwise have to pay.

A HIRING SERVICE

445. I would extend this idea in every possible way. I should like, for example, to see the Partnership putting a lot of capital into things that could be hired out to members for a charge that would make available to them important pleasure or other benefit that they could not have otherwise. I should like to see the Partnership buying and hiring out to its members valuable pictures, costly books of reference, first-rate musical instruments and similar things.

In some cases the arrangement might be a really great and intensely appreciated boon even if the charge was a reasonably good rate of interest and a full cover for incidental expenses of transport, insurance, depreciation and so on. But I suspect that such provision may be a peculiarly good field for deliberate subsidy.

MONEY OR THINGS?

446. There must, I think, be many cases in which a gift of some particular thing would be a much greater benefit than a gift of its value in money. There is, I believe, much impressive testimony that a small legacy is quite often a disastrous misfortune and there must, I think, be very many people who from ignorance or thoughtlessness or unfortunate habits of mind are such incurable fritterers that they would never succeed in saving the money in question or in screwing themselves up to use it in the particular way in which in fact they would be wise to use it.

Obviously all this kind of thing is deep water and partnerships should be very careful to keep well inside a line, up to which results seem to be quite unquestionably good. But for my own part I think that, so long as human beings differ so very greatly in natural ability and in education and—even among the expensively educated—in possession of particular knowledge, there may be in this way really important scope for such a community, as we are here considering, to increase its own efficiency by making the lives of some of its members a good deal happier in the best sense than otherwise they would be.

JEALOUSY

447. Expenditure upon individuals and groups must tend to raise jealousy and this may be a good place to discuss that problem of partnership. One occasion, upon which it arises, is the matter of

Partnership Discount. Obviously the giving of discount will be of greater advantage to those who are able and willing to spend more upon things with which the Partnership can supply them than it will be to others. Equally obviously Partners, who at only unimportant expense of time and trouble and money can frequently visit one or more of the Partnership's more important businesses, will get in this way much more advantage than those whose homes are much further off.

It is held by some that this difference of advantage is unfair and improper and that Partners should not make purchases from the Partnership on terms more favourable than would be given to strangers, so that the profit, that would be made out of a stranger, may be made out of the Partner by all the Partnership's other members. The actual purchaser would still get a tiny advantage, that is to say his own share through the Partnership Benefit of the net profit upon his own purchase.

Now let us take a particular example. Let us suppose that a Partner desires to get the best piano that he can for £100. Let us suppose that the Partnership can offer him his choice between a piano that anybody can buy from it for £100 and another for which anybody else would have to pay, say, £133. Are the other members of the Partnership to say to this would-be purchaser, "We shall not actually lose anything if we let you have for your £100 this piano for which an outsider would have to pay £133. If you decide to save your money instead of buying any piano at all, we shall not have the slightest right to complain but, if, instead of saving your money, you choose to buy a piano, then in our opinion you ought to buy it from the Partnership, if it can offer you at least as good value as you would get otherwise, and in our opinion you ought to give us £100 for a piano that will have cost us, say, £75. We will let you have a tiny bit of that £25 back in the form of Partnership Benefit but, apart from this, we take the view that those of us, who choose to save our money, are perfectly free to do so but, if any of us chooses to put his into a piano that his partners, without appreciable damage to themselves, could supply to him for £75, he must hand over to them another £25 to be divided among all of them because they and he get their living by trading in such things and they do not see why the fact, that any one belongs to the Partnership, should cause him to escape having to pay that profit either to themselves or to some other similar traders"?

SHOULD FRIENDS GAIN AT EACH OTHER'S EXPENSE?

448. To my own mind this is plainly quite wrong. For years I was inclined to it partly because of the danger of various abuses but partly, I must admit, from the idea, that seems to me now to be quite false, that, because some Partners are not able and willing to spend so much as others upon things that the Partnership might supply to them on favourable

terms, therefore those others should be deprived, of an advantage that the first set could give to them without damage to themselves.

Personally I should not be willing to make a profit out of my own brother and I should not admire any of my friends for feeling differently. More than that, I would not make a profit out of anyone whom I regarded as not a mere acquaintance but definitely a friend, that is to say I would not make a profit if I should either not wish to replace the thing or should be able to replace it without disadvantage.

If I were to be sorry to be asked to part with the thing at all, then I might feel that the profit was no more than a fair and reasonable compensation for letting my friend have something that I really wanted to keep for myself but I should, I think, feel a little uncomfortable about it.

NO DOG-IN-THE-MANGERISM

449. This question of jealousy is, of course, always difficult and dangerous in any community. Years ago it occurred to me that on Saturday mornings a good many Departments could let one or more of their team be away because on Saturday morning business ceases before any of the Partners go off to lunch and therefore there is no period during which one-third of the team of any particular Department will be off duty.

A rule was made accordingly that in any Department, in which someone was thus superfluous on a Saturday morning, he or she might be allowed to stay away without loss of pay. When the rule was announced, I remarked with some bluntness that it could operate only in particular cases, hardly anywhere outside the Selling Staff and perhaps not in all Departments even on the Selling Staff and certainly not to an equal extent.

I said that the Partnership was not intended for people with a dog-in-the-manger unwillingness to see other people getting things that they themselves could not have.

The Partnership called this new arrangement "Chairman's Leave" and it was very popular indeed, partly, I imagine, because it was regarded as a step towards the Partnership's professed aim of a five-day week but largely, I suspect, because there is, if I am not mistaken, a very general consciousness or half-consciousness that many of the disagreeables of life are quite unnecessary and are maintained for no sufficiently good reason and that one case in point was the practice of asking a full staff to attend on Saturday morning, when there would be no real disadvantage at all in letting some of them be away.

CHAPTER 27

PARTNERS AND PUBLIC SERVICE

450. THE Partnership professes to aim at behaving towards the general community and its representatives, that is to say all public authorities, as would a thoroughly good citizen. It aims at being not merely strictly honest but as actively helpful as possible. Questions of any difficulty do not arise often. But a war raises one of great importance. What is to be then the Partnership's attitude upon the question of volunteering for public service?

The public authorities would obviously call up anyone whom they wanted to be sure of getting. If they depended for a time upon volunteering, their reason for doing so must presumably be to enable their first intake to consist of people who otherwise would be doing nothing or who could be so well spared from their ordinary occupations that their volunteering would not be too bad for the business or other organisation to which they belonged.

In a multitude of cases the consequent saving of working-expenses would be extremely welcome and, if in some cases an employer or the responsible managers of some other organisation objected unreasonably to somebody's volunteering, then in that case he or she must of course act according to his own conscience and the law.

PATRIOTISM OR AN EYE TO THE MAIN CHANCE?

451. But it is perfectly plain that many people, especially women, might have very strong selfish motives for volunteering early. The early birds were obviously likely to get in the end the best jobs with the prospects of a decoration and so on. But, if in fact everyone dropped his or her normal employment and volunteered, then to the extent, to which they were accepted, the effect would be plainly precisely the same as a general strike. The country would break down completely. That being so, there is a plain duty upon all workers to consider carefully whether their real duty to their country is in the direction of volunteering before they are called up or of continuing for some time at all events in the work that they are doing already and that is presumably more or less necessary to the country.

The Partnership has taken accordingly the line that volunteering without permission must be treated as resignation but that on the other hand in cases, in which permission was asked, it should be given immediately or with the least possible delay.

There was of course a great deal of volunteering but very little without permission.

SUBSIDY OF WAR SERVICE PAY: THE FAMILY SPIRIT

452. What ought the Partnership to aim at doing for those of its members who did not cut themselves off from it? Obviously in the first place it must maintain their employment: it must take the greatest care that War Service did not avoidably injure their civilian careers. In the event reinstatement was made legally compulsory. But the principles of the Partnership would have required in any case much the same procedure.

In the next place, so far as the money could possibly be found, no Partner should be allowed to suffer during the war excessive hardship from any fall of his income.

Whenever a partnership of this type, however large, finds itself confronted with a grave problem, it should in my view always ask itself what would be the natural behaviour under such circumstances of an affectionate, intelligent family whose general material position was upon much the same level as the partnership's though of course comparatively tiny in total size.

The partnership should ask itself how far and in what ways it would be natural for the members of such a family in such a case to stand by each other and to help each other and the partnership should try to behave in the same way to its own members.

The General Strike of 1926 was such an emergency. As has been mentioned elsewhere, the Partnership immediately gave notice that it would keep the income of all its members going as long as it had the means. It appealed to its account-customers to give any help, that they could by paying their accounts, and the customers responded very usefully.

The war was another emergency. There was no means of knowing beforehand how far the Partnership's earnings would shrink or to what extent its members would be called away or what pay they would get from the Government. But the principles of the Partnership plainly required that, so far as it might have the means, it must not allow any of its members to suffer excessive hardship.

The difficulties arising from the war should be, so far as possible, shared, so that they would not fall too heavily upon any particular Partners who in one way or another were specially unlucky.

£125,000 GIVEN AWAY BY DEMOCRATIC PROCESS

453. As has, I think, been mentioned elsewhere, in this last war the actual cost to the Partnership of this subsidy was approximately one hundred

and twenty-five thousand pounds. The administration was controlled entirely by the Central Council and their Committee reported that they found the Partners with whom they had to deal very satisfactorily frank in their disclosures and modest in their suggestions.

I received myself a somewhat peremptory intimation from one young bachelor that in his view the Partnership should subsidise him substantially in order that he might take a commission in the Guards rather than serve his country in some other branch of the Army. "Other employers," said he, "were to his knowledge feeling the provision of such subsidies to be incumbent upon themselves."

But I have no doubt that the broad judgment of the Committee was well warranted.

The Government are putting upon employers a substantial financial burden in the continuance during Territorial training of the civilian earnings of young men whose training, being for the benefit of the nation as a whole, might perhaps be thought to be something for which the nation as a whole should pay. This is welcome to the Partnership because we were already arranging to do much the same thing and are glad that in that respect our competitors will not have over ourselves the advantage that they will so far as they do not feel called upon to subsidise, as we are doing, the amounts to which are to be limited for the present the Family Allowances from the national purse.

454.   In the same way the Partnership early in this war resolved that, when peace should return, it would spend not less than a thousand a year upon subsidising the real earning-power of a certain number of partially disabled workers of whom a certain number should be carried without any limitation to those who had been previously members of the Partnership.

Here again the Government has put upon employers a charge that it might perhaps have been thought more honest and therefore more patriotic, though perhaps less fruitful of votes in future elections, to take upon the public purse. But, so far as the Partnership is concerned, the effect is to diminish what would have been otherwise a voluntarily assumed handicap.

It is certainly true that these charges would have merely diminished the amount available for distribution as Partnership Benefit and I suppose it would be more strictly accurate to say that, but for the decision of the Government that these charges are to be enforced upon all of the Partnership's competitors, the Partnership would have lost some part of such economic advantage as would have flowed otherwise from its own special system.

Continuance of pay during absence on jury service is another such case. Here again the Partnership would not let its members lose by public service undertaken compulsorily or with its own consent.

It may be that the advantages to the efficiency of the Partnership of the effects upon the minds of all concerned of its making a considerable expenditure upon providing employment for partially disabled workers or upon encouraging Territorial training or upon paying people for working for it in its business, when in fact they were working for the State in its Courts of Law, would be at least as great as the addition of that money to the general Partnership Benefit. There is no means of knowing the exact truth of matters of this kind.

PARTICIPATION IN PUBLIC AFFAIRS

455. Service in war and upon juries is not, of course, all of the part-time or temporary whole-time public service that workers in private enterprise may desire to render or that the Law may require of them. The recent general tendency to put upon employers charges, that being required by the public interest should, it would seem, be met from the public purse, appears in, among other things, a suggestion that employees, whose sense of public duty or private ambitions or both incline them to enter municipal politics, shall not only be given leave of absence at no matter what inconvenience to their employer's business but shall also draw from their employer pay for the time that they thus spend in satisfying their conscience or starting upon the career of a professional politician.

Just as the Partnership takes the view that the rearing of the children of each generation should be a charge upon the whole community but provides for its own members Family Allowances so long as the whole community does not provide them sufficiently, so the Partnership takes the view that it is very highly desirable that public affairs shall not be conducted entirely or even nearly entirely either by whole-time professional politicians or by people who have no need to make an income and who are able and willing to give their time to public affairs and that, so far as the public purse is not opened sufficiently, the Partnership should meet the need.

456. The Partnership is accordingly not only entirely willing to make in its own arrangements all possible adjustments to enable members to give to public affairs a substantial part of their time and energy without avoidable disadvantage to their careers in the Partnership but furthermore, if the public work is unpaid or if the rate of pay would involve a financial sacrifice that the Partner could not afford, the Partnership is very willing to provide any subsidy that is lawful.

In all such matters there must be no departure from the principle that the Partnership in its collective capacity keeps itself completely aloof not merely in appearance but in reality from every political party. Just as a broad-minded family may be conceived as giving equal help to each of two or more members, who belong to different political camps, and as arguing that these are matters upon which good men can differ deeply and that it may be a real public service to enable anyone, who is sufficiently good, to secure election under the auspices of any party that does not aim at despotism or, as it is called nowadays, totalitarianism, so is the Partnership willing to give whatever financial or other help it feels it can afford to the fostering among its members of intelligent interest in public affairs and active participation in them.

CHAPTER 28

TRADE UNIONS

457. IN the past, when I used sometimes to find myself addressing bodies like the Marshall Society at Cambridge and gatherings of students of the London School of Economics, I used generally to find that at a fairly early stage of the meeting I should be asked in perhaps a slightly aggressive tone and with some appearance of expectation that the question would bring to light a cloven hoof, "What was the general attitude of the Partnership to trade unionism?"

I have always given the same answer. The attitude of the Partnership to the officials of a trade union is precisely the same as it would be to a firm of solicitors. We wish to believe that they are not out to get for their clients more than they themselves really feel to be fair and right and, since that is precisely what the Partnership wants to give to everyone with whom it has any dealings, its Management are entirely willing to do their best to see the thing through the eyes of the trade union officials or solicitors concerned.

The Partnership has no more wish to influence its members against belonging to a trade union or against belonging to any particular trade union than it has to dissuade them from consulting solicitors or any particular firm of solicitors.

SCOPE FOR TRADE UNIONISM IN PARTNERSHIPS

458. It is obviously unlikely that a business, that gives to its workers the whole of its profits, will afford much scope for trade unionism as between Managers and Managed but it may quite conceivably afford substantial scope as between different sections of workers. This is a principal field of strife among trade unionists and therefore of opportunities of professional advancement for union officials and friction of that kind between sections of a partnership would of course be likely to involve its Management.

It is plain that, if in a genuine partnership any group of workers are overworked or underpaid or have any real grievance, one of two things must be true.

Either the business must be giving to some or all of its customers excessively good value, so that in effect the business is acting as an agency whereby those customers "sweat" those workers, or else the business must be overpaying some of its workers, present or future, at the cost of those who have the grievance.

That is plainly perfectly conceivable and it is likewise perfectly conceivable that the particular workers, who were overpaid, might be the principal Managers or some of them. Accumulation of reserve funds might be such overpayment of future members. Allegations of excessive conservatism in the management of its funds have been a cause of serious friction in, I believe, many a trade union. It would be absurd to suggest that in a world, in which the Partnership system was general, there would necessarily be little real scope for trade unionism. The middle classes have shown that there may be great scope for extremely powerful and active organisations in professional occupations into which capitalism does not enter at all.

459. But it is plain that workers, who strike against a partnership, will be striking against their fellow-workers. There will be no one else against whom they can strike, for the whole of the profit would go to them and to those fellow-workers and they must accordingly be the only losers.

That may make it much more difficult for unions to put pressure upon partnerships than they would find it to put pressure upon ordinary businesses and partnerships will need to be very careful indeed that they do not take any improper advantage of that fact.

A worker, who is a member of a partnership, may well feel that it is his duty as a citizen to belong to a certain union. He may feel that, even if he is very certain indeed that there is no real likelihood of his ever losing his place in the partnership. But, unless he does feel extremely secure in that respect, he may very reasonably feel that, though he may wish to continue in the partnership and may hope to do so, he would be very imprudent to give up his union membership or to get into bad relations with his union, even though his motives in that respect are purely selfish.

That being so, he may find himself called out on strike not against his own partnership but in order to put pressure on the general public for the benefit of other members of the same union.

STRIKE-ABSENCE AND SICK-ABSENCE

460. Then there would arise the question whether the action of the union was so unreasonable that the Partnership must say to workers of that kind: "Either you must persuade this union to allow you to continue at work, your conditions here being what they are, or you must disobey it or you must find some other union to which it will suit you to belong or you must leave this partnership."

Obviously individual cases will differ by degrees that will be almost infinitely subtle. There can be no exact measurement of the particular facts. The decision will be a matter of mere judgment, mere feeling. In such matters it always seems to me very desirable that the decision shall, if possible, be left to the Council or to some committee appointed by the

Council and for my own part I should be inclined to advise the Council to treat the obligations of union membership as on a footing with sickness. The Partnership cannot retain anyone whose sick-absence is too bad for its teamwork. Purely from the Partnership's own selfish interest it may be wise to tolerate an infrequent absence, however long, because the sight of that toleration gives everybody else a feeling of safety and increases their own inclination to stay in the Partnership and to do their best. But a worker must have very uncommon quality to be desirable in a first-rate team if his health obliges him to be frequently absent at awkward times. In such a case the degree of toleration must be affected by length of membership and other considerations but there will come a point at which the Management must say to the Council that they must make to this Partner any leaving-gift that they think fit, but that his membership must be terminated.

The same would apply to union membership. If a union called its members out only once in a way, membership of that union might not be a disqualification for membership of our partnership but, if the absences were too frequent, then, if good enough workers could be got whose value to their partners was not thus handicapped, the Partnership would have to proceed accordingly.

One would hope of course that unionists, who were members of a genuine partnership, would not be called out but would be allowed to continue at work even if the union levied on them some special contribution.

BREACH OF CONTRACT

461. But here we come up against another question.

If somebody, in order to get into the Partnership or to stay in it or to get some particular post in it, has given a written undertaking that he will not withdraw his services at less than a certain notice, is he to be allowed to go on strike without first of all giving that amount of notice?

For my own part I should be inclined to fight against that tooth and nail. But then labour-organisers may say to the Partnership: "Will you give employment to our members on an engagement that can be closed at a minute's or a day's notice so that without breach of contract they can engage in a 'lightning strike'?"

What is the Partnership to answer? I should be inclined to answer that the Partnership would go to any reasonable trouble and expense to make arrangements suddenly to replace such workers with temporary substitutes, but that, if it could not do that, (and of course such replacements might defeat an aim of the union to cause inconvenience and even suffering to the general public) then I should be inclined to say that, if the Partnership could get satisfactory workers who were able and willing to enter into a more substantial contract, it would not give employment to any who were not.

A SHADOW THAT PASSED

462. As labour-conditions steadily improve, so that grievances are only in respect of a margin of comfort and not in respect of necessities, these problems will presumably become less difficult. The Partnership so far has never had any troubles but there was a rumour just lately (1947) that some of its members, whom it took over with a business that it bought some years ago, might be coming out on strike not upon any complaint against the Partnership but as part of a concerted action in Smithfield and elsewhere.

I was asked whether those in charge of that part of the business could notify any absentees that they might lose their positions in the Partnership unless they returned within twenty-four hours.

I answered that if, as I imagined must be the case, they had promised in writing that they would not leave the Partnership at less than a certain notice and they did in fact strike in a way that broke that promise, they must be informed that they could not come back at all except upon a clear understanding that their re-engagement would be subject to a day's notice on either side until the Partnership's Central Council should have decided by secret ballot whether on this particular occasion their breach of their contract could be overlooked.

I asked that the inquiry and that answer should be gazetted.

The trouble blew over and I was then asked to agree that the notice should not be gazetted but that it should be held in reserve in case trouble should arise again.

I answered that to my mind such things are best said in cool blood rather than in emergency and that I wished the inquiry and my answer to be gazetted, so that thenceforward there should be no uncertainty in the mind of anyone concerned.

The gazetting may lead to discussions that may cause some modification of the. Partnership's attitude but that is what has actually happened so far.

463.   The actual notice was as follows:

"Memorandum 29833. Dated 15.1.47. From the Chairman to the Director of Selling

"1.   You have just told me by telephone that you have just heard a rumour that certain members of the Partnership may stay away from work to-morrow and you have asked me whether in that case I am willing that they shall be informed that, if they are absent for more than twenty-four hours, the Partnership will not retain them.

"2. My answer is that, if they behaved in this way, they would be breaking a contract into which of their own free will they have entered with the Partnership.

"3. If the Partnership on its own side tried to treat that contract as a scrap of paper, these Partners would quite rightly say that behaviour was not only dishonourable but unlawful. They would certainly go to law against the Partnership and they would certainly win.

"4. If any of them do break their contract in this way, they will not be retained in the Partnership unless they can offer some excuse that in the opinion of the Central Council, voting by secret ballot, the Partnership can properly accept. The Partnership is not intended for those who do not keep faith with their partners but break their contracts and dishonour their signatures if they think it will pay them to do so.

"5. If any of these Partners go off duty and then wish to return, they may be reinstated pending the decision of the Council but each of them is to be given notice in writing that, if he starts work again, it can only be on the understanding that he is on a daily engagement until the Council shall have decided whether he is to be allowed to return permanently.

"6. Trade unionism has done immense good. But trade unionism depends upon bargaining and bargaining is impossible unless on both sides there is good faith.

"7. All freedom and decency depend upon law. To strike without proper notice is to break the law and to try using force. That is a game at which two can play.

"8. The Germans submitted to victimisation by Hitler's gangsters who persuaded other people to break the law. In the end the will of those gangsters replaced in Germany all law and order. The people of Germany found themselves enslaved and driven to their present frightful ruin.

"9. The time to stop such things is at the beginning. Breaking of contracts is the beginning."

The following notice was gazetted on the 5th April 1947.

"STRIKES

464. "In the bad old days of the Combination Laws it took very great courage to create or lead a trade union. You might find yourself in jail for fourteen years and, even if you escaped jail, you might find yourself unable to get any employment.

"Nowadays the formation and management of trade unions is an attractive profession. At worst it means a tolerable income and a good deal of fun. At best it means a four-figure income and a title.

There is corresponding competition to get on to that ladder and this competition has given rise to a new development, the unofficial strike.

"A constant drawback of democracy is the tendency of the general mass to keep on changing their leaders, in the hope of getting results still better than they are expecting to get otherwise.

"This inclination is, of course, fostered and exploited by those who want to push the leaders out and to take their places. It is a very easy game to play. Whatever the leader has got or says that he is going to get, you simply say that it is by no means all that could be got and that, if the men will follow your lead, you will get them more.

"In human affairs any bargaining must stop somewhere but it is generally possible to go a bit further than any point at which it actually does stop. So, if the officials of a trade union have made some bargain, it is often possible, if you choose your moment well, to start fresh trouble at some particular point and thereby to get a bit more. In the long run the trouble may not pay. In the end it may drive trade elsewhere or it may lead to some development of machinery, with a reduction of labour-requirement.

"That may be good for the general community but it may not be good for some of the workers who caused it to happen.

"But, on the short view, if you have succeeded in starting an unofficial strike and you can claim that that strike succeeded in getting something, then you can hope that you yourself will be presently elected to one of the official jobs that you are after so that you will have a place on the ladder that may lead to a four-figure income and a title.

"Other people will then try to play the same game on you. But your own experience will make you very wide awake in that direction and you will hope to succeed in keeping them out and in staying in yourself.

465.   "It is notorious that, some big unions have been made by ruthless poaching upon little ones. It is said that in some cases commission has been paid to people who could bring in new members. It may have been quite a good thing for the general community that a lot of little unions, keeping up perpetual unrest by their efforts to beat each other's achievements and so to gain members, should be replaced by a much bigger union and, once the big union has succeeded in coming into existence, those leaders commonly show themselves extremely touchy at any sign of a beginning at their own expense of the poaching by which their own big union was created.

"But this state of affairs does not necessarily bring peace in industry. Instead of the former competition between small separate unions, you now get the unofficial strike, the attempt of ambitious outsiders to muscle in to the official ranks and to get for themselves places on that ladder.

"In view of what can come nowadays of a successful career in trade unionism, it is small wonder that there is ceaseless fierce competition to get places on that ladder. But for everyone except the competitors that competition has the drawback that industrial unrest is fostered by the ambitions of those who want to muscle in to official appointments as well as by Communist influence exerted from motives that are not trade unionism at all but purely political.

"Our prospects therefore of industrial peace are by no means secured by the substitution of big unions for little ones and by the natural policy of the established unions to restrict the formation of new ones.

"By themselves those things should make for stability and so they would in Russia, where the unions are part of the machinery of government. In Russia anyone, who tried to start an unofficial strike, would be killed or sent off to some frightful prison-camp. The present great and growing relation between the Trade Union Congress and the control of the House of Commons may mean that we shall presently find ourselves going along that road. You are getting near to it when you see a Labour Government using troops to thwart an unofficial strike. But, as yet, there is in this country nothing to prevent ambitious persons, who may or may not be helped by money from Moscow, from starting unofficial strikes. And that means that no agreement between employers and trade unions will necessarily ensure that strikes are avoided.

"That may put members of a partnership into a very difficult position. A genuine partnership will be giving the whole of its profits to its workers, so there are only three ways in which they can get more. One way is by charging more to customers. That would tend to kill their business. Another way is by cutting the total staff down so that those, who are left, can have a bigger share-out. Broadly speaking that is hardly possible because the cutting down would mean at best a fully proportionate loss of the earnings that could be shared out. The third and last possibility is to diminish the share, that some workers get, in order that some others may get more.

"That is plainly a perfectly legitimate field for trade union action and it might be the only field that would remain if the partnership-system became universal.

"I say 'might be' because it seems conceivable that trade union action might secure that all the partnerships in a sheltered industry raised their prices to the general community. But I doubt if the possibilities in that way would turn out to be important.

467. "Anyhow, there can never be an end to the possibility of organised action by workers of one kind to get for themselves at the expense of other workers a bigger share of what customers pay for the team-work in which both kinds of workers are engaged.

"To that extent there will always be scope for trade unionism. So, if partnership becomes general, you will have a world in which some people will be making a living by creating and running trade unions while others are making a living by creating and running partnerships.

"If nationalisation goes far enough, the two may melt into one, as has virtually happened in Russia, though that is looking a very long way ahead. The people, who in Russia got possession of the Czardom by promising the peasants the land and who managed to keep the Czardom after the peasants woke up to the fact that they were not going to get the land, took over an extremely ignorant public, taught them to read and write and kept absolute control of the printing-press, the schools, the wireless and all coming and going between Russia and the outside world. That has enabled them to get away with a very great deal that would probably be impossible in this country.

"At all events, as yet, though the Trade Union Congress has been able to stop the starting without their consent of any new unions, they have not discovered how to prevent unofficial strikes and that means that members of a partnership may always find themselves asked to join in such a strike.

"What are they then to do? From an unselfish standpoint they will wish to be loyal to their partners. But they will also wish to be loyal to outsiders with whom they feel sympathy.

"From a selfish standpoint they will be likely to lose by leaving the Partnership and therefore they will want to stop in it. But, on the other hand, the people, who are promoting the particular unofficial strike, may be in a position some day to victimise any non-strikers who are then no longer in the Partnership.

"The Partner may think that that might be serious for him if he were to find himself outside the Partnership, so he will have both an unselfish and a selfish motive for thinking that he ought to join the strike if he is asked.

"Now what are his partners to do? Are they to say to him: 'Play the game of these outsiders if you choose but in that case look to them for Partnership Benefit, four weeks' paid holiday a year, big sick-pay and a pension. Stick to our show or join theirs but don't expect to have it both ways.'

"What else can they say? Can they say that they will treat an impulse to go on strike as they would treat illness, that is to say reckon that it is something that their partner cannot help and that they must keep going without him as best they can and take him back whenever he is ready to come?

"If anyone took sick-absence again and again, the Partnership would in the end say to him, 'We have stood an awful lot because, when you are on the job, you are such a good Partner. But this really is more than we can stand. We are so uncertain whether you are going to be here or not that we cannot keep you in our team. We are sorry for you and we will make you a pretty handsome leaving-gift on top of all the sick-pay that you have had but this partnership set out to be a team of first-rate workers, not a refuge for crocks. A man, who wants to play first-class football and who has not got the health, cannot expect to be taken into a first-class team or kept there if his health goes wrong after he has joined it and in just the same way we cannot keep you.'

468.   "For my own part I am inclined to think that the Partnership's best course through this puzzle may be along this general line. If somebody's sense of loyalty to some outsiders obliges him to go on strike just once in a way and *without breaking any undertaking that he has given to the Partnership not to withdraw his labour at less than a certain notice,* then for my part should be inclined to say: 'Let us treat it the same as we should sickness. Let us assume that he is unwilling to let the Partnership down but feels that he cannot help himself. So long, as it does not happen too often, let us make such a temporary arrangement as we can to carry on and let us re-engage him whenever he wants to come back, just as we should if he was ill.' But, if he takes himself off without giving proper notice to close his engagement, then it seems to me the Partnership ought to think very, very carefully before it takes him back.

"He most certainly would go to law with the Partnership if the Partnership behaved in the same way to him and he most certainly would win his case and get his money. All happiness and decency depend upon reasonable law and order and all law and order depends on keeping faith. If a man gets a job by giving a written promise that he will not leave that job at less than a certain notice and he breaks that promise, then there is an end of law and order.

"That is precisely what happened in Germany. The Nazis in their early days defied the law and got away with it and then, when they were strong enough, they set up a terrific secret police-force, just like Mussolini and the Russians did, and took very good care that there was no more law-breaking.

"If in some particular case the Council held that there was for some reason sufficient excuse, then I should be in favour of doing what the Council advised and waiting to see what came of it.

469. "That actually happened when one Partner knocked out another's teeth and his General Manager pressed me very strongly to forgive him and I refused and then the Council made the same recommendation and I agreed at once, for, as I said, it seemed to me that it was one thing for the Management to forgive for their own convenience a good worker, whom it would be difficult to replace but who did something that might be intolerable to the self-respect of one of his partners, and it was quite another thing for the elected representatives of that partner to say, as the Council did, 'We think there was so much excuse that the thing ought to be forgiven' (the Partner, who lost the teeth, very sportingly said the same thing).

"But I think that *any Partner, who goes on strike in breach of his contract with the Partnership,* must not be readmitted except on a day-to-day engagement until the Council have decided whether he shall be forgiven or not. If the Council voted against it, then, whatever trouble and difficulties it might mean for the Partnership, he would not be readmitted.

"I imagine that no union would call upon him to strike in breach of his agreement. It would merely call upon him to give proper notice and then withdraw his labour. In that case, as I say, I am inclined to think the Partnership ought to treat it as illness and, if in the particular case the Council so recommended *but not otherwise,* I could agree that he should draw pay just as if he had been ill.

"That seems to me to be about as far as we can go. The problem is plainly real and serious. There is a genuine conflict of unselfish loyalties and there is genuine conflict of selfish interest as well. The Partnership ought to take as sympathetic and broad-minded a view as it can, just as it ought to be as patient as possible with good Partners who have for a time persistent trouble with their health.

"I should be glad if any people in the Partnership or outside it, who have any views upon this matter, would write to THE GAZETTE or to me. It is very desirable that Partners shall know where they are. The Partnership ought never to bluff and, as far as it can, it ought never to leave its members uncertain what will be the consequences if they take some particular course."

REASONABLENESS ON BOTH SIDES

470. I have been glad to get from recent correspondence in the Partnership's journalism a strong impression that these suggestions are entirely satisfactory to keen trade unionists. I have been advised that upon these matters feeling in some sections of the Partnership runs high and that on each side, the pro-unionism and the anti-unionism, there are some Partners who do not seem to have very much capacity for

dispassionate, much less sympathetic, consideration of the ideas upon the other side.

The letters, that I have mentioned, seem to show that in the pro-union camp my ideas are thought reasonable. There were, indeed, expressions of rather warm appreciation of what seemed to me a very obvious and natural suggestion for the Partnership to make, that it might in certain cases regard the absence due to a strike not directed against the Partnership itself as equivalent to sick-absence and that it might in such a case conceivably continue pay.

I was thinking, as I made, I think, clear, of the possibility that in a particular case one or more Partners might be quite genuinely constrained by their consciences to make a certain use of their legal right to put pressure upon the general community by ceasing to do work of a certain kind even at the cost of injuring their fellow-workers in such a partnership as our own.

It seemed to me then and it seems to me now that there might conceivably arise a true conflict of genuine loyalties.

471.   Another suggestion of my own, that seemed to make a somewhat similar impression, was that, if members of the Partnership desired that one or more of the professional officials of some trade union should visit the Partnership's premises, they might not only be entertained like any other guests but provided, if there seemed sufficient reason, with transport. It is interesting to notice how many years it takes a community to realise that things, that they have been told over and over again in ways that involve permanent public record, really do mean what the words appear to mean.

It is noteworthy how apt quite intelligent people are to fail to realise that there cannot possibly be some disingenuous intention in publishing such announcements and, above all, in publishing them in such a way that the record will always be easily available to anyone who wants to make use of it.

PROBLEMS ARISING FROM SECTIONAL ADVANCES OF PAY-RATES: WANTING TO HAVE IT BOTH WAYS

472.   There is, of course, always a chance that trade union action may produce an apparently unjustified difference between the pay of certain workers and that of others who follow a different occupation. Trade unionists are no better or worse than the general run of mankind. They are apt not to have much difficulty in persuading themselves that they will be justified in being pretty ruthlessly selfish.

Naturally, if members of a union get into our own partnership, they want the Partnership to take the view that, if the union did not exist, it would nevertheless feel that it ought to give those particular workers just the same rates of pay and everything else to which on other occasions they will point as an example of what trade unionism does for the worker. They will go on to argue that, since they are not really getting from the Partnership by reason of the existence of the union any more either in pay or in anything else than the Partnership would give to them in any case, it follows that on top of these rates, that are in fact fixed not by the Partnership but by some outside bargaining, the Partnership ought to give to them everything else that it gives to any of its other members whose rates in those other respects have been fixed entirely by bargaining between them and the Partnership itself.

473. Obviously this may be mere dishonest humbug. On the other hand, it may be perfectly true that, if the union did not exist or if the rates it had been able to get were lower, the Partnership would be paying for the work in question just what now it is paying. There may be sections of the Partnership's business that it would be very awkward to drop out because of the ill-effect upon other sections and it may be that, if these sections, that it would be awkward to drop, are retained, it will be difficult or impossible to staff them satisfactorily except from the ranks of trade unionists.

Of course there is nothing to prevent the Partnership from giving them no more than it thinks fit beyond their union rate and union conditions and, if it did give them nothing more, they would lose heavily—a fact to which they are by no means blind.

On the other hand, if the Partnership makes any difference at all, then, human nature being what it is, you get much more resentment of the difference than gratitude for whatever they are still getting over and above their union rates and conditions. Suppose, for example, that you give unionists their union pay and conditions and full Partnership Benefit and Pension-prospect but in the matter of, say, paid holidays or sick pay or both you give no more than the union has been able to secure from other employers. You will be apt to find that resentment of the fact, that other Partners get more sick pay or more paid holiday, is much more conspicuous than gratitude for the Partnership Benefit which will be itself a very large addition to the union pay and conditions. The Pension-prospect is sure to be ignored.

474. Any such persistent sense of grievance, however unreasonable and however deliberately cultivated, is, of course, very undesirable in a team. In organising work you should, if you possibly can, either give each worker whatever he thinks it reasonable to ask or else get rid of him. My own view, therefore, is that in cases of this kind the Partnership should go as far as ever it can towards accepting the view that, if the union did not exist, it would still give the union members the union pay and conditions, in which case there is, of course, no reason why they should not have on

top of those things the full additional benefits of partnership. But, if the Partnership does this, it should get as far as ever it can towards taking care that the work given in return is reasonably good value.

I raised the pay of Buyerships out of sight of my father's figures but only a few of the very best of my father's Buyers would have had the slightest chance of being appointed to any of my Buyerships or of holding it for more than a very short time if he were in fact given a trial.

That seems to me to be the line that the Partnership should take as far as ever it can in face of union demands that may seem to be rather near to extortion and therefore unfair to all of the Partnership's other workers who are not clients of the professional officials of some particular union.

REQUIREMENT MUST BE PROPORTIONATE TO PAY

475. The Partnership should give what is asked but it should be proportionately strict in its requirements. That may quite easily include refusing to keep on duty throughout the year workers whose services at busy times may be worth a high figure but who cannot be carried through slack seasons. In such cases it may be wise to pay season-rates. If you give an average, you will be apt to find it will be accepted through the slack season but, when the busy time comes, you will receive a resignation.

There is, of course, a marked tendency for workers to get out of employment in which they are engaged by the job into employment that will be continuous. They do so precisely because they want the continuity when work is slack, they want to be carried then in some light, standby occupation or half-occupation with no effect upon their regular rate of pay. But, when they have got that advantage, a good many of them will be inclined to suggest that they have a serious grievance if that continuous rate of pay is not the full rate that is customary for employment by the job with a corresponding likelihood of periods of unemployment between one job and the next.

All this is, of course, merely human nature but it needs to be watched carefully and handled firmly if a partnership is to have a general sense of fairness that is essential to general happiness and to friendly relations between different sections.

THE CLOSED SHOP

476. The problems of trade unionism include that of the Closed Shop. The Partnership had lately some reason to think that one of the large unions who are at present conspicuous for their disregard of the Labour Government's appeals to their patriotism in the matter of refraining from pressing for increases of pay-rates except as production rises, might aim at creating that position in some at least of the Partnership's Branches. My own answer was that at first sight and subject to what other members

of the Partnership might have to say, I could see no reason why the Partnership should not agree that it would give none of its posts of a certain kind to people who were not willing to belong and who did. not in fact belong to some particular union but in that case the Partnership must make three stipulations: first, the union must admit to membership anyone whom the Partnership saw fit to engage, second, there must be no restriction at all upon the Partnership's freedom to require any or all of those workers to accept any terms of tenure that are lawful and that the worker is willing to accept, third, the union must refrain absolutely from making the slightest effort of any sort or kind, overt or covert, to induce any of its members to break any contract that he or she has made with the Partnership.

477. In other words, if the Partnership can find suitable workers, who are willing to enter into a legal contract that will prevent their being called out on strike in some quarrel that is not a quarrel with the Partnership itself, the Partnership must be to that extent secure against inconvenience to its own customers or injury to its own interests in any other way.

When I made those suggestions, I lost sight of another point and, if the case were actually to arise, I should, subject always to the views of the Partnership's other members, feel that I must insist upon that point. Workers of that kind, who are already members of the Partnership and who object on principle or who, to use another expression, have a conscientious objection to belonging to any trade union or to that particular trade union, must be allowed to remain in the Partnership and to stay outside the union, provided that the Partnership is willing to pay their union dues, so that, if the refusal of the Partnership's member to join the union is not really a matter of conscience, the loss may fall not upon the union but upon the Partnership.

Subject to these stipulations, I can see for my part no reason why the Partnership should not accept the principle of the Closed Shop.

CHAPTER 29

BUSINESS POLICY

SERVICE TO CUSTOMERS: NEVER KNOWINGLY UNDERSOLD

478. THE length, to which the Partnership has adopted hard and fast rules that give to the Managed not only more than the present Law of our land gives to them but more than trade unionism is as yet even asking, seems to be quite feasible, for it has not prevented the Partnership from holding, quite strictly to the policy, that it has always professed, of never knowingly allowing itself to be genuinely undersold by any real competitor.

When it serves a customer, it conceives itself to be saying in effect to that customer: "To the best of our knowledge and belief you cannot get this same thing cheaper anywhere that is so within reach of this present place, where you are standing at this moment, that, if you knew of it and were a sensible person, you would go there for it rather than come here".

The Partnership constantly keeps a substantial team of competent whole-time workers watching ceaselessly for any case in which some competitor is giving better value. The activities of this whole-time team of workers are supplemented by standing offers of reward to any Partner who discovers any such case and makes it known to the Partnership.

Up to now the Partnership has found it practicable to apply without any exceptions at all an absolute rule that, whenever such a discovery is made, the Partnership either ceases to trade in the article in question as something in which somebody else is for some reason able and willing to give better service or else it puts its own price down to that other price, no matter what loss that may involve in its supplying that particular thing.

COMPETITIVE VALUE

479.   More than this, the Partnership has constantly aimed at giving in as many cases as possible value so much better than is offered anywhere else, that no sensible person, no one who was not grossly extravagant or lazy, would get that thing from any other source if the Partnership's own branch was not so far away that the cost and trouble of the journey would outweigh the difference of value. The extent, to which the Partnership has been able to follow that policy, has allowed it to build up without any appreciable use of advertisement a business of which the yearly turnover now exceeds sixteen million pounds and that seems likely to grow fast and far.

A business, that depends thus upon value and upon the recommendation of customers in place of all other forms of advertisement, must obviously be serving the general community efficiently. It would seem therefore that, so far as the Partnership does give to its members more than does the present Law of our land and more than is as yet even asked by trade unionism, that betterment is genuinely feasible, economically sound.

In considering these things, we must keep in mind not only such material gifts as twenty-four days of paid holiday, leaving-gifts and so on, but also those things in which substitution of the Rule of Law for the exercise by individuals of their own discretion, that is to say for the exercise of power, gives to the Managed more security, more freedom, more equality.

FINANCE

480.   I hope I shall be forgiven for not attempting to extract from other places in this book and to gather together here things that really belong to financial policy but that it seemed reasonable to place where now they are.

In the matter of finance the Partnership's policy can, I think, be summed up as follows.

Provide amply for sufficiency, accuracy and promptitude of all accounts and related statistics.

Watch them constantly and publish them promptly and honestly to the fullest extent that will not reveal to competitors business secrets that really are too important to be thus given away. Use this publicity to keep yourselves up to the mark. Criticism from the outside world and from inside the Partnership will be a most valuable safeguard for a management with such strong tenure of their own powers.

Restrict your business-operations absolutely to the extent of your ability to make all payments not only absolutely punctually upon their becoming due but earlier to any extent for which a just sufficient discount or other consideration is offered.

Never use short-term loan capital for any but strictly self-financing short-term purposes. By short-term I mean any loan that the lender has power to recall at notice that will not give the Partnership ample time to raise the necessary money without serious waste, such as may occur if money has to be provided by selling something somewhat hurriedly.

Never engage in your operations so much of your capital, including your power to borrow upon long term, that you have not a reserve that you can feel to be really ample for any unforeseen emergency. In judging such things remember the possibility of a coincidence of a number of unwelcome surprises.

481.   All this amounts only to saying: Never let a prospect of extraordinary gain or the satisfaction of doing big things draw you suddenly or gradually

into running a risk of any really great disaster, much less of such disaster as would destroy the Partnership's financial independence, so that the Partnership itself would be or might be brought to an end.

A man, whose luck is sufficiently good, may take with impunity such risks for a time, even perhaps for the whole of a lifetime. Just possibly his son and even his grandson may be equally lucky. But the pitcher, that keeps on going to the well, will be broken at last.

The Partnership is designed for more than one or two or three generations. If it never takes major risks, never opens a flank to Fortune, it will get in the end so much that to hurry would be merely foolish. If others by successful venturing outshine us, let them. Let us do all we can without ever putting ourselves at Fortune's mercy but let us be patiently content with what we can have in that way. For more let us bide our time. Let us think of the Partnership in the days of our successors as still ours and let us take no risks with it.

This may be as good a point as any other for me to put upon permanent record for the Partnership my most earnest advice that in every possible way they will always endeavour in their conduct of their business-affairs to preserve what I call liquidity. Never tie your hands more than you can possibly help. Human foresight is very limited. Your utmost efforts to look ahead and the utmost efforts of any number of first-rate advisers will still leave vast possibilities of complete surprise. Try your utmost to see every possibility of reserving to yourselves freedom comparable to the freedom to distribute cash instead of giving some particular Stock. Never mind that there seems to be no chance at all that you will ever regret giving up some freedom that you might retain. Retain it. You can always give it up if on some future occasion there seems to be sufficient reason. But, once you have parted with it, you may be unable to get it back or only at a cost that will be more or less cruel.

JAM TO-DAY OR TO-MORROW?

482.   Right up to this present time the Partnership has been steadily aiming at enlarging its affairs, its buying power, the size of its team, the calibre of its leading posts and the breadth and diversity of its interests. It has been working in fact for jam to-morrow. In any new enterprise there is apt to be a period during which the owner or owners live as thriftily as they can bear to do and draw upon the business as little as ever they can. They do this in no spirit of self-sacrifice but because it is the way to make that business as fruitful for themselves as they are hoping that in due course it will become.

When the business has reached a certain scale, then those abstainers reap their reward.

Though the business, from which the Partnership has arisen, is now eighty-four years old, really rapid growth did not begin until eighteen years ago. Thenceforward long strides followed each other quickly but those strides took the form of the acquisition of enterprises that were out of health and that took time to become satisfactorily profitable. All of that meant working, as do commonly the starters of a new enterprise, for jam to-morrow. It means forgoing, as they do, jam to-day.

Obviously such a policy could not continue for ever. If there is never to be any harvesting, why farm at all?

At first our policy was governed merely by a general feeling that the whole thing was not yet as large as was expedient for security. The policy was always safety first. Be content with a hope of jam to-morrow so long as there is any doubt whether jam can prudently be drawn off to-day.

SIZE-FACTOR IN POLICY OF SAFETY FIRST

483.   But, as the years passed and the whole thing became larger and larger, there arose with increasing insistence the question—where are we getting to? When is this policy of expansion to stop? When are we going to increase the well-being of existing Partners rather than to keep on adding to their number?

For some time the answer had seemed to be in the increase of buying and employing power. But a stage was beginning to be reached at which buying-power seemed quite sufficiently large for really first-rate service of the Partnership's customers. That left employing-power. What was upon that side the corresponding line at which it would be possible to say, "Now we are safe: now we can begin to feel that the Partnership is large enough and that so long as it seems to be keeping quite healthy and vigorous, we need not accept still further opportunities of expansion that will tend to increase expenses especially the pay-sheet without an immediate equivalent increase of the amount available for Partnership Benefit?"

The answer seemed to be that a business consists of three factors, relations with a set of consumers, relations with a set of suppliers and, finally, relations with the occupants of a set of posts that are key posts in respect of the maintenance of those relations.

If any business lost simultaneously from the top level downwards more than a certain number of its most important workers, those, who were left, would be unable to make sufficiently soon a sufficiently good set of choices to fill the vacancies. Some of them might be genuinely promotable to some of the vacancies and with luck some outsiders might be secured who sooner or later would be as good or better than their predecessors.

NEED OF CONTINUITY OF MANAGEMENT

484. But no business can afford to lose simultaneously more than a certain proportion of the most important of its leading spirits.

Over and over again it happens that the loss of some one person brings to an end quite a large business. The whole thing may actually run down and be liquidated or the control may pass into other hands who convert the enterprise into something more or less importantly different from what it was before but, so far as that happens, the old business will have really come to an end. Many of its old customers will no longer get from it the service that they used to do and a good many of its workers may find themselves displaced or so ill at ease that they resign.

From the standpoint of those, who finance a business, such a change of policy may not matter at all. The income, that they have been accustomed to receive in dividend, may be as large and as safe as previously—perhaps more so—but from the standpoint of those workers, who are displaced or whose happiness in their work is at all events seriously diminished, the change is deplorable and of course, if the business comes altogether to an end, though the shareholders may get all their money back, the workers will have, lost their employment.

For all these reasons the Partnership's policy of safety first required that it should not merely continue from the standpoint of the Money Market but it should also continue from the standpoint of its own workers. There should be as little risk as possible of any sudden sharp change of policy and character. This finally emerged as the real steering-mark by which the Partnership could know when to shift its helm from the initial, temporary course of jam to-morrow to the ultimate permanent course of jam to-day.

REQUIREMENTS OF A POLICY OF SAFETY FIRST

485. The policy of safety first would be satisfied when two positions were achieved. Adequate buying-power. This had been achieved already. And adequate employing-power in a certain special sense, namely in the sense that the true principal management of the business, the functions upon which depended the real policy and character of the whole thing, were so far divided that the sudden loss of any one or two or even three of those particular members of the team would leave a mass sufficiently substantial to maintain the continuity of the policy, the general character of the business.

If that mass, that central core, were sufficiently substantial, then, if newcomers consciously or unconsciously sought in effect to change the real nature and character of the business, one of two things would happen. Either they would encounter such opposition as would cause them to drop out again, so that their places would be again vacant, or else in their own ideas and methods they would make consciously or unconsciously such adjustments as would maintain sufficiently the existing policy so that the Partnership would still be as congenial as before to all those of its workers who were used to that policy and to whom it was presumably congenial.

BLUE WATER

486. In the course of these last few years it came to be felt that this position had been reached. The Partnership could at last reckon that the requirements of safety had now been satisfied. So long as in that respect general conditions did not seem to be changing too seriously and so long as there were no symptoms of decline in the vitality of its existing business, that business could be reckoned sufficiently large. The supreme consideration could now be to make membership of the Partnership as advantageous as possible to those for whom it had already scope instead of continually adding to their numbers without any important immediate advantage to most of those who were already inside it.

But for the war this position would have been reached some few years ago.

We have yet to see what will be in normal conditions our system's fruitfulness for our members. At present very much of our floor-space has been bombed out of existence. Of the remainder seriously large parts are still requisitioned. One of our chief advantages, the efficiency of our buying and our relations with our suppliers, is immensely reduced by, on the one hand, restriction of profit, no matter how well you buy, and, on the other hand, restriction of supplies. Of any profit, that nevertheless we do succeed in making, the tax-collector takes a great part.

In a future edition of this book or in some supplementary publication we may perhaps be able to give some information upon this question of fruitfulness, the effect on the incomes of workers of all grades of stopping what is here called the cancerous distortion of the proper working of capitalism in the team-work of private enterprise but at present the precise facts are so unsettled that it seems better to say upon this no more than the statement at the end of Part III of what has actually happened up to now and the broad fact that upon the total capital of the Partnership the dividend-claim is no more than 4.36 per cent. and all other earnings must necessarily go sooner or later, somehow or other, to the Partners themselves.

PART THREE

THE PARTICULAR INSTITUTIONS THAT HAVE
ARISEN FROM THE GENERAL IDEAS

CHAPTER 30

THE PARTNERSHIP'S PUBLIC OPINION
AND ITS WRITTEN CONSTITUTION

487.   THE Partnership's present institutions have been devised gradually during the last forty years or nearly so. As they stand now, they may seem over-elaborate and likely to be excessively costly but it must be remembered that they have been devised for this particular partnership, which has already twelve thousand members and seems likely to grow fast and far.

As was explained in Part II, in paragraphs 306 and 7, the real essence of a partnership of this general character might exist in the case of no more than two members possessing no capital and making their living by hawking fruit in the streets.

The organisation described in this final part of this book seems to me likely to be final. So far as I can see, this frame-work should suffice for an enterprise of any possible size and complexity, no matter how large and various its operations or how widely its branches were scattered over the world.

As for cost, it appears from the confidential figures mentioned in paragraphs 720 and 721 that at this present time the Partnership's total pay-sheet is much heavier in proportion to its total turnover than the average figures for these last two years of a great number of other organisations in the same way of business but from such analysis, as is given, of those total figures the cost of the Partnership's management seems to be remarkably light.

"Management" is a vague term and all, that we know as yet, is that something, that the experts, who collected and issued these figures, thought proper to be described as "management", has in these two years cost on the average substantially more than the amounts that in our own partnership are considered to come under that head. In this connection it must be remembered that my own whole-time work is done without charge.

To return for the moment to the question of elaboration, I hope that I have made it absolutely clear that I have not the slightest inclination to suggest that the broad aim of securing that all the advantages, moral, intellectual and material, of ownership shall be shared as fairly as possible among all the workers of an enterprise can only be achieved by means of an organisation of the same general kind as that which is described in this book. To me it seems, on the contrary, very highly probable that, even if this particular organisation is capable, as of course I hope that it is, of giving results that will not be very importantly inferior to the best that, so far as mere organisation apart from the quality of particular persons goes, can be achieved in other ways, there are a host of real possibilities of getting first-rate results by methods that would be extremely different both in appearance and in reality.

As I look back, it strikes me as interesting that the notions, that are embodied in our own present organisation and that, as has just been said, have been evolved gradually during the last forty years or nearly so, have differed so very widely in the time that they have taken to arise from the experience that is the subject of the first part of this book.

Within the first five or six years I had got as far as the few elementary notions that form the core of the whole thing and that are perhaps rather of the nature of an aim, an end, whereas the later ideas are rather of ways to achieve that aim, means whereby that end might be reached.

Those first notions have never wavered at all.

THE END

488. Divide as fairly as possible among all the workers in the enterprise all of the advantages of ownership for a wise owner—someone to whom money is not everything. In deciding how far to be enterprising he will never bring upon himself the worry and danger of risking excessively the safety of his business and in deciding how much leisure to take and how hard to work he will be careful not to let his mind get dull and not to overstrain his health but within those lines he will do his best.

Divide as fairly as you can all the advantages in this sense of ownership and do your utmost to get in return the very best work that can be got for those attractions whatever they may be.

SOME OF THE MEANS

489. To this extent the plan took shape very quickly. But this was hardly more than the broad aim. The problem, how to achieve that aim, consisted of a great many separate questions and some of those questions were to my mind so difficult that until a very few years ago I was still waiting for experience to suggest answers.

Rather slowly after the first five or six years there arose such notions as the Committees for Communications between the Rank and File and the Principal Management to bridge the gulf that develops as soon as the workers in a business are too many to be all in frequent personal contact—a gulf that, if it is not bridged sufficiently, must be fatal to proper efficiency.

Some years later still there came the notion of using journalism with its priceless advantage of allowing utterance to be anonymous and yet to be heard by everybody with simultaneous answer anonymous or otherwise.

About the same time there arose the idea of calling the thing a partnership and the members partners but that of course is not of essential importance. It might have been called a brotherhood or by any name whatsoever and still have recruited the same people, asked of them the same efforts and made to them the same return.

Something in the way of a general council elected in the main by secret ballot was a plain need. Obviously there must be some representative body that could ask and answer questions on behalf of the Partnership as a whole. But, so far as I know, it was a really important innovation to give to elected representatives of all the workers absolute control of an important amount of money—absolute, I mean, in the sense that any power of veto would be strictly limited by the written Constitution to the minimum that might seem consistent with the Partnership's general interests, a limitation that would very probably mean that the veto would never be actually used. It was still more of an innovation to use that power for the particular purpose of giving compensation for disturbance, so that the public opinion of the Partnership could give through the Council (voting by secret ballot) such compensation in a case in which the Courts of Law would not award damages for wrongful dismissal or would award less than would satisfy the public opinion of the Partnership.

THE MORE DIFFICULT PARTS OF THE PROBLEM

490.   As the years passed, the plan became more and more complete, rather like building an arch. But quite a number of problems of essential importance, gaps in the crown of the arch, remained unanswered until these last few years. Year after year they remained empty and I had to go on hoping that, if they were never filled in my own time, the thing would be done sufficiently well by those who would come after me.

If I died before the first irrevocable settlement in trust had been supplemented by a second, that would complete the foundation of the Partnership, the particular shares, the twelve thousand Deferred Ordinary shares of John Lewis Partnership Ltd., that controlled the whole enterprise, were to pass to my wife. I have always thought and think still that that would have given my own lifework as good a chance, as it could well have, of being in due course completed satisfactorily.

I never felt any doubt that I had better leave my arch still waiting for a key-stone or indeed for several stones rather than finish it off in a way that to my own mind would be a mere stop-gap, something that certainly would have to be scrapped and replaced with something else.

Of course that may still happen or the Partnership itself may come for some reason to an early end. All that is as may be. What I am saying now is that to my own particular temperament it was possible to continue year after year with a prospect that, if my own career were cut short, my lifework would be frankly incomplete in certain respects of cardinal importance.

But it was not possible to me to give the whole thing a kind of sham completion. I could bear to leave almost any amount of gap to be filled after my own time but I could not bear to do any filling that I could not feel was really likely to be final and was about as good a job as I could hope to do.

In these last few years the mist, that in my own mind covered these gaps, has somehow cleared away. Answers, that rightly or wrongly I feel to be satisfactory, have at last occurred to me.

SOME YEARS LOST

491. If the war had not occurred, those particular ideas would, I think, have arisen upwards of five years ago. At all events, as I look back, it seems to me that for these purposes our experience was by then complete and I think that ideas substantially the same as those, that have arisen in these last five or six years, would have occurred that much earlier, if the war had not stopped, as it did for that time, all further thought upon these matters of main construction.

But it does seem to me interesting that, though the core of the plan was settled upwards of thirty-seven years ago and though ideas of substantial importance, that, when they came, stood firm (there has never been any important change in the Committees for Communications or the Council or the Journalism or, so far as I can remember, in any developments of similar importance), have been arising every few years, like additional parts of a growing building, it has been only so lately that the plan has been, as at least it seems to me, completed.

LONG-STANDING GAPS FILLED AT LAST

492. The final set of notions, that have filled the long-standing gaps, seems to be made up of a good many that are in a sense separate. They must be, I think, related to each other for, when at last they began to come, they seemed to follow as if they were linked together, but, so far as I can see, some of them might just as well have occurred long before. If they are in fact related, they are not so connected that, if some of them had come to light, it would have been impossible that the others should never have arisen at all. For example, there is the notion that the true ultimate purpose of an enterprise of this kind is the advancement of the interest of those who are worst off and that everyone, who gets more than the Minimum Wage, should be considered to stand to them somewhat in the relation of a professional guide to a party of climbers. He is more skilful and he is probably stronger but that skill and strength are to be

used to help the others. They are not to be used simply to get him up the mountain—never mind what happens to the rest of the party.

In some ways this idea is surely very important? It tends to produce clearness of purpose and to people of the right sort it will be very highly congenial, exhilarating, productive of energy and of good team-work in every way. It was in fact only quite lately that we came to look in this particular way at the whole plan and I have somehow a feeling that this development of our ideas was in some way related to the notions that arose at more or less the same time for answering the supremely important technical problems of which any solution, that seemed sufficiently hopeful, had been so slow to suggest itself.

But, so far as I can see, we might have got as far as that conception, that the supreme purpose, the centre of gravity of the whole thing, was in the interest not of the controllers but of the controlled and, moreover, of those of the controlled who were worst off, without ever hitting upon any such solution, as now we have, of certain technical problems that for us had been for some reason , the toughest of all.

The outcome of all the waiting for experience and so on, of which I have just spoken, has been that in this partnership ultimate authority, supreme responsibility, supreme power, sovereignty or whatever you may choose to call it, is divided much as it is in the British democracy. Consciously, at all events, there has been no intentional copying of that example. There has been a truly separate development and a truly separate, though, as it happens parallel, solution of problems that in spite of the enormous difference of scale were sufficiently the same.

PUBLIC OPINION

493.   In a certain sense, that I will not try here to put at all completely into words but that will, I think, prove to be sufficient, the supreme authority in the Partnership is to be the public opinion of its members.

That public opinion is to be informed, developed and expressed partly by and through the Partnership's own journalism, of which something will be said presently, and partly through a whole network (that in a smaller partnership would be proportionately simpler) of representative institutions and partly by arrangements to secure, by means of social gatherings under pleasant conditions, informal personal contact between all ranks.

Apart from the Committees for Communications, the principal representative institution will be the Central Council and all other representative bodies, except the Committees for Communications, will be financed and therefore to some extent controlled by that Central Council. The Committees for Communications need no separate financing. Their functions are merely to enquire, discuss and suggest expenditure and other action.

As I have said, the formation and expression of general public opinion will not depend solely upon the journalism and the representative institutions. They will be supplemented by informal general contact among the Partnership's members—contact that will be facilitated and fostered as much as possible by systems of moving Partners from one post to another and by social gatherings and in any other ways that seem desirable.

This public opinion will play upon the conduct of the Partnership's business and social affairs partly directly through discussions and through the journalism and partly indirectly by pressure upon the minds of the holders of particular positions—the members of the Council, the members of the Central Board and a host of others.

THE CONSTITUTION: ARTICLES, RULES, REGULATIONS

494. The whole of the Partnership's activities, whether impelled or influenced by waves of general public opinion or by the genuinely separate initiative of particular individuals or groups, will have to flow through the Constitution, as the waters of a river may flow through an embanked channel and through sluice-gates.

It will not be in the power of the Partnership to behave unconstitutionally. The draft of the new Constitution, which at present is being considered by the lawyers and is near completion, is intended to be in general accordance with the following principles. The Articles of the Constitution, with which all of the Partnership's Rules and Regulations and the whole conduct of its affairs must be in accord, will be in writing and they will have two custodians, the chairman of a trustee-company, that will be mentioned further in a moment, and the Central Council, of whom at least two-thirds will be elected yearly by secret ballot of the whole partnership. The Council will elect each year three of the five directors (the other two being the chairman and the deputy chairman) who will form the Board of a Company that will be a Corporate Trustee holding the Deferred Ordinary Shares of John Lewis Partnership Ltd. that carry the control of the whole enterprise. The chair of the trustee-company will have the same occupant as the chair of the Board of Directors of John Lewis Partnership Ltd. and will be in the Partnership the position of chief individual responsibility. Under the settlement, by which I shall thus give up my own present possession of those shares, their voting-power will have to be used to elect each year to the Board of Directors of John Lewis Partnership Ltd. (the Partnership's Central Board of Management) five Partners recommended by the Central Council and five others recommended to them by the Chairman of John Lewis

Partnership Ltd. who in my time will always recommend the five Heads of the Partnership's Critical Side. This notion was a very late development but for my own part I like it very much. It seems to me a satisfactorily neat way to give to the elected representatives of the Managed continuous inside knowledge of the conduct of the whole enterprise and in so doing to achieve two things, first, that the powers of the Chairmanship shall be sufficiently great and his tenure sufficiently strong, and, second, that, if there arises a state of affairs in which under the Constitution the Council through their Trustees displace the Chairman and appoint whomsoever else the Trustees may think fit, the new Chairman shall be assured of the support of the Central Board (the Board of John Lewis Partnership Ltd.) immediately and without need of a fresh appointment to any position but his own.

STABILITY OF THE TENURE OF THE POSITION OF CHIEF INDIVIDUAL RESPONSIBILITY BUT EASY TRANSFERENCE OF ITS POWERS IF OCCASION ARISES

495. So long as the Chairman performs his undertaking to maintain the Constitution and without any breach of that Constitution keeps the business-results up to a certain level, seven of the twelve directorships upon that Central Board will be held by the Chairman himself and by the occupants of six posts to which the Chairman will have the power of appointment. Thus in the theoretically possible event of intrigue against the Chairman by the five directors, who got on to the Central Board by acquiring influence in the Council, the Chairman would have a majority-vote upon his side.

But, if the Chairman were to lose his own tenure, none of his six supporters need be displaced. The new Chairman would be appointed by the Corporate Trustee. That would bring a sixth vote to the side of the representatives of the Council and, if the other six directors voted solidly the other way, the casting-vote of the new Chairman would give the control to him and the five Trustee-members, who had just appointed him. If the Chairman were not personally very active in the business, the real transference of initiative might really be rather from his nominees on the Board to the nominees of the Council. But the effect would be the same.

It is plainly very much to be hoped that the Partnership will never get within sight of such a situation but we must obviously provide for every conceivable contingency and from that standpoint this arrangement does seem to me to be good.

496. The Articles of the Constitution, that the Chairman will have undertaken to maintain, cannot be altered in his time without his consent and equally they cannot be altered without the consent of the Council.

The Chairman upon taking office will undertake in writing to maintain them as they stand at that time. If in the judgment of the Council he breaks that undertaking and if the Council do not choose to disregard that breach, they will be entitled to direct the Trustees to call upon the Chairman to resign and in that case he must either do so or else he must apply successfully to the Courts of Law for an injunction to restrain the Trustees from declaring the Chairmanship vacant and from appointing to it whomsoever they shall see fit. Of course his application to the Courts must be on the ground that the Council are wrong in thinking that he has broken his undertaking.

Since the Chairman will have undertaken to maintain the Articles, he will be liable to displacement if he fails to do all that he should to prevent any breach of them by anybody. All Rules and Regulations of the Partnership must be in accordance with the Articles. So long as they are, they will themselves be part of the Partnership's Constitution and as such binding upon all of its members.

PUBLIC OPINION AND ITS PRINCIPAL AGENTS

497.   As has been said already, the Partnership is genuinely intended to be as completely as is really possible a democracy, that is to say that in the Partnership, as in the British or any other democracy, the real supreme authority, the real sovereign, will be public opinion operating through the Constitution, written or unwritten. But, except for a possible use of the referendum, as in Switzerland (an institution that may quite possibly arise in this or some similar partnership), the action of public opinion in exercising supreme authority must be as vague and invisible as the action of the wind that cannot be seen and that has no edges that can be felt and that can yet exercise enormous force and leave behind it such permanent effects as, for example, the arrival of ships across vast distances or the permanent bending of trees.

CHAPTER 31

THE PRINCIPAL AUTHORITIES (THE CENTRAL COUNCIL, THE CENTRAL BOARD AND THE CHAIRMANSHIP OF THE CENTRAL BOARD) AS A WHOLE

498. IN a democracy there must be a secondary supreme authority: some visible, tangible holder of power subordinate only to the invisible, intangible sovereign, public opinion.

In the Partnership this secondary supreme authority, public opinion's principal agent, that can be seen and felt and called to account for any breach of the Constitution, is divided in three, a Central Council, a Central Board and the Chairman of that Board.

THE POSITION OF CHIEF INDIVIDUAL RESPONSIBILITY

499. Division of power between the Council and the Board might not be very difficult. The real puzzle was the functions of the position of chief individual responsibility, its remuneration, its tenure and so on. In any democracy there must be some position of chief individual responsibility. Conceivably that responsibility may be reduced very narrowly but whatever remains must be in a sense the keystone of the whole arch, on the cricket-field the umpire, in the House of Commons the Speaker, in the British Cabinet the Prime Minister, in the United States the President.

When you come to think of it, the functions of the position of chief individual responsibility in a business enterprise, that is not in the very fullest sense of the phrase a one-man management, are the residue of the functions of the owner-manager of a business so small and of such a kind that one person can be truly its "head" and the others can be truly "hands". As such a business grows, its head can no longer do all of its brain-work and, if the business becomes so large as is now our own partnership, his functions should in my view be reduced to the absolute minimum. This reduction seems to me to be necessary to the stability of the whole thing and I suspect that in the long run it will be found that the possibility of continuity for any particular enterprise will be proportionate to the extent to which it is really possible for the functions of its position of chief individual responsibility to be restricted.

Consider, for example, the team-work that is said to have arisen around some of the great painters of the Renaissance. A lot of the painting, that was sold as that of the master himself, may have been by other hands but, once he was gone, the team must collapse. Is it not plain that, so far as any one position is essential to the permanence of a team, that team's own prospect of permanence must depend upon how far the qualifications for filling that particular position properly are such as it is always easy to get?

DIVISION OF THE POWER OF THE PURSE BETWEEN THE COUNCIL, THE BOARD AND THE CHAIRMAN

500. To decide what was the very smallest part, that the Chairman could be called upon to play, was therefore to decide how much power and consequent responsibility could be put upon the Central Council and the Central Board.

The power thus divided in three is of course largely financial. In any business—even national affairs—control must be largely financial, it must be exercised largely through the Power of the Purse.

THE COUNCIL'S SHARE OF THE POWER OF THE PARTNERSHIP'S PURSE

501. Upon the financial side of this three-fold division, the Council has a voice in the Partnership's taking any financial decision that in the judgment of any three of the Council's five representatives upon the Central Board ought to be referred to the Council because it is (1) of more than a certain size and (2) being above that size either seems to involve such financial risk, as ought not to be taken except with the Council's knowledge, or else seems to involve the termination of so many existing memberships and this for reasons so questionably sound that the thing ought again not to be done except as aforesaid. The idea of this right of the Council to be consulted by the Board is that all members of the Partnership shall feel as safe as possible against any grave rashness or unnecessary changes of policy tending to ˉweaken the general sense of security of tenure and shall moreover know as, if the Council thought fit, they would of any conflict of opinion between the Council and the Board.

Of course in business public or private secrecy is often essential to taking some good chance and, so long as any three of the Council's representatives on the Central Board consider the proposal good, there need be no such publicity.

502. Apart from this possibility of an influential voice in the Partnership's largest operations, the Council has also virtually absolute control of almost all of the Partnership's expenditure upon help to its members in special need. So far as all of the Council's fund is not so used, it is available to the Council for any other purposes whatsoever. It is the duty of the Chairman to veto any proposed expenditure by the Council that he reasonably holds to be too dangerous to the Partnership's interest but, if at the instance of the Council the Trustees of the Constitution, whom they elect each year, obtain in a Court of Law a ruling that the

veto has been used unreasonably, the Chairman can be displaced. The vacancy will be then at the disposal of the Trustees. All this is still merely in contemplation because it is taking so long to make the second, irrevocable settlement in trust and it seems undesirable to delay further the publication of this book but this is what is intended. There are naturally difficulties in using to enable Labour to hire Capital laws that were created from the opposite standpoint but it is believed that by some such means as this projected creation of a corporate trustee the broad intention can be achieved within the framework of existing legislation and of the present requirements of the London Stock Exchange.

If partnerships (or Producer-Cooperatives) become as numerous and important as, according to the Webbs, they are already in Russia and as Consumer-Cooperatives are in this their country of origin, the Law will presumably be adjusted as it has been already to Consumer-Cooperatives but in the meantime the technical difficulties are real and serious and now, that this partnership's experience has at last enabled its plan to be worked out sufficiently completely, the finding of ways to achieve the plan by means of existing Company Law is taking so long that the second settlement has not been, as was intended, made in time to be included in this first edition of this book.

Publication could, of course, have been delayed but it is felt already to be really several years overdue and, since this problem of partnership for all at which we have been working for so long, is now a matter of such special public concern and since these technical details are not of really fundamental importance, it seemed better to wait no longer.

THE BOARD'S SHARE OF THE POWER OF THE PARTNERSHIP'S PURSE

503. The second part of the Power of the (Partnership's) Purse belongs to the Central Board. The whole of the Partnership's affairs are managed by budgetary control and that control belongs to the Board down to the point at which the estimate of the revenue has been settled and also all outgoings except to the Partners themselves.

THE CHAIRMAN'S SHARE

504. That residue after providing for every other expense of carrying on the Partnership's affairs goes in one undivided total to the third of the Principal Authorities, the Chairman of the Central Board. Subject therefore to the Council's right to be consulted in some cases of very special importance to the Partnership's general safety and peace of mind, the Board control all of the financing of the Partnership's business except the patronage, the pork-barrel, to use a term of American politics, that is to say the Pay-Sheet, the Pension Fund (itself fixed very completely by an

Article of the Constitution), such Amenities as are not financed by the Council and the Partnership Benefit.

All of these things are the third division of the Power of the (Partnership's) Purse, the division that is the Chairman's affair.

INDIVIDUAL OR GROUP RESPONSIBILITY

505. The question arises very plainly whether a Chairman with life-tenure (up to the age of seventy-five), so long as there is no breach of the Partnership's Constitution and in particular no failure in punctuality of payment of interest or dividend due upon any of its capital, and with control of the whole of the Partnership's patronage cannot spoil the whole thing. In theory he certainly might but to my mind it is reasonable to reckon that in practice he will not. In all organising you must trust somebody, some person or group of persons. To put your trust in a group is to open the door to the politician. He may be very wise and very good but he may be a conceited fool or a cunning knave, a conscious or an unconscious misuser of a gift for spell-binding or for intrigue or for both.

And it must be remembered that such gifts are likely to be possessed by several competitors for place and power. Then you are apt to have a grim demonstration of the wisdom of Napoleon's remark, that in war (which, after all, is only a specially testing kind of business) one bad general is better than two good ones. A single policy, though devised and carried out by a mediocrity, may be better than the results of two or more conflicting policies operated by persons individually abler but interfering disastrously with each other. It is all very well to say that a man or woman, who knows his or her mind, can always swing a committee but what happens when there is upon a committee more than one man or woman who knows his or her own mind?

Inevitably you get bargaining. It becomes the duty of Mr. A. to vote with Mr. B. for something that to his judgment is wrong. Why is it his duty? Because that is the only way in which he can secure the vote of Mr. B. for something else that in the judgment of Mr. A. is still more desirable.

506. Not only do you get conflicts of opinion that arise from genuine differences of judgment. You are also very apt to get conflicts out of mere jealousy, mere desire for self-assertion, mere disinclination to be everlastingly letting Mr. A. take the lead and simply saying "Ditto" to whatever he says.

National communities with their enormous margin of financial and other strength can pay for the advantages of democracy a price far beyond the strength of any community so small as would be a partnership many times larger than is, as yet, our own. At a level below that of national affairs great municipalities are immensely stronger than any partnership is ever likely to be. Yet we see that in the United States, with their passionate love of democracy, the great municipalities are tending to place their trust in the City Manager rather than in a group of elected persons.

Other partnerships may find a way to achieve in the conduct of their affairs satisfactory efficiency without putting nearly so much trust, as for the present the John Lewis Partnership will be putting, in one member of its team. But the real (and crucial) contribution of the Rochdale Pioneers to the success of the Consumer-Cooperative. was, I believe, that they restricted drastically the trust that in previous ventures of the same kind had been placed in the good sense and good faith of the members of the Society. Thereby they avoided the bad debts that had wrecked all previous ventures of the same kind.

I suspect that, if Producer-Cooperatives are to become similarly important, they must be similarly drastic in their restriction of trust in the good sense and good faith of voters and of vote-catchers.

BUT USE VOTING WHEREVER YOU REASONABLY CAN

507. Carry that trust by all means as far as ever you can. There are purposes for which voting, even if it may go disastrously wrong, is yet so much the best course that the risk must be taken. But voting can easily destroy itself, if the freedom, that it represents, is pushed too far so that the voters are out of their depth. No human arrangements can be wholly free from risk. If voting is not used, there will be other dangers and I would use it wherever the matters to be settled seem to be sufficiently certain to be within the qualifications of the voters and there does not seem to be too much risk of their being misled by quacks, conscious or unconscious. In a partnership voting upon anything, on which feeling is at all strong, should I think be as a general rule secret. In a community so small and in which it is, on the one hand, so important that the holders of power shall not be avoidably exposed to suspicions of misusing it, while, on the other hand, it is no less important that those, who would suffer from such misuse, shall have no fear that it may occur, secret voting must often be best for everybody. Certainly it has the very great drawback that the electors in some constituency may not know how their representative voted and of course discussion cannot be secret except so far as it can be conducted by anonymous journalism. But secrecy in the actual voting must be, I think, often desirable.

All votes by our own Central Council and by any others of our representative institutions have to be given secretly if any member so request or if it is requested by any Partner who is specially concerned in the matter at issue. But I hope the Partnership will be always very cautious how it uses voting in matters in which mistakes would be too serious and in which the voters are likely to be out of their depth. If they are, they will be at the mercy of the quack.

MUCH EXPERIMENTING NEEDED YET

508.   It is obviously not in the least likely that the plan of this particular partnership, as it stands, is the last word that can be said rightly upon these problems. For years I hoped vaguely that our plan would involve very much less trust in the holder of any one position or even in any small group. But in the end I have not been able to see how to go further this way without taking what seemed to me to be worse risks. For my own part I believe that the holder under this plan of the position of chief individual responsibility, the Chairmanship, will wish to play the game and that, if he does not so wish, traditions, that his own partnership may have developed by then, and the example and competitive efficiency of other partnerships in business of the same kind may be fairly potent influences upon him.

If in spite of what is really grave abuse of his powers he gets team-work good enough to keep himself in office, that particular partnership will be for his time and perhaps afterwards a more or less poor thing of its kind, a more or less complete return to the evils it was designed to prevent. But the occurrence of railway-accidents does not mean that railways are no good.

A bad chairman of a partnership, that had been healthy and that had developed sound ideas and traditions, would presumably lose the help of many of the best of its members. He might even arouse such organised mass-resistance that he failed to maintain the punctuality of payment and so lost his own tenure.

AN EASY POST MEANS A WIDE FIELD OF CHOICE AND LESS RISK OF CHOOSING WRONG

509.   But let us suppose that, if a partnership of this general type has the bad luck to get a bad Chairman, the other members may in the end find themselves little, if any, better off than in the ordinary exploiting employment that this plan is designed to supersede.

Even if this can happen where a Chairman does not choose to play the game, it may still be useful to have a plan that works satisfactorily when the Chairman is sufficiently well-meaning and, before we leave this part of the main plan as it stands at present, let me draw particular attention to a feature that may, it seems to me, prove to be very important indeed. The line, that it is proposed to draw between the functions of the Board as a whole and the separate functions of the Chairman as a sort of Managing Director of the whole Partnership is intended to prevent the Chairman's needing more than common sense and common decency, qualities in respect of which it is comparatively easy to choose well.

SUCH A POST SHOULD NOT REQUIRE CLEVERNESS

510.   If the Partnership is to be really stable, this particular post must, it seems to me, need character rather than cleverness. It must need honesty, kindliness and grit but beyond those I think it should not absolutely need more than a fair degree of common sense. For all their frightful blundering the people of this island are among the most sagacious this world has seen so far and they may be wise in their marked reluctance to put much trust in the clever.

Cleverness may be, of course, wholly good but experience has given rise to the saying that there is no fool like a clever fool and, moreover, cleverness is simply one kind of power. So far, as it goes, its possessor is independent of other people. He has that much less need to win and hold their respect and affection. All power, we have been told on very high authority, tends to corrupt. That must be as true of cleverness as of any other power.

If an organisation can be so devised that the holder of its position of chief responsibility can play his part quite satisfactorily without much of what is commonly called cleverness, the team-work may be all the better divided, the organisation itself may be all the more truly a partnership.

THE MINIMUM FUNCTIONS OF THE CHAIRMANSHIP

511.   In the core of the whole conception the notion for securing that the division of its ownership need not make a business any less self-financing came last of all. It formed, as it were, the keystone of an arch. So also in the planning of the details for giving effect to that original fundamental conception has come likewise last of all the notion for meeting in this way the need in all organising to trust somebody, some one person or some group. The notion, I mean, of making the functions of the Chairmanship as nearly as possible judicial, those of an umpire and perhaps of a selector, rather than of a player. The Partnership is to depend upon other people for initiative and drive and so forth. In a cricket-team judgment, whether someone ought to be invited to play, rests with a captain who is "getting up a team" or with a selection committee and judgment, whether in the actual game that player has got himself out, rests with the umpire. The Chairman may or may not undertake to make some appointments. What he must do is end appointments of which the results are not good enough.

THE CHAIRMAN MAY HAVE TO MAKE SOME APPOINTMENTS

512.   Anyone, however, who must take responsibility for making vacancies, may find himself obliged to take also that for filling them.

In effect he may find himself told that, if he is thus dissatisfied with appointments made by other people, he must make them for himself. Obviously that will not happen in the case of posts that are not at the top level. But, if the Chairman asks the holders of some of those positions, that come next in responsibility to his own, to fill vacancies at their own level and if he is then dissatisfied with the results, he may find himself told in effect that his colleagues have done their best and that he must either do that particular work for himself or else he must get other colleagues.

If he feels that, so far as all the rest of their functions go, the change would be bad for the Partnership, he will be driven to do this particular thing himself as best he can and the same position will arise if they keep on trying and he keeps on feeling that the appointments are too bad to be continued.

The plan of the Partnership puts upon the Chairman those two functions and it is designed to ask of him as little as possible beyond this.

ENCOURAGINGLY JUDICIAL CHARACTER OF THESE FUNCTIONS

513.   I had not foreseen at all that the plan would work out to this correspondence between the functions of the position of chief individual responsibility and those of the judiciary in a political democracy. When I saw that that was happening, I was a good deal encouraged, for the plan required that the tenure of this position should be the most permanent of any under the Partnership's Constitution and I thought there might be very highly satisfactory significance in the fact that in a political democracy the most permanent element, the element that has the strongest tenure, is precisely the judiciary.

If I am asked "What about the British monarchy?" I shall answer that that is a special case. That institution has survived from a polity that was not democratic. As a matter of fact its requirements and functions have surely tended quite plainly towards the conception that we are considering here? But, if we leave the British monarchy aside and look at the other great Anglo-Saxon democracy, what do we find the most permanent element in the political structure of the United States? The Supreme Court. And we find that it is so immensely strong that even President Franklin Roosevelt, when at the height of his power he moved in an important way against the Supreme Court, was unsupported by the public opinion that for his sake had just then broken its immensely strong tradition against re-election of a President for more than a second term.

This notion may be merely fanciful or at all events unsound but it does seem to me a real encouragement of hope that the plan, that has worked out in this way, may be more than a mirage.

514. Thus there are three Principal Authorities, a Council, of whom at least two-thirds are elected every year by secret ballot of the whole Partnership, a Board of twelve Directors, of whom five are chosen by that Council and six by the Chairman and finally the Chairman appointed by his predecessor and holding office for life (unless he lives beyond seventy-five or chooses to retire earlier) but holding it only so long as he maintains the Constitution and keeps the business of the Partnership from falling below a certain level of prosperity. If he fails in that, the Council can, if they choose, cause him to be replaced by anyone chosen by the Corporate Trustee, a board of directors of the Council's own choice.

So much for the Principal Authorities considered as a whole. Something remains to be said upon each of these three organs of the Partnership, taking them separately in turn.

CHAPTER 32

THE CENTRAL COUNCIL

515. AT present the Central Council has altogether one hundred and eighteen members. Of these eighty-four are elected, twenty-eight are ex-officio and six are nominated.

Who are at present the Council? Not more than one-third of them are either the holders of particular positions to which the Chairman has ruled that ex-officio membership of the Council shall for the present attach, or else are Partners appointed by the Chairman because they have not been elected and their presence in the Council is thought by him to be desirable for the Partnership.

The original aim of this ex-officio membership was to ensure the presence on the Council of everyone who ought to be available there as a source of information and also to ensure that the Council would include those who were considered to possess the general ability necessary for the most responsible posts. There was originally no intention that any Partner should be in the Council otherwise than either by being appointed to one or other of certain posts or by being elected for one or other of the constituencies into which the whole of the remainder of the Partnership was to be divided.

NOMINATION OF COUNCILLORS

516. After a few years, however, it began to happen occasionally that Partners, who had been conspicuously useful in the Council, were for one reason or another not re-elected. The President at that time of the Council and some other Partners, who were specially interested in this question of representative institutions, pointed out that the number of posts, to which ex-officio membership had been attached, was less than one-third of the Council's total membership and they urged that, so long as there was no breach of the rule, that the elected members must be at least two-thirds of the whole Council, the Chairman's power to attach ex-officio membership to a particular post should be used to bring into the Council particular Partners who were likely to be specially useful there.

It could of course have been done by attaching ex-officio membership to whatever particular post such a Partner happened to be holding. But it was thought better to adopt frankly a new practice of nominating particular Partners, provided that the total number of ex-officio members and of the nominated members should be still no more than one-third of the whole Council.

All the other members of the Council, that is to say not fewer than two-thirds, are elected each year by secret ballot of the whole Partnership divided for that purpose into constituencies by the three Trustees of the Constitution appointed each year by the Council.

THE FUNCTIONS OF THE COUNCIL

517. What are the present (or prospective) functions of the Council? (1) To appoint their own President: (2) to appoint three Partners to be for the coming year Trustees of the Constitution and to nominate five others for appointment to the Central Board: (3) in certain cases to decide whether the Chairman of the Board shall be invited to continue in that office or the Trustees of the Constitution shall appoint a new Chairman who may be anyone they think fit who is not yet seventy-five: (4) to amend but only with the concurrence of the Chairman of the Board the Articles of the Constitution of the Partnership. (It seems likely that a Chairman, who is near retirement and who has always followed voluntarily some rule in certain cases in which the Articles of the Constitution gave him discretion, may, before he retires, suggest to the Council that the rule, that he has thus in effect laid down for himself and has followed of his own accord, shall be added to the Articles, so that it will be compulsory upon his successors. The Council on their side may not agree but on the side of the Chairman it seems likely that, when a Chairman is near retirement even if not at any other time, there may be a quite sufficient readiness to develop the Articles): (5) to consider and express an opinion on any financial proposals of the Central Board that are beyond a certain degree of importance and that in the opinion of at least three of the Directors nominated by the Central Council ought not to be adopted by the Partnership without the knowledge of the Council. This applies equally to proposals that are positive, that is to say that involve financial risk for the Partnership, and to those that are negative, that is to say that involve a reduction of the Partnership's membership: (6) to dispose in any way whatever, that they think fit and that the Chairman does not reasonably in the view of the Courts of Law hold to be too undesirable for the Partnership, of a fund of which the amount is fixed by the Constitution: (In the Constitution of the United States a presidential veto can be overruled by a two-thirds majority of Congress. But that is the constitution of a sovereign state and therefore has to be secured wholly upon institutions internal to that state. A partnership, being a state within a state, can anchor itself externally upon the law of the land. The good faith and good sense of a veto or of a series of vetoes by the Chairman of this partnership can be challenged in the Courts of Law. If

that happened, the Chairman would have to satisfy the Court that his veto was given in good faith and reasonably. If the Court held otherwise, then the Council could, if it chose, cause its Trustees of the Partnership's Constitution to displace the Chairman and appoint someone else): (7) to make of the Board or of the Chairman any inquiry they think fit and with or without such inquiry and in the light of such reply, if any, as they receive, to discuss openly or privately any matter whatsoever and to make to the Board or to the Chairman any suggestion whatsoever.

SAFEGUARDING BUSINESS SECRETS

518.   Thus the Council have an unlimited right to discuss and to make suggestions but they cannot be used as a means of access to any of the Partnership's business secrets that in the judgment of the Chairman ought not to be thus discussed.

In British democracy the corresponding safeguard is the good sense of the House of Commons in refraining from pressing the Government to answer questions of which the Government says that the answering would be contrary to the public interest. But the House of Commons is a massive body of immense political experience. There is correspondingly little risk that a traitor or a fool would succeed in persuading the House to insist upon any disclosure that would be in fact really gravely undesirable.

Experience may show that the constitutions of such partnerships as this can with advantage place the same responsibility upon the Central Council. But experience has yet to show what in the way of real requirements for a sound balance of divided powers will be the differences between such a community as the British democracy in domestic and international affairs and such a community as this partnership in its internal affairs and in its relations with business competitors and all the rest of the outside world.

I cannot be sure that as yet the Council has never made an inquiry that has been left unanswered and it remains to be seen whether upon this point there may arise some day a question whether the Chairman has so failed in his undertaking to maintain the Constitution as to have forfeited his tenure of the Chairmanship.

Obviously, if there is not in all concerned enough of good will and of good sense, a split must come somehow. No constitution can secure successful team-work in spite of no matter what deficiencies of good will or good sense. A constitution can only be a ship that will keep afloat and sail satisfactorily so long as her company behave appropriately.

519. The Council was started almost thirty years ago by a notice that was gazetted on the 20th September 1919. At that earliest stage it had only eighteen members. The notice contained the following paragraphs:

"The House Committees were a first step towards our development of representative institutions. They represent only the rank and file and each of the three is quite separate from the other two.

"It seems to me that it is now time that we advance another step by arranging that for certain purposes the three existing Committees, or delegates from each of them, shall meet as one body and that that body shall include representatives of those sections of the Staff who do not elect Members to the present Staff Committees, that is to say the Buyers, Superintendents, Chief Assistants and other officials.

"The new body may, perhaps, be called 'The Staff Council'. Its functions will be to decide such questions as the Board may leave to its discretion, to make suggestions and to give advice to the Board upon other matters.

"It should in particular be invited to express its opinion upon every item in the first edition of the Code of Rules, which we hope to draw up in the course of the next twelve months, and, of course, upon any new rules that may be adopted thereafter. A very large number of the rules can be left to the absolute decision of the Council. The line should be drawn, for the present, at rules which, in my own opinion, have a vital bearing upon the Company's commercial success.

"All matters of that kind must, for the present, be settled by the absolute discretion of the Board, and the Staff Council have no power to do more than express an opinion on it, exactly as the House of Lords is debarred from interfering with any decision of the House of Commons which is certified by the Speaker to be a Money Bill.

"There are, .however, a multitude of questions, some of which are matters of acute concern to the Staff, which need not be thus withheld from absolute decision by the Staff Council.

"For example, the rule that Sick Pay is only given to those who consult a Dentist at regular intervals so as to safeguard their health from being unconsciously undermined by tooth trouble, is not a rule which can be called vital to the commercial safety of the Company.

Every Doctor and every Hospital Nurse, to whom I have ever mentioned it, agrees that it is a most valuable rule and ought to be enforced by law upon everybody, but it will never be my policy to enforce against the consent of those concerned regulations which I for my own part should like to see them adopt, unless those regulations seem to me to be of vital importance to our commercial safety.

"It is my own and the Board's business to be the most expert Members of the Staff upon the Company's commercial policy. In that regard we are paid to know better than anybody else, and it would be just as wrong that we should shirk our responsibility by giving up the casting vote on those questions as it would be wrong for a Doctor to give up his own opinion against his conviction and to adopt his patient's.

"But, in my belief, it is of the utmost importance to the healthy and, therefore, peaceful evolution of society that those who, in virtue of special skill on certain matters come to occupy positions of authority, should be scrupulously careful not to push the exercise of that authority beyond the matters which are strictly their own special business.

"It is quite true that good government is not a proper substitute for self-government and, therefore, the Staff ought to be made self-governing as fast and as completely as the actual facts of existing trade-conditions allow.

"So, if the Staff Council were to resolve by a majority that the Dental Certificate Rule should not be put into the new code, the Board would accept their decision, though I should deplore it and should never cease to try to get them to reverse it whenever I thought I saw a chance that they might be persuaded to do so."

"I hope that in one shape or another this Staff Council will turn out a real success. I shall be very disappointed if it does not come within a few years to play a very large part in the actual management of the Company.

"It seems to me at present that we ought gradually to evolve an organisation not unlike that of the United States, in which the Chairman will correspond to the President, the Staff Council to the House of Representatives (if that is the proper name of their Lower House) and the Board will double the parts of the Secretaries of State and the Senate, just as in this country the Heads of the Government Departments are also Members of one House of Parliament or the other.

"It would be a mistake for the House to imagine that it is necessarily wrong or unnatural to model the organisation of a little community of a few hundred people on that of a great nation. Nature follows precisely the same plan for a gooseberry-bush as she does for an oak, and gets her pound of gooseberries by just the same methods as she gets her tons of acorns.

"J.S.L."

NEED OF NURSING INTO REAL LIFE

520. The Council did not take root easily. In the early days, when I was still acting as President, I had often to supply an agenda so that there should be some sufficient occasion for meeting and, when I thought that the Council could now stand alone and I gave up the Presidency to somebody else, the whole thing died away and had to be started afresh. The colleague, who took it over from me, did not see the need to develop it into a customary habitual element in the life of the Partnership and for some time I did not realise what was happening.

In my own view there is all the difference between arranging some sort of special meeting to deal with some special problems and having a permanent organ to deal with all such problems as and when they arise.

To secure that state of affairs, the meetings must become a fixed custom, a settled habit. If at first there is a shortage of topics, then suitable topics must be provided specially. In fact the agenda may have to be created so as to give occasion for a meeting instead of the meeting being held because there is an agenda. For many years now our own Council has been steadily busy and very much alive.

If no such established organ exists, many things, that ought to be done in that way, will in fact be done quite otherwise. To bring a regular permanent organ into existence, it may be a help not only to take care that there is always something sufficient to meet about but that the meetings are good fun, interesting and pleasant. Pains should be taken to prevent their being dull and in its early days I think our own Council owed quite a lot to the provision of a pleasant meal with wine for those so disposed.

FOOD, DRINK AND EFFICIENCY

521. From time to time this was attacked as an improper luxury but against those attacks I always stood firm. The cost seemed to me a trifling return for the sacrifice of leisure and my own personal opinion is that a good many people are better tempered, broader minded, more imaginative and altogether more efficient as members of representative institutions if they have had a glass or two of wine.

As I have to keep on saying, the general development of the Partnership has been paralysed almost completely for several years by the war. Whether or not this is a great part of the reason, it is certainly a fact that as yet the Council does not play nearly so large a "part in the actual management" of the Partnership as in 1919 I hoped that it would "within a few years". Nevertheless it seems to me to show quite satisfactory promise.

On many occasions it has been extremely useful to the Management to be able to refer some matter to the decision of the Council and on many other occasions the advice of the Council has been valuable in things that were not thus completely handed over to them. They played, for example, a great part in the settlement of the pension-system.

I think that on the whole they have done less than I vaguely expected that they would in the way of making enquiries and suggestions in practical matters of the management of the business. But of course, the more the Management try to keep in close touch with the Managed and the more pains the Management take to consider as far as they possibly can the wishes of the Managed, the less occasion has any such body as the Council for asking questions and for intervening in one way and another.

But the fact, that a safety-valve may come only rarely into use, does not mean that the valve is not needed. Any genuine partnership must have ample machinery for discussion, enquiry and recommendation—in fact for freedom of speech. We are a tongue-tied people. Our safety-valves are terribly apt to stick and rust, so that steam, that ought to be blown off, is accumulated into a dangerous sense of grievance or at all events of breakdown of proper team-work.

FREEDOM OF SPEECH NEEDS FOSTERING

522. It is, therefore, very much a function of Management not only to provide ample means of freedom of speech but to get those means used. It is not enough to dig wells and keep them unchoked. You must also provide pumps and get those pumps used quite sufficiently. Don't wait for the Managed to utter. Question them and do it sufficiently often and searchingly. Some sort of a council and some sort of a newspaper will both be needed and so will some way of meeting the Rank and File of the Managed in freedom from the shyness and nervousness—or excessive irritability, a common result of nervousness—that is apt to hamper them in talking in the presence of intermediate authorities. This last need is, I suspect, in many cases the greatest of all and our own Committees for Communications between the Rank and File of the Partnership and the Principal Management were devised to meet it.

THE COUNCIL AT WORK: CHRISTMAS CLOSING IN 1935

523. To my mind the Council have shown on the whole an ample degree of hard-headedness. There is, I believe, always a tendency for self-government in industry to be either too lax—a thing that has repeatedly ruined experiments with the Self-Governing Workshop—or, on the other hand, excessively strict. I am not quite sure that the Council did not make lately a mistake of this latter kind. Christmas in 1946 fell on a Wednesday. When that happened in 1935, the Council were asked to decide whether the Partnership should close its shops on the Friday and Saturday.

In those days the business consisted almost entirely of John Lewis & Company and Peter Jones. The four provincial branches were only a small percentage of the total turnover and there was no provision trade at all. It was a remarkable innovation for such a matter to be decided by elected representatives of the whole of the workers but in face of the year's results it seemed clear that the Partners could afford to treat themselves, if they liked, to a couple of days of extra holiday and, that being so, it seemed plainly right that the Council should make the choice between leisure and money, between business and pleasure.

The Council decided to close and I heard that among the Rank and File there had been great anxiety that the thing should be decided in that way.

AND IN 1946

524. Now in 1946 the same question arose again. This time it was decided the other way. A subsequent angry correspondence in THE GAZETTE included the following letter:

"Sir,   "25.11.46.

"As an ex-Service Partner who some months ago returned to the Partnership I would like to voice a strong protest against the news contained in last week's GAZETTE regarding after-Christmas opening. I am sure also that I am voicing the opinion of other Partners who, like myself, have been in the Forces. I served in the Army for six years, four of those years being spent overseas. I have not had a Christmas at home for five years, nor a decent Christmas holiday for five years. Now that other ex-Service Partners and myself have our first chance of a real Christmas holiday at home we are greeted with the information that the store will be open on Friday the 27th and Saturday the 28th December. As a fairly old Partner I very much regret to state that I shall not be at work on Friday or Saturday.

"Yours, etc.,
"Ex-8TH ARMY."

Upon this I wrote to the Director of Selling a paper that was likewise gazetted. That paper included the following paragraphs:

"2. The notice, that the Council was going to deal with this matter, was gazetted on the 9th November. The notice made it perfectly clear that the Council would have a completely free hand. They might close every branch and give every Partner his ordinary pay. Or they might close some branches and open others and in that case give ordinary pay to those who had the extra holiday and double pay to those who had to be on duty. Or they might simply keep open for the convenience of customers and for the difference of about £13,000 to the Partnership Benefit that will be distributed next Spring.

"3. The Council meeting was expressly fixed for the 18th November so that after this notice Partners should have a clear week in which to communicate with their Councillors and another GAZETTE to which they could write before the Council met.

"4. 'Ex-8th Army' should have written his letter then and not waited until now and, if some accident prevented his writing to THE GAZETTE, he should at all events have communicated with the Councillor for his constituency if, as I gather, he is not himself a member of the Council.

"5. He does not seem to have taken the trouble to do any of those things and now he writes to THE GAZETTE a letter like this.

525. "6. The decision of the Council surprised me and made me rather uneasy. In 1935, when Christmas was likewise on a Wednesday and people were not so strained and hard-driven as now they are, the Council had the same discretion and they closed the whole business. I quite thought they would do the same this time and I thought they would probably be wise. I thought the prospect of the long holiday would help people to work better through the Christmas pressure.

"7. It is not easy for the members of a big team to realise that every penny, that they make, will go to themselves. If people were sensible enough for that, they would have been sensible enough to prevent this war, as they very easily could have done.

"8. But the Council had to take into account some important facts that did not exist in 1935. Through the war shop-keepers as a whole have behaved badly and the public are pretty sore about it. The Partners in the main have behaved very well indeed. That has been much appreciated by customers. The Partners have reaped some harvest already and they will reap a lot more in the future. The public has a pretty long memory. Many forget such things quickly but many do not.

"9. The Council had to reckon that, if the Partnership closed its shops when customers had been looking forward to shopping, there might be rather serious resentment that might undo some of the good of the courtesy and good humour that the Partnership as a whole has shown to its customers through these specially trying years.

"10. Furthermore, the Partnership has now a good few shops in which Saturday is the most important day of the week and it has a lot that sell provisions. To close either of these groups on the Saturday might have been specially serious from the standpoint of losing the goodwill of our customers.

"11. The Council had to take account of all these facts. And there was also the fact that no member of the Partnership had taken the trouble to send to THE GAZETTE in advance of the Council's meeting any such letter as 'Ex-8th Army' has sent now.

"12. The Council has discussed the matter at considerable length and twenty-two members spoke. At the end of the discussion the Council adopted the following:

"Resolution 83: That the following decision be taken with regard to the Christmas Closing—Excluding food shops and food departments, all of which will be open as usual on Friday 27th December and Saturday 28th December, shops which normally close on Saturday afternoon will work as usual on Friday 27th December and Saturday 28th December: shops that have an early-closing day mid-week will close on Friday 27th December and open on Saturday 28th December.

"13. Eighty-four members voted upon this Resolution. Sixty-five were in favour and only nineteen were against. That is a majority of more than three-quarters and it is a well settled principle of British Law that in Company matters a three-quarters majority is to be reckoned decisive for most purposes.

"14. I am sorry that it did not occur to the Council to include in their Resolution a recommendation that special leave should be given in as many cases as possible and that there should be no loss of pay without the knowledge and consent of a special committee whom the Council would appoint for that purpose. But it is easy to be wise after the event. I never thought of this until I read this letter in THE GAZETTE and, if I had been one of those members of the Council, perhaps I should not have thought of it any sooner, though, when you come to think of it, it is pretty obvious.

"15. My purpose in writing to you now is to ask that you will take extreme care to hear of any case in which any Partner is absent on either of these days without previous leave or an explanation that is considered acceptable. Anyone, who is thus absent, is to be dropped from the Partnership as soon as possible and the Council must be asked to say whether he is to be admitted to Partnership Benefit next Spring.

"16. On the average income of the Partnership the Benefit seems likely to be somewhere about fifteen pounds. The Council would be perfectly free to allow Benefit in some of those cases and to withhold it in others but democracy is bound to be unworkable if people are going to decide for themselves how far they will comply with the decisions of their own elected representatives.

"17. At a time, when war was spoiling the Partnership's unbroken and very valuable record for invariable punctuality in the payment of its dividends, it nevertheless found eighty-eight thousand pounds for subsidy for members on Service and at the suggestion of the Board the Council voted unanimously that after the war the Partnership should deliberately lose year after year up to £1,000 in order to enable a decent living to be made by men or women, not necessarily already members of the Partnership, who had lost some of their earning-power by war-injuries.

"18. Actions speak louder than words and, if all this does not convince 'Ex-8th Army' that the Partnership sympathises with him, then he must be so stupid that to try to reason with him would be a waste of time.

"19. But democracy cannot succeed if those, who rightly believe that they will have sympathy, are going to defy the authority of their own elected representatives.

"20. I hope that 'Ex-8th Army' will apply for leave. If he does, I cannot think that he will fail to get it but that is not a matter for me. If he thinks he is being refused improperly, let him ask the help of the Partners' Counsellor. If the Partners' Counsellor thinks the case ought to come to me, I shall deal with it. If he does not, then 'Ex-8th Army' will have to choose between complying with the constitutional decision of the Partnership or leaving it.

"J.S.L."

526. Later still THE GAZETTE published the following letters, one anonymous and the other not, with my own attached comments:

"CHRISTMAS CLOSING

"9.12.46.

"To the Editor of THE GAZETTE,
"Sir,
"I write with a sense of urgency on a subject about which the Chairman has confessed to feeling uneasy. I feel certain that he would feel even more uneasy if he knew the full extent to which disappointment is felt at the decision of the Central Council to remain open on the two days after Christmas. I can testify as a result of recent visits to several Partnership Houses that there is a widespread discontent on this point.

"The method by which 'democracy' operated in arriving at the decision is best exemplified by the case of Peter Jones. Two representatives of that House actually proposed and seconded the resolution to open in direct opposition to the view of their constituents, the majority of whom certainly desired to close. The amazing reply given by these members when tackled by their constituents afterwards was that 'they were not elected to the Central Council to put the view of their House but purely for their personal qualities and to use their own individual judgment'. Frankly, I cannot escape the conclusion that the Central Council contains a majority of sycophants who, in their eagerness to echo the Chairman's supposed wishes, have miserably failed to interpret the views of the Partnership. They appear to have based their sycophantic voting on the Chairman's note mentioning the £13,000 cost of closing. As a member of John Barnes was heard to say after the meeting, 'We all knew the Chairman wanted us to open'. They must have been dismayed to read the Chairman's notes in subsequent issues of THE GAZETTE!

"Other members of the Central Council were heard to say after the meeting that, of course, they had voted for the opening but would not be in themselves!

"So much for your democracy, Partnership—it's up to you.

"Meanwhile may we appeal to the Chairman to make some ruling on the lines of his own views which will relieve the feeling of discontent that has been caused by this unfortunate episode?

"I, also, could sign myself 'Ex-something or other' but will be content to sign what I believe I am, in this matter,

"Yours, etc.,
"VOX POPULI.

"*CHAIRMAN'S COMMENT*:
527. "This is obviously just silly claptrap. Nobody, who knows the members of the Council, can seriously pretend that a majority of them are sycophants. If it is true that a member of John Barnes was heard to say after the meeting 'We all knew the Chairman wanted us to open', what earthly reason had he for saying so? Self-government is bound to have teething troubles but they will not be made any easier if, whenever people disagree about what ought to be done, they are going to start calling each other sycophants instead of giving each other credit for wanting to do what will be really best. For my own part I simply do not know how much there really is in the argument that to close for those two days would be too likely to annoy too many customers too seriously. That is, I gather, the main reason why the Council decided to open this time, though in 1935, when they had to decide, the same question, they decided to close.

"Anyhow the Partners will gain about £13,000 by keeping open and they will be doing the safer thing from the standpoint of their future business interests. They will all be getting a week's paid holiday in the Spring and, until we started that years ago, nobody dreamed of such a thing.

"In these days we are all tired and strained and for that very reason we ought to be specially careful to keep our tempers.

"J.S.L."

"A CRAWLING OF SYCOPHANTS"

528.   Later still one of the two representatives upon the Central Council of the Branch Council of Peter Jones, who had been thus criticised by "Vox Populi", replied in a letter of which the opening, fifth and last paragraphs were as follows:

"Sir,   "22.12.46.

"The Chairman, in labelling the letter from 'Vox Populi' silly claptrap, let him off very lightly: I shall not do so . . . . . .

"Let 'Vox Populi' refer to THE GAZETTE of the 20th July, p. 305, par. 29 and he will find that 29 sycophants out of 61 voted for this proposal. Let him refer to Resolution 44 in the same issue of THE GAZETTE, and he will see that 31 out of a total of 63 sycophants voted against this. Then let him turn to Resolution 64 in THE GAZETTE of the 12th October, and he will be astounded to find that the whole crawling of sycophants unanimously voted for this proposal. . . . .

"This statement of 'Vox Populi' is nothing but a malicious slander: but perhaps his biggest mistake of all was to dare to imagine that he was what he signed himself. 'Vox et praeterea nihil' would have been more appropriate.

"Yours, etc.,
"EDMOND PECK."

Upon the broad question of expediency I wrote as follows on the 21st December 1946, to the Financial Adviser:

"As you have seen, I have left the Council free to decide whether we should open or close. Rightly or wrongly I should have voted with the minority. I gravely doubt the wisdom of trying people's tempers to the extent of letting some other big shops be shut while we are opening. It is all very well for the big guns, who necessarily get the lion's share of the satisfaction of good figures. The loss of a day or two's holiday is the same to everybody and indeed it is actually more severe on those whose lives are much less pleasant. But their individual share of the proceeds of renouncing that holiday is by no means the same. It is very far smaller. Nevertheless, I took the risk that the Council would go wrong and I have stood by what they have done. I am by no means sure that they were wrong. My own judgment is very far from infallible and, if my detached position has some important advantages for seeing the wood, it also has some important disadvantages for knowing what is really happening among the trees."

I am printing this correspondence here as a useful indication of the extent to which the Partnership's general system for the fostering of public opinion and of freedom of speech gives rise to sustained strenuous discussion. This correspondence began with a letter dated the 25th November 1946 and closed with one dated the 22nd

December. Between those dates it occupied in each week a substantial part of THE GAZETTE's space.

MANAGERS AND MANAGED IN JOINT REPRESENTATIVE BODIES

529.   A problem, that is still very much an open question for our own partnership and in respect of which individual partnerships may differ widely, is that of securing in such a Council a balance acceptable to general public opinion between the representatives of the Managers and those of the Managed.

This must be, I think, an extremely important problem in the future of this particular partnership and of the Self-Governing Workshop in general. There is bound to be a certain conflict of interest between the Managers and the Managed. It does not matter how the Managers are chosen. If they are a good choice at all, they must necessarily have more than average imagination and energy. They must necessarily get more various and more intense fun out of their work than do as a general rule the Managed. Their incomes are bound to be larger and that alone must affect substantially their inclination to work rather than take a holiday.

When there arises some question of this kind, upon which feeling is strong, how is it to be decided? There is no means of splitting the difference. It is a question either of business before pleasure or else of pleasure before business.

BUSINESS OR PLEASURE?

530.   If the Management have in fact a majority in the Central Council, then business will come first. But, if the Managed have in fact a majority, then they will tend to put pleasure first. By persuasive speeches and by energetic canvassing and perhaps by something very near to intimidation the Managers may get a sufficient number of the Managed to vote with them. But, all the same, the conflict will be there. Experience has shown again and again that, if the Rank-and-File are asked to play in the conduct of a Self-Governing Workshop a part that is too difficult for them, the result is ruin.

531.   Of course you get over the difficulty to some extent by giving the self-governing workshop, the partnership, a written constitution and then saying to everyone "This is our deed of partnership. If you do not like it, do not become a partner in this business. If you have come into it without realising that this deed of partnership would work in this way, find for yourself some other business in which to work. Go out of this one. We shall wish you luck, but we cannot keep on altering our written constitution, our deed of partnership, to suit everybody who wants it to be altered. As fast as we pleased one, we should displease somebody who was already satisfied."

But, although this does in a sense meet the difficulty in any particular case, it does not solve the fundamental problem. It does not give any means of being sure that in any particular partnership the balance will be held properly between the Managers and the Managed. The greediest and harshest of employers can say to the worker: "This is the way I run my business. If you do not like it, get out. You will find that I shall be able to fill your place well enough to keep my business going."

TO BE HEALTHY THE SELF-GOVERNING WORKSHOP MUST BE ROOTED IN THE GOOD OF ITS CUSTOMERS

532.   Certainly the self-governing workshop might be so conducted that Managers had too much personal power. The root of the problem, the true centre of gravity of any such enterprise, is in the interest neither of the Managers, nor of the Managed. It is in the interest of the general community. They ought to be given in every way the best service that will leave a good enough life to those who render it.

The whole team, managers and managed alike, should be all of first-rate capacity for that particular work and the work should be done in the best way that will give them a good enough life, sufficient income including pension, sufficient leisure including sufficient early retirement, sufficient sense of security and all the rest of it.

INTUITION

But all this is only words. How are you to judge what is the real meaning of these words when in any particular case you get down to brass tacks and try to make up your mind what you are actually going to do? You get back to mere intuition and in each particular case there will arise the definite question: "Is the constitution of this particular partnership really good? Does it hold well enough the balance between the needs and wishes of the sort of people whom it ought to get for its Managers and the needs and wishes of the sort of people who ought to be the clients of those Managers—the Managed whom the Managers are there to serve?"

IN A MONEY-SOCIETY DEMOCRATISATION WILL DEPEND UPON THE POWER OF THE PURSE

533.   From time to time anonymous writers to THE GAZETTE, mostly of the rather shallow-witted, Johnny-head-in-air type, have found fault with the Council as insufficiently self-assertive and generally active. On such occasions I have commonly answered that the Council would never come fully to life until it had to deal in a really important way with money.

When the Council had to decide whether at this particular Christmas-time to put business before pleasure, in this particular case the Council actually was dealing with money, an amount of £13,000. It decided that in present circumstances the Partners could not afford to throw that amount away. Immediately there were symptoms of rather serious trouble with the electorate.

LIMITATIONS OF THE MANAGED

534. Our own Partnership has now almost exactly twelve thousand members. Many of them are young and inexperienced. Many of them have had little education. Many of them would not be very wise, however much education they had had. For the most part they are honourable people, miracles of intelligence and energy compared to any of the more backward races of the world. But they are no more capable of grasping the problems of a big business and of managing it in the real sense of the word than most of us, no matter how long and carefully we were trained, would be capable of holding our own in the professional boxing-ring.

Among the clients of a great lawyer or the patients of a great doctor there may be some few with just the same natural ability for the Law or for Medicine but very, very few of us, had we taken to the Law or to Medicine, would have reached that level of competence or anything like it.

All the same, the great lawyer or the great doctor exists to serve us and, though his social prestige may be far higher than ours and his income likewise far higher than ours, it is nevertheless true that he is our employee and we are his employers.

535. The same state of affairs exists in a partnership. The Managers may have similar advantages of social prestige and of income but they exist to serve the Managed. They hold their position not by a property-right but by service. In that sense they are employees of the community to which they belong. Within the constitution of the particular partnership their orders have to be obeyed.

But our lawyer or our doctor cannot serve us unless we obey his orders. If we refuse to follow his advice, we are likely to lose our law-case or our health. It is conceivable the advice may be bad. However great the great man, he will be human and therefore fallible. But that is a risk we have got to take. We may decide to follow somebody else's advice but we have got to follow somebody's. We ourselves are out of our depth. In fact we, in matters of health or of law those of us, who are not physicians or lawyers, must submit to be managed.

THE CONSTITUTION MUST BE FIRM ENOUGH

536. Where is this to stop? In the sudden or gradual drafting of the constitution of any particular partnership how are you to find the right line between business and pleasure? And how are you to find the right line between the interests of one section and the interests of any other? What can the Partnership reasonably and properly ask of its van-drivers

or of its ledger-clerks or of its principal managers or of any other of its various sets of specialists? And how far should the Rank-and-File decide by and for themselves whether they will go to work on two particular days at Christmas time or whether they will treat themselves to a bit of extra holiday?

We believe that, if a partnership is to have any real chance of permanent prosperity, it must be very strict indeed about upholding its constitution. If you once start paltering with the Law, the end will be disaster for everybody. Alter the Constitution by all means if it seems to you to need altering, but whatever it is at any particular time, uphold it. Alter it, if you feel that you really should, but be very, very careful how you start on that sort of thing.

BEWARE OF BEGINNINGS OF REACTION

537.   Before you make any rule, think well. Once you have made a rule, try your hardest to make do with it. Be very, very careful how you yield to the temptation to chop and change. But above all, keep every rule quite firmly, so long as it has not been properly cancelled or amended. Too much changing of your rules may perhaps ruin you. Too little enforcement certainly will.

People differ so much in temperament, one from another, and the same person varies so much in different moods that it must generally be wiser to invite apparently desirable newcomers or even those, who are already inside your team, to find elsewhere a partnership that will suit them better than it will be to start chopping and changing the constitution that you have already. But you quite certainly cannot afford to be insufficiently vigilant and discerning in perceiving offences against your current law, whatever it is, or insufficiently firm with yourselves and with each other in upholding the law. Alter it, if you must, but alter it by proper constitutional process. Do not let it simply rust and rot away either from mere carelessness or from lack of moral courage or from other weakness. The current law of our country has made it necessary that certain portions of this partnership's constitution shall be fixed by irrevocable Settlements in Trust but outside that line everything has been left changeable.

NO DEAD HAND

538.   No man, whatever his wisdom in relation to any present state of affairs, can foresee the future and in my view no partnership, that is intended to last for very long, should be left under what is sometimes called the dead hand.

In the constitution of this particular partnership the present law of taxation in our country has made it necessary that certain things shall be irrevocably settled in trust. Apart from any question of taxation, there might have been other sufficient reason why that should be done. However that may be, it has been done but with whole-hearted care to leave the Partnership's future members the utmost possible freedom to alter the Constitution—and, if necessary, to alter it very quickly—to any extent that some day might seem to them to be necessary.

BUT SUFFICIENT STABILITY

539.   However, I hope they will think very carefully before they start any chopping and changing at all and that, if they feel they must do some, they will constantly try their utmost to keep it as infrequent and as small as ever they can. Because of the great hindrances, that the Partnership's development has encountered, the Council is still very immature. But it has done a good deal in various experiments, that the Partnership has tried and that have come to an end, and I hope that, as experience gives rise to new developments, the Partners will find the Council takes over more and more of those matters that in themselves are comparatively small but that are very highly important to individual Partners.

RECENT LONG STEPS TOWARDS DEMOCRACY

540.   In bigger things there have been lately two very great developments of the Council's powers. The fact, that the Partnership has now got to that length, is indeed a great part of the reason why it is now at last time for this book to be written.

541.   One of these developments is the very recent decision that the Council should choose each year three Trustees of the Constitution and recommend five Partners for election to the Central Board. This comes within the field of the second Settlement, of which the technical problems are still being studied, but this is intended and will, it is believed at present, be found practicable. Obviously such technicalities do not affect the motive, that is to say the aims, of the Partnership. They are merely a particular way of achieving these aims.

Another development at the same level of importance is the decision that followed quickly upon this last, that consultation with the Council should be necessary on certain financial decisions of more that a certain gravity in relation to the general scale of the Partnership's affairs.

These arrangements will bring the Council into consultation on certain matters of the very highest business importance, decisions that might either mean that the Partnership was taking a big business-risk or that, on the other hand, it was cutting its business down in a way that would oblige it to reduce substantially the size of its own team. As can be seen from the terms of the Settlement in Trust of 1929, that is the first appendix to this book, exclusions from Partnership Benefit have from the beginning required the consent of the Council. The same is true of the pension system, of which the rules are likewise in this book.

DEMOCRATISATION OF MINOR ADMINISTRATION

542. My broad hope has been and is still that, as the years pass, the Council will take over from the Management a very great deal of matters of discipline. Years ago the Council took over almost the whole of the work of deciding what financial help should be given to Partners who had a long illness or some serious private loss or who needed for any other reason a special gift or loan.

In the same way, when we were trying to make a success of substituting small penalties for the possibility of dismissal as a factor in efficiency, the Council had absolute power to make good any small penalty that anyone would otherwise have had to pay if he wished to stay in the Partnership.

But I have always hoped that some day we should get still further than this and that in the distribution of bonuses and increases of pay and minor promotions the Council might come either to share or to do the whole job.

If a community like this partnership has been educated into the habit of reading week after week a newspaper, that deals quite frankly with those things in business life about which people care really strongly, it is perfectly possible to make important and far-reaching experiments and to modify them and to drop them without too much ill effect on general contentment and efficiency.

DEVELOPMENT OF THE CONSTITUTION OF THE COUNCIL—PROSPECTIVE DEMOCRATISATION OF POWERS RESERVED AS YET TO THE CHAIR OF THE CENTRAL BOARD

543. The arrangement, that is here contemplated, might develop into something that would be pretty highly constitutional. The Chairman's powers, though in the last resort they would be concentrated, would necessarily be devolved to a very substantial extent upon various individuals and groups. In the last resort, however, it would always be possible for the Chairman to take back into his own hands whatever discretion he had given to some individual or to some group and to decide the thing according to his own personal judgment, a judgment of which the exercise will be always open to public criticism through the obligation of THE GAZETTE to publish any anonymous communications that are relevant to the affairs of the Partnership and that in the House of Commons would be reckoned "parliamentary".

544. From the beginning the Partnership has tried to secure that the constituencies were so arranged as to give adequate representation, that is to say an adequate voice, to every section of the whole of our community. In other words constituencies have been vocational. The question of the number of seats was more difficult. At one time we tried to base it upon pay, so that, for example, a group of Partners, who formed its whole team of workers of a certain kind and whose total yearly pay-sheet was, say, £30,000 would have about as many seats as another group who likewise formed the whole of the Partnership's team of workers of another kind and whose total pay-sheet was about the same, though the number of persons, among whom that pay-sheet was divided, might be much larger or much smaller than in the case of the first group.

The idea was, of course, that pay-rates could be used advantageously to secure that the Council was well composed from the standpoint of the Partnership as a whole. From time to time there have been some symptoms of jealousy on the side of the Rank and File. My own impression is that it has been felt by few and that those, who have shown it and who have seemed to have some inclination to foster it in others, have been moved in some cases by vague but real public spirit, a vague notion of being properly democratic, but in some cases perhaps by a mere spirit of mischief, mere impishness, and in some cases by real malice, jealousy and a destructive impulse of a definitely poisonous kind. They have been in my opinion few, but they have not been wholly absent.

545. The same spirit has been shown persistently, though only infrequently, in the anonymous letters to THE GAZETTE. THE GAZETTE began thirty years ago and the Council twenty-nine. In all that time there has never been any real trouble at all, any such discord as might end in the loss of valuable members or be otherwise injurious to the common interest. But it must be remembered that for a pretty long run of early years the Partnership was quite small and in several of those years Benefit flowed at a quite high rate. In a good many years it increased a full year's earnings by upwards of two months' pay.

This combination of a small sized community with high immediate Benefit was of course favourable to the development of general understanding, good will and good temper. It may be, perhaps, a quite serious trouble of genuine partnerships that people, who are more or less angrily discontented or addicted to spiteful mischief-making, will not resign, as, if they are so ill-pleased, they might be expected to do, but will continue and, while accepting on the one hand whatever benefits may make them feel that they had better stay where they are, will, on the other hand, make mischief in various ways.

PRIVILEGE MUST BE SAFEGUARDED BUT THE PERSISTENTLY DISCONTENTED MAKE BAD PARTNERS

546.   It is plainly extremely important to do nothing that any reasonable person can possibly regard as a breach of the privilege that must plainly be attached to utterances in representative institutions, such as our own Committees for Communications and Councils, or to the right of anonymous publications through THE GAZETTE.

But, so far as they can be identified otherwise, I should for my part favour strongly the elimination of people who appeared to be persistently and seriously dissatisfied. No one partnership can possibly please everybody. The better it suits some, the worse must it suit others. People, who are persistently and gravely dissatisfied, will neither be happy themselves nor allow others to he as happy as they would be if the discontented were to resign and to transfer themselves to some other community and I think they should be eliminated.

But in this respect it is necessary to be very careful to distinguish between well-meant criticism, however frequent, outspoken, unconventional and occasionally mistaken, and expressions of such discontent as cannot be removed without unfairness to other members of the Partnership or a departure from its real policy.

REAL FREEDOM OF SPEECH CAN BE ACHIEVED

547.   Some years ago one of the more energetic of our "tribunes of the people" remarked in the Council that some newcomers to the Partnership thought that, if they criticised the Management, they might lose their engagements. "We," said the speaker, "know very well that that is not true. If it were, I should have been gone long ago"—a remark that was greeted with much friendly laughter, as was the exhibition on the stage during one of the Partnership's own revues (of which some account will be given shortly) of a newspaper placard—"Daniels defies Chairman" succeeded in due course by another—"Chairman defies Daniels". Mr. Daniels, a member of the Rank and File, was another of the more energetic of our Tribunes.

The real point here is that to me, it seems possible that in future years, when the Partnership is much bigger and the activities of the Council may be much wider and of a kind to be felt more poignantly, as they were in this recent matter of deciding against a long holiday at Christmastime, there may be at times some more or less serious trouble over the question of the Council's composition.

The settlement of the constituencies for the next Council-election is now to be a function of the three Trustees of the Constitution, whom each newly-elected Council is to choose for that new Council year.

THE COUNCIL APPOINTING ITS OWN OFFICIALS

548. I have a strong hope that this will work well but the composition of the Council and the development of its functions are deep water and, though the Council is nearly thirty years old, it is in fact still very immature and there may be some tough problems and some surprising developments still to come.

Another recent step towards maturity has been the abandonment of the old arrangement that the officials of the Central and of the Branch Councils (the President and the Clerk) and the Chairmen and Secretaries of certain Committees, notably the Committee for Claims, were all appointed by the Chairman of the Central Board. In future the Presidents and Chairmen are all to be appointed by the Councils or the Committees or by the Presidents of the Central Council or Branch Councils.

I suspect that my own choices have been very much those that the Council would have made and I believe that the initiative in these developments has been almost wholly my own rather than from the side of the Council or from the electorate, the Partnership as a whole.

But these developments seem to be quite clearly required by the principle, that the Partnership professes, of steadily democratising as completely as possible all those of its affairs in which that seems safe enough from the standpoint of the business-efficiency upon which depends the existence of the whole thing.

If a partnership is organised on the main lines, that are contemplated here, then broadly speaking its development, as it matures, should be towards enlargement of the powers and responsibilities of its Council and diminution of those of its Board and of that Board's Chairman. As matters stand at present in our own partnership, the scope for such a transference seems to me to be almost entirely in the functions of the Chairmanship and little, if at all, in those of the Board. But that is as may be.

One of the most successful developments of our own Councils has been the function that they normally discharge through standing Committees for Claims.

SUCCESS OF THE CLAIMS IDEA

549. Now and again Managers of other businesses having seen THE GAZETTE. or heard otherwise something of the Partnership have come to look into our methods with a view to considering whether they would

make some use of those ideas. They have commonly thought well of this particular notion. We ourselves think that it has been a great success.

The essence of the idea is that elected representatives of all workers in a business should control that giving of help in special need that the most ruthlessly selfish of managements must undertake to some extent and that is commonly carried to a quite considerable length. However the thing is done, there ought obviously to be an effort to achieve consistency. But cases vary so widely that mere judgment of what is right and proper, mere intuition, must play a very great part. Wherever that is true, favouritism is apt to be suspected and, moreover, it is much easier for the unscrupulous to impose upon the heads of affairs in any considerable organisation than it is to impose upon a fairly representative body of their own fellow-workers.

550.   Furthermore, such a committee is in some cases much better able to judge of the reality and seriousness of some particular need and they may have information that will enable them to avoid causing embarrassment or even pain by such enquiries as might have to be made if the machinery for such grants were of a different kind.

In the early days, when we had no idea what total volume of claims would arise or what would be their nature, I presided over this Committee and, until precedents began to accumulate, gave a strong lead wherever that seemed to be desired. After some years my place was taken by another of the Partnership's principal leaders, Mr. (now Sir Metford) Watkins.

When he had held that chairmanship for a good while, he remarked to me that he had found the work extremely satisfactory and would be sorry to give it up. Eventually the development of his other functions made that necessary and his successor seemed in course of time to feel much the same.

In dealing with all ordinary kinds of trouble and special need the efficiency of these committees has always seemed to me quite first-class. They meet weekly for quite a long time and there is, I believe, keen competition to serve on them. The Central Committee for Claims at all events has a whole-time secretary with now a whole-time assistant. Much of their work is visiting chiefly, of course, in illness and this, I understand, is very much appreciated.

DANGERS OF THE PORK-BARREL

551.   The giving of help in exceptional trouble, the administration, in effect, of a free insurance, is, of course, essentially different from providing money for social entertainments and other purposes of pleasure.

In work of that kind elected representatives are, I think, very much more inclined to go wrong. I think they are apt to be too submissive to what politicians call pressure-groups and to be rather unimaginative in failing to distinguish between deprivation that is an important misfortune—as, for example, to some people good music may be not merely a pleasure but in a real sense a need—and such gratification as is not in nearly the same sense a real need.

A good many people are apt to feel that, if money is going to be spent upon anyone, it had better be spent upon themselves. The real gratification may be in the mere sense of acquisition, of self-assertion and achievement. The actual provision itself, when it has been obtained, may be used little or misused deplorably.

552. My own personal impression is that such representative institutions, as we are here considering, can very safely be left virtually unwatched to use ample funds for the relief of hardship and misfortune. When, however, it comes to spending money upon pleasure, it is very highly desirable to foster great freedom of speech and to give very careful attention to suggestions from every quarter but there is far more need of some sort of watch and criticism and even of some measure of control.

My own feeling at present is that the Council should have ample funds from which to finance dances, concerts and indeed social activities of every sort and kind that the Chairman or some other competent authority does not reasonably hold to be too dangerous to the Partnership's business-interests. But such expenditure should be limited to things that will leave no material residue at the end of the Council-year.

553. If the Management provide a billiard-room or a tennis-club, let the Council by all means give, if they see fit, prizes for billiard- or tennis-tournaments or pay for expert coaching or do anything else to foster those recreations. But in theory two-thirds of the Council are in office for no more than one year and at present I feel that the decision, whether the Partnership should acquire material assets that will not be consumed within the year, must remain with the Management.

NO LOBBYING FOR SELFISH ENDS

554. Furthermore, I feel very strongly that the success of partnerships of this type may depend upon their concentrating upon a single post those responsibilities that expose their holders to log-rolling and to temptation to play the patron—always excepting as aforesaid relief of hardship and assistance in exceptional misfortune.

I think it might be very unhealthy if a Partner's chance of getting an important promotion or a large increase of pay depended upon the fact that he could get some particular member of a controlling board to espouse his cause and that member were then to say to some other member: "I will vote to-day for So and So, for whom you want to get this or that, if you will vote to-morrow for somebody else for whom I want to get something."

I do not see how that kind of thing could possibly be avoided, if decisions affecting what Americans call "the pork barrel", the gain or loss, the advantage or disadvantage, pleasure or displeasure of particular individuals or groups, depended upon group-voting, especially if it need not be unanimous. The stronger a member's conviction of the merits of a proposal, for which he desired to secure a majority, the clearer his duty not to be careless or perverse or narrow-minded in the way of failing to strain his own conscience, as far as without real impropriety he could, in the direction of making some concession whereby his own objective would be secured.

In just the same way it seems to me there may be danger if it is possible for some greedy or mistakenly fanatical minority to form a clique in the Council, with perhaps such results as in America the Prohibitionists to the immense injury of their country achieved in Congress.

You would then have the leaders of the cliques bargaining in just the same way: "Vote with us to-day for a billiard-room and we will vote with you to-morrow for a tennis-court."

PREVENTION OF INTRIGUE

555. I do not pretend to see nearly to the end of problems of this sort. In such matters the development of the Partnership will perhaps take within my own time or at all events thereafter a line very different from that which I am now contemplating. But at present my own feeling is that things specially apt to give rise to "political" activities by individuals or groups "on the make" and working with the energy of those who have an axe to grind, should not depend upon group-voting and especially not upon majority-voting by Councils or Boards or any groups. A group can be split. Its existence can give rise to undesirable bargaining. For things of that sort responsibility should, I think, be concentrated upon a single post. One person cannot make bargains with himself. He cannot agree to something, that he feels to be wrong, but to be comparatively unimportant, because such agreement is the only way to get something else that he feels to be right and to be more important.

PERFECTION IMPOSSIBLE

556. In group-authority that kind of thing is bound to happen. To such a concentration of responsibility and power, as is here contemplated, there are plainly substantial objections.

But human ability is so limited and human nature is so full of flaws that in such matters as those you cannot devise arrangements that will not be open to objection—and to grave objection.

The choice is not between good on the one hand and evil on the other. It is between different combinations of good with evil.

The work of the Central Council and of the Branch Councils gives rise, of course, to a variety of standing and special committees but only the Committees for Claims seemed so unusual in their nature and so important as to need mention here.

The Committees for Communications between the Rank and File and the Principal Management have been described in Part I, in paragraphs 70 to 77. They are independent of the Central Council and have no executive functions.

CHAPTER 33

THE BOARDS OF DIRECTORS,
ESPECIALLY THE CENTRAL BOARD

557. FOR better or worse, the business of the Partnership has been organised as a group of companies under what is commonly called Company Law.

A question arose whether there should be a single very large company or an association of several separate companies. The latter course was taken as on the whole the more likely to prove convenient.

Every such company must have a Board of Directors and it is obviously not in the power of the Partnership to relieve any holder of any of its Directorships of any of the part that the Law requires that Directors shall play in the conduct of the business of their company but that minimum part can, in fact, be played in a very small amount of time.

Broadly speaking, the Partnership does not ask more of its Directors as such and broadly speaking it reserves its Directorships for whole-time members of its own organisation.

DIRECTION MADE EASY

558. The Partnership's policy of never accepting short-term loans and of never failing to take all discounts, that are sufficiently attractive, for premature payment and of making all other payments absolutely punctually automatically relieves its Directors of one of the principal anxieties of those who undertake to hold such positions.

Their responsibilities are further lightened by the Partnership's constant strict adherence to a policy of never being knowingly undersold and also by its policy of carrying publicity in its accounts and reports to the very greatest length that seems just sufficiently safe from the standpoint of the need that in competitive business your business-secrets (sources of supply, rates of profit and some few other matters) must not be disclosed to your competitors.

PART-TIME POSTS OTHER THAN DIRECTORSHIPS

559. But, though these things have made it easy for the Partnership to entrust Directorships to any of its members, there is a real difficulty in the fact that part-time Directors may be extremely valuable as sources of information. Their continuous contact with other parts of the business-world may be very valuable to each of their several companies and, so long as those companies are genuinely not in competition actual or potential,

such a spreading of information and ideas is obviously wholly desirable both for them and for the general community.

The Partnership has intended to overcome this difficulty by creating, as it has now begun to do, a number of part-time posts for certain work that can be done quite satisfactorily in that way.

Companies on a large scale tend to give rise to committees, of which the members need not be Directors of the company. Membership of such a committee, especially its chairmanship or deputy chairmanship, may be posts of as high or higher prestige than an ordinary Directorship and, whereas a company is not free to pay its Directors as such as much as it thinks fit without disclosing those arrangements to its competitors and others, there is no such limitation upon posts that are not Directorships.

RESERVATION OF DIRECTORSHIPS FOR PARTNERS

560. In the vast flock of Company Directors there is a sprinkling of black sheep. Their misbehaviour tends to be news for sensational journalism. The honesty and efficiency of all the others is not similarly advertised to newspaper-readers. In consequence the words "Company Director" and even the title "Director of such and such a company", unless the prestige of that particular company is very high, tend to be less and less desired for merely social reasons.

But in the little world of a particular business its own workers, its suppliers, its customers and its business-connections generally, the holding of a Directorship gives some real prestige.

An invitation to join a Board is to that extent a real compliment and desired as such and there may be corresponding advantage in reserving most, if not all, of the Partnership's Directorships for its own whole-time members.

AVOIDANCE OF INTERLOCKING DIRECTORSHIPS

561. Partly with a view to sharing the Directorships as widely as possible from the standpoint of their having these attractions and partly because there seems to be a tendency to dislike of "multiple Directorships" though there might be no such dislike of seeing all of those separate enterprises grouped in a single company and therefore under a single set of Directors, the Partnership aims as far as it can at avoiding what are called interlocking Directorships. In cases in which there seem to be sufficient grounds of practical convenience it asks some particular Partner to hold Directorships of more than one of its companies. But it seeks to avoid this as much as possible.

For that avoidance there is another reason that may perhaps be hardly more than theoretical. If a business is to be organised in separate companies at all, there should be of course care to get from that state of affairs as much advantage as may be possible. Such advantage must obviously arise from the fact that certain sections of the enterprise are in fact separate companies. If the advantage of that separateness is to be secured fully, it seems desirable that the Board of Directors of each of those companies shall not hold avoidably Directorships of any other of the Partnership's companies between which and the first company there may be from time to time some inter-company transactions.

THE CHAIR OF THE MORE IMPORTANT BOARDS

562.   Up to now it has been thought desirable from the standpoint of the investing public that I should hold the Chairmanship not only of the Central Board but in all of those of the Partnership's companies in which the investing public are interested to a substantial extent. I have regretted that the Partnership's technical advisers felt that they must take this view. I should have preferred to set personally an example of the Partnership's aiming at complete separateness in the manning of the Boards of its several companies so long as it has more than one.

The essential functions of the Deputy Chairman are rather like those of the Vice President of the United States. When the post is not vacant, its occupant is available to act for the Chairman in his absence. The Deputy Chairmanship might be coupled with any other post in the Partnership. At present it is not because its holder is my own wife.

In the course of her career in the Partnership Mrs. Lewis has been at various times Editor of THE GAZETTE, Goodwill Director, Head of the Department of Staff Advice (this has now developed into the Partners' Counsellorship), Chairman of the Committee for Administration (a long tenure at a time when this committee was in chief charge of the execution of policy that was the field of another that met under my own chairmanship) and very lately Chairman of the Committee for Education from the time when the Partnership began the experiment described at the end of Part I.

Up to now she has always followed my own example of renouncing Director's fees and other remuneration, the cumulative total of which renunciations, when at the end of a considerable term of years it dawned upon her, produced an emotional reaction not easily distinguishable from pain and grief.

DIRECTORS' FEES

563.   Up to now few, if any, of the members of the Partnership have drawn remuneration as Directors. In cases where the Articles of Association of a Company provide certain Directors' fees, Partners holding any of those Directorships have signed each year a letter of renunciation of those fees. This has been because, so far as my wife and I were concerned, we were

content with what we had already and preferred to make the Partnership a present of any work that we did for it, just as people do in many public positions and the other Directors all drew incomes from the Partnership for whole-time services in another capacity and it was not thought desirable that the holding of a Directorship should increase an income that was being drawn already for whole-time service.

There is, however, nothing to prevent the drawing of Directors' fees and nothing to prevent the Partnership from availing itself of the help of part-time Directors whose work for it might be confined to the functions of Directors in the very narrowest sense of that word.

THE CENTRAL BOARD

564. Experience will show whether the advantages of part-time Directorships can be secured sufficiently by other means.

As matters stand at present the functions of all of the Partnership's Boards of Directors are little, if any, more than the absolute legal minimum except in one case only, the Central Board, that is to say the Board of John Lewis Partnership Limited.

This is the holding company that was created at the time of the first settlement twenty years ago to give sufficient unity to the whole group and to all their various operations. Now that the time is come for the second settlement, it seems very probable that a new company will have to be created to be a corporate trustee of this new settlement. If that is done, the new company will share with John Lewis Partnership Limited this function of giving unity to the whole group.

POWERS OF THE CENTRAL BOARD

565. The Board of this company is limited to twelve. It is intended that under the new settlement five of those twelve Directorships shall be filled each year by the Partnership's Central Council as promptly as possible after the election of the Council itself. Technically the Council will, I suppose, recommend five names and the voting control of the Partnership, that is vested in the twelve thousand Deferred Ordinary Shares of John Lewis Partnership Limited, that belong at present to me and that are to be the subject of the new settlement, will be used accordingly.

If one of these five Directors ceases to be a member of the Partnership, he will not be thereby disqualified from a Directorship of John Lewis Partnership Ltd. for the remainder of the year for which he was appointed. That is to ensure that, if during their year of office one or more of them ceases to be a member of the Partnership, he can, if he chooses, retain his Directorship until the end of that year, so that the intention of the Council in securing his election to that Board may not be thwarted by a termination of their nominee's membership of the Partnership itself.

The other seven members of the Board of John Lewis Partnership Limited are the Chairman and six others by his nomination. In my time the Chairman's power to dispose of these six seats will, I think, be used, as it is at present, to bring on to this board in addition to the Deputy Chairman, the five Heads of the Critical Side, an expression that will be explained presently, namely the General Inspector, the Chief Registrar, the Internal Auditor, the Financial Adviser and the Partners' Counsellor.

Of the functions of the Central Board enough has, I hope, been said already in the description of the division of the Principal Management between the Central Council, the Central Board and the Chairmanship.

Until very lately the Central Board (the Board of Directors of John Lewis Partnership Ltd.) was in certain ways at the top of the group of companies through which the Partnership's business is conducted. As, however, has just been said, there has arisen very lately a prospect that to these there will be added a new company created to be a corporate trustee of the impending second irrevocable settlement in trust that will supplement the settlement of 1929 and complete the foundation of the Partnership.

The Partnership has already one such company, John Lewis Partnership Pensions Trust Ltd., the corporate trustee for the pension fund. The Partnership's legal advisers have very lately suggested that the creation of this new company will be the best means of meeting the technical needs of the second settlement. If these suggestions are, as seems highly probable, adopted, the occupant of the position of chief individual responsibility in the Partnership will be Chairman of the Board of this corporate trustee.

He will be also the Chairman of John Lewis Partnership Ltd. but, if the new plan goes through, it may, I think, be well that he shall be known as the Chairman of the Corporate Trustee because that immediately indicates that the Partnership is governed by a settlement in trust for the benefit of the Partners.

As I have said elsewhere, it is obviously a great pity that this second settlement, whatever is to be its actual form, was not completed before this book was published. But the book itself is so very much overdue and in legal work of this kind there are so apt to be such long delays that it seems better to wait no further. After all, the exact details of the legal methods by which effect is given to the intentions that the book expresses cannot be of much moment to any but the Partnership's own members and hardly even to them, if, as will presumably happen, the lawyers succeed again at this last stage, as they have succeeded up to now, in finding some way of fitting these new ideas quite satisfactorily into the framework of the law as it stands at present.

CHAPTER 34

THE CHAIRMANSHIP

566. WHAT is the Chairman ordinarily to do? As little as possible. That is of the essence of the plan. In theory the Partnership should get along perfectly well without any chairman. His part is merely negative. He is not there to play but only to contribute to the game the umpiring that is necessary for the game to be played properly. He is merely there to prevent things from going wrong, as is in a modern democracy the judiciary, though all wise people try to avoid going to law and most of us succeed.

What does the umpire on the cricket-field do? In a sense, nothing. He does no playing at all. He merely makes the laws of the game, its constitution, effective for those who do play.

To an individual player he says: "If you choose to retire from the game, you are free to do so and, if I say you are out of the game, you are out of it. That's cricket. If you don't like it, don't play it and, if you like cricket but you are not satisfied with my umpiring, find another game with another umpire. In this game, I'm umpire and what I say goes".

567. In cricket, an umpire, who does not give satisfaction, gets no umpiring to do and the head of a partnership, who played his own part in a way that prevented his getting together and keeping together a sufficiently capable and energetic team, would find himself without any business.

That is what would happen if someone unfit to occupy such a position tried to create a partnership. It is what happens already when someone incapable of starting a new enterprise, that requires team-work, tries to do so. The venture comes to a more or less early end.

But it is necessary to provide also for the possibility that a new chairman in an established partnership might fill his own position too badly. In the present business-world, if a man or woman does not own a controlling interest, he or she will probably be displaced before the damage to the business has gone very far. If he or she does own a controlling interest and does not part with it of his own accord, then the business suffers and may collapse altogether.

The constitution of a partnership, its laws, must therefore provide for getting rid of an unsatisfactory chairman and for filling the chair if it is vacant.

AVOID LOADING THE CHAIRMANSHIP

568. But the less the Chairman has to do, the better. Don't ask him to be your Director of Expansion or anything else. Let him do nothing but watch the game and on the other hand let the Chairman prevent the dismissal from the Partnership of anyone who wishes to stay in it and who is not really disqualified for membership and let him send off the Partnership's field of play anybody who in his judgment is out according to the laws of that game. These laws require of each Partner a certain efficiency, a certain compliance not only with the letter but with the spirit of the laws. A cricketer can be declared "out for obstruction". What is "obstruction" in cricket? What the umpire says it is. What is unfitness to come into a particular partnership or to stop in it? What its chairman says it is. These things cannot be measured. They cannot be "proved". They have got to be settled somehow and the only way to settle them is to use as a touch-stone, an indicator, a gauge, the mere judgment of some person or group of persons, fallible though humanity is.

Perhaps an individual will be best. Perhaps a group. If partnerships become numerous, many ideas may be tried out for this and for many other things. Our own partnership is organised at present upon the idea that this is one of these matters for which it is best to use a single mind and to concentrate responsibility.

A WHOLE-TIME OCCUPATION

569. But, though I am entirely serious in urging that the executive functions, the routine work of my successors, should be as light as possible, I rather hope that they will give to it all of their time that is not spent upon genuine recreation or in ways that, so far as they are not wholly recreation, are likely to bring some advantage to the Partnership.

In my early years I thought that to take part in affairs outside would help to keep one's mind fresh and to give useful contacts and knowledge. I imagine that for some temperaments and for some partnerships that might well be so. But it is now a good many years since I came to feel that for myself and for this partnership any such diversion of working-energy would be unwise.

There is no limit to the really important good that the holder of the position of chief individual responsibility, even I think in a quite small partnership, can do without any approach to inexpedient interference in the field of any colleague. It is no light matter to undertake to play in some important ways the principal part in such a community. Those, who embark upon such undertakings, may well, I think, so long as they continue, give to them all of whatever working-energy they have.

RAISE NO SUSPICIONS OF BIAS

570. At all events they should in my view be most careful that any outside interests are not so weighty and responsible as to prevent the Chairman's being constantly available to give virtually the whole of his mind to any sudden grave concern of the Partnership and he should be also most careful to avoid any external relations that may raise doubts of his impartiality.

If the Partnership does not profess frankly to cater specially for members of some particular race or religious community or political party, let its Chairman and its Deputy Chairman avoid most carefully arousing or, if they have been somehow aroused, fostering any doubts of their absolute impartiality, their exclusive care in all of its affairs for the good of the Partnership itself and for nothing else at all.

THREE QUESTIONABLE FEATURES OF THE GENERAL PLAN

571. I conceive that there are three features of the present plan of this particular partnership that will be particularly disagreeable to many theorists with whose general values and aims I should sympathise entirely. One will be the provision that the Chairman's tenure is to be so secure as this plan can mean that it is. Another will be that the Chairman is to have power to name his own successor. The third will be that, just as an umpire or referee may, and indeed in theory must, simply upon the strength of his own judgment, send out of the game anyone who in his opinion has broken in a certain way the laws of that game, so one particular member of such a community, as we are here proposing to build up, can and in theory must drop from its team anyone who has so far lost his (the Chairman's or whatever he is called) confidence that he would feel no doubt that, if that Partner tendered his resignation, it ought to be accepted without any attempt to persuade him to withdraw it.

PERHAPS THEY ARE REALLY AMONG ITS CHIEF MERITS IF IT IS GOOD AT ALL

572. For my own part I suspect that, if the Self-governing Workshop achieves along these general lines such success as hitherto it never has achieved, the reason of the success will be precisely in such provisions as these.

The Rochdale Pioneers made a success of the Cooperative Society of Consumers precisely by taking the hard-headed, uncomfortable, unattractive line in those respects in which their predecessors had been soft-headed and had yielded to temptations to take a course that seemed pleasanter but that led to disaster by reason of certain facts of the Nature of Things, certain facts of human nature.

The Chairman's tenure and functions are in fact based upon three Ideas:

first that at the core of any such organisation as is here suggested there must be one position of which the occupant's tenure must be absolutely secure so long as without breaking the rules of the written constitution of the organisation he or she achieves a certain degree of business-success but that, if this is not achieved, the members of the organisation should have power to displace the Chairman and to appoint whomsoever their representatives shall think fit;

second that except in this last case the occupant of this position must have power to appoint his own successor;

third that the Chairman's functions should correspond as nearly as possible to those of the Judiciary in Anglo-Saxon democracy.

A RELUCTANT DECISION

573. Let those, to whom this power, as thus qualified, of the Chair seems unnecessarily and therefore improperly great, devise something better and let them try out their device and demonstrate its soundness.

If that happens, the new arrangement, whatever it was, would, I hope, be adopted promptly and wholeheartedly by the John Lewis Partnership. I wish very much indeed that I had been able to devise something more democratic. For years I have racked my wits to hit upon some plan that would be in reality of the nature of trial by jury, even though the jurors might be elected to serve as a standing tribunal. For many years I hoped that the Chairmanship could be relieved of the very invidious function of being the Partnership's ultimate authority in questions affecting the individual interests of its members, their admission, remuneration, promotion, demotion and perhaps the termination of their membership. But it has seemed to me impracticable. It has seemed to me that any arrangement, that would genuinely relieve the Chairmanship of this duty, would open the door to troubles that might be disastrous.

In all my reading and contacts I have tried to be always sharply on the watch for helpful ideas in this direction but such information, as has come my way, has seemed to me to be all in the other direction.

RUSSIAN EXPERIENCE AND THE EXAMPLE OF OUR OWN LABOUR GOVERNMENT IN NATIONALISED INDUSTRY

574. Such news, as we get from Russia, suggests that, in order to achieve efficiency in large-scale team-work, they are more and more abandoning government by groups for concentration of responsibility upon one person. Our own present Labour Government is composed of men who have been thinking about these matters all their lives. They must be presumed to be in the main genuinely anxious to promote equality

and to take the utmost care of the interests of the Managed as against the Management. Nevertheless, in all of their schemes of nationalisation we see them concentrating managerial power into very few hands and concentrating a very great deal of it into a single post, that of the Minister concerned.

Certainly it may be argued that Ministers may in theory be called to account in Parliament (though of late the present Government seem to be aiming at preventing that in the case of Fuel and Power and of Transport and presumably of the other "nationalisations" that they intend) and possibly to some real extent through the newspapers and certainly we are not entitled to feel quite sure as yet that these general tendencies will mean that among the most responsible of the permanent officials, the people in the line next below the transient politicians, there will be a substantial tendency for some one person to have in such matters, as we are here considering, a very high degree of one-man control.

SUCH CONCENTRATION OF POWER PROBABLY UNAVOIDABLE

575.   But to my mind all the symptoms look like that and, however objectionable it may be in theory, I am not at all sure that in practice it will not be found the most satisfactory to the Managed themselves. There is real substance in the objection to group-control that a group has neither a soul to be damned nor a body to be kicked.

At all events, this is the arrangement that to my own mind seems on the whole the best that I can devise and, as has been said, if one or more other partnerships arise with some different plan in this respect and if that plan seems to be on the whole better than ours not only in theory but in practice, I hope that this partnership will not be too slow to recognise that and will adopt it.

HOLDING AND EXERCISE OF POWER: AN UNPLEASANT JOB

576.   The possession of power over the fortunes of other people is pleasant enough when you and they feel that merit is getting its due in a case in which otherwise perhaps it might not. But in the main it is not. It is indeed a function that no one should desire except in the sense that people should desire to be surgeons. Our whole object is to get rid of the need of surgery. As long, as the need exists, there must be surgeons and, as long as some group or individual has got to exercise such power as we are here considering, the job must be done. But it is a job that strictly speaking ought not to exist and that should be eliminated as far as possible.

Apart from accident, the need of surgery arises from ailments of the body and the need of managerial controls, though required for co-ordination, even among equals, arises largely from foibles of the mind.

As health and education improve, there should be less and less either of surgery or of controls.

Some readers of this book may think that this passage represents humbug or self-deception. I can only answer that for years I have reduced so very greatly my own personal exercise of power of this kind that at this present moment there are among the Partnership's most coveted posts a great many people with whose engagement I have had nothing to do and who were in the Partnership for months and years before I ever met them. I was perfectly free not to set up that state of affairs. If I really enjoyed the exercise of patronage, I could have kept all that in my own hands.

SOME INTERVENTIONS

577. It may be thought that that state of affairs sounds as if there was not much reality in the problem that we are here discussing but for my own part I should not agree. It is perfectly true that, the holders of certain posts in the Partnership being the people that they were, there have been hardly any cases in which I have felt called upon to intervene but the fact remains that I always could and sometimes I have felt that I must.

The cases, in which I have intervened to any substantial purpose, have been very few indeed and it is quite conceivable that some group-arrangement would have been substantially more effective.

Of course all this will be done in the main by an elaborate network of subordinate authorities. That would happen whether the ultimate authority was an individual or a group. But ultimate authority can and should be more than a figurehead and the question, whether the ultimate authority is to be an individual or a group, seems to me and will, I imagine, seem to a good many people very important in principle.

578. What are at present the functions of this post, the Chairmanship of the Central Board? (1) Those normally belonging to the chair of such a board; (2) to maintain the Constitution of the Partnership to the satisfaction of the Council subject to appeal to the Courts of Law; (3) to amend but only with the concurrence of the Council the Articles of the Constitution; (4) to use or to cause to be used to the Partnership's best advantage according to his judgment such amount as under the Partnership's system of budgetary control, as operated by the Board, shall not be at the disposal of the Council and shall be available for consumption by the Partners themselves either collectively or individually as pay, pensions, amenities, Partnership Benefit (if distributed in cash, otherwise the consumption will be only to the extent of the interest upon that capital) or in any other way whatsoever; (5) to decide, subject only to the law (including the Partner's legal contract with the Partnership) the question who shall be admitted to the Partnership or retained in it and upon what terms.

That decision is to depend upon two persons alone, the particular Partner (for himself) and the Chairman (for the Partnership) but the Chairman cannot cause the Partnership to commit itself to any contract of membership that it cannot end by giving at most twelve months' notice or by paying in lieu of that notice or of any unexpired remainder thereof one-half at most of the amount to which the Partner would be entitled if he were required or allowed to continue on duty.

The Partner on his side is, of course, always free within the terms of his own particular agreement with the Partnership to resign from it. He is under no obligation to justify that decision to the Partnership, however unfortunate may be for it his decision to withdraw at that particular time and however ungenerous his action may seem to be in view of some special circumstances and of the extent to which the Partnership may have served him as a ladder by which to climb to a better position in life.

In precisely the same way, the Chairman can at any time say to any member of the Partnership that in his judgment the Partnership would be so much better without that particular member that he, the Chairman, cannot acquiesce in that member's continuing.

Ideas, upon which the Chairman should play this part, are suggested under "Admission and Advancement" and "Tenure".

LEAVING GIFTS

579.   In connection with this matter of tenure of membership it must not be forgotten that the Constitution gives the Council absolute discretion to make up to the limit of the very large funds at their disposal any gift they think proper to any Partner or ex-Partner and their vote upon that as upon any other matter whatsoever must be given by secret ballot if that be requested by any member of the Council or by anyone else concerned in the particular affair.

A Partner has three safeguards against the effects of misuse of this power of the Chair to terminate membership or to proceed so as to induce resignation. First, the possibility of a compensatory award by the Council from the funds of the Partnership. These funds extend to many thousands of pounds and the award might be a large pension for life.

THE REQUIREMENTS OF THE CONSTITUTION

580.   Second, the possibility that the Council may consider that the Chairman has so broken his undertaking to maintain the Constitution of the Partnership that his tenure can and should be ended and may require the Trustees to proceed accordingly and that the Chairman, if he be unwilling to resign, may not succeed in the application that in that case he must take to the Courts of Law for a declaration that that procedure of the Trustees will be *ultra vires* and for an injunction to restrain it.

Third, that misuse of the Chairman's powers would tend to diminish the general efficiency of the Partnership's team-work so that the success of its business-operations might fall to the not very low point at which the Chairman's tenure can be ended on the indisputable ground that there has been a failure in that punctuality of the Partnership's payments that is required by the Constitution that the Chairman has undertaken to maintain. If that point were reached, the Chairman would have no ground upon which to appeal to the Courts of Law.

PERSONAL CONTACT BETWEEN THE PARTNERSHIP AND THE CHAIRMAN

581. The journalism and all the machinery for representation are designed to ensure a lively and well-informed public opinion and to secure its due expression but of course all this machinery is in a sense merely supplementary to informal contact between Partners, which likewise is deliberately fostered, and there is, I think, a chance that in the near future there will arise a definite system for regular meetings between the Chairman and as many as possible of the holders of particular positions and between the Chairman and representatives of all those positions that are too numerous to be included among the former. These regular meetings with individuals or groups of various sizes may, I think, become a chief part of the Chairman's personal functions and perhaps grow into a definite formal development of the Constitution.

582. In February of 1941 I felt that I must do something fairly substantial to renew the personal contact, that years ago had been very adequate, between the occupants of the more important positions and myself. In 1935, when I died experimentally, I reckoned that my withdrawal would be much less complete than it proved to be. I had reckoned that I should get a stream of requests for a casting-vote that would amount in the aggregate to a fairly sufficient continuance of personal contact. In fact, all those, whose opinions might have come thus into conflict, contrived to agree. Presumably they felt that such give and take, whether it was pretty even or pretty one-sided, would be on the whole better in various ways for the Partnership and for themselves. At all events, whatever the reason, the thing happened.

When the war was beginning to draw near, I was beginning to be conscious of this. And now I felt that something substantial must be done. Accordingly I started asking the holders of certain positions to come down to Hampshire for lunch and a general chat. That gave us two or three hours for leisurely talk. Generally, if not always, I made, as I used to do in the old days when I reviewed the buyerships, a pretty full note for future reference and in a good many cases our talk led me to make some enquiry or some other move.

This continued at the rate generally of two visitors a week until February of 1943. In the course of that time I had such talks with a hundred and twenty-three holders of Buyerships, General Managerships, Divisional Managerships, Registrarships, Managerships of Counting Houses, Workrooms, the Members of the Medical Service and others.

A CONTRIBUTION TO FREEDOM OF SPEECH

583. As the talks proceeded, I felt more and more that they should be a permanent element in the Partnership's normal life. For some very important purposes people can talk to whoever holds the position of ultimate responsibility more easily than they can to anybody else, and he, on the other hand, can say to all and sundry things that could hardly be said so well, if at all, by any one who did not hold his own particular position. He can, in fact, act as a clearing-house, an information-exchange, and that can be a most useful function, a most valuable supplement to other means of securing real freedom of speech and sufficient communication between all ranks.

For many years I had felt quite uncertain what would seem to me to be the ultimate functions of the position of chief individual responsibility but now I. began to feel that the mist was beginning to clear away.

HARVEST

584. I enjoyed the talks very much. Some of my visitors were old friends whom for years I had known very well but whom for a long time I had not met. Never before had I had the sense, that these visits gave me, of harvest. Always before I had felt that my own career was still in front of me and that my own work was just beginning, still experimental, still an effort that might or might not come to something. But now I found myself talking to people who had held for so long posts carrying incomes of such a size that one could feel that, even if the Partnership were to come soon to an end, they at all events would have had out of it something really considerable. Their careers were not finished and the Partnership was still, as for me, I think, it always will be, a mere embryo of future possibilities. But here were these Partners to whom it had afforded worthwhile careers. To a really substantial extent their particular ships had come home.

585. From the beginning there had been the possibility that the Partnership might have a serious importance for the general community, something of the importance of the Rochdale venture in the Cooperative Movement. But, apart from this, there had been the alternative and surer hope that our venture would at all events while it lasted give to those, who took part in it, a pretty good life, a life that for most of them would

be perhaps on the whole quite a bit happier and more prosperous in the money sense than they would have had otherwise.

It was extremely pleasant to meet one after another people, who had helped to get the Partnership going and to make it succeed to the extent that it had, and to feel that out of it they themselves had done well enough to be pretty happy and content and to be firmly settled upon continuing. They seemed to me to have a thorough sense of security and to look back with pleasure upon the career that the Partnership had afforded them up to now and to look forward with pleasure to continuing in it until their retirement.

CONTACT MUST BE METHODICAL: A RIGHT OF HOLDERS OF SOME POSTS

586. Along with those, whom I had known more or less well, there came others whom I had never met before. Some were comparatively newcomers to the Partnership. Some had been in it for a good few years. It was extremely interesting to meet week after week a whole succession of people of more than average ability and varying pretty widely in personality and in the nature of their work and to see in all their different minds, as if it were in a set of differently placed mirrors, the general picture of the Partnership as in their memories it had been and as in their view it now was.

As the talks progressed, I was more and more impressed with the usefulness of such personal contact and I felt more and more that there should be an elaborate system for maintaining it. In the case of holders of certain posts there should be meetings of a certain frequency. In the case of others the frequency should be different. In some cases it might be as high as monthly or even somewhat higher. In others it might be as low perhaps as once in three years without being so infrequent as to have no real importance. The frequency should be a matter of the particular post. It should be a right belonging to the holding of that particular position. It should not depend upon merely personal considerations and the contact should not be limited to the holders of positions of a certain importance.

A GROUP-RIGHT OF HOLDERS OF MORE NUMEROUS POSTS

587. There should be similar contact between the holder of the position of chief individual responsibility and representatives of groups too numerous to be all seen separately. The larger the Partnership becomes, the more must such representation take the place of personal contact with, say, everyone who holds a Buyership. Talks in complete privacy, that is to say one at a time, should be supplemented by talks with groups and such meetings might have to some extent both characters. A few minutes of quite private, that is to say quite separate, talk, might be combined with general chat among several at once.

The total possibilities of such personal contact between the holder of the position of chief individual responsibility and all the rest of the Partnership will, I believe, prove to be very important indeed. They must certainly be methodical and I should think the more definite the routine the better. They will be a most valuable supplement to the Committees for Communications, which now, that the Partnership is so large, the holder of the position of chief individual responsibility can no longer meet as a general rule personally but only by deputy.

The Chairmanship of the Committees for Communications has become a whole-time post and already has outgrown even that arrangement.

CONTACT BROKEN AFRESH

588. The beginnings of this new institution, this regular organised personal contact between the holder of the position of chief individual responsibility (I am purposely avoiding giving it any particular title because whatever its title the function would remain), were broken off for a time by the very great difficulty that I had in making satisfactory progress with the writing of this book, a thing that I felt must be virtually finished before I could properly take the risks involved in committing the Partnership and myself to a second irrevocable settlement that would so supplement that of 1929 as to complete the foundation of the Partnership.

Because of that pressure I very reluctantly discontinued this series of meetings instead of beginning again upon a second cycle of them and supplementing them with such other arrangements as I have suggested. I hope that in the near future they will begin again and that within my own time they may grow into a routine pretty adequate and well established.

Rightly or wrongly I feel very sure that, however large the Partnership may become, whoever holds in it the position of chief individual responsibility ought to give to this particular function a really large part of his own working-time. If he is too busy, he ought not to be. This work must be supremely important. He should be relieved of other things not of this.

VALUE OF PERSONAL CONTACT

589. Obviously there must be fairly narrow limits to the extent to which any one person can have such contact with others. However excellent the arrangements for meeting with groups, there must be an ultimate limit. The number of hours available must be more or less fixed and there must be a definite limit to the number of people with whom really satisfactory contact can be achieved within that space of time.

The limit may perhaps vary rather widely according to personal temperament and aptitude but, though it may vary, it will still be there.

Within that limit, however, I feel very sure that the worst job, that any holder of my own particular position can do in this particular way, will still be extremely well worth doing, extremely important to the Partnership's general health and happiness.

GENERAL MEETINGS

For some years before the war I followed a fairly definite practice of holding once in each year a "General Meeting" in each branch. It had, of course, to be held after working hours. No one was required to attend, but in practice most people did. Anyone was welcome to raise any question either by letter, anonymous or otherwise, before the Meeting or in the course of the Meeting itself.

The Meeting generally lasted about an hour and, if discussion of any matters raised by questioners occupied about that length of time, then I should probably say little more. If, on the other hand, there were, as sometimes happened, no questions at all or only such as took little time, then I would talk to the Meeting of any concerns of the Partnership that might, I thought, interest them.

MASS-MEETINGS DESIRABLE BUT THEIR POSSIBILITY LIMITED

590. It is, I suspect, very desirable that from time to time all members of an organisation shall have an opportunity to come to this extent into personal contact with the occupant of its position of chief individual responsibility. From time to time they should have a chance to see him or her for themselves and to hear his or her voice and to judge for themselves the sort of person he or she really is.

On such occasions the giver of the address may sometimes have the pleasure of making immediately some welcome communication. I had that pleasure once at Southsea. A questioner asked in what was perhaps a slightly complaining not to say aggressive tone whether it could not be arranged that Partners in provincial branches should have some share of certain amenities available to those who worked in London. I was able to answer that there was nothing to prevent the gratification of that wish. The amenities included a very successful Chess Club and chess can be played by correspondence. From the laughter, with which this suggestion was welcomed, I was glad to infer that the audience found the prospect satisfactorily delightful.

But, jesting apart, personal contact of this kind is in my view very highly desirable. On the other hand, as branches become more and more numerous and very widely scattered, such visiting will be a more and more formidable call upon the Chairman's personal time and strength.

THE LAST RESERVE BEHIND A THINLY HELD LINE: SOME RESUMPTION OF
MASS-MEETINGS

591.   In 1940, a tour of the new branches, that the Partnership had just
acquired, ended for me in pneumonia. After that I gave the Meetings
up for the opening years of the war. I could never know from day to
day when one or more of my principal colleagues would be lost to the
Partnership. They and I together constituted a desperately light core for a
thing so large, so complex and in many ways so immature. I was the very
last reserve and I thought that I ought not to use up my own strength in
any way that I could possibly avoid.

After the war I was a good deal pressed to start the Meetings again
and I did in fact hold four in London. But nowadays that sort of thing
takes a great deal out of me. In 1908, before my chest was damaged, I
used, so far as I can now remember, to feel hardly any fatigue in making
a two-hour impromptu speech in a large room to a strange audience
but nowadays I find any public speaking a quite serious undertaking
physically. Perhaps the after-effects of the operations are more important
that when I was younger or perhaps the pneumonia has left a subtle
weakness. At all events, I doubt if I shall do much more of this spell-
binding, as the Americans call it.

NOT TO BE LIGHTLY OMITTED

592.   Nevertheless, I strongly recommend my successors to do in this way
as much as they feel that they really can. It is true that, the more you get
into touch with your audience and the more interested you are in talking
to them and the more pains you take to be lively and audible, the greater
the strain. But we see many politicians making considerable speeches
at ages beyond seventy-five, the absolute limit that our Partnership is
setting to active membership, and I hope that the giving of addresses of
this kind will be generally a substantial and a very valuable part of the
Chairman's personal functions.

For my own part I favour discussion rather than the mere giving of
an address and before the war I used to combine these Meetings with a
previous inspection of the particular Branch. In talking afterwards to the
Meeting I would refer to anything that in the course of that inspection
I had seen or heard, the reference being congratulatory or as the case
might be.

The substance of these addresses or discussions can of course be
reported and published to the Partnership in the central GAZETTE or in
the local CHRONICLE if in the particular instance that seems desirable.

593. In any team-work upon a fairly large scale the holder of the position of chief responsibility will need informants and advisers. Even if his temperament and ability make him extremely active, so that he does an immense amount of executive work, he will need information and advice. Suppose, on the contrary, that the constitution of the organisation or his own choice or sheer lack of capacity limit extremely his personal activity, he will still need information and advice if his playing of his part, no matter how narrowly it may be limited, is to be good enough to maintain his position.

It remains to be seen how far in a partnership, that exceeds a certain size and that is really mature, the functions of its position of chief individual responsibility, that we are here calling the Chairmanship, can be restricted to those of the umpire and of the selection committee in cricket and how far they must on the contrary correspond to those of a managing director in an ordinary company. Certainly the work might be done by the Board or conceivably by the Council. In that case the Board or the Council would have to get information and suggestions from someone or other and they would have to take the responsibility for the actual decision what was to be done.

DEMOCRACY'S TENDENCY TO GIVE RISE TO SOME POSITION OF CHIEF INDIVIDUAL RESPONSIBILITY

594. The advantages and disadvantages of placing responsibility and power upon groups of minds rather than upon individuals vary according to the particular kind of matter that has to be settled and according to the particular circumstances of each case. British democracy has substituted a great division of powers for such one-man rule as existed in the case, for example, of Henry VIII, but in the course of hundreds of years very great responsibility and power have come to be concentrated in the Prime Ministership.

In the United States the passion for equality and security against misuse of governmental authority was even stronger than in our own country. In consequence the American Constitution is an extreme example of checks and balances devised to secure that no individual or group of individuals can be excessively powerful. Nevertheless the powers of the President are so great that the holder of that office is commonly said to have the greatest real powers of any single man in the whole world.

DIVISION OF POWER AND RESPONSIBILITY MAY REQUIRE A MARGIN FOR ERROR

595. Great nations, in the conduct of their affairs, plainly suffer from a vast amount of blundering, a vast amount of trial and error and a vast

amount of sheer inefficiency in the way of personal friction in team-work and of such slackness as concentration of responsibility is designed to prevent. But the resources of great nations are so enormous that except in very special emergencies such as a life and death war they can afford to pay that price for certain advantages that their arrangements are designed to secure.

In conditions of genuine competition no private enterprise could stand the strain of such inefficiency. Private enterprise is always incomparably nearer to the possibility of real disaster. In comparison with the affairs of a nation the affairs of a competitive private enterprise are in a perpetual state of emergency and in all emergencies all communities concentrate power and responsibility.

It is, I suspect, true that in almost all private enterprises, that succeed and in which the chief power is apparently exercised by some Board or Committee or other group, that group is guided by the views of some one person to an extent that comes very near to restoration of one-man management.

However that may be, experience has made me feel that the safest course for this particular partnership will be to divide the functions of Principal Management between the Central Council, the Central Board and the Chairmanship in a way that will mean that the Chairman can, if he chooses, play pretty fully the part of a strong and trusted managing director in a large company, so that, if things go wrong, the Partnership can content itself with changing its Chairman and can, if it chooses, carry on with the same Board and the same Council.

A PARALLEL DEVELOPMENT IN PUBLIC AFFAIRS

596.   In this last fact there is a quite accidental parallel to the development of British democracy in the management of public affairs. Mr. H. E. Dale in his book upon the Higher Civil Service of Great Britain remarks in his first chapter that in each separate department "most Ministers gather round themselves naturally and without any fragment of formal constitution an inner ring of chief advisers", a ring of which the exact composition depends on the Minister himself and "varies with the character of the Minister and of his principal permanent subordinates" but "normally consists of or is selected from the Permanent Secretary, the Second Secretary, the Legal Adviser, one Principal Assistant Secretary or Assistant Secretary and the Minister's Private Secretary".

Mr. Dale goes on to say that:

"Around this cabinet there is an outer ring of Principal Assistant Secretaries, Assistant Secretaries, and specialists other than the Legal Adviser, numbering for a large Department 15-25 and for the whole Service about 450, whose powers and influence are confined to limited provinces. In every Department the Minister for the time being is the sun round whom revolves this system of planets—with the not unimportant difference from the physical universe that in the official world a recurring convulsion casts down the sun from heaven and sets another luminary in his place but does not shake the planets from their accustomed orbits."

A further accidental parallel is the fact that, whereas according to Mr. Dale the "inner ring" of which he speaks tends to consist of "five men", the Partnership's Critical Side has been divided into five Departments of which the Heads are to be the Chairman's principal informants and advisers upon all matters whatsoever. They are to give him all the assistance that he will need in that way to make up his own mind properly upon all questions that come to him from the whole of the remainder of the Partnership, the Central Council, the Central Board, the Journalism and the whole of the Partnership's Executive Side. They will in fact correspond pretty closely to Mr. Dale's "inner ring of chief advisers" that "most Ministers gather round themselves naturally".

AN INNERMOST MANAGERIAL RING

597. At this level of organising we encounter a certain absolute limitation that arises from the nature of the human mind. Throughout history right down to quite recent reports from strong commissions appointed to study and advise upon the question of the right size of the Cabinet in the British Government, there seems to have been steady agreement that a dozen or fewer is the largest number of minds, that can achieve really satisfactory team-work. Even among a dozen there seems to be a strong tendency for fewer than half-a-dozen to form a sort of core, almost a cabinet within a cabinet.

Now, if in a partnership as large as our own there is good reason to divide among so many as five separate posts the function of knowing all that ought to be known and of keeping the Chairman properly informed and of giving him proper advice, then we have no more than six posts left for the remainder of the Partnership's innermost managerial ring.

Because of the aforesaid absolute limitation of the capacity of the human mind for team-work, if the Chairman is going to need five Critical colleagues to inform and advise him in his dealings with all the rest of the Partnership, then the representatives of "all the rest" have got to be fitted into these six remaining places.

CENTRAL AUTHORITIES MUST BE JACKS OF ALL TRADES

598. In any large organisation, the nearer you get to the centre, the more will it tend to be difficult to set out the functions clearly and completely. They must be in some ways unspecialised. The centre has to

deal with matters of every kind and arising from every part of the whole organisation.

Moreover, its actions must tend to be merely part of a chain or, to express the same thing in another way they must tend to be one element in a combination, one ingredient in a mixture. It is much easier to give a clear and complete description of, say, a particular quantity of salt than it is to indicate how you are to decide how much salt to put into some mixture of many things for all the purposes that the salt has to serve.

This body, that we are here calling the Partnership's innermost managerial ring, will be in a sense executive as far as it affects the Chairman's use of his own powers. He may adopt in preference to his own opinion that of a majority of the group or perhaps that of a minority, even a minority of one. But so far as the Chairman takes a line of his own, the functions of the group will be merely advisory. This is, I understand, the practice that in our own country, with its quite exceptional gift for self-government, has arisen in the conduct of our public affairs. The Prime Minister can and sometimes does decide after discussion in the Cabinet that the policy of the Government is to be one that he alone favours and to which all other members of his Government are opposed.

The members of the Cabinet must either support the Government policy to the best of their ability or else they must resign. Cabinet decisions, therefore, are not a matter of majority opinion except in cases in which the Prime Minister considers that they ought to be. It is in this sense that the members of the Chairman's regular conference can be said to be the Partnership's innermost managerial ring.

JOURNALISM

600.   In addition to the five Heads of the five Departments, that make up the Critical Side, of which the composition and functions are about to be described, this innermost ring will include besides the Chairman and the Deputy Chairman, the General Editor of the Partnership's Journalism and the Heads of the three Executive Departments, Maintenance and Expansion, Personnel and Financial Operations.

The inclusion of the Head of the Journalism may seem odd but, after all, the real management of a newspaper is a function of very real power and corresponding responsibility. If the Partner ship's policy of freedom of speech requires journalism that will correspond pretty closely to the Free Press in a modern British or American democracy, will it be really possible to avoid including the Head of the Journalism in this innermost ring of no more than twelve?

The Partnership's use of journalism was one of my own inventions and right up to this present time it has been so much in my own hands that on this point of the real nature of a separate chief editorship and of its holder's consequent position in the Partnership's structure I cannot put any conclusions forward a: a result of experience but I do in fact feel pretty sure that it will be found highly desirable, if not absolutely unavoidable, that in such an organisation, as we are here contemplating, the Head of the Journalism shall have a place in this regular conference.

THE DIRECTOR OF MAINTENANCE AND EXPANSION

601. Though for brevity the Department of Expansion may be known by that name, it would be obviously wrong for a business to lose ground needlessly in some directions while it was expanding in others. The Department is really a Department of Maintenance as well as of Expansion. As a sheep-dog gets a flock along by watching for laggards and supplying sufficient impulse, so this Department should watch and listen for any symptoms of flagging and get promptly busy as gently and pleasantly as possible but with quite adequate effect.

The Partnership must, I think, do all that it can to build up definite rules that will enable the holders of high executive positions to feel that, so long as their results are kept, whether by luck or by judgment, up to a certain level, they will be quite secure against any interference from the Department of Maintenance and Expansion. Some of them may with good reason consider themselves every bit as expert, as able and as hardworking as anybody in the Partnership and, the abler people are, the more apt they are to wish to be left quite alone to paddle their own canoe. In a civilised community the ablest of us must keep the law. That is the price of the advantages of civilisation and in a partnership the ablest must keep the rules, whatever they may be,—that is the price of having behind you the resources of that partnership.

602. A partnership must get along somehow without the help of anyone who is too ill-tempered to be to that extent a team-worker. But within that line the Department of Expansion should leave executive chiefs alone, as, when we are in health, our doctors refrain from asking to feel our pulses and look at our tongues and from telling us to go to bed or to take some physic.

The Department of Maintenance and Expansion exists partly to deal with early but definite symptoms that something is going wrong and partly to start new ventures and get them to the stage at which they can be handed over to somebody else as a separate charge. It is partly that bit of the mind of the owner-manager of a pretty big one-man business that is devoted to keeping a sufficient eye on the results of all of its separate sections with a view to keeping all of them up to the mark and it is partly that other bit of the same mind that is devoted to being on the watch for need to start new ventures, new departments or branches or whatever they may be called and to attending to them until their success seems to be sufficiently firmly established.

THE DIRECTOR OF FINANCIAL OPERATIONS

603. Besides this, I think that these regular conferences must include a representative of the Executive Side in respect of finance. The executive function of providing capital ought, I think, to be separated from the related functions of the Financial Adviser.

I think there should be constantly in the Partnership's innermost ring a Director of Maintenance and Expansion or whatever he or she may be called to whom the Partnership's Prime Minister, the Chairman of its Central Board, can say "You are responsible for perceiving at the right time any disquieting symptoms in any part of the existing business and for securing that there is an appropriate investigation and, if necessary, proper action and you are also responsible for the Partnership's being sufficiently alert for new possibilities and enterprising and efficient in starting and in making a success of them." But I think there should be someone else (at present the Partnership calls him its Director of Financial Operations) to whom, if the Director of Maintenance and Expansion asks for capital, the Chairman should be able to turn and ask, "Can you produce that capital and, if so, upon what terms?"

THE DIRECTOR OF PERSONNEL

604. This seems to me to be a function of such importance and so special in its nature that it ought not to be within the field that the Director of Expansion has to cover. In the same way, it seems to me that this innermost ring should include the post that the Partnership calls its Directorship of Personnel, the highest individual authority next to the Chairman himself in all matters whatsoever of personnel-administration.

If the Director of Expansion wants the Partnership to do something, that thing will be apt to require both capital and personnel. If the Director of Financial Operations says that he can find the money, there will remain the question whether the Partnership can find the necessary workers and, when that question arises, the Chairman ought to be able to turn to the Director of Personnel for the answer. Everything, that affects the Partnership's members from the standpoint of its business-efficiency, everything that affects its power of recruitment from that standpoint and its power not only to attract new members of the right quality but to retain them and to secure their best efforts, everything whatsoever of that kind should be the concern of the Director of Personnel and it seems to me that the Directors of Financial Operations and of Personnel should supplement really importantly the Director of Expansion as a source of creative initiative. This is what I mean when I say that this last is primarily (but not exclusively) the Director of Expansion's affair.

THE CORE OF THE PARTNERSHIP'S EXECUTIVE SIDE

605.   It seems to me that the Director of Financial Operations should of his own separate initiative say to the Chairman in conference ("conference" is the term that the Partnership uses at present for this innermost ring), "The Partnership has such and such an opportunity to get additional capital. Cannot that opportunity be used?"

Equally the Director of Personnel should say, "The Partnership has such and such an opportunity to get such and such an additional and apparently importantly desirable member or members. Cannot scope be provided for him or for them?"

In either case the Chairman should turn to the Director of Expansion and ask whether he can make some suggestion. In other words the Director of Expansion will be upon some occasions stirred up and propelled by the Director of Financial Operations or of Personnel or by both of them though as a general rule the position will be the converse of this.

Thus these three will form an entity, the ultimate core of the executive side. The Director of Financial Operations and the Director of Personnel will on the one hand say to the Chairman, "The Director of Maintenance and Expansion is proposing such and such an initiative that would require additional capital or additional workers but the capital or the workers or both cannot be provided." Or on the other hand the Director of Financial Operations may say, "Such and such additional capital is available. Cannot the Director of Expansion find a good enough use for it and cannot the Director of Personnel find the necessary workers?" Alternatively the Director of Personnel may say from his side the corresponding things.

AN INNERMOST RING OF ELEVEN

606.   If these ideas are sound, the Partnership's innermost ring will consist of the Chairman, the Deputy Chairman, who may or may not hold some particular other post, the five Heads of the Critical Side, whose business it is to know everything and to advise wisely but whose power and duty stop at that line, the Director of Expansion, the Director of Financial Operations and the Director of Personnel, providing between them creative initiative, executive energy or, if the word be preferred, "drive" and efficiency in the finding of ways and means to give effect to executive decisions, whether those ways and means be capital or personnel, and finally the General Editor or whatever may be the title of the head of the Partnership's journalism.

If the Deputy Chairman holds none of the other posts, you have here a cabinet of ten members. Even if, as I am about to suggest, there be added an eleventh, the General Secretaryship, we are within what is said to be in such a case the absolute limit for first-rate team-work and yet, I believe, we have here enough of a team for conducting with sufficient safety and sufficient vigour a business of no matter what size or complexity.

POSSIBILITIES OF MODIFICATION

607. Perhaps the Chief Registrar and the Internal Auditor will eventually drop out. Perhaps their function of supplying information may be achieved sufficiently through the other three posts on the Critical Side and the General Editor.

There may be here two possibilities of modifying the innermost ring without enlarging it. But an Executive Side, that is not sufficiently watched and informed and criticised, must in the end go wrong and to me at present it seems quite likely that it will take six really first-rate Partners all their time to enable the Chairman to play properly his own part in relation to the Executive Side of a partnership of several thousand members.

THE GENERAL SECRETARYSHIP

608. There remains the question of something in the way of a secretariat and I think the Partnership may find it a good plan to let the holder of a post, that has arisen lately and that at present is called the General Secretaryship, act as the secretary to these regular conferences but take a member's full part. When we deal later with the Executive Side, something will be said there of the functions of the General Secretaryship. Obviously, as the business grows, the holders of all these posts will need in their respective functions more and more assistance.

SMALL DEPARTMENTS OF TOP LEVEL QUALITY

609. In some or possibly in all of these Departments one or more of the posts technically—and perhaps in some ways quite importantly—subordinate to its chief's may carry the Partnership's "ceiling" rate of pay, that is to say that there may be absolute equality so far as income goes between the lieutenant and his chief.

For my own part I hope that all of these central departments, whether upon the Critical Side or upon the Executive, will tend to develop teams very high in quality but in quantity the smallest that will give sufficient assurance of continuity if the Head of the Department or any other of its very important members is by illness, accident or otherwise suddenly lost to the Partnership.

610. Thus some questions for the Principal Management of the Partnership will go to the Central Council. Some will go to the Central Board, where the Chairman may be present and may play fully a chairman's part but decision will be as the Board may vote.

Finally, matters, that have to be settled by the Principal Management but that are outside the field either of the Central Council or of the Central Board, will belong to the Chairman as in an ordinary company they might belong to the Managing Director.

The Chairman will be free to take any advice, that he thinks desirable, but, whatever other advice he may take, he will—at least I long have and always shall—if the thing is of major importance, discuss it with the members of his regular Conference. No doubt that will happen often in the case of matters that have to go to the Central Council or to the Central Board.

Before that happens or perhaps while the thing is still under consideration by the Council or the Board the Chairman may consult the members of his regular Conference upon the question what line he ought to take in his own dealings with the Council or in his playing in the Board-room his part as the Board's Chairman.

ELASTICITY OF THE SCOPE AND REQUIREMENTS OF THE CHAIRMANSHIP

611. This arrangement should, it seems to me, make the Chairmanship acceptable to an able energetic occupant. He will be able to keep well within the Constitution and yet have ample scope for genuine initiative. On the other hand, a Chairman, whose qualifications were limited to thoroughly good intentions and fair commonsense, could confine himself to his minimum functions and the Partnership might still draw ample vigour from the initiative of holders of other positions.

Perhaps I should mention that for many years I have never attended a meeting of the Central Council. My successors may think it better to proceed otherwise but I have thought that during this part of my career the Council would develop better if I left it as much as possible to itself. Reports in THE GAZETTE of the procedure of the Council are generally accompanied by an expression of my own views and I have commonly gazetted replies of my own to attacks anonymous or otherwise upon the Council.

THE CHAIRMAN MUST BE QUITE SUFFICIENTLY ACCESSIBLE

612. As was, I think, indicated a few pages ago, I think it is impossible to exaggerate the desirability of personal contact between the Chairman and all of the Partnership's members. In practice this must mean all

holders of certain posts and adequate representatives of all the remainder, including every section of the Rank and File.

I am very far indeed from suggesting that the Chairman, either in respect of his functions in the Board-room or in respect of the remainder of his functions that I have compared to a Managing Directorship, should be accessible only by ante-rooms, passage through which can be prevented or at all events obstructed by some other authority. But the absolute need to keep down to about a dozen the membership even of such bodies as the British Cabinet, that has to deal with all the affairs of many millions of people scattered all over the world, makes it necessary that, when the Chairman has to deal with some communication from someone who is not a member of the Central Board or of the Chairman's regular conference, the Chairman shall have available to him information and advice from some body of that size whose help he is accustomed to use in that way.

Obviously it will be necessary to be careful that the holders of other positions in the Partnership or that the members of particular sections do not feel that they themselves have not full proper access to the Chairman. That is of course a principal problem of all large-scale team-work. But it is equally plain that whoever has to fill the position of chief individual responsibility in any organisation, that is fairly large and complex, must have regular informants and advisers who are used to helping him in that way and with whom he is used to working.

THE CHAIRMAN'S ABSOLUTE RESPONSIBILITY TO THE PARTNERSHIP EMBODIED IN ITS COUNCIL

613. At meetings of the Board the Chairman will have with him, in addition to the Deputy Chairman, the five Heads of the Critical Side. In Conference matters he will have all of those six and in addition the Head of the Journalism, the Heads of the three Central Executive Departments, Expansion, Personnel and Financial Operations and, finally, the General Secretary whose function it is to secure the efficiency of all of the Partnership's committee work at the top level.

But, before I leave the Chairmanship, get me emphasise again that the Council can displace a Chairman whose decisions turn out too badly. He cannot claim that he is entitled to exemption because the real fault was somebody else's. He cannot argue that he was misinformed or ill-advised or that his intention was thwarted. Certainly the Council may choose to take the view that in the particular case there was some sufficient excuse and they may choose to refrain from exercising their power to displace him and to appoint whomsoever else the Trustees, whom they will have elected, may think fit but that will be a matter for the absolute discretion of the Council.

CHAPTER 35

JOURNALISM AND THE REVUE

613a. THIS Chapter upon Journalism has been placed immediately after the Principal Authorities because it is intended to be both for the Managers and for the Managed a really powerful means of influence for each upon the other. It is intended to vitalise the whole of the Partnership so as to maintain in every direction the utmost general awareness. The larger an organisation, the greater the risk of a deficiency of such vitality, as it is said that the vast animals, that are now extinct, perished from failure to develop a nervous-system adequate to their bulk.

614. Among our means of creating and maintaining an atmosphere of candid disclosure, freedom of speech and general partnership, I should put very high indeed the device, that in the spring of 1918 the Partnership adopted and has continued ever since, of publishing a weekly newspaper that accepts freely anonymous communications.

A newspaper, that publishes anonymous communications, can be a most potent means of achieving real team-work throughout a team no matter how large.

VALUE OF ANONYMITY

615. The anonymity is the point. From time to time writers to THE GAZETTE have attacked it as "un-English" but I have always answered that in the world outside the Partnership any of us can use a newspaper to speak our minds publicly upon, say, our local police or post office. The editor is quite likely to accept the letter for publication and, though he will require us to give as evidence of good faith a name and address, that he may or may not verify, he will allow us to write, if we like, over a *nom de plume* and he will strenuously guard the secret of our identity. Not only does that enable us to indulge in public criticism without fear of ill consequence to ourselves, it also safeguards the criticised from appearing to be revenging themselves upon their critics.

It would be awkward for a management to let slip a chance of promoting or to dismiss for reasons, that might be absolutely imperative and yet were not generally known and could not be published, someone who had lately contributed to the Partnership's newspaper some caustic criticism or very "awkward" enquiry. On the other hand, if he is himself a decent-minded person, he may be thereafter uneasy lest he seem to be taking unfair advantage of the presumable reluctance of the Management to appear to be biased against him. Moreover, it is very difficult for someone of senior standing to deal as thoroughly and as bluntly, as may be really desirable, with some communication that is signed by someone of very much more junior standing. But, if the communication is anonymous, no such difficulty arises.

Furthermore, many people, especially newcomers, would be shy of writing in their own names, lest they should seem to be conceited or excessively self-assertive or to have some other wrong motive.

Anonymity cuts both ways. It makes possible plain speaking to the Management but it also makes possible plain speaking to the Managed. Things, that deserve blame, may be known to happen but the identity of those injurers of the Partnership may not be known to the Management or, if they are, there may be no sufficient proof.

With no mention of names or any such indications, as might be challenged, of personal identity, frank speaking upon such matters in a community's own newspaper may be very highly effective.

GENERAL VALUE OF SUCH JOURNALISM

616.   In my own view Journalism of this kind is absolutely indispensable to real efficiency in large-scale team-work. In this last year or two I have heard vaguely of similar developments in America and for all, that I know, they may be long-established.

Partnership or no partnership, I would most earnestly advise all organisations, that are too large for really close, continuous contact between all of the Managers and all of the Managed, to provide themselves with this means of achieving such contact.

It is immensely salutary that critics shall be able with perfect safety to express their minds within the hearing of all concerned and that the answer to that criticism shall be known equally widely. It is immensely salutary that the worker's family or other friends shall be able to see the actual words of the Management instead of being given some possibly extremely inaccurate report of what somebody said in a speech or of some notice that has been posted up.

617.   "Wall-newspapers", said to be much used in Russia, are much better than nothing but they are utterly inferior to a newspaper that the worker can keep in his pocket, study at his leisure, produce in a discussion and show to his friends and they lack the immense advantage of a newspaper that it provides and makes accessible to all a permanent record of whatever is thus published. Everyone can point to any passage upon which he wishes to base some contention and on the other hand, if he denies that something was ever communicated to him, you have only to prove that the announcement was within his easy reach. Before the present paper-shortage limited so very awkwardly the space of THE

GAZETTE, the front page bore constantly a reminder that on a certain date the Council had resolved that publication in THE GAZETTE must be considered sufficient notice to everyone who at the time was a member of the Partnership.

SHOULD SUCH A NEWSPAPER BE ISSUED FREE? IN ANY CASE SHOULD IT BE CATCH-PENNY?

618.   At one time we tried issuing THE GAZETTE without charge. If you do that, a copy must be available for everyone and many will be wasted. A charge, however small, gets rid of that wastage. Circulation has tended to be about fifty per cent. of our community. No doubt very many copies are soon thrown aside and lost. On the other hand, a good few have several readers. A fifty per cent. circulation is, I think, very ample. There is some constant pressure to make the thing catch-penny. Those, who have difficulty in grasping ideas unfamiliar to them or in following a chain of argument that is at all complex, and those, who could, if they tried—but who resent any suggestion, that they shall—undertake "the intolerable toil of thought", will supply you with a stream of anonymous criticisms, some plaintive, some contemptuous, some ill-tempered. Do not play down to them. So far, as you can, let your paper give pleasure with bits of fun and with some things that, though not really necessary to the paper's functions in the business, will interest your readers.

But never forget that those functions are what really matter and that, so long as the paper is in those respects what it should be, it will achieve its real object.

GRATIFY ALL PROPER CURIOSITY AND DON'T BE ANY TOO MUCH AFRAID OF RESENTMENT OR DISAPPROVAL

619.   So far, as the law of libel will allow, and so far as you can without giving to competitors too much of your business-secrets, publish above all other things those that are likely to arouse strong resentment. Set them out candidly and invite your readers to say what they would do if they had to play your own part. Use your paper to make the business-life of your partners or employees or whatever they may be as interesting as possible. Talk to them as if you were talking to a meeting of shareholders or to a board of directors. Gratify, so far as you can, their mere curiosity. Any live-minded worker will be curious to know all sorts of things about his or her own business. If you want your team to work in the spirit of owners, you must give them the feelings of owners. Full information supplied constantly and in such a way, as to be as interesting as you can make it, is quite indispensable to the creation and maintenance of a general sense of ownership. Human nature being what it is, the unconventional and

anything on which feelings tend to be strong are apt to be especially interesting.

THE PARLIAMENTARY STANDARD

620. It is a matter of individual taste and skill how far you can go towards unconventionality without giving too much offence, being too discouraging or doing too much harm to discipline.

The aim of our own GAZETTE has been to go quite as far as and never any further than in the British House of Commons is reckoned fully permissible, the freedom of speech that is achieved by those particular members who to a rather extreme degree have the knack of hitting really hard in debate and yet of preserving good fellowship outside the Chamber.

From the strong disapproval and at times grave displeasure, that my own use of THE GAZETTE has aroused from time to time in my colleagues, I infer that none of those critics would have gone nearly so far towards trying to reproduce such disclosures and comment as in the world outside arise from the existence of representative institutions, especially the House of Commons, and from a free Press.

It is alleged that someone particularly well placed to judge of that matter (as a matter of fact a lady, a certain Mrs. Spedan Lewis) was once moved to observe: "Spedan has one great advantage. He has no sense of decency". The truth of the allegation is denied but I am afraid that if the tale was invented, the invention was not wholly without felicity.

A NECESSARY CONSEQUENCE OF A PROFOUNDLY NEW THING, INDUSTRIAL DEMOCRACY

621. Such objections arise perhaps from failure in imagination. The objectors are not able to feel that a large partnership has sufficient reason to seek to reproduce within itself the general structure and consequent practices of the national community. They feel that to keep alive in the memory of the Partnership certain mishaps is needlessly offensive and altogether inexpedient, though it would seem to them perfectly proper to quote in the House of Commons utterances or writings of a statesman of which the recalling at that time might be intensely unwelcome to him and, though it would seem to them likewise legitimate and perhaps highly desirable that public opinion should not be allowed to lose sight of the fact that on such and such occasions Mr. Gladstone or whomsoever you will had shown that in certain respects he was not infallible.

622. Obviously this sort of thing is thin ice and difficult going. On the other hand, the vitality and the real usefulness of a paper must depend very much upon the extent to which it plays successfully with fire and with edged tools, the extent, to which it sails close to the wind of what is for

one reason or another not permissible without allowing itself wrongly to be frightened into refraining from saying something that ought to be said.

In public life there has grown up gradually a long tradition of acceptance of general freedom of speech. The too thin-skinned are ridiculed and reckoned unfit for public life. People, who rise to high places in a business community, may be thin-skinned and they may be unshakably convinced that, however reasonable it may be to say that persons of their temperament should not enter public life, it is quite improper to say that such persons should not undertake to play their part in the conduct of the business of a partnership so large that proper unity of mind cannot be achieved without the need of something in the way of a newspaper.

SOME PRICE MUST BE PAID

623.   There is, I think, a tendency for some of those, who are most inclined to think that our partnership has some really great merits, to under-estimate the extent to which those merits could have been achieved without some real discomforts. The fitness, in which an athlete delights on the day of competition, was bought at the price of many aches and pains, many reluctant risings and goings forth to practice, many reluctant abstinences from this and from that. It is unquestionably true that our own partnership, so far as it is good at all, could have been just as good and it is quite possible that it might have been very importantly better if our Journalism had been less unseemly and annoying than at times it has been reckoned to be.

In a modern democracy Journalism has to keep within whatever laws are made to prevent abuses—libel, improper intrusions upon privacy and so on—but within those laws Journalism in a modern democracy can and does speak its mind very freely indeed upon the very highest authorities individual or collective.

624.   The enterprise of journalists in finding things out and in making them generally known and the ideas that journalists by their comments and criticisms may raise or spread or keep alive may be exceedingly disagreeable to political parties or great personages of one sort and another and may do much grave harm. Partnerships will presumably differ widely in their ideas of what is desirable and, if desirable, practicable in the way of democracy. In this particular partnership such democracy, as it conceives to be practicable, is thought to be on the whole expedient for efficiency as well as right for other reasons.

If democracy is to be genuine, then journalism must have a very high degree of such freedom of speech, for in a large community Journalism takes the place of talk among the members of a family, talk that is indispensable to the team-work of family life. Here and there freedom of speech will do harm and in some cases that harm may be really grave but that price may, I think, have to be paid.

625. As I have said already, it was prophesied that in our part of the business-world in which technicians like Buyers and Managers were quite unused to having their results published for all the world to contemplate, those technicians would be excessively discouraged or antagonised if those results were published at times when at first sight they did not tend to the personal glory of the technician. In practice that has not happened: On the other hand, it has happened on a good many occasions that publication of papers, that to my mind were quite unquestionably "parliamentary" or such as would have been thought perfectly proper and natural in the most respectable of our newspapers, have been resented with pain or anger or both as a quite unnecessary and more or less grossly improper procedure in the conduct of such a business as ours.

GRIT NEEDED HERE

626. Here we have one of the reasons for which to me it seems conceivable that the functions that in the course of many years I have gradually come to feel ought to be attached to some one post in such a partnership as our own, may turn out to give the Self-Governing Workshop that element of hard-headedness that, when it was achieved by the Rochdale Pioneers, made the success of the Cooperative Society of Consumers.

I conceive that the General Editor of its Journalism should be one of the Partnership's most important members. Its Journalism should be to the Partnership what the more respectable organs of the British Press have been to the life and especially to the politics of Great Britain.

The General Editor should be responsible to nobody but the Chairman and the Chairman, if forced to choose between a personal friendship and maintaining the proper depth and breadth and general liveliness of the Partnership's Journalism, should put duty first. He should maintain the Journalism and forgo the friendship.

627. The truth is apt to be unimportant except when it is more or less unpleasant to somebody and this may unfortunately be true even of well-deserved praise because that so easily excites jealousy. Public praise, that can be shown to friends and that will be on permanent record, is an immensely valuable stimulant and a most important function of such journalism as we are considering here.

Clearsightedness and grit in the maintenance of proper publicity may be vital to the success of partnership on more than a pretty small scale. Immunity for great personages from unwelcome publicity would be privilege in a peculiarly poisonous form, unless it were accompanied with equivalent immunity for small personages: in other words a total abolition of real publicity in respect of things that really matter.

I believe that some of those, who have resented my own practice in this respect, have resented it all the more because their own ideas of their duty to the Partnership and indeed of what was right and seemly, their own self-respect in fact, has not allowed them to make any similar use of THE GAZETTE either over their own signature or anonymously.

I think that in the main they have been wrong. I think that freedom of speech is a sham unless it is carried pretty well as far as in this country we carry it in our House of Commons and in our newspapers and I think that a very substantial amount of genuine freedom of speech is probably indispensable to the creation of a proper atmosphere of such equality as is really possible in a human community. And I feel rightly or wrongly that to the extent of that possibility sense of equality is for all concerned essential to the good life.

RELATION OF MANAGEMENT TO JOURNALISM

628. Editorial functions in the Journalism of such a community must obviously differ in some important respects from the corresponding functions in the world outside, where newspapers depend for their existence partly upon the payments of readers and partly upon selling advertisement-space, which sales depend upon the nature and extent of the paper's circulation.

A newspaper's course is governed to a considerable extent by need to get in this way a living and at the same time to keep within certain laws and perhaps certain requirements of Trade Unions or professional organisations of the same kind. On the other hand, it has a certain freedom, a certain real separateness from those who are the subject of its utterances.

But the Journalism of a partnership must be financed by the Partnership itself. Its procedure must have sufficient regard to those business-interests upon which depends the Partnership's existence. If the Journalism did in fact antagonise to an extent, that the Partnership simply could not afford, persons either inside or outside of it, then by indulging in such Journalism the Partnership would be cutting its own throat. To that extent the Management must watch the Journalism and take care it does not run too much risk of doing too much harm.

So does the general community in the world outside restrain libel by laws that are frequently declared by journalists to be needlessly strict and formidable in their penalties and to be gravely injurious to such freedom of newspaper speech as for the general community's own sake ought to exist.

MALICE MAY BE UNINTENTIONALLY HELPFUL

629.   Need of restraint in these respects is no reason why a partnership must despair of creating and developing within its own community sufficient general confidence that its own Journalism is quite sufficiently free, quite sufficiently independent, well-informed and outspoken.

As I have often said in THE GAZETTE, scurrilous communications are in many cases welcome because their publication proves to the simple-minded that in the matter of freedom of speech the Partnership really does live up to its professions.

It is odd to find yourself sacrificing the whole of what would have been a very large income and letting a part of the money be used to provide anonymous enemies with the means of throwing mud at you and endeavouring, so far as they can, to poison and thwart your life-work. But I have never seen any reason to doubt that the policy was sound.

Occasionally there has been a volume of protest, that I have felt to be rather formidably large, against the publication of what the protesters have felt to be particularly stupid and unpleasant attacks upon myself or (what has been felt, I think, to be really the same thing) upon the Partnership or of communications that, without being rather disgusting in that way, were so very silly as to be in the view of the protesters a gross waste of THE GAZETTE's space and too much of an annoyance to its readers. But, as I have said on such occasions, it has always seemed to me that the Partnership's only safe course was to err a really long way towards giving too much space to mud-slingers and fools.

If the total volume of contributions was impossibly large, publication would have to be refused to some of them but, until this war restricted very severely our supplies of paper, contributions to THE GAZETTE have hardly ever been more than could be printed fairly promptly and, so long as that has continued to be the case, I have felt that, while the Partnership was still comparatively young, it would be better to print pretty well everything rather than run the slightest risk of failing to build up general extreme confidence that THE GAZETTE never withheld publication from anything that ought perhaps to be published.

PRIVATE PERSONS ARE ENTITLED TO PRIVACY. THE MANAGED ARE ENTITLED TO USE THEIR JOURNALISM TO ATTACK THEIR MANAGEMENT BUT NOT FOR MERELY SPITEFUL ATTACKS UPON EACH OTHER

630.   For many years from THE GAZETTE's first start almost the only suppressions were a very few anonymous letters, that were written not against the Management or any section of the Management but simply with the object of giving offence or causing pain to someone on the writer's own apparent level. We do not allow the House of Commons to be used for attacks upon the sense or good faith of private persons. In

such matters those, who enter public life, must be prepared to give and take but, so long as the procedure of private persons is not in the common opinion so much a matter of public concern as to justify criticism in Parliament, we recognise that private persons are entitled to privacy.

Our Law allows to newspapers a right of fair comment upon a matter of public interest. It is a matter of public interest whether certain things are true of somebody who chooses to enter public life, even to the extent, for example, of entering into contractual relations with a Public Authority. But a newspaper could not use that plea as a defence to a claim that it had unwarrantably defamed or otherwise injured a private person.

THE GAZETTE has accordingly distinguished between anonymous communications that appeared to arise from ill-will of one member of the rank-and-file or holder of some junior position to another. THE GAZETTE's has not allowed itself to be used as a tool for such purposes merely because the writer of the letter made in it some pretence that the publicity would be justified by the matter's importance to the Partnership as a whole or, alternatively, that in such a case a Partner was entitled to the satisfaction of such publicity.

But these cases have, as I say, been very few indeed—no more, it is believed, than three or four in all of THE GAZETTE's thirty years.

CENSORSHIP

631.   It has always been intended that this function of censorship should belong as much as possible to the Council but, in my view, the Chairman must always have power to safeguard the Partnership from indulging in publicity that at a particular time would be too gravely dangerous to its own welfare. The risk is not confined to possible offence to customers or potential customers.

Suppose the Partnership was engaged or was expecting to be engaged in a very important operation for which the zealous services of some particular Partner were necessary. Certainly, if he were suddenly killed by some accident, the Partnership would have to manage without him. But it seems very doubtful whether the Constitution ought to allow a bare majority of the Council to make of THE GAZETTE some use that at that particular time would discourage or antagonise that particular Partner in a way that might be exceedingly unfortunate for the Partnership.

In framing constitutions for organisations intended to be permanent you must allow for some rather fantastic theoretical possibilities. It is true the Chairman can drop from the Partnership anyone whose continuance in it would be in his view too dangerous to its welfare. But it seems extremely undesirable to create any avoidable risk that the Chairman may be forced to use that power to prevent what he might judge, perhaps rightly, to be a very grave misleading of the Council. Moreover, the most resolute and far-reaching action of that kind might not be in time to prevent the damage.

632. I hold therefore that the functions of the Chairmanship must include those of Principal Press Censor and that the Partnership's safeguard against misuse of that power must be in the possibility that a Court of Law might hold that the power had been abused. But I would most certainly urge that the occupant in any partnership of its position of chief responsibility should take the utmost care to make in this matter all proper use of the assistance of the Council and should take the greatest pains to maintain constantly throughout the Partnership absolute confidence that its Journalism has all the freedom and as much as possible of the efficiency of such newspapers as "The Times", "The Manchester Guardian" or "The Economist" at their best.

IMPORTANCE OF THE GENERAL EDITORSHIP

633. I have often said that if I wished to make a career in our own partnership and I were offered the General Editorship of its Journalism on condition that acceptance was to disqualify me absolutely from ever occupying in the Partnership any other position, I would accept immediately, with no fear at all that I might fail to make a competent Central Management feel that my services in that capacity were worth at least as much as they could have been in any other.

In my view a really good Editor should make the Partnership's Journalism an unceasing spring of vitality and an immensely effective force both of impulse and of restraint.

Being in a fool's paradise, mere inadvertence, is one of the chief dangers in the practical conduct of human affairs. Anything, that serves as eyes and ears, a thoughtful brain and an effective tongue, can play in that way a priceless part and on top of all those functions you have the immense possibilities of publicity as a general galvaniser, a general encourager and a general sweetener of tempers, though, as has been mentioned, there have been occasions on which the Journalism of this particular partnership has appeared to have in this last respect effects of another kind.

In the matter of galvanising, it is, in my view, difficult to exaggerate the importance of seeing in public print your own performance or that of your particular group. A GAZETTE that in this respect was managed with real resourcefulness and vigour, would do an immense amount to prevent stagnation and slackness, conscious or unconscious, in every hole and cranny of all the Partnership's thousands of posts.

634. Ever since THE GAZETTE was started I have contributed a very great deal of signed copy and some that has been anonymous, things that I have thought had better appear as anonymous editorial pronouncements.

For many years THE GAZETTE has had a whole-time Editor and the successive occupants of that post, most of whom are still in the Partnership but who have moved to functions of more importance than what was really an assistant editorship, have played what I have felt to be a quite important part.

Some of THE GAZETTE's present regular features were created by them and THE GAZETTE has owed much of its success to their work as well as to the great helpfulness of its printers, The Bucks Free Press, but almost every week I have read it pretty closely and have almost always sent the Editor some critical suggestions.

I have taken responsibility for all the more dangerous of its publications and in such things the initiative has generally been my own. The Partnership would be far more securely self-supporting and correspondingly more sure of continuance without any serious change of its general character if my part in its Journalism were reduced extremely.

635. Journalism of this kind can serve many purposes. In 1940, when France was tottering, I began to feel that THE GAZETTE ought to be used to help the Partners to stand the strain of the war and so to maintain and indeed to heighten throughout the Partnership the sense of unity, the family spirit, at which we had always aimed. The War-articles, that developed from this idea, became a rather formidable undertaking. They appeared almost every week from the 25th May 1940 until the 20th February 1943. Between those dates there were 138 and then again between the 6th May 1944 and the 24th February 1945 there were a further 7.

They had to go to the printer by the first post on Monday morning, so they had always to be a week in arrear of the news, a formidable handicap in trying to write upon such a thing as war news a commentary that the Partnership would feel to be worth reading. This meant that they had to be written on Sundays, so that to inferences drawn from the newspapers of the previous week there could be added any from those that appeared on Sunday mornings. The articles became a decoction of "The Times", "The New Statesman", "The Economist", three Sunday newspapers, "The Contemporary Review", and occasionally some other "monthlies", "The Round Table" and some miscellaneous reading of writers upon military matters, notably Ludendorff and Captain Liddell Hart.

Week after week the dictation lasted until the small hours of Monday morning and week after week the typing was done after that. In February of 1943, when the real danger seemed to be over, I said so and added that

that article would be the last. But the pressure, particularly from Partners on Active Service, to continue them was so strong that I felt that, heavy though the work was, it ought to be kept going for some months further.

Many Partners on Service made a point of having THE GAZETTE sent to them and, as the paper-shortage began to restrict our circulation to two thousand a week or something of that sort, Partners made among themselves quite elaborate arrangements to pass THE GAZETTE on from one to another.

I think there is no doubt that, though, as I endeavoured to keep pointing out, the articles were merely the efforts of a layman to get what he could from the newspapers and books that were quoted, they were a boon to many Partners and their families and did a corresponding amount of good in keeping people happier and in maintaining the Partnership's family spirit. In any long continuing period of great public anxiety I would urge the Partnership to follow this precedent and provide again a frank weekly review of a reasonably wide set of respectable sources of information.

I made a point of remarking frequently that the articles were intended to be the equivalent of family talk upon the latest war news. From time to time there were suggestions that after the war these articles should be published as a whole.

The copyright of THE GAZETTE belongs to the Partnership and the articles will be there if it is ever thought desirable to republish them. Perhaps some day some people, who read them week by week through the war, may like to have them again in that form. But so long at all events as the present paper-shortage lasts, I should not for my own part vote for this. If space had allowed, it might, I think, have been worth while to reprint a few of them here as a memorial of those days and as examples of the use that a business-organisation can make of its own newspaper in times of great general anxiety.

IMPENDING DEVELOPMENTS OF OUR JOURNALISM

636. My own retirement in the main from all this writing and editing was one of the many developments for which we were just about ripe when the war began. Indeed, some time before that I made one or two efforts to get this particular work off my own shoulders. Those efforts came to nothing but I hope that it will not be long now before we shall succeed.

This book itself should go far to help an Editor to comprehend the functions of the Partnership's Journalism and to lighten for me the task of handing over. But for the war that ought certainly to have been achieved some years ago and it is now the more urgent because the Partnership is starting under the name of Chronicles local newspapers in its larger Branches and in the groups of smaller Branches.

There clearly must be something of that kind. From 1918 until 1924 THE GAZETTE itself was confined to Peter Jones. The galvanising function, that seems to me so exceedingly important, involves dealing with very small details. They may be of ample interest to a sufficient number of the Partners in one particular Branch or group of little Branches that are sufficiently of the same kind but, if such details were gathered into one central GAZETTE, it would be impossibly large and the greater part of it would be of no interest to any one reader.

Apart from the other disadvantages, it would be too monstrously wasteful to print pages and pages of local affairs costing altogether several pence per copy and then to sell all that for one penny, to each of all THE GAZETTE's thousands of readers. Clearly we must have a central GAZETTE corresponding to the national press and branch GAZETTES corresponding to local newspapers, for those local affairs of which the publication will be a powerful stimulant to effort and a strong enhancement of the interest of the daily work but that would interest very few of the Partners in other branches and would, moreover, if such details for each of all our many branches were published as a single whole, make a newspaper quite impossibly large.

All this will make the Journalism a much heavier mass of work than hitherto it has been. These "Branch Gazettes" have now begun to come into existence and have been named Chronicles for distinction from the central Gazette and to retain the convenience of a single word that can serve either as a noun ("It is in the Chronicle") or as a verb ("That must be chronicled"). Next year the Partnership's Journalism is expected to cost about £30,000, a full one per cent. of the Partnership's total Pay-Roll, but I would far rather undertake to keep the Partnership's business healthy for a Pay-Roll smaller by one per cent, than without such means of constant direct communication between all and sundry as the Journalism provides. Such a team has many of the qualities and needs of a live multi-cellular organism, an animal or a plant, and Journalism is a large and an indispensable part of its nervous system.

WEEKLY PUBLICATION AND SOME PROSPECTIVE EXPERIMENTS

637. After THE GAZETTE had grown from less frequent publication to appearing every week, we tried issuing it twice a week. That seemed unsuccessful. Weekly seems to be often enough but for our present requirements it seems very highly desirable that the frequency shall be no less.

I hope we shall try before long various methods of illustration. I believe we shall find the cost amply justified.

Our acquisition of the Suburban & Provincial Stores, increasing, as it did, our business by more than fifty per cent., might have cheapened such things as THE GAZETTE. Most of its expenses could have remained the same. In the main the difference might have been merely the extra paper. In my view that policy would have been quite wrong. In such a case we ought not to say to ourselves that in the course of years our GAZETTE has developed in a way that now requires a certain subsidy and that we have been pretty well satisfied with the success of our business and that therefore, so far as that success has depended upon THE GAZETTE, the subsidy must have been sufficient. We ought on the contrary to say that we have been getting out of our business a profit that has on the whole contented us and that has been achieved in spite of a GAZETTE-subsidy of so much a year on each member of our Partnership. A sudden enlargement of the Partnership should not be used to reduce the rate of such charges as that subsidy. The rate should be at least maintained and the amount thereby increased.

638. From that increase we should do our utmost to get the best possible results and so, as the Partnership grew, we should continue until some day we should feel presumably that THE GAZETTE was now about as valuable as it really could be to the efficiency of our business and as a source of pleasure.

Then, if the Partnership grew further, we should cease to maintain the rate of the subsidy and should instead let THE GAZETTE become cheaper in its proportion to the Partnership's total revenues. Here is an excellent example of thinking of a business is a living organism of which the various organs must have a proper proportion to the size and complexity of the whole thing and must be enlarged or diminished, as may seem to be right, in relation to changes in the real scope for each of them.

THE BEGINNING OF OUR JOURNALISM   1918

639. The first issue of THE GAZETTE began with a letter that is reprinted here. As will be seen, answers were invited but there was only one and that not very appreciative or encouraging. At that time I had been for four years risking almost half of all that I had in the world (and incidentally forgoing a quarter of the profits of John Lewis and Company) and working desperately hard, all to try out this plan of partnership when I might have been jogging placidly on at Oxford Street with a large income and a virtual certainty of being my father's sole heir.

The starting of this newspaper and the contribution to it of this opening letter were in a way the most dramatic move that up to that time I had had an opportunity to make. I had taken corresponding pains with it and I might have hoped that the response would indicate both that the idea of THE GAZETTE was welcomed and also that the trouble and money, that I had poured out upon Peter Jones in immense improvements for the comfort of the staff, had produced some warmth of good will that would now show itself.

I mention all this for the encouragement of other people who may start partnerships and who may find that, until they are able to distribute partnership benefit on a pretty substantial scale, the response is chilly, suspicious and unhelpful.

640.   I am very far from suggesting that, so far as I was concerned, the general atmosphere of my daily work was as bleak as might be supposed from the solitary response to the invitation of cooperation in starting this GAZETTE. But, anyhow, you cannot have it both ways. If the average mind were pretty lively, we should have a totally different world. Man is, we are told, still in his very early infancy and the brightest of us is no doubt very dull compared to the ultimate possibilities of mankind. But already the average members of the civilised nations deal easily with ideas that could hardly be got into the heads of those primitive races of whom some survivors linger on in the depths of tropical forests and here and there at the extreme edges of the great continents.

If people are in some ways unappreciative, on the other hand they are often very generously tolerant and, when something does light up their minds, their response can be very warm. All the same, I would urge anyone who thinks he sees the way to some promised land and who seeks to lead others there, to be content with the gardener's reward. He does not expect the plants to clap their hands when he comes in sight. His reward is in their prosperity.

641.   If it is your fate to be the founder or chief leader of a partnership you are not dealing with plants but with people whose capacity may be in some very important ways greater than your own and, if they are really lit up, not importantly inferior in any way. But all the same, you may at times be pretty badly disappointed by what you may feel to be inertia and unhelpfulness. If you are, you may be wise to reflect that no expressions of appreciation from the plants ever gladdened the ears of a gardener. Better not to say so; some uncharitable person might accuse you of arrogance. But in your private mind you may be wise to get so far as you can the habit of feeling that, as I have sometimes remarked in THE GAZETTE, the only popularity truly worth while is the sort you get when you are dead. If the unacknowledged and apparently unfelt results of your work will not be for you a sufficient reward, you may be wise to choose some other occupation, lest your energies be too far weakened or your mind soured by disappointment of your possibly unreasonable expectations of understanding, sympathy and appreciation.

For my own part, I have met with all the understanding and friendliness that I ever hoped. The particular use I have made of my own life has been more rather than less fruitful of such pleasures as I reckoned it might yield. But it has surprised me that after so many years there are still in such a community as the Partnership quite a few people whose good sense and good temper do not prevent their writing to THE GAZETTE such anonymous letters as they do. Just as I did not expect that in such a community there would be so much, as there has always been and is still, of stealing of the private property of the Partners themselves, so I reckoned that, if in time we should have so many, as now we certainly have, of Partners who understand the Partnership very well and whose feelings for it seem to me to be all that I ever hoped they would be, association with them would produce in pretty well all of the others enough understanding to prevent their having such feelings as are shown in those letters.

642.   My own impression after forty years is, that in that part of the business world, in which my own life has been spent, there are a great many people who are all that I ever hoped to find them but that, on the other hand, there are far more, than in my early years I expected, who are impervious to influences no warmer and stronger than our particular partnership generates for people of their sort.

The following was the opening letter in the first issue of our GAZETTE, (the 16th March 1918). One of the reasons for which it is reprinted here, is to show the extent to which at that time the ideas, from which the Partnership has arisen, were already settled and published.

"Ladies and Gentlemen,
"The main purpose of this paper you will see in a general way from the paragraphs on the last page, which are intended to appear always, or at least frequently. But I think it may be useful if in this first issue I try to put my ideas with regard to it more fully before you than can be done there.

    "There can be no doubt that large-scale industry has come to stay. Whatever may be the ultimate economic cause or causes, it is certain that in our own, as in many other occupations, men and women achieve their purpose better, that is to say they get a greater result for any given amount of effort by working in large teams than by working in small ones. We cannot help seeing that the big factory can produce exactly the same thing cheaper than can the little factory, and that the big shop can likewise beat its little rivals by offering the public greater variety or better value or a combination of both. Some people argue that cheapness is not everything, and that the world might contain more happiness if goods were dearer but more men and women worked 'on their own account'. I think these people are wrong. I think they fail to see that cheapness is really human liberty: that, if everything were to be had absolutely free of charge, everyone would be absolutely free, so long, of course, as the law restrained mere bodily strength as it does now; and that, this being so, cheapness is in itself wholly good and desirable.

"Look at it like this:

"Suppose 1,000 men, in order to support themselves and their families, have to make 1,000 wardrobes every year. Suppose that each man working by himself must be at work sixteen hours a day, seven days a week all the year through, to finish his one wardrobe. Is that man really free, although he is working in his own home and on his own account? Is it freedom to be obliged, on pain of starvation, to work sixteen hours every day of the year?

"Now, suppose that those 1,000 men combine into one team and become each of them a specialist in one or two of all the different jobs that go to the making of a wardrobe, and use in one factory such machinery as cannot be separately set up in each of 1,000 homes. And suppose that in that way to turn out their thousand wardrobes they need work only eight hours a day, six days a week, forty-eight weeks a year. Are they not incomparably freer than they were before?

"You will agree that they are, but you will go on to point out that large-scale industry is not so simple and innocent as all this sounds. In practice it produces two new kinds of men: the capitalist, who wants an unreasonable share of the factory's takings, and the managers who likewise want an unreasonable share and who, moreover, instead of trying to interfere with the workers as little as possible, and to be as fair as possible in that interference, tend to interfere as much as ever they can and trouble very little about fairness, and in plain English become more or less offensive tyrants.

"My answer to this is that it is undeniably true, but that there is no reason, apart from unnecessary human folly and unnecessary human wickedness, why these by-products of large-scale industry should have arisen at all and that, having arisen, they are perfectly capable of being entirely abolished.

"After all, this is only a repetition of the trouble we had in working out a decent system of government. Men had to have governments because, if they did not, every strong or clever man made the lives of his less gifted neighbours unbearable. And for ages and ages the men and women who, whether by accident of birth or of natural talents, happened to be in the governing positions, misbehaved outrageously. Here and there you got a real sportsman, who had a first-rate sense of decency and acted up to it, but he or she was a very, very rare exception. Very nearly all of them all over the world for ages and ages were comfortably confident that their countries existed first of all for their own benefit, and they were playing the game quite creditably if they were neither extraordinarily extravagant of the public revenue in their personal and court expenditure nor extraordinarily slack in the work they were really paid to do, namely conducting the public business.

"Thus, over and above this comfortable confidence that it was perfectly natural and right that they should spend pretty well any proportion of the public revenues that they thought fit on their fancies, they commonly allowed themselves to break the laws to almost any extent.

"And this went on all over the world for thousands of years. Men could see no way of getting a government at all except at the price of tolerating more or less gross abuses of power by the governors, and, since they found it impossible to do without government, they grumbled and groaned over the abuses but just made the best of it and pitied for a crank anybody who argued that such things need not be at all and presumably would some day pass away.

"Now, if you think of it, this is exactly the situation to-day of the world of large-scale industry. The chiefs, under whom our 1,000 wardrobe-makers placed themselves for the sake of the overwhelming advantages of large-scale organisation, have been just like so many old-time kings. They have helped themselves to a quite unreasonably large proportion of the revenues of the business.

"They have made a regular practice of giving fat jobs to their own kinsmen or favourites, and now and then, when a sufficiently strong fancy seized them, they have done things which are clean contrary to any sound rules of business, just as the old-time kings allowed themselves to break their country's laws.

"And the modern captains of industry do all these things with just the same comfortable confidence, as the old-time kings, that it is perfectly natural and right, and mankind in general just makes the best of it and pities for a crank anybody who argues that such things need not be at all and presumably will some day pass away.

"Yet it is so.

"The day will certainly come when no man will be free to take out of the earnings of a business five or ten times as much for himself (over and above a fair interest on his capital) as he could get for the same year's work if he were a paid manager instead of the owner.

"To whom the difference will go is a very interesting question.

"The co-operators say the consumer should get it.

"I agree that it will come to this in time, but I very much doubt if that time is come yet. The social organisation of mankind is a very slow-growing tree, and, if you contrive somehow to force a premature shoot, it always withers, and in the long run time is not gained but lost.

"For my own part I am very much inclined to think that the natural next step—with which, precisely because it is natural, we now shall be wise to be content—is the just distribution among the other trades of the industrial world, to each in proportion to its true earning-power, of the unfair part of the present share of capital and management.

"If you ask me how I propose to decide what is fair and unfair, and what is the relative earning-power of different grades, e.g. of a window-dresser and a motor-driver, my answer is that I have no idea.

"But no more has anyone who sets himself to invent a new machine or a new pudding or a code of laws or anything else that requires to be built up bit by bit with constant experiment and consideration all the time.

"All you need ask yourself to start with is, 'What am I driving at, and will it be worth having if I get it?' Now, I am quite clear what I am driving at. I am trying to build up a system of business which shall serve the public not less well than the ordinary type of the present day but which shall differ from the ordinary type in the very important respect that it shall be carried on not for the benefit of the capitalists, to whom it will pay for such capital as it requires no more than it finds that it must, or yet for the benefit of the Managers—including myself—to whom it will pay no more than the full market-rate for our services, but for the benefit of the staff as a whole, Managers and all.

"This obviously means that, when once we are making profit enough to pay all our dividends and to provide proper reserve funds against a rainy day, all further profit will belong to the Staff, and that it will, therefore, be for the Staff to decide whether they will work a shorter day or week, down to whatever may prove to be enough to pay the dividends, or whether they will have the extra money. There is no powder hidden in this jam: no conditions of having been so many years with the company or of having to give up this or that on leaving. The business will be run by the Staff for the Staff, subject to scrupulous care of the capital and the dividends, just as a modern state, however democratic, has to be scrupulously careful to play the game with regard to its National Debt.

"Of course it will be a long time before my cautious and intensely conservative temperament (this policy is profoundly conservative though you may not think so: it is really in the long run the natural alternative to anarchy) will allow me to hand over beyond recall the supreme authority in our affairs to whatever organisation may grow up to take it over. But such growth can only be by means of the exercise first of all of advisory functions, and the sooner and the faster we get to work in this direction, the better.

"Our own Parliament, which now governs the Empire, not so well as we could wish but still better than any great Empire has ever been permanently governed hitherto, grew up from a small advisory body that used to meet in the Chapter House of Westminster Abbey long, long before this world had outgrown the idea of the Divine Right of Kings, and long, long before a strong king need trouble himself much about laws or public opinion or private rights or anything else but the attachment of a handy body of soldiers. In the same way our Board of Directors which, unlike most Boards, is drawn entirely from the Staff, and our elected Staff Committees may perfectly well develop in time into a thoroughly adequate Governing Body, amply skilful and able enough from the standpoint of management, and at the same time genuinely representative of all sections of the Staff. Such a general Governing Body would of course deal with much of its business by means of Committees, either permanent or temporary, but all these questions must be left to Time.

"I have told you all this in order that you may have a general idea of my ultimate object, namely, the evolution of a new social organism, an efficient self-governing community of business-people of all sorts and kinds, all free to leave whenever they like, just as any Briton can become a citizen of another country if he likes, but all sharing in its prosperity, so long as they are in it, in the just proportion of the value of the work that each does, i.e. in proportion to their pay, and all having an influence upon its administration of the same kind as that which we all have upon the government of our country.

"Now I come back to the GAZETTE.

"To the healthy development of a white community, we see all over the world that two things are necessary.

"First: Representative Institutions. Of these we have already made a beginning with the Staff Committees.

"Second: a Newspaper Press. And, just as the Institutions to serve their true purpose must be well manned with honest and capable representatives, so the Newspaper Press to serve its true purpose must be honestly and sensibly conducted in the public interest.

"It must not admit contributions on one side of a public question and exclude those on the other side. It must not try to mislead the community as a whole for the benefit of certain interests. It must not foster in the public temperament an appetite for empty, vulgar and morbid sensationalism. It must not allow itself to be used, as it is in Paris and elsewhere, as an instrument for diminishing by lying insinuations the influence of honest men. Above all it must not allow itself to curry favour with its readers by taking 'the popular' line when it really thinks it is the wrong line.

"On the other hand, it must not allow private connections or even friendships to hinder it from publishing anything that may be unwelcome or even seriously painful to individuals, if such publication seems likely to be for the general good.

"That is the easy and modest programme of our GAZETTE

"If you think it over carefully, you will see why it must be a thing apart from the Management and independent, and why it must be prepared to publish anonymous communications which are not on the face of them such as clearly ought not to be published. Experience will no doubt enable us to work out a more or less clear code of rules, but the general intention is to publish anything that conceivably would not be refused publication by any respectably conducted paper.

"For example, if a letter is received which says that the writer thinks that it would be better for the House if the Staff of such a department were not in such a hurry to leave at nights, or if such and such a Buyer did not go in so exclusively for such and such a kind of goods or particular wholesale House, or if the Chairman did not rely so much, as he seems to do, on the advice of So-and-So in such and such matters, or were to pay at least one visit a week to such and such a part of the premises, anything of that kind would be published without hesitation.

"Honest criticism is good for all of us, and the higher our position the more we are likely to lose for the lack of it. If the rest of the Staff will tell me and my principal colleagues where we fall short of what seems to be possible, we will not be backward in returning that good service: I will not be, at all events.

"It seems to me that this ought to do a tremendous lot of good. To see ourselves as others see us: to hear in good, plain words how intensely some possibly necessary, possibly unnecessary, change of system, or dismissal, or what not, is resented by at least one person, can never do harm and must often do great good. For example, I dare say the next number will contain some very strong objections, signed or unsigned, to some or all of these rather unusual ideas, and very likely some of those objections may lead to useful changes in the GAZETTE's policy as it stands now.

"But to provide everybody with a convenient means of 'talking straight' to the Powers-that-Be will be only one of its important functions.

"It will pay well for contributions of any real interest from the standpoint of business, such as an article on 'Things that are Better Managed at Gorringe's' or 'Drawbacks of Drapery Life in London compared to Denmark' or Montreal, or Manchester, or New Zealand: or 'Changes I should Make if I were Buyer of . . . . . Department'.

"There is clearly no reason why questions of this kind should not be discussed in the House Press just as the 'All Big-Gun Policy' or the Food Orders are discussed in the Public Press. But, apart altogether from business, it will pay in the same way for good contributions on matters of general interest, such as 'An Easter Holiday in the Peak District', or 'Impressions from Letters Home from the Argentine' or 'Half an hour with a German Prisoner'. I may remark here that, whenever the writer desires it, literary style, etc., will be 'touched up' for publication, but of course with great care not to alter meaning.

"This letter is already so enormously long that I suspect that, if I do not stop soon, the Editor will cut me down, so I will leave the rest unsaid.

"Of course, it may be that factors for which I have not allowed will defeat this notion of giving to the House, by means of a publication conducted on these lines, the advantages which society at large derives from the general Newspaper and Magazine Press, but I hope that it will be successful. For I do think that it could fill an important need, that is none the less real because from long use we are unconscious of it.

"I am,

Yours faithfully,

J. SPEDAN LEWIS.

"(We should be glad to publish correspondence on the questions raised by this letter.—Editor.)"

643.   In addition to this invitation there was printed on another page of the same GAZETTE the following notice:

"*Competitive Contributions*
"Subject I.—Prize one guinea.
"What do you consider the good and bad points of the policy of this paper as described and exemplified in this issue? What changes or additions would you advise?"

To the note at the foot of the letter there was no answer at all. For the competition the following was the only entry:

"Dear Mr. Editor,
"THE GAZETTE, if it has come to stay, must alter its style in a few points, and should be, as doubtless it will, far more racy and interesting.

"It would be better if it were called *Our* GAZETTE, and the title of the Company put only on the outside.

"The statement as to whether it is to be issued weekly or monthly should have been made. Personally, I hope weekly (sic) as life is too brief (my leisure I mean) for me to take in and assimilate all the complex matter, and exuberant verbosity, which flows from the pen of the writer of the opening statements. The said writer also addresses us, his servants, as fellow-employees; c'est camouflage, n'est-ce pas? For I cannot allow myself to think of the Chairman of the Board of Directors being such. Can we not know the name of the Editor, and should not the address of the publisher be affixed at the bottom of the outside page?

"Why on earth do you insert three pages of Cookery Recipes? Every daily paper gives half a column of these! Obviously, to fill up! Please don't —the space is far too valuable. Our firm never allow Haberdashery to be shown in the windows.

"Those two wrong dates on page 15 are glaring errors. You want a good type reader, but, as this is the first number, we accept the apology. The bank is a good idea, and should be well patronised."

Upon this solitary response to the requests in my opening letter the following comment was made editorially but, in fact, by me.

"We are very much obliged to the writer of this anonymous letter because he (or she) has furnished us with what we were afraid we might not get, namely, an opportunity to give a striking example of our entire readiness to publish any anonymous communications that appear to be written in good faith, even though they may not be expressed with good humour or good taste. With the criticism, that our first number might have been racy and interesting, we have no quarrel. On the contrary, we quite agree that a paper of this kind should cultivate variety of interest. A first number, however, or even any early number, is bound to be rather different in many respects from the general character which the paper may, in the long run, develop with actual experience. We do not agree that "The Gazette of Peter Jones, Ltd." should be called "Our Gazette", any more than the "Army and Navy Gazette" or the "Manchester Guardian" should be called "Our Gazette" or "Our Guardian". The statement whether it was "to be issued weekly or monthly" was omitted, as our correspondent might have guessed, for the very good reason that only experience can show how often we had better publish.

"The letter suggests that the Chairman's address of his letter to "My Fellow-Employees" is camouflage. But this is not the case. The Chairman has just begun, now that the Company is making a profit instead of running at a loss, to charge it a salary for his own services, and so is, therefore, perfectly entitled to call himself our fellow-employee. Certainly it so happens that he has a controlling interest in the Company, which employs him and us, but that is another question altogether.

"It is not usual in this country for organs of opinion to publish the names of the editors. The same applies, we think, to the name of the printer, though it is possible that on both these points our practice, though general, is not universal.

"The Cookery Recipes are not published, as our correspondent so hastily assumes, for lack of other matter, of which, on the contrary, we had to hold over a part for future issues. We published these war-recipes because we thought that they might be welcome in some of the homes to which, we presume, the GAZETTE will find its way. We should be very glad if any of our readers who would like such articles occasionally, will let us know. This is just the sort of thing on which we must be guided by experience.

"The errors in proof-reading we deplore. How easy it is to fall into such misfortune will no doubt be more fully realised by our correspondent when we point out to him (or her) that his own manuscript also contains an error. It is quite clear that where we have printed (sic) he intended to write either "monthly" or else "not weekly", since "weekly" by itself does not make sense. We think that our readers will sympathise with our inability on making this discovery to refrain from chuckling.

"This error, however unfortunate, will not disqualify the writer for the prize, which we shall be glad to offer him, as his contribution was the only answer to Subject 1. In such cases we shall award the prize if the solitary contribution has, as this one certainly has, some real merit. Editor, THE GAZETTE."

644. Twenty-eight years after this first issue of THE GAZETTE there appeared in it the following correspondence. It is reprinted here for two reasons. It shows the general confidence in freedom of speech that enables a Partner in the Workrooms to write thus polemically upon an utterance of the Director of Selling, a Partner of very long standing and holding one of the most important positions in the whole organisation. It shows also the extent to which the general character of the Partnership is congenial to all the four main lines of political thought at this present time, Conservative, Liberal, Socialist and Communist, a thing that seems to justify hope that this may be one of those innovations that are not premature and that have a corresponding chance of being useful.

(From THE GAZETTE of the 26th October 1946)
"Politics
"(The Chief Editor has sent to me, in case I may have some comment
to make upon it, the following letter dated the 9th September from Mr.
Arrowsmith. I have looked up in THE GAZETTE of the 30th August
the comment by the Principal Director of Selling that has aroused
Mr. Arrowsmith's 'surprise and disgust'. As that comment and the
letter, upon which it was written, are not very long, I have suggested
to the Chief Editor that they shall be reprinted here, together with
Mr. Arrowsmith's own letter and the comment that I am now about
to make upon that.—J.S.L.)

"Discouragement of Shop-Lifting
"13.6.46.
"To the Editor of the GAZETTE,
"Sir,
"I believe it is true to say that more people are now indulging in shop-
lifting than ever before. Quite a number of these obviously are not the
professional kind—but are victims of a sudden temptation; it looks so
easy and it does save a few coupons.

"Would not a great many of this type be deterred if they realised
that it was not as easy as it looked; that we were on the lookout
for it and that the risk of being caught was considerable, as their
predecessors had found to their cost?

"At present there is nothing to show how great are the risks they
run in attempting it—nor how grave the results may be. A notice of
a similar kind to that adopted by the London Passenger Transport
Board to deter irate passengers from beating up their conductors,
would show that breaches of the law can have terrible consequences,
and might save some of our customers from a sudden lapse into crime,
and ourselves from this irritating and costly way of losing stock.
"Yours, etc., 'CAVEAT EMPTOR'.

"The Director of Selling has commented as follows:
"I am afraid that I do not like the suggestion of 'Caveat Emptor'. If
his suggestion were adopted, it would create a bad feeling amongst
most of the customers; after all, it is only a very few who fall to the
temptation of shop-lifting.

"The whole suggestion smacks of Nazism; these are the sort
of tactics that the late Dr. Goebbels would employ, and I am not,
therefore, in the least surprised that such practices are indulged in by
the London Passenger Transport Board, which is a child of socialism

and nationalisation, and very much in keeping with National Socialism.

"J. M. FITZROY NEWDEGATE, Director of Selling.

"9.9.46
"To the Editor of the GAZETTE,
"Sir,
"Ever since our store became a member of the Partnership I have seen it inferred in THE GAZETTE that, rightly so, political opinions had no place in the internal affairs of our community. Therefore I was surprised and disgusted to read the Director of Selling's vitriolic attack in his reply to 'Caveat Emptor's' letter in THE GAZETTE of 31.8.46.

"I quite agree with him that the suggestion was not good for civil business, but this was no occasion for a direct assault upon what is probably the most efficient transport service in this country.

"If we are thus to transcend the unwritten laws, then we can clearly state that the whole conception of this great Partnership of ours was and is a revolutionary, socialist design with well-nigh nation-wide aspirations; and if Commander FitzRoy Newdegate does not consider this a great step in the direction of a planned social economic State in which all industries are plied for the benefit of all classes, then I, for one, would like to know his precise view of the structure and application of the Partnership scheme.

"Yours, etc.,
"A. LOUIS ARROWSMITH, (FF Workrooms, Peterborough).

"Chairman's Comment:
"The Partnership *as a whole* must under its present Constitution (which is not to be alterable without the consent of the Council) refrain from taking sides in Party politics. The same restriction applies to the Chairmanship of the Central Board because its holder is so likely to be regarded in the world outside as representative of the Partnership *as a whole*.

"But the Constitution of the Partnership does not restrict it at all from including in its ranks ardent and active party-politicians and from facilitating their participation, direct or indirect, in public affairs.

"By 'indirect' I mean, for example, work to secure the election of persons of their own way of thinking. By 'direct' I mean standing themselves as candidates for election.

"The rule, that the Partnership as a whole must not take sides in party politics, obviously requires that it shall be in the judgment of competent impartial persons strictly fair in the extent to which it gives leave of absence, official help or other facilities to any of its party-politically-minded members. That is to be part of the Constitution that each successive Chairman is to undertake to maintain.

"In such matters the words 'judgment of competent impartial persons' must mean the judgment of the Courts of Law. If the Council is ever of opinion that the Chairman of the day is falling or has fallen short of proper impartiality in this matter of party politics, the Council will have power to call upon the Chairman to resign and, if he declines, they will have power to ask the Courts of Law to turn him out.

"The Council's agents for doing all this will be the five Trustees of the Constitution whom the Council will appoint each year.

"So much for the distinction between politics and party politics. A really civilised family, if it finds that one of its members is a convinced Conservative, another a convinced Liberal, a third a convinced Socialist and a fourth a convinced Communist, will be apt to say 'All these four people are to our minds well-meaning. By a three-quarters majority they *all* agree that in matters of politics *each* of them is insane. That is a matter of which we do not undertake to judge. But to us they seem sane enough in other matters and, since human beings are fallible, it is conceivable that *none* of them is either wholly right or wholly wrong. Let them all, therefore, if they can find voters whom by lawful methods they can induce to elect them, get themselves elected to anything to which they want to be elected. Let us give *each* of them the *same* help, so far as we give any of them *any* help, and let us in fact give them such help as we can, for it might not be good for the country if it came to be governed wholly by whole-time professional politicians in whose ranks the disinterested and intelligent might sooner or later be swamped by the self-seekers and the stupid.

"Under its present Constitution that is the Partnership's present attitude to politics and party politics.

"For my own part I do not agree with Mr. Arrowsmith that our partnership is socialism. I think it goes deeper than any party politics and I suggest that this view is supported by four interesting happenings.

"Nowadays there are four main parties—Conservatives, Liberals, Socialists and Communists.

"About fifteen years ago the then leader of the Liberal Party, Professor Ramsay Muir, with whom I had no previous acquaintance, wrote to me a long letter of warm commendation of our system and of earnest request that in a general Parliamentary Election then impending I would publish a statement that our system was essentially Liberal in the Party-politician's sense of that word. Because of the spirit of the rule, that I have mentioned, I declined, though the temptation was sore for the thing might have been kept within the letter of that rule and the Partnership might have got much valuable publicity.

"In the Spring of the present year the Headquarters of the Conservative Party pressed me in very kind terms to deliver a certain lecture to their trainees for political work. The theme of the lecture was to be our own system and the reason, why I was asked to give the lecture, was that in the view of those, who sent me the invitation, our system would be a good Election plank for the Conservative Party. Again I felt obliged to decline.

"As for the Communists, in the Webbs' great book upon Russia, "Soviet Communism," many pages are devoted to a description of what the Russians call Incops—organisations that seem virtually identical with our partnership except that they are not left free to distribute as much Partnership Benefit as they like. They may give it to their members in other forms like country-clubs and colleges and it is said that some of them have colleges that are finer than anything provided as yet by the government. But, so far as the individual incomes of their members go, the Incops are not allowed to make their own members better off than the Trade Union rates for workers in Government organisations (the Trade Unions being, we must remember, in Russia government-controlled).

"Now we have Mr. Arrowsmith telling us that to his mind our system is a 'revolutionary socialist design'.

"In face of all this it seems to me reasonable to think, as for my own part I always have, that our system is one of those things that are not really a matter of party politics at all but something upon which *everybody* can agree. After all, if there is such a thing as common sense, it must *be* common to *all* men who are not so very crazy that even in the present early infancy of mankind they are accounted mad.

"If THE GAZETTE were already illustrated, as I hoped that before long it would be, I should look forward to the result of the efforts of the Chief Editor to secure a close-up of Mr. A. Louis Arrowsmith registering surprise and disgust at his idea of the views of Commander the Hon. J. M. FitzRoy Newdegate and a close-up of that eminent member of the Partnership registering disgust and possibly surprise at his idea of the views of Mr. A. Louis Arrowsmith.

"I am asking the Chief Editor to give the Principal Director of Selling an opportunity of adding his own observations to those of Mr. Arrowsmith and to this comment of mine. But perhaps Commander FitzRoy Newdegate will feel that this matter has now reached the stage at which the British genius for genuine partnership enables and requires us to agree to differ.

"I ought, I think, to add on behalf of all the Partnership a word of gratitude to the Commander and to Mr. Arrowsmith for thus enlivening the Partnership's journalism.

J. S. L.

"(The Director of Selling has written that he has no further comments to make.—Editor.)"

Before I close this Chapter, I will mention one past development of our Journalism that will be, I hope, revived in the near future and maintained thenceforward—the publication of a yearly Census of Membership.

CENSUS OF MEMBERSHIP

645.   A sense of security of tenure is so extremely important to happiness that the Partnership must obviously do all it possibly can to develop and maintain such a sense to the very greatest extent that will not do too much harm to efficiency. That risk is real. Over-nervousness can be very bad for efficiency but overconfidence can very easily be ruinous. To steer the right course between these two risks is far from easy.

Among the devices the Partnership invented and used for this purpose was the yearly publication in its GAZETTE of a census of the whole of the Partnership with the names arranged in order of length of membership. This census was thus published from 1919 to 1928 inclusive.

The idea was to safeguard all concerned from false notions, so that nobody should imagine that the Partnership's "labour turnover" was either much greater or much smaller than it really was. The rapid growth of the Partnership's numbers made this publication more and more difficult and, as those difficulties coincided with a time of lean trade, when there is always a temptation to use the desirability of all possible savings, large and small, as a reason for not tackling some rather bothering job, the thing was simply dropped.

The total numbers at the foot of the columns, that showed the longer memberships, were, it was thought, pretty satisfactory in their proportion to the remainder but it was not at all easy to be sure of that because the continual rapid growth of the business meant that every year there were a great many newcomers whose appearance in the list did not mean that other memberships had been terminated.

VALUE OF HARD FACTS

646.   I have always been sorry that the census was dropped and I think that in some sufficiently condensed form it ought to be revived and kept going.

If Journalism is to play in team-work the immensely valuable part, that it should, there must be ceaseless care to keep it as full as possible of hard facts. Nothing, that will strongly interest any appreciable number of readers, should be omitted.

The publication of things, that make disagreeable reading and that may cause bad feeling, is hardly less desirable than the publication of things of the contrary kind. Genuine frankness and nothing else will win confidence.

If team-work is to be really good, the Managers and the Managed must talk to each other—and in fact everybody in the team must talk to everybody else—with the frankness of real partners.

Of course the thing must be done with common sense. There may be some need of prudence in timing and of tact in presentation. But there should be the utmost possible avoidance of real suppression of information, real withholding of knowledge, that would be desired if those, to whom it might be given, knew it was there to give.

THE REVUE

647.   Another institution, that, like the Journalism, has arisen from the Partnership's aim of fostering freedom of speech and general cheerfulness and that has been, I think, a very great success, has been the Partnership's Revue. This was a spontaneous growth. It was started in 1929, in a very small way by a member of the Rank and File, Mr. Guy Inglis, to whom there would, I believe, be very general agreement that the Partnership owes deep gratitude. By the time the war stopped the Revue (it was revived again in 1947) it had grown into a performance that required the hiring of one of the smaller theatres and played for four nights to full houses, so that it was seen altogether by about two thousand people.

Now, that the Partnership is so very much larger and that a really substantial part of it is outside London, we may perhaps have either a number of regional Revues or else some arrangement for sending the leading artists on tour to give local performances with a local orchestra and chorus.

From 1929 to 1939 there was a Revue every year and by the end of that time experience had given rise to a fairly definite art form, designed to be played within a definite space of time. The thing has always been intended, like the Athenian Comedy, to make fun of everybody, Customers and the Partnership, Managers and Managed. At first the whole thing was entirely amateur but in two years one General Manager found it necessary to use the help of a professional producer to get the timing right and we regularly have a professional orchestra to get the right rhythm for the dancers. With these exceptions the Revue is still entirely home-made. The book, the music, the dresses and all the company are from the Partnership.

648.   At the dress-rehearsal before the three nights, for which tickets are sold, admission is free and reserved for certain of the less wealthy sections of the Partnership. About six months ahead someone is appointed to be the General Manager of the next Revue. I think this should be a Council appointment but up to now there has been so much consultation that it would not be easy to say whether the appointment was really made in the end by the Council or by myself. Like the Athenian Choregus, he has a completely free hand. The cost of production rose to about £1,500, most, if not all, of which was recovered eventually from the sale of tickets. With this money the General Manager does whatever he thinks fit. He selects the book from such items as are offered to him. He engages the Company, arranges for the rehearsals, which continue through a great part of the winter and in fact controls the whole thing.

In some years the advertisements on the programme alone have seemed to some of us to be well worth the cost of the seat. They generally refer to some of the more flagrant of the Partnership's scandals in recent months or are in some other way highly agreeable to the irreverent.

The Revue makes fun of everything and everybody in the Partnership and it has been very pleasant to see to how extreme a length eminent personages could go in playing some part without the least subsequent ill-effect upon their personal prestige and the discipline necessary to the team-work of the Partnership's ordinary affairs.

The most cheerful informal family in the most intimate of merry-making could hardly go further. I have seen one of the Partnership's principal leaders portraying in a lady's dress a wax model of comic appearance with such success that, until the model came to life, I think that all the audience were as completely deceived as I certainly was. And there was an occasion on which an Oriental sage exiguously attired but appreciatively garlanded and accompanied by colleagues, whose own dress indicated eminence in the Public Services or the Academic world, appeared to recall somehow to the mind of the audience the Chairman of the Partnership's Central Board.

On one occasion an artist, whose talent for mimicry gave in successive years great delight, achieved so perfect an imitation of the laugh of a retired Admiral, who held at that time one of the Partnership's leading posts, that I was told that on the evening, on which the Admiral was in the audience, his response was so perfect an echo that the duet became a kind of extra turn and the appreciation of the audience approached delirium.

CHAPTER 36

THE SECONDARY MANAGEMENT—THE
PARTNERSHIP'S CRITICAL AND EXECUTIVE
SIDES: THE FORMER CONSIDERED IN DETAIL

649. SUBJECT to all, that has been said so far in this Part III, the Partnership may be regarded as consisting of two main parts—the Executive Side who do things and the Critical Side who watch the doing and play the part of the bystander who is proverbially apt to see most of the game.

The function of the Critical Side is to safeguard the Executive Side from inadvertence. The Critical Side provides the Executive Side with the salutary if not always pleasant services of a candid friend, the fulfilment of the poet's wish that we could see ourselves as others see us.

The Critical Side do more than this. It is also their function to be the Partnership's and especially the Chairman's eyes and ears and to a substantial extent their memory and their judgment. In a small enough partnership there would be no Critical Side. The Chairman himself would do all that. In a still smaller he might do also the whole or some large part of the high-level work on the Executive Side.

All these, that the Partnership calls "principal" posts—all these posts of which the holders deal directly with the Principal Authorities—the Council, the Board and the Chairman—are really fragments of the total functions of the one-man manager in a business small enough to require no more than one person, who decides what is to be done, and some others who help him to do it. If their work is sufficiently simple, it is not unreasonable to think of him as the head and of them as the hands.

THE CRITICAL SIDE

650. As team-work grows, specialisation necessarily develops. The Partnership has now reached a stage at which its team-work requires that the Chairman shall have the assistance of five specialists whom the Partnership calls the five Heads of the Critical Side. As, was mentioned in an earlier Chapter, they are the General Inspector, the Chief Registrar, the Internal Auditor, the Financial Adviser and the Partners' Counsellor. They extend the Chairman's personal sight, hearing, memory and judgment. Moreover, they extend these without limit, for there is no limit to the quantity and quality of the assistance that each of them may have.

Here it may be well to mention in passing that the Partnership rather likes its rising members to have some experience both upon its Executive and upon its Critical Sides and in as many different sections as possible of those. For example, the Executive Side includes what are called at present a Selling Side and a Buying Side. The Partnership likes a rising member to have experience in each of these, so that on the one hand he can sympathise with difficulties that he has shared and, on the other hand, he can be up to tricks that he has helped to play or that he has at all events seen played. The five Heads of the Critical Side are appointed by the Chairman and are responsible separately and directly to him. They have no executive authority outside their own Departments, though they may achieve it in effect by the competence and prestige of their advice to holders of executive power.

651. The work of the Critical Side is divided to give the advantages of specialisation and it is hoped that its five existing Departments would enable a Chairman to fill adequately his own post in a partnership no matter how large, how various or how spread over the world and would moreover be able to render adequately to that partnership all other services that the Critical Side should.

A chief advantage of the existence of the Critical Side is that it gives the Partnership a separate organ of high potentialities upon which can be put great pressure towards carefulness. Within a fairly wide margin it is in practical affairs difficult to quarrel with executive workers whose performance is ordinarily high, their qualifications rare and their knowledge of the affairs of the particular enterprise and their personal relation to its existing members such that any replacement must have very great disadvantages. But, if there is a separate organ having no such executive responsibilities to related parts of the organism, it becomes possible to say that inadvertence or improper reticence cannot be tolerated. To prevent them is in fact the supreme reason for which that other organ exists at all.

A lyric poet, who was presumably upon the Executive Side, contributed to the Revue of 1936 a song that ran:

"The Critical Side, the Critical Side: that is the Side to be.

As soon as you join it you lay aside responsibility.

Whatever you do is always right, whatever you say is true,

And never forget, the week's GAZETTE will always see you through".

He erred. In old times, when much chastisement was deemed indispensable to the education of the young, the scion of a family too august to undergo that process personally shared his tuition with a companion who was known frankly as the whipping-boy. His sufferings for the sins of his august fellow-student were supposed to incline the latter towards righteousness.

In some cases the association led to lasting friendship and gave an advantageous, if at first uncomfortable, start in life to the companion of the future Great Personage.

So the Partnership, if it finds that it has suffered gravely from some persistent or recurrent shortcomings of one of those major Executives, who are apt to be so difficult to replace, may say to itself that it is just possible to refrain from shooting the prime sinner but may soothe its own feelings and foster very desirably future vigilance by shooting a secondary sinner, somebody on the Critical Side, who could and should have seen what was about to happen or was actually happening and who could and should have prevented or stopped it.

One has a vision of a constantly growing host upon the Executive Side of major entrepreneurs all sleeping the sleep of the comfortably confident that the general value of their services will enable them to get away occasionally with murder while in the watches of sleepless nights cold dews break out, upon Critical brows, racked with effort to think of all the things that the Executive Side may be up to and to devise ways of catching them at it before too much milk shall have been spilt.

Perhaps in time among the five Heads of the Critical Side and their lieutenants there will develop a fine art of judging just how unimportant a member of the Department the Partnership can, if the presentation is sufficiently skilful, be persuaded to accept as a target for the firing-party.

It is plainly a matter of some—and possibly of very great—delicacy to achieve in this respect sufficient safeguards and yet avoid an atmosphere of espionage. But this is one of the things in which those, who undertake to plan team-work or to play a certain part in its conduct, must by luck or judgment achieve sufficient skill.

It must be remembered that the functions of the Critical Side not only leave more time and energy for thought, that is to say for avoiding failures in wariness, but they also allow of the appointment of people temperamentally specially well fitted to avoid such failure. Wariness is apt to be the weak side of those whose executive ability is great. Their vitally important work requires supremely swiftness and self-confidence, qualities peculiarly apt not to be combined with first-rate excellence in wariness. The converse also is true. The best research-workers, critics and theorists are apt to be deficient—perhaps very deficient indeed—in the "practical ability" of the able man of action.

THE GENERAL INSPECTOR AND HIS DEPARTMENT

652. The General Inspector graduated at Oxford with first-class honours in History. He came into the Partnership twenty-one years ago, in September 1927. In the absence of the Chairman and Deputy Chairman his office carries the first Vice-Chairmanship of the Central Board. His Department exists to secure that the Partnership's rules are not dead letters but are either rescinded or effective. It investigates symptoms of any trouble. It maintains a routine-watch for need of action.

It is by no means limited to things that have gone wrong or that appear to be in danger of doing so. It calls attention to merit and recommends recognition and reward. The Department includes an Intelligence Department that ceaselessly watches the Partnership's competitors and draws attention to any matter in which they seem to be excelling the Partnership in any of its affairs.

THE CHIEF REGISTRAR AND HER DEPARTMENT

The Chief Registrar (the second holder of this post) graduated at Oxford with first-class honours in Politics, Philosophy and Economics ("Modern Greats"). She is a newcomer but she succeeded another Oxford Graduate with first-class honours in English Literature. That first holder of the Chief Registrarship had been in the Partnership nineteen years, when she reached retiring-age. The Chief Registrar's Department does the whole of the Partnership's secretarial work other than accountancy. It is the duty of the Chief Registrar to provide in each Branch a Registrar who can and will be an adequate informant and counsellor to anyone who desires to ask any question about the Partnership's rules, regulations and precedents either their letter or their spirit. Except within her registry, she has no executive authority. Those, who seek her advice or that of any member of her team, are in the position of any of us who consult, say, a lawyer or a doctor or an engineer. We are responsible for any action we take in the light of that advice but the facts, that we obtained it and acted reasonably in respect of it, will probably help us a good deal if in the end we find ourselves in trouble. Moreover, whether the Registrar advises him to do so or not, a Partner can always get rid of responsibility by going to his own chief who may, if he chooses, do the same thing until at last the problem gets right up to the Chairman who, if he likes, can consult the Council.

Registrars have another function besides giving information and advice and providing adequate secretarial service and taking charge of papers. They must keep the Principal Management aware of what is in those papers. They are to the Partnership the nervous system by which the big horse feels the little fly. Inadvertence, ignorance, unawareness are a chief danger of team-work and, the larger the team, the greater the danger. How is general awareness to be achieved without an atmosphere of espionage, of tittle-tattle? By requiring everybody to put upon paper whatever he ought to put upon paper and by keeping a sufficient eye upon what he writes. If in a little business the owner-manager watches closely the papers, the correspondence, the invoices, the factory-dockets and so forth, his team may say he is a tartar but they will respect him for a hard-working, lively-minded, efficient man of business. But, if, when they are talking together, he tries to overhear what they are saying or if he makes what they feel to be ungenerous use of something he overhears by accident, they will not respect him. They will feel that is an improper invasion of privacy to which they are entitled even when they are on duty. Some things, that are said, cannot be disregarded but, as far as possible; speech should be free. Mere talk should be ignored. Pay attention to what is done and to what in the course of duty—but only in the course of duty—is written but so far as possible ignore mere talk. That is the Partnership's broad aim. But within this limit the Registrars exist to ensure that the Partnership's team-work is not thwarted by irregularities intentional or unintentional. The Partnership seeks to give to every one of all its members as much as ever it can of the freedom of anyone in business for himself but such rules, as it does make, must be kept.

PREVENTIVE RATHER THAN DETECTIVE

654. This may sound as if Registrars will have a somewhat invidious and unpopular function of observing and thwarting inclinations to break the Partnership's laws or of bringing crime to light. In practice, however, I think that their work in this way will be so largely preventive and the prevention will be felt to be so advantageous to those whom it affects, that the Registrars will have, on the contrary, something of the popularity that is said to make a nurse's uniform an ample safeguard in districts where police-constables do not venture singly.

It will be the function of Registrars not only to know the letter but also to understand the meaning of the Partnership's current Rules and Regulations. And they will tend, I think, to be extremely helpful and much appreciated counsellors to executive officials, especially to those who are still more or less newcomers in their posts. Such counselling functions are, I think, a specially good field of work for women. Does not many a successful man owe much of his success to the discernment and advice of a shrewd wife, though, if she had had to take the responsibility and carry the worry of deciding for herself to act upon her advice, the strain might easily have been too much for her, not in the sense that she would have broken down but in the sense that her temper and judgment would have suffered and her efficiency along with them?

PUGNACITY AND TOUGHNESS OF NERVE

655. Is not a great part at least of the fundamental difference between masculine and feminine abilities the outcome of the need for millions of years that the female should be alert for danger and bent upon avoiding it while the male should be upon occasion ready to fight? For all, that I know, this may be a platitude among modern psychologists but, platitude or not, it is an idea that organisers and administrators, who have to deal with teams of both sexes, may be, I think, wise to bear in mind.

Much of the impatient tendency to under-value the potentialities of women for important work arises, I think, from an unreasonable expectation that they will have a certain particular kind of toughness and nerve, a certain equanimity and balance, a certain imperturbability, that is by no means necessary in work of every sort and kind and that is precisely one of the qualities that should least of all be required of women. At all events, I suspect that the Partnership will find that really high efficiency in managerial work will be attainable much more easily by letting a zealous, energetic and forceful but not very clever or perhaps very experienced man in a Managership work with a really intelligent and well informed woman Registrar than it would be by trying to find their joint qualities combined in one man or in one woman. Moreover, such an arrangement allows of permanency in the executive post but change, say every third year, in the other with the possibility of bringing in fresh knowledge and ideas.

THE INTERNAL AUDITOR AND HIS DEPARTMENT

656. The Internal Auditor graduated at Cambridge with second-class honours in Languages and Law. He came into the Partnership in June 1946. He is a chartered accountant and is the Board's and the Chairman's means of dealing with the Chief Accountant and his 1,200 assistants and to some extent with outside accountants, especially the auditors of the Partnership's various companies.

THE FINANCIAL ADVISER AND HIS DEPARTMENT

657. The Financial Adviser graduated at Cambridge with first-class honours in Economics. He came into the Partnership in August 1947. The position was held previously for some years by the present General Inspector and for two periods by the present Director of Maintenance and Expansion. The Financial Adviser's functions were expressed as follows in a paper dictated on the 7th February of this year (1948) and slightly amended here for the sake of greater clearness.

"The Financial Adviser is the Partnership's supreme safeguard against waste. It is of the essence of his functions to be extremely wary and extremely penetrating in his judgments.

"So far as he considers that consultation between himself or one of his staff with someone outside his own Department would be wasteful for the Partnership, let him by all means have the courage of his convictions and let him not create that waste because somebody else would differ from his own view that the consultation would be in fact wasteful.

"Whether the Financial Adviser and his team rely upon their own knowledge and judgment or whether in the particular matter they seek to supplement that from outside their own Department, let their responsibility, so far as in each particular case they are willing to take it, be as great as possible.

"Let the margin, within which they have discretion to commit the Principal Management, be as wide as the particular part of the Principal Management feels justified in making it and within that margin let the Financial Adviser take all the responsibility that in his own judgment it will be on the whole expedient for the Partnership that he shall.

"When I speak of the Principal Management, I mean the Central Council in respect of the funds at their own disposal, the Central Board in respect of the whole of the Partnership's Budget down to that financial residue that I call the pork-barrel, the residue from all those appropriations that do not accrue in one way or another to the personal gain of Partners themselves in cash or kind, including in kind such comforts as a pension prospect, prospect of financial help in exceptional need or any amenity that is intended to be in any way gratifying to one or more of the Partnership's members.

"It is for the Council in their field and for the Board in theirs to decide what, if any, discretion they will invite the Financial Adviser to exercise on their behalf.

"They have no power to require him to take any such responsibility at all. They are not entitled to require of him more than that he will study properly any financial problem that they refer to him and that he will advise them upon it to the best of his ability.

"He is entitled to insist that they will take formal cognisance of the view that he favours and that they will take the responsibility for deciding whether that view is to be adopted or no.

"On his side the Financial Adviser will not be entitled to say that in his view a particular matter ought not to have been left to his own discretion and that he, being requested to deal with it, 'did the best he could'.

"If he exercises discretion in a way that is in a sense executive, he must never make any grave mistake, any more than a member of the Fighting Services, who takes it upon himself to disobey orders, is entitled to expect that he will not be held responsible if his disobedience is judged to have been unjustified.

"In such a matter it is his duty to be right and to be wrong is a failure in duty, no matter how conscientiously he may have done his best to decide correctly.

"The professional batsman, who loses his wicket too cheaply, must take the consequences, no matter how desperately hard he may have tried not to lose it.

"If the Central Council or the Central Board considered that a Financial Adviser was excessively wasteful of their own time and trouble in the extent to which he declined to take anything at all in the way of what would be really executive responsibility, their remedy would be to complain to the Chairman that the Financial Advisership was not filled satisfactorily for the general interests of the Partnership.

"If the Chairman declined to do anything about it, they would have to make the best of that, unless the waste was great enough to cause the Partnership to fail in the punctuality of some payment in which such failure would entitle them to appoint a new Chairman.

"We are dealing here with matters of supreme importance and therefore I am going right down to the ultimate implications of our system as that seems to me to be now developing.

"Three courses will be open to the Financial Adviser upon any matter that is referred to him and that is within the discretion that at the time he holds from the principal spending authority concerned, the Council, the Board or the Chairman.

"In the first place, he may give sanction, a green light as the traffic-controllers would say. In the second place, he may give an amber light, that is to say he may answer that he is not willing to take the responsibility of sanctioning the thing but that he is likewise not willing to take the responsibility of discouraging the applicant to the extent of replying that, if the application goes further, the Financial Adviser will oppose it.

"In this case, that is to say if the Department of Financial Advice gives the applicant an amber light, the applicant will be entitled as a general rule to carry the thing no further. If he does so and he is afterwards asked to justify his decision, he will be entitled to expect that great weight will be attached to the excuse that the view expressed by the Financial Adviser made him feel that there was too much risk that, if he pushed the proposal further, he would be merely wasting time and trouble.

"If the dropping of the proposal was held to have been a grave mistake, that answer might or might not be held to be a sufficient excuse.

"I am setting all this out thus completely because these things are so important to the general sense of security of tenure.

"The sense of security, that the Partnership seeks to offer, is comparable to the sense of security of a climber who knows himself competent and who knows that he will be climbing upon sound rock and with no danger of avalanches or falling stones.

"That seems to me to be the very highest security that is compatible with first-rate efficiency which itself is plainly indispensable to full potential earnings.

"As you will see in all this, my object is to keep as great as ever I possibly can the number of matters upon which the Department of Financial Advice can instantly give a green light and I am further providing that, when the light is amber, the applicant cannot break off the proposition. In other words responsibility is to be upon the Financial Adviser for preventing the breaking off of a proposition to which in his own view he cannot properly give a green light but that is such that in his own view the applicant would be wrong to let the thing drop at that stage.

"The third course open to the Department of Financial Advice is to give a red light, and say: 'Go on with this if you like but, if you do, we shall oppose it'. In that case the Department are not taking the whole of the responsibility for a breaking off of the proposition but they are saying to the applicant: We are quite definitely of opinion that, if you decide to break off at this point, you will be justified in doing so. The final responsibility is yours. But for what it may be worth to you, you will have this written evidence that we advised you that, so far as we could see (and it is your business to be in some respects a better judge than we can be) you would not be in danger of finding eventually that you had incurred blame if you abandoned at this point the intention with which you came to us'.

"Obviously the Department of Financial Advice must keep really adequate records of all that it does and must make such reports to the three principal spending authorities that they are to that extent continuously aware of the use that is being made of the discretion that they have given to the Department of Financial Advice and of the consequences that are accumulating in the way of frequency of refusal or volume of sanctions or risk of discouragement for some particular applicant and so on and so forth".

THE PARTNERS' COUNSELLOR AND HIS DEPARTMENT

658. The Partners' Counsellor graduated at Oxford with first-class honours in English Literature and for twenty-two years, until he resigned it at the Partnership's invitation in January of 1942, occupied in the University of Bristol, where he was Dean of the Faculty, the Winterstoke Chair of English Literature. In the Partnership's organisation the Partners' Counsellor is that part of the owner-manager's brain and time that in the staff-management of a small business is given to the claims of humanity. The motives of care for health and happiness may be high or low. They may be merely intelligent selfishness but an efficient leader will care to some extent for the health and comfort, bodily and mental, of every member of his team.

There is obviously a special relation between the Partners' Counsellor and the Director of Personnel. The claims of economic efficiency and the claims of humanity tend to coincide. A management bent quite ruthlessly upon profit but very highly intelligent in that selfishness will tend to treat its workers very well indeed up to a certain fairly high point. It will give them not the tiniest thing beyond what is required for economic efficiency but within certain limits that requirement itself will go quite a long way towards satisfying the claims of humanity.

Nevertheless there is a very real difference between the functions of the Director of Personnel, which strictly speaking should stop at this last line, the line of economic efficiency, if that line were in fact accurately discernible, and the functions of the Partners' Counsellor, which have been devised from precisely the opposite standpoint. This is considered further in paragraph 683 in the description of the Directorship of Personnel.

MONEY NOT EVERYTHING

The supreme purpose of the Partnership is simply the advantage of its members. Only fools put business too far before pleasure, especially health and happiness in the more important senses of that word. The functions of the Partners' Counsellor are correspondingly important.

OVERWORK MORE DANGEROUS THAN SLACKING

One of my own chief doctrines is that, if a business is rightly organised and has a good atmosphere, the Principal Management will have more need to be on the watch to prevent over-work than to prevent slacking. Unselfish zeal for the good of the Partnership and personal ambition and pride will all tend to cause people to over-work both in the more ordinary sense and in the way of staying on duty when they ought to go on sick-leave or take a precautionary rest and to return to duty when they are not properly fit to do so.

COMFORT

659. Beyond all this, there is the almost infinite variety of ways in which the management of an organisation like the Partnership can promote happiness. There is an almost infinite scope for imagination and energy. To notice that somebody has to work in a draught, to ask if a different chair or a bit of carpet over cold stone would be welcome, to provide pleasant decorations, pictures, flowers, to take care that food is of the right kind and served in the right way, to experiment with the provision of things that may turn out to be extremely welcome though it would never have occurred to the beneficiaries to ask for them, to be on the watch for over-driving or needless harshness or preventable troubles of any kind, all this is the field of the Partners' Counsellor and his assistants. Certainly it is also very much the field of the Director of Personnel but he has got to take care that the Partnership is not too soft. It should be some one else's supreme aim to secure that it is not too hard. That is what the Partners' Counsellor is for.

RIGHT TO KNOW

He has a right of access to all of the Partnership's papers and can see for himself the facts of any matter in which there is some allegation of grievance. He should not wait for complaints or for questions. He should, as for as possible, forestall them. He and his team should be extremely well aware of all the Partnership's precedents that can be cited to the present advantage of some individual or group. As his title implies, he should be constantly available personally or by sufficient deputy to any Partner who upon any matter whatsoever desires counsel and cannot or does not wish to get it otherwise. He can pledge himself to secrecy from everyone but the Chairman but he is an extension of the Chairman's own mind. No man can keep secrets from himself and in the concerns of the Partnership its other leaders must have no secrets from its Chairman.

660. But the Counsellor can promise to do his best for his client and in that way the Partnership should in my view give the Partners' Counsellor all the influence and all the consequent prestige, popularity and confidence that it can. A wise manager will be as careful not to be needlessly severe as a good surgeon will be not to operate needlessly or to be rough and heavy-handed. The Partners' Counsellor should do a very great deal to secure that the Partnership is imaginative and energetic in making the working lives of its members as happy as possible. He should be ceaselessly watchful for good ideas elsewhere and for possibilities of our own. His clients will tend to be in the main those whose earning-power is small and whose status is proportionate but he should be always on the watch for any chance to say or do something that may create happiness or prevent unhappiness in any case at all. Obviously his work must overlap a good deal that of several of his colleagues. For example from the standpoint of business efficiency the General Inspector will watch the records of staff-changes for suspicious frequency or individual cases that seem to call for enquiry. As has just been said, the Partnership's supreme aim is the happiness of its members. Business-efficiency is only one of the means to that end.

NEED OF COOPERATION BY THE MANAGED

661. The planning of devices of this kind and the provision of an adequate budget are very far from being enough to ensure adequate results. Those, for whose benefit the arrangements are intended, will be very apt to fail to give the cooperation that would be a very important help and that is indeed indispensable to any fairly complete achievement of the broad aim.

It is one thing to provide a Counsellor. It is quite another to get people to consult him when they should. A community of any size takes a tremendous lot of educating into ideas that are not familiar and into understanding and remembering to use machinery that is at all complex.

Many a well-educated man has got himself into disastrous trouble by failing to consult a lawyer or a doctor in a case in which it would very probably have occurred to him to advise a friend to do so. But as yet the great majority of British citizens are not well-educated and, whereas the notion of consulting a lawyer or a doctor is very familiar, the notion, that the management of your business may be quite genuinely on your side and quite genuinely anxious to know your wishes and to be in various ways of help to you, is not at all familiar.

HELP MUST BE GIVEN WHERE NEEDED

662. The dull tend rather to pride themselves upon their dullness—to make a virtue of it. Their attitude to the rest of the world is not that they themselves failed to play their own part as they should have done but that the rest of the world ought to have prevented their failing.

In the main this view is quite reasonable. They are what they are and their behaviour will be what it will be. Those, who undertake any responsibility for them, must discern their limitations and must make such arrangements as will in fact achieve the result desired.

But, whether his clients are dull or bright, whether they seem to be quite exceptionally deserving of sympathy, affection and correspondingly liberal help from their partners or whether their real dues seem to be no more than the minimum of anyone who has been allowed in fact to come into the Partnership and to continue in it for whatever may be the period in the particular case, it is, I think, very important indeed to the general happiness of the working life of the Partnership's members that they shall be constantly seeing and hearing of instances of its being intelligently and painstakingly kind and helpful now to one member and now to another.

PSYCHOLOGICAL IMPORTANCE TO TEAM-RELATIONS OF THE SIGHT OF KINDLINESS

663. This psychological value is not, I believe, merely confined to the creation of a conscious or subconscious confidence that in comparable circumstances the Partner, who is feeling the pleasure, would get similar help.

I think that it is extremely important to the mental climate, the happiness of the general mass mind of a community, that it shall be proud of itself. It has been suggested already that pride in the business efficiency of the team to which they belong, the quality of its merchandise, the excellence of its value, the honesty and general efficiency of all parts of its procedure, is quite genuinely important to the happiness of most workers.

I am sure that the same thing is much more true of what they feel to be sensible and proper—even if in this hard world very surprising—kindliness to any of themselves or indeed to any outsiders with whom they are inclined to feel much sympathy.

The sight of very good treatment of others is of real importance to the happiness of workers and that largely for reasons higher than its encouragement of expectations of like benefits.

The functions of a Partners' Counsellor, a Principal Welfare Worker (a term that for my own part I dislike as savouring of patronage) or whatever you may like to call him, are really very difficult indeed. They afford scope for first-rate energy, resourcefulness and general efficiency. Done well, the dynamic importance of the work may be very great indeed but it is not work for amiable mediocrities. It calls for acute intelligence, a firm mind and first-rate energy.

ADEQUACY OF THE CRITICAL SIDE

If these five posts are properly occupied and their five occupants have proper assistance and if the Journalism and the Representative Institutions are healthy, the Chairman, as I said a little while ago, should, I believe, be able to play his own part satisfactorily in a partnership of any size and complexity and no matter how widely scattered about the world.

CHAPTER 37

THE EXECUTIVE SIDE

664. WE now come to the Executive Side. We are assuming that in a large partnership the Chairman must have five colleagues for the work of the Critical Side. The General Editor must be a sixth. The Journalism is a vitally important part of a partnership's nervous system. It must be quite sufficiently welded into the Chairman's own mind. It must be operated, that is to say the real editorial work must be done, by someone who is thoroughly in the Chairman's confidence and between whom and the Chairman there can be quite sufficient understanding.

The Executive Side will comprise almost the whole of the Partnership. There should be no limit to the number of its posts that can carry the Partnership's highest rate of individual income and any post, in which there is scope to earn such an income, must have such freedom of discretion and must dispose of resources so large as to make the post attractive to men and women as able as any in the Partnership.

REPRODUCTION ON A TINY SCALE OF A NATIONAL COMMUNITY

665. Here we see again how a partnership, as it grows, must tend to reproduce on a tiny scale the general community, a national democracy.

We have already seen that in our own case at all events a partnership gives rise to representative institutions, a Free Press and (in the Department of the Partners' Counsellor) the embryo of a legal profession available to assist the individual partner to secure his rights under the partnership's constitution including the relevant precedents in the recorded decisions of its various authorities.

In this possibility of an unlimited number of executive positions, affording scope for as able people as the partnership can ever attract and offering a corresponding income and amenities of all kinds, we see arising within our own partnership positions corresponding to those of the entrepreneurs in the general community. To their number there is likewise no limit. That number depends upon the supply of persons of sufficient ability and energy. The more there are of them, the better for the national income. Whatever their number, they are still served by one set of representative institutions (Parliament and so forth), one Free Press, one Civil Service (the Partnership's Central Departments), one legal profession, one medical profession and so on. If the number of important entrepreneurs grows greatly, there will need to be some enlargement of the Civil Service and of each of the various professions. But they will remain unities to which upon occasion each separate entrepreneur will have recourse.

DEMOCRACY NOT A ONE-MAN ENTERPRISE

666. To my mind this conception seems very important indeed. A business organisation is usually a pyramid. There is some one ruling spirit to whom everyone else is more or less completely subordinate. No really important risk can be taken without the previous knowledge and consent of that one person. Initiative is in the main confined to his own ideas. The enterprise as a whole grows as he thinks fit. If some extraordinarily able and energetic subordinate continues for very long in that organisation, he will generally be found to have acquired in reality the same dominance. The business will have become "his". Partnerships could perfectly well develop on these lines and it remains to be seen whether there are really important possibilities along the quite different lines that are here suggested.

For my own part I suspect that there are, although my father's especially long retention of control of the business in Oxford Street and now this war have reduced pretty narrowly my own chance of seeing whether this general idea will prove really important. Rightly or wrongly, I do in fact believe that, in partnerships conducted with sufficient intelligence, it will be found that this diffusion of ownership will make possible a scale of operations far different from any that has been achieved as yet by any enterprise free from the limitations of administration by politicians.

DEMOCRATIC TEAM-WORK

667. If the soil is suitable, there is no limit to the size of a healthy woodland, wherein each tree has enough of light and air but all join in breaking the gale for each other and in drawing down moisture and in keeping the forest-floor clear of competing herbage that would cut nourishment off from the roots of the trees.

Such a conception assumes that there will be no limit to the number of genuine leaders, true entrepreneurs. Their separate initiatives, their separate applications for finance, will complete the partnership's principal management in the true sense of those words.

National governments will presumably prevent individual partnerships from becoming too powerful but up to that line they will presumably be allowed to grow to any scale that results in better service to the general community. They are obviously consistent with "the American way of life" and apparently they are no less acceptable to the present rulers of Russia.

668. I am not going to attempt to suggest in this book the range of enterprises that might exist to their reciprocal advantage within the same partnership and, while helping each other in various ways, be so far separate as to afford adequate and congenial scope to leaders of great ability and energy and of the masterful temper that goes commonly with gifts of that particular kind. My subject here is not those executive specialists, the true entrepreneurs, but the central, executive officials who will be the co-ordinating frame of all those separate but mutually helpful enterprises.

As has been said already, it seems to me that a partnership so large as ours should have upon its Executive Side a Department of Maintenance and Expansion, a Department of Personnel and a Department of Financial Operations. These three will be the core of the Executive side.

THE DEPARTMENT OF MAINTENANCE AND EXPANSION

669. The Director of Maintenance and Expansion and his Department will play the part that has been indicated already. He graduated at Cambridge with first-class honours in Mathematics and came into the Partnership twenty-two years ago, in 1926. He and his Department will be watching constantly for the first important signs of flagging in any part of the whole of the Partnership's affairs. They will investigate those symptoms and take such steps as may seem necessary and, apart from this work of Maintenance, so far as desirable initiative does not arise from one or other of the Partnership's entrepreneurs, one of the Directors of Buying or the Head of one of the major sections of the Selling Side, the Department of Expansion may perceive the opportunity and take steps to start that new enterprise and to bring, it to the stage at which it can become a whole-time occupation for a chief adequate to take it off their hands. Both Maintenance and Expansion will require that the Director shall have control of a good deal of capital.

For all but very large operations spending authorities who need supplementary warrants beyond their current sanctioned estimates will apply in the first instance to this Department and not to the Board or the Chairman.

THE DEPARTMENT OF PERSONNEL

670. Next to the Chairman, the Director of Personnel is in supreme and sole charge of the whole of the Partnership's Personnel-administration. He graduated at Oxford with first-class honours in Literae Humaniores in 1921, and was from 1922 to 1947 in the Indian Civil Service, in which he was finally Secretary, Home Department, Government of India. He joined the Partnership in 1948. It is his business to take care that

the Partnership is at all times adequately manned for a cost no greater than the current budget provides. In practice some posts are so highly technical that the relation to them of the Director of Personnel is merely theoretical and formal. He cannot undertake to be an authority upon the very numerous, very various and constantly changing kinds of expertise that the Partnership requires. In certain matters an extremely free hand must be exercised by other people—managers, for example, of buying, manufacture and so on—who are not members of the Department of Personnel, but who, nevertheless, within their own fields of work are in effect agents of the Director of Personnel and agents so nearly plenipotentiary that the Director's own functions in respect of them are really rather critical than executive. He has to watch that their use of their powers is consistent with the Partnership's own principles and policy. Beyond this he may have some scope for helping them in various ways. He may for example be able occasionally to help with their recruiting or to arrange a transference for someone with whom they wish to part but whose membership of the Partnership they do not wish simply to terminate.

In the field of the Director of Personnel the Partnership is feeling very specially the consequence of the years of paralysis that this war has imposed upon our development. It has frozen completely the growth of trial-arrangements, that would have given long ago effect to the experience that we had been gathering up to 1938 or 1939, arrangements that ought to have been ready for dealing smoothly with all the requirements of the vast enlargement of our business that has occurred in these last seven years.

RELATIONS OF THE DIRECTORSHIP OF PERSONNEL TO SECTIONAL AUTHORITIES AND TO THE FIVE HEADS OF THE CRITICAL SIDE

671. We have yet to see how much of our engaging, training, transferring, promoting and dismissing will in a few years' time be done centrally by the Department of Personnel and how much will be done locally by someone who in comparison with the Department is in the position of the Man on the Spot, though he may be in fact the general manager of a branch numbering, perhaps, thousands and having a correspondingly elaborate organisation of its own.

The five Heads of the Critical Side, the General Editor of the Partnership's Journalism, the Director of Expansion, the Director of Financial Operations and the Chief Accountant are at present and perhaps will always be each quite independently responsible to the Chairman. None of them, it seems, should be able to excuse inefficiency in his own team by contending that that team is not what, had his own hands and the Chairman's been quite free, he and the Chairman would have made it. In other words, so far as responsibility for the efficiency of that particular team is not upon the Chairman personally it should be wholly and solely upon the team's own Head.

The Critical Side as a whole must be what the Chairman himself makes it. Over the principal members of that team none of their colleagues in the Partnership should have any power at all. This plainly means that in respect of his own department every member of the Partnership, whose functions require that he shall be separately and directly responsible to the Chairman, must be himself a Director of Personnel.

But there may and should be friendly cooperation between the Director of Personnel and the Head of any of these independent Departments and it is theoretically conceivable that, if the Director of Personnel felt gravely concerned at the extent to which the Personnel-administration of one of these independent Departments was in his view endangering the Partnership's reputation in the world outside, that is to say its prospects of satisfactory recruitment, or was endangering in some way its internal peace by arousing jealousies or setting an example of some grave disorder, the Director of Personnel might decide, however reluctantly, that he must protest privately to the Chairman.

672. But although this possibility exists, it is hardly more than theoretical. At all events, the Chairman's devolution of his own supreme responsibility for Personnel-administration must be in fact split. Very far the greater part of it must go to the Director of Personnel but in Departments of the kind that has just been mentioned it must go to the Head of that Department.

As has just been said, this need not prevent their having relations with the Director of Personnel. Imagine two heads of separate businesses quite independent of each other. Either may say to the other: "I have a vacancy: can you help me to fill it?" Or: "I have someone whom I do not wish to carry further but whom I should like to help if I can to a fresh position". In either case the head of the second business may answer that he has in his own team someone whom he can recommend and with whom, even if only as a very great favour, he is willing to part. Or he may answer that there is in his own team no one whom he can recommend and with whom he is willing to part but that he knows of such and such an outsider who might be just the right person for the position in question.

Now in such a case the head of the first business will be completely free to please himself whether he accepts the suggestion or takes some quite different course. And that, as I see it at present, is the relation to the Director of Personnel of Heads of such independent Departments as we have just been indicating. But in almost all the rest of the business the Director of Personnel has responsibility and authority.

673. Suppose that the Head of a Department, that itself forms part of a Branch, decides that he cannot carry further some member of his team. It is for the Head of the Branch and not for the Head of the Department to say whether that Partner shall be given the refusal of some other position in that Branch. Suppose that the Head of the Branch decides that he cannot carry the Partner. It is for his own chief, the Head, say, of the Selling Side, or the General Manager of Workrooms, to say whether that Partner shall be given the refusal of some other position in that portion of the Partnership. The "Chief" in this sense may be not the holder of a single post but the members of some committee, the Principal Executive Committee, for example.

But suppose that even at this very high level it is still held that no offer can be made to the Partner. It is still conceivable that the Partnership as a whole, embodied in the Director of Personnel, may say to that Partner: "The Head of the Selling Side (or the Principal Executive Committee) has decided that there is no place for you among all the thousands of posts for which he is (or among the much fewer specially important posts for which they are) responsible. It is my function to be in touch with such matters and I have thought it reasonable to make to the Head of the Selling Side (or to the Committee) certain suggestions. He has (or they have) considered those suggestions and turned them down. I might protest to the Chairman that that decision was bad for the efficiency of the Partnership's business or was too seriously incompatible with the principles that the Partnership professes, too likely to be held by competent impartial judges to be an indefensible failure in the degree of kindness and care and competence that we profess to give our members in the matter of retaining them if they wish to be retained.

674. "If there were to be such failure on any considerable scale, the general atmosphere of the Partnership would become unhappy. Some of its more valuable members would begin to look for chances to leave it and would resign. Some might even resign without waiting to be sure of any attractive fresh position outside. Moreover, there might be a gravely ill effect upon recruiting. The best candidates might cease to offer themselves. These things are my own responsibility. For these things the Partnership depends upon the Chairman and myself. The Chairman gets certain help from the Heads of the Critical Side. In personnel matters he gets that help especially from the Partners' Counsellor, the General Inspector and the Chief Registrar but on the Executive Side in the case of anyone like you he depends upon me. I do not consider that I ought to make such a stand in this case. I think that it is by no means grossly unreasonable that my colleague, the Head of the Selling Side (or the General Manager of the Workrooms or whoever it may be) should take the view that he is

taking. The case is perhaps rather near the line and, if a very great many decisions of this kind were all to be taken in the same direction, that is to say in the direction of strictness, I might have to argue that discretion used so one-sidedly is misused and that in cases, that are not really very clear, there should be a middle course. The answer should not be always 'yes' or always 'no'. It should be a blend of the two, sometimes the one and sometimes the other, with an effort to be as fair and reasonable as possible. But in this particular case I can see no sufficient reason why I should not simply accept my colleague's view.

675. "On the other hand I consider that it would be wise for the Partnership to give you, if you like, such and such a chance of continuing in a position that will be outside my colleague's own field—outside it so completely that it cannot be reasonably said that your continuance in that other position will be in any too serious way dangerous to the efficiency of the field for which my colleague is responsible. That being so, the question, whether you shall be given an opportunity of continuing, is entirely a question for me. It has nothing whatever to do with my colleague and I am willing to give you a further chance, if you like, and moreover I am willing to cause the Partnership to continue your pay for a certain period and to spend a certain amount upon giving you training because, though I may be disappointed in this particular case, I believe that on the whole that procedure in such cases as this will not be so gravely hurtful to the Partnership that the disadvantage will outweigh the advantage of the extra general sense of kindliness and care and consequently of individual security that will be created by the Partnership's taking all this trouble to carry you further if you want to be carried."

PERSONAL INCOMPATIBILITY

676. The Director of Personnel embodies, as has been said, the Partnership in those cases in which the single-handed manager of a business, in which there were a number of subordinate chiefs, might take the view that he could not properly and wisely ask the head of some particular section to persevere further with some particular worker but he could wisely and properly ask the head of some other section to give that same worker a real trial and to do his best to make that trial turn out well.

In such a case the principal manager could ask for no more than a fair trial and a genuine effort to make it succeed. If he was not going to undertake personally the management of the section, he must not be unduly exacting in asking the person or persons, who were going to do that job, to carry in their team someone of whom the principal manager might think that he could make a success in work of that kind but whom they in fact could not.

If he feels that they have not a proper desire to give in such cases a real trial and to do all, that they reasonably can, to make it succeed, then he will presumably decide that they are not fit for their own functions. But, so long as incompatibility of temperament does not occur too often, he must expect to find that there are some people with whom the head of some particular section cannot work and, if a fair trial seems to show that some particular worker is one of those cases, then the principal manager will have to say to that worker that ability to fit into that particular team is one of the qualifications for belonging to it and that the experiment can go no further.

677. The Director of Personnel has in respect of most of the Partnership's business this power to require that somebody shall be given a fair trial, and, if the Director of Personnel were to report to the Chairman that in his own view a fair trial had not been given or there had not been a proper degree of skill in the efforts to make that trial turn out well, then the Chairman would presumably take a very grave view of that reason for feeling that the head of the section, in which the broad policy of the Partnership had been thus thwarted, was not well enough suited by his own post.

As has been said, this power of the Director of Personnel does not extend to departments of which the heads are responsible separately and solely to the Council, the Board or the Chairman and it does not extend to posts above a certain rate of pay (at present £1,499 a year). With these last the Chairman deals at present but the line may rise a long way yet. With these exceptions this power of the Director of Personnel extends to the whole of the Partnership except so far as some posts are of such a special nature that in general the Director of Personnel can hardly be anything more than a rubber stamp for the particular expert concerned.

CENTRAL SUPERVISION TO SECURE CO-ORDINATION

678. In cases of that kind the Director of Personnel will in effect give a completely free hand to some specialist but it will still be the Director's duty to watch the results. Suppose, for example, that the Director of Personnel arranged with the Director of Catering or the Manager of the Hairdressing that they would make or would authorise other people to make all engagements of in the one case skilled kitchen workers and in the other skilled hairdressers. It would still be the duty of the Director of Personnel to keep an eye on the broad results and to see that they were not such as to be injurious to the Partnership as a whole.

If the rates of pay for some particular grade were to be made extravagantly high, that might cause serious jealousy and trouble in other sections of the Partnership where otherwise there would be contentment and efficiency. Or if there were to be gravely excessive harshness in dismissals or in other ways the general reputation of the Partnership might suffer. Harm might be done not merely in the particular field for which the Director of Catering or the Manager of the Hairdressing was responsible but also to the Partnership's recruiting for other sections.

In exactly the same way, a single-handed head of a business would keep an eye on the exercise of powers that he might entrust to the head of some section of that business. He would still be responsible, of course, for the general atmosphere of the business and for its general reputation and he would have to watch to see that there were no serious signs of trouble from the exercise by somebody else of power that he himself, the principal manager, thought it better not to keep in his own hands.

CENTRAL KNOWLEDGE OF EACH PARTNER'S QUALIFICATIONS

679.   Furthermore, it is the function of the Director of Personnel to watch by means of his Department the whole of the Partnership's team with the limited exceptions mentioned already and of which the total number is relatively small. It is for example the business of the Department of Personnel to discover that somebody in one of the kitchens desires intensely to become a hairdresser and has a real talent for such work. It is the function of the Department of Personnel to know enough of every member of the Partnership's present team.

If, for example, a Branch suddenly enquires whether there is in the Partnership anyone who can speak some uncommon language, it is the function of the Department of Personnel to be able to answer that question very promptly. It seems possible that this function of giving information of this kind may pass to the Registries. In such things our organisation is not yet so firmly settled as, but for the war, it might have been by this time.

CENTRAL FUNCTIONS IN PROMOTION

680.   It is likewise the function of the Department to make a really first-rate job of building up promotion-lists not merely within separate sections but for the Partnership as a whole and the Department must be consulted and its views must prevail to such extent as the interest of the Partnership as a whole may require. The head of a section may want to give a certain promotion to one of his own people but the Partnership may have someone with a better claim to that promotion. It is for the Department of Personnel to know whether that is so. The claim may arise from equal capacity with longer membership or from greater capacity though with shorter membership. In either case a really efficient head of a business might decide that the proper person in his business to have that promotion was so and so and, if he took that view sufficiently strongly, then he would feel that he must request the head of the section concerned

to accept that view loyally and to do his utmost to make the promotion turn out well.

VOCATIONAL TRAINING

681. Related to this matter of promotions is vocational training. It is for the Department of Personnel to take care that the Partnership makes in this way all the provision that is desirable for its own efficiency. And of course that includes whatever may be required by the principles that the Partnership professes. If those provisions are intended to raise in the minds of those, who come into the Partnership, and of their friends a hope that they will be given a certain training and a certain chance of advancement without having to leave the Partnership, then those hopes must be fulfilled even though equally efficient workers for the higher grade could be obtained outside without any need to make within the Partnership arrangements for vocational training of that particular kind.

How far such an arrangement is to go is a matter of general policy for which at the top level the Chairman must be personally responsible. But, whatever the Partnership does profess to do in the way of vocational training will be a function of the Department of Personnel.

Vocational training is one thing. General education is another. But they shade into each other. The acquisition of any skill, however narrow, has some general cultural value and general culture will tend to increase a worker's efficiency in almost anything whatever.

Nevertheless it is broadly true that the acquisition of a certain skill, a certain expertise of body or mind, does not affect general perception and intelligence as do other things of which the value for material achievement and for money-making is wholly indirect.

EDUCATION AS DISTINCT FROM VOCATIONAL TRAINING

682. Because of the war the Partnership's experiment with adult education has begun so lately and its development of vocational training has been likewise delayed so much, that it is not possible as yet to judge how far these things may go. But it seems clear that they should be functions of the Department of Personnel and that the general culture, while most strictly non-vocational, should be frankly open to those who are hoping that it will increase substantially their earning-power as well as to those whose motives have nothing to do with money.

It must, however, be arranged and conducted most strictly from the standpoint of the latter group. There should not be the very slightest concession to those whose motive is not culture but material gain.

So far, as general culture will in fact increase their earning-power, let it by all means do so and let us hope that consciously or unconsciously they will get from it much benefit besides increase of income. But, if it does in fact increase earning-power, it should do so precisely in those respects that depend upon genuine culture and not upon such knowledge or skill as according to the inclination of its possessor can be used either for good purposes or for bad.

THE MEDICAL SERVICE

683. This also is within the Department of Personnel. At present it is costing the Partnership about £9,000 a year. In almost all cases newcomers have to pass a medical examination and admission sometimes depends upon the candidate's getting some treatment first. All the larger Branches have Medical Rooms and the Partnership aims at securing the early taking of sick-leave that tends to early recovery and to prevent infection. This is one of the motives of the very liberal sick-pay rules. In the past we experimented with the support of the Council in pressure towards proper dentistry. It was made a condition of sick-pay. It was dropped but may perhaps be revived. As yet, we have not done as much as I hoped we should in the way of preventive medicine. There have been various difficulties but in the end I hope we shall do a very great deal.

The Department of Personnel is plainly closely akin to that of the Partners' Counsellor. But, whereas the Partners' Counsellor and his assistants have no duty to think of anything at all but the interests of the individual Partners, the Department of Personnel must, of course, have full care for the Partnership's efficiency in the services that it undertakes to render to its customers and so to the general community.

The Partners' Counsellor must not mislead the Partnership. His advocacy of the interests of his clients must be that of an advocate clear-headed and scrupulously honourable but up to that line he must not keep silent upon matters of which the Partnership should wish to know.

He is, however, entitled to use all fair and proper means to secure that the view taken of those matters is the most advantageous to his client or clients. So long as he is punctiliously honest, he has no duty to go further towards securing the general interest of the Partnership as a whole as against that of any particular individual members.

The Director of Personnel, on the other hand, has to think of the Partners as in war a general has to think of troops. It is his duty to take the utmost care of them and to promote to the utmost of his ability their happiness but only so far as may be consistent with their duty as champions of their country. The supreme consideration is not their pleasure or safety but the interests of their country.

The Director of Personnel is entitled to feel that, so long as he gives the Partners' Counsellor the full proper opportunity to know what is intended or is being or has been done, he, for his own part, in cases that in his own view are really doubtful, can give the benefit of the doubt in favour of the interests of the Partnership as a whole and against those of the individual Partner for the Partners' Counsellor exists to secure that in such matters the Partnership is in fact not false to the principles that it professes. He has unlimited right of access to all of the Partnership's records and unlimited access to the Council, the Board and the Chairman.

If in a matter, of which he has been informed properly, he without adequate protest allows the Director of Personnel to take a course that is excessively favourable to the Partnership as a whole and excessively unfavourable to some individual or individuals among its members, past, present or future, the Director of Personnel and the Chairman will both be entitled to say that the Partners' Counsellor has failed to give them help for which they were depending upon him.

THE DIRECTORSHIP OF FINANCIAL OPERATIONS

684.   In a large sense the Director of Personnel has to find and manage the workers necessary for the carrying out of the Partnership's current programme.

The Director of Financial Operations has to find the money. As it is the function of the Director of Personnel to take care that the Partnership's procedure is expedient for its recruiting and retention of those whom it ought to wish to retain, so the Director of Financial Operations has to take care that the Partnership's procedure is expedient for its financial credit, its ability to obtain as thriftily as possible whatever capital it needs now or may need in future.

Next to the Chairman's, his views must prevail upon all matters of that kind.

With one unfortunate exception (the trouble mentioned earlier with certain jobbers on the London Stock Exchange) the Partnership's relations with the investing public have been extremely satisfactory. The unusualness of those relations in the matter of extraordinarily informative accounts and reports to our shareholders and the satisfactoriness of the results of that policy have been set out elsewhere in this book.

The Directorship of Financial Operations has not grown as yet into a separate, whole-time post. Perhaps it never will. At present it is combined with the Directorship of Maintenance and Expansion.

PUBLIC RELATIONS

685.   At this point we pass outside the set of posts that carry membership of the Central Board or of the Chairman's Regular Conference. We are getting near to such specialised fields as the Directorships of Buying and the major sections of the Selling Side, the two groups of posts that correspond to the private entrepreneurs in the general community. But,

before we get to them, there must be some mention of certain central positions.

One is the Directorship of Public Relations. In some enterprises this might require regular membership of the innermost managerial ring, the Chairman's Conference or whatever it was called, since the functions are so closely related to Financial Operations, Recruiting, Sales Promotion and even upon occasion Supply, that is to say the purchasing of merchandise.

In our own business this particular post has not yet become heavy but it may.

ACCOUNTANCY

686.   Among the central posts one, that must be always of extreme importance, is the Chief Accountantship. The keeping of the Partnership's accounts is at present a full-time occupation for approximately twelve hundred people, scattered among the separate Counting Houses of the various Branches.

The relation of the Manager of such a Branch Counting House to the Head of the Branch is that of a partner, a junior partner but a partner.

In the old days of the private firms the chief position in the Counting House was commonly held by a member of the firm, who was commonly known as the counting-house partner. In a family business, if no member of the family was available, a Counting House Manager, felt to be satisfactorily competent and to be permanently settled in his post, was often admitted to membership of the firm. That is the position at which the Partnership aims.

In a large business the outside auditors may keep one or more of their own staff permanently at work in their client's business. Those outsiders are not employees of the client. They are employees of the auditors. If their behaviour is in some way inconvenient to the client, his remedy is to protest to the offender's employers whom he himself employs as aforesaid, for a client is of course one of several employers of the professional firm of whose services he avails himself.

687.   We have yet to see whether this relation between local Counting Houses and Branch Managements will work well enough. The problem did not arise to any important extent until in 1940 the Partnership acquired fifteen new branches, some of them large and far from London. Since then the war has prevented any gathering of conclusive experience. The Chief Accountant has within his own field all the responsibilities of the Director of Personnel up to the rate of pay (£1,499) and up to the length of membership (seven years) beyond either of which lines decisions of really high importance to the Partner, whatever his or her

position in the organisation, require at present the Chairman's personal concurrence.

The Chief Accountant is responsible directly and solely to the Chairman. That position will, I feel sure, be permanent for my own time and I expect thereafter also. It is plainly questionable whether a tenth of the whole of the Partnership's workers ought to be occupied in keeping accounts and it may be that, as we recover from the tremendous upheaval of a sudden sixty per cent. increase of our business by the acquisition of fifteen new branches under the extraordinary conditions of this war, we shall find that there is room for great improvements in this field. Here, as everywhere else, the aim of the Partnership is to carry the fewest possible workers consistent with stability and avoidance of overstrain and then to pay them in one way or another as much as possible, for, since the dividend-charge is absolutely fixed, there is nowhere else for the Partnership's earnings to go.

SOME OTHER CENTRAL DEPARTMENTS

688. Among other Central Departments of high importance are the Department of Legal Advice and the Directorships of Building and of Research. Their names will indicate sufficiently their functions, except that it should perhaps be mentioned that the services of the Department of Legal Advice are available not only to holders of administrative positions who may have need of such help in their work but also to Partners upon their private affairs. The extent, to which Partners requested this free legal advice, became too formidable a charge upon the Partnership and it is now given in those cases only in which the Central Council or some body responsible thereto considers that it should be.

Still other examples of Central Departments on the Executive Side are the Directorship of Services (Planning, Plant and Stores, Transport, etc.), the Directorship of Catering and the Central Management of the Hairdressing. The holders of such posts as these two last may be in executive charge of separate Branch businesses of their own kind or of Departments in Branches not thus highly specialised.

689. In some cases the executive charge of such a Department may be undertaken by the Head of the Branch, of which it forms part, and the Central Specialist may act merely as an expert adviser upon technical matters.

If the Head of one of the Partnership's Department Stores was unable to cooperate satisfactorily with one of these Central Specialists, the Partnership would obviously have to choose between either, parting with one or other of them or else saying to the Head of the Branch that, if his Branch was to continue to include that particular Department, he must contrive to get good enough results without the assistance of the

Central Specialist, just as he would have to do if the Branch were his own property and, so far as he was concerned, the Central Specialist did not exist.

Cases of such conflict should be very rare. If two people cannot pull together in such a relationship, it is unlikely that each of them can be really desirable in his particular position. But now and again there may be an unlucky incompatibility between the temperaments of two people who ordinarily are quite sufficiently good team-workers.

In such a case the Partnership's policy could be thus elastic.

SUPPLY (MANUFACTURE AND BUYING)

690. Some of these Central Departments of the Executive Side fall entirely or almost entirely upon one side or other of the line that divides at present into two main parts all that still remains to be considered of the Partnership's present organisation, namely the Buying Side and the Selling Side.

Buying includes production. Broadly speaking the Buying Side decides what is to be made or to be bought in order to be put on sale and at what price and with what warranty or warning, and in which Selling House the goods are to be sold.

In any of these matters the Buying Side may reconsider from time to time their own original decision and may then change it. This includes the very important function of lowering selling prices in order to liquidate stock-in-trade that does not sell satisfactorily.

Except in these respects the Selling Side from the time of its accepting any stock-in-trade is wholly and solely responsible for its safe-keeping and for all dealings with it.

The separation requires of course great care that Buyers shall not get out of touch with public demand, present and prospective. But it is plainly inevitable if a number of selling establishments are to get for their customers the advantages, that may be great, of combining their making or buying of merchandise. We have however yet to see how far it may seem practicable and desirable to arrange for some things to be bought locally. Those Buyers would be presumably in constant touch with their customers and would really do a great deal of selling.

TEAM-WORK IN SUPPLY

691. Central manufacturing and buying will tend to give rise to team-work. First-rate judgment, whether to manufacture or to buy and in what quantities, and first-rate skill in bargaining, with at the same time the wisdom to resist temptations to be unfair to the supplier, are apt not to be combined in one person with a first-rate sense of design or of the tendencies and intensity of public demand.

Furthermore, possessors of really high ability of this former kind, the man of business as opposed to the artist or to the clever gambler upon the ceaselessly varying whims of the consumer, will tend to be too expensive to be available for the detail work of constantly renewed diligent search through a particular market. The broad control of manufacturing and buying policy requires, moreover, great experience and that tends to mean that the worker is no longer of an age to be fully energetic in hunting out individual opportunities, many of them not of great separate importance.

Furthermore, a field of supply that ought to be under a single chief may require simultaneous buying-activities in widely distant markets. Altogether, buying must tend to give rise to team-work, a Director of Buying directing the activities of a team of Buyers, some of whom may be themselves very great experts, equal colleagues rather than junior partners of the Director. Below these again there will be in some cases people of much less experience or smaller ability who may know a market well and be excellent at hunting out minor opportunities.

Besides these there may be one or more designers, factory managers and others working within the field of a particular Director of Buying or possibly for more than one.

BUYERS' COUNSELLORS

692. There must be some liaison-officers to secure proper team-work between the Directors of Buying themselves, of whom some must draw trade to others and in the same way satisfy demand drawn to them by those others, while there will be also joint operations, as for example Directors of Buying of Garment Departments may draw supplies from colleagues trading in materials. In such joint operations there may be important advantage to both parties. Such liaison-officers by their very knowledge of the inner operations of several Directors of Buying and by the experience that they will accumulate will tend to be highly influential advisers both for the Directors of Buying themselves in their own work and for the Partnership when it has to appraise that work.

Nevertheless, I have rightly or wrongly a strong feeling that at this level the function of co-ordination, liaison, information and advice should be not managerial but secretarial in the sense that these Buyers' Counsellors, as the Partnership is at present calling them, should have no executive responsibility, no power over Directors of Buying except in the sense that the counsel will be upon record and, if it is not followed and the results are bad, the Director of Buying will not be able to plead that that particular idea could hardly have occurred to him and in fact never did.

The function of securing the completest possible liaison between the work of all of the Directors of Buying and their teams, so that knowledge gained by any of them is passed promptly and adequately to any of the others, to whom it will be useful, is extremely important and requires that the Buyers' Counsellors shall be as few as possible. At present there are only two. One graduated at Cambridge with first-class honours in Geology and Mineralogy and the other at Oxford with first-class honours in Literae Humaniores (commonly called a First in Greats).

THE ENTREPRENEURS

693. The Directorships of. Buying seem destined to be one of the greatest groups of top level posts in which a partnership may be capable of expanding without limit. The war has prevented our starting as yet to experiment with the problem of combining Local Buying with Central. Before 1940 our Branches were too few and small to give much scope for this and since then difficulties of recruiting and scarcity of supplies have prevented any considerable developments.

For my own part I think that in this direction the possibilities may be great. We are just setting to work upon them.

694. On the Selling Side the problem of top level organisation is very much more difficult because there is hardly any limit to the possible number of selling points or to their variety of function and size and, whereas the Central Buying tends to be based in London, the principal divisions of the Selling Side must be territorial: they must be based in their fields of work.

The real entrepreneurs upon the Selling Side, the opposite numbers of the Directors of Buying, will be the Managing Directors or General Managers or whatever they may be called who will be in charge of selling territories (whether the "territory" be a single large unit or a group of several smaller units) capable of a volume of business large enough to carry the Partnership's top rate of individual income.

As these posts become numerous, we shall have to make somehow some arrangement corresponding to the Buyers' Counsellors, posts of which the holders will be few enough to be a really satisfactory means of securing that on the Buying Side the Directors of Buying and on the Selling Side the Heads of major territories are so far in touch with each other that valuable discoveries are shared to the best advantage and possibilities of mutual help are not wasted. The first of these "Sellers' Counsellorships" has come already into existence.

In the end it seems to me that the real centre of gravity of the Partnership's business-management, its real vitality, must be in these bodies of entrepreneurs, these leaders of the actual Buying and of the actual Selling.

Such Central Departments as Personnel and Financial Operations will exist to supply them, precisely as in the general community the

Courts of Law, the Money Market and such professions as architecture exist to supply the needs of all the individual entrepreneurs.

The ultimate objective of all these activities will be the advantage of all members of the Partnership with a favouring, so far as there is any favouring, of those who are worst off. But the core of the Partnership's vitality, as a team of manufacturers and traders, will be in these major entrepreneurs. I say "major" because there may be within the Partnership some enterprises that are genuinely separate and desirable and yet not large. But, large or small, it will be upon the heads of these enterprises that the Partnership as a whole will depend for its security and its prosperity.

THE MANAGERSHIPS OF DEPARTMENTS

695. It is said that the real backbone of the armies by which the Romans brought long-lasting peace to the world of their day was the centurion, the leader of one hundred and twenty men. Some commanders-in-chief were brilliant, some were mediocre, some were fools. But the quality of the Roman army did not depend upon them. It depended upon the centurion.

I think that in the same way the Partnership's solidity and success in the long run may depend supremely upon the skill with which it recruits, trains and deals with the occupants of the positions that at present it calls the Managerships of Departments.

The broad idea is that the holders of these positions shall be in charge of no more than about a dozen workers. Unless these positions are filled really well, the creative imagination, technical knowledge and energy of the major entrepreneurs will be largely thwarted. If, on the other hand, these positions are filled really well, then I think the Partnership will be able to stand a very great deal of bad luck in the way of failures to provide itself constantly with a sufficient supply of the quite uncommon qualities that the posts at the top, the posts that I am calling the major entrepreneurs, will require.

696. It seems to me that upon the Buying Side the Director of Buying and his team are the opposite numbers of the specialist manufacturer or wholesaler, asking the retailer for orders but at the same time advising him, in the light of their own knowledge and experience.

On the Selling Side the head of a major territory, which may be a single very large shop or may be a lot of Branches scattered over a considerable area, will be the present-day opposite number of the owner-managers of the Department Stores when they were private firms or of the Managing Director of such a business after it had been turned into a public company.

The Managers of little separate Branches, of which some day we may perhaps have very many, and the Manager of the individual Selling

Department within the Department Store will be the present-day opposite number of the owner-manager of those little specialist shops, the silk mercer, the linen draper, the haberdasher, the glover and so on whom the creators of the Department Stores gathered under one roof to the great convenience of the public. The convenience was not only in their being brought side by side and under one roof so that the customer's purchases could go all into one parcel and be charged to one account. There was in addition the advantage that the buying of each of those formerly separate little shops was now co-ordinated pretty closely to serve a particular clientèle.

The system proposed in this book does not eliminate all competition, all conflict, but in that direction it may take us a step that is perhaps the longest possible as yet.

Competition between partnerships will remain.

DYNAMOS MUST BE USED APPROPRIATELY

697.   There is not space here to describe the various posts that in a large Branch exist at present between its Head and its Rank and File, the Partners who have no official responsibility for the work of other people but who are themselves in the strictest sense "the workers," the people who actually do things instead of getting others to do them.

Here I think it may be enough to say that for my own part I feel very strongly indeed that in such team-work Managers of business should profit by the example of armies. Armies avoid, so far as they can, wear and tear for their officers, not as a matter of privilege but because it is essential that right up to the end of the march the officer shall have all his wits about him and plenty of nervous energy with which to hearten his men in any emergency. That is why an army does not ask its officers to carry a heavy kit and, if it can, it lets them ride.

In business the holders of key positions should be given likewise, so at least it seems to me, good pay, easy hours and freedom from all avoidable strain, not as a matter of privilege but in order that they may be able to put into their own work the energy that it needs.

698.   The best occupants of responsible positions will tend to be people of exceptional vitality, able to carry a great deal of wear and tear and yet to feel and seem fresh and lively after long hours day after day. It may be wasteful to prevent the working of such hours by such people. If they are prevented, little or nothing may be achieved. They may use the leisure for something that is not sufficiently recreation and that on the contrary diminishes rather than increases their fitness when they return to duty.

But people of that strength are few. There are very many who can achieve for a rather short while at rather long intervals high excellence in something that needs strength and skill or great mental effort, like successful public speaking, for one who can make such exertions day after day without flagging too much.

The Partnership should, therefore, I think, be very careful not to let the holders of key positions of any kind sacrifice consciously or unconsciously quality to quantity. These things are subtle and difficult but for my own part I believe there are really important possibilities in the idea that almost all of us do much more than half of our real work, our real achievement, in the first half of our working time, and that, if we go on too long, we may very easily lower grievously the real value of our performance.

AVOID THE WASTEFUL FRICTION OF NEEDLESS CURTAILMENTS OF FREEDOM

699.   One other thing I would say here that applies to work of every kind. Avoid unnecessary regulations. Let everything be as free and easy as ever you can. Where regulation seems to be necessary, enforce it with the utmost firmness. There is much less friction, much less wear and tear if there is no doubt at all what the regulation is and no hope at all of getting away with any disregard of it. But, the greater the strictness where there has got to be any strictness at all, the greater the desirability of having free and easiness wherever you possibly can.

When the Partnership abolished years ago fixed working-hours for Buyers, we were told the results would be very bad. There was never any trouble whatever.

Let the partnership regard every single one of its members as an intelligent worker, working by and for himself and solely because he chooses to do so. Let it give him in every possible way the very utmost freedom that in the same occupation an intelligent entrepreneur, who was really sensible, might allow himself. Those, who from choice or necessity set themselves to make their living by team-work must accept necessities of team-work. But let the Partnership refrain most carefully from making any regulations beyond those necessities.

A few years ago we asked ourselves whether we could not cease in many, if not all, cases to use attendance-clocks. I was delighted to hear then that the idea had arisen already in the United States and that the experiment had succeeded. Our own experience has been the same.

OVERLAPPING NECESSARY IN ORGANISATION

700.   In such picture, as this book, written in the conditions in which it has had to be, gives of the present structure of the Partnership and of some ideas for its development, there may seem to be much overlapping. That is, I think, inevitable in such team-work, as is here in question. In some team games, football, for example, or cricket, a competent set of

players move freely in relation to each other and are always on the watch to come to the rescue if a colleague makes some mistake or has some misfortune.

Poaching—usurpation of the functions of a colleague—is bad play and will only be tolerated on any considerable scale in players whose general value to the team is very high indeed. But failure to back up properly is still worse.

It is of the very essence of good team-work in a game or in anything else to understand quite thoroughly what is your own proper part and to judge it correctly from moment to moment and to help it wholeheartedly to the very utmost of your ability.

This duty of backing up your colleagues will mean a certain overlapping. On one occasion you will be in a certain sense doing somebody else's job and on another occasion he will be doing yours. A player, who in this respect is dull or grudging, is a bad player and so equally is a player who is jealously resentful of help of which the giving is not unreasonable and that he therefore ought to take in good part, even though he may feel that he could have done without it.

It is extremely necessary to sound organising and sound administration to recognise the need of overlapping in this sense and it is likewise necessary to be constantly most careful that the common interest shall not depend excessively upon any particular individual or individuals. All members of the Partnership should be free to die at any moment untroubled by a feeling that their departure will be an unnecessarily serious misfortune for the Partnership.

DEVOLUTION

701. The structure and practices of the Partnership, as they stand at present, are the result of many years of aiming at devolution. If I do not deceive myself, my supreme aim from my earliest days has been to make the Partnership tough and solid, to give it the utmost possible prospect of continuing smoothly after my own time. For that reason, if, again, I do not deceive myself, I have striven to give up power to other people, to give it up both in reality and in appearance. The latter is, of course, important for questions of prestige and psychology. A man, who feels himself responsible, will tend to rise to that occasion but his tendency will be all the stronger if he not only feels himself responsible but is also conscious that he is so in the eyes of others.

If one does not own, as I have done, a controlling-interest, it takes real unselfishness not to wish to be indispensable and the Partnership must expect that it will suffer from such selfishness the more it fails to make holders of desirable positions feel very sure indeed that there is no risk whatever of their losing those positions undeservedly.

It was all very well for me with an absolute voting-control and a serene, howsoever mistaken, conviction, that the work suited me so well and that I knew it so thoroughly that in case of need I could carry on well enough with almost any amount of such substitute-help as might be available if a whole lot of my principal colleagues were to be killed in a single accident.

To welcome and train a lieutenant of your own calibre and to keep nothing avoidably to yourself is a very different matter if you do not own a controlling-interest in the enterprise to which for the time you are giving your working-life and from which, as the years pass, it may become, if only as a matter of personal associations, more and more important to you that you shall not have to move to whatever new field might then be available.

A PERSONAL TRIBUTE

702.   Here, though I am afraid that he may dislike it, I feel that, if for no other reason, I ought for the sake of the Partnership's future traditions to pay tribute to what through the last twenty years I have constantly felt to be in this immensely important respect the unfailing wisdom and courage and generosity of Sir Metford Watkins, now the Partnership's Director of Maintenance and Expansion. To join us he gave up a scholastic career in which he was prosperously started and his prospects were excellent. Fifteen years later his success in our own business and his standing in our part of the business world were such that at the request of the President of the Board of Trade he created the Directorship of Civilian Clothing and in so doing originated the "Utility" idea.

It has always seemed .to me that in those years, that obviously were likely to be supremely important to the Partnership's development of the right atmosphere and traditions, no one could have set a better example of genuine team-work, genuine and perfectly good-humoured acceptance of organisation, genuine and perfectly good-humoured acceptance of the functions of others and therewith unfailing candour in recognising the occasional occurrence in his own field of work of such failures, such mistakes and misfortunes, as none of us can hope wholly, to escape, and moreover in recognising the full extent of their real ill-consequences for the Partnership.

Such an example is, of course, immensely influential and correspondingly valuable. Wisdom and generosity of that kind are tested more or less constantly in any team-work between posts of which the individual functions are important but the test is peculiarly searching in an organisation growing so fast and so far that some individual functions have to keep on contracting and eventually to contract, in appearance at all events, so extremely as did those of Sir Metford when the growth of the Partnership, after splitting ten years earlier my own functions, the functions of the Chairmanship, so as to carve out of them for Sir Metford the Directorship of Trading, with its very great share of real responsibility, patronage and so forth, split that Directorship in its turn so that the immensely increased weight of the Partnership's affairs and the far greater increase, that seemed plainly to be coming, would be carried thenceforward not by two principal posts, the Chairmanship and the Directorship of Trading, but by a whole team of separate posts and groups of posts forming between them about as numerous a body as the limitations of individual human ability allow to be capable of sufficient integration for real intimacy of mind, that is to say somewhere about a dozen persons.

DUALISM IN ORGANISATION

703.   To return to general matters, it may be well to mention here that the organisation of the Partnership is based as completely as possible upon the idea that on every important occasion there should be at least two separate parties each qualified to make things go right and of whom either or both can be held responsible if things go wrong. For example, either the General Inspector or the Director of Expansion could properly be held responsible for failure to perceive in certain cases some signs of flagging. The Partnership could quarrel with either and could secure sufficient continuity by retaining the other. Moreover in all such cases the Partnership will get the very important advantages that have given rise to the sayings that two heads are better than one and that the bystander sees most of the game.

In the matter of the Partnership's not failing in awareness of what is happening in the world outside and of generating new notions of its own, the Director of Maintenance and Expansion has no such sharer of responsibility and there would seem to be at present a weakness at this point. Perhaps it may be made good by a development of the Department of Research.

704.   At all events it is at present the general policy of the Partnership that at all points of major importance real responsibility shall rest upon each of at least two separate posts, so valuable that their holders will presumably be anxious to run no risk of losing them and so separate that the holder of neither can hoodwink or obstruct the holder of the other in the performance of his duty. Of course in very many cases the safeguard will consist of the responsibility of more than two such separate posts. But the present aim is that, whenever anything goes seriously wrong, the Principal Authority, whether in the particular case that be the Central Council or the Central Board or the Chairman, shall be able to hold responsible either or both of at least two people.

705.   The policy of devolution requires that holders of posts other than that which carries the chief individual responsibility shall have very great discretion. Opinions are bound to differ upon the question just where the line is to be drawn. The Managers will tend to say: "Draw it widely. We cannot do our work if too many of our decisions are subject to appeal and we and our average successors shall be just as competent and careful and anxious to be as kind as will be the average Chairman."

The Managed, on the other hand, will say: "Draw it narrowly. To have proper peace of mind we must be able to feel that in anything, that matters very much to us, and above all in any case, in which our membership and perhaps our pension-prospect are at stake, we shall have, even if we do not choose to use it, a right of appeal to whoever holds in this Partnership the position of chief individual responsibility."

CHAPTER 38

THE PRINCIPAL EXECUTIVE COMMITTEE—THE COMMITTEE FOR APPEALS—THE GENERAL SECRETARYSHIP

706.   THIS seems to mean that, if the Partnership is to ask of its Chairman as little as it can, there must be some provision for diminishing as much as possible the passage to him of matters from the next highest level of individual responsibility. With this aim there have been instituted two Committees, a Principal Executive Committee (of four) and a Committee (of three) for Appeals. The chairman of the former is a representative (normally the Director) of the Department of Maintenance and Expansion. The other members are a representative (normally the Director) of the Department of Personnel, a representative of the Buying Side (one of the Buyers' Counsellors) and a representative (normally the Sellers' Counsellor) of the Selling Side.

Four are required for a quorum. If any of the regular members is unavailable, he must be represented by a sufficient deputy. Decisions must be unanimous. If the committee cannot agree, then the matter must pass to the Chairman of the Partnership. If they do agree, their decision is final so far as the collective interest of the Partnership is concerned. But, if one or more Partners, who come directly into contact with this committee, consider that, however expedient the committee's decision may be for the Partnership as a whole, it is so unfair to himself or to themselves that they must appeal against it, they can ask the Committee for Appeals to certify that the matter ought to have the personal attention of the Chairman of the Partnership. If the three members of the Committee for Appeals unanimously refuse to give that certificate, then the thing will go no further and the Chairman's own time will be saved. But, if any of the three members of the Committee for Appeals considers the certificate ought to be given, then the matter must pass to the Chairman of the Partnership.

VALUE OF REQUIREMENT OF UNANIMITY

707.   The arrangements, that the decision of each of these two committees must be unanimous, would enable the Chairman to suggest to any of the members that he ought to have dissented and thereby obliged the Chairman to examine the details personally. When the Committee was unanimous, the Chairman's position would be strong against criticisms that he ought to have examined such a thing for himself. It is one thing to say that you relied upon the advice of ·some one person of whose

functions and competence the critics (a Court of Law for example) may know nothing. It is quite another thing to say that you relied upon the unanimous opinion of four or of three people each voting with the knowledge that, if he concurred in the view of the other three or two, he would be taking the responsibility involved in the fact that, if the Committee were not unanimous, the Chairman of the Partnership must examine the thing for himself.

708. Whereas the Principal Executive Committee consists of four principal leaders of the Partnership's Executive Side, the. Committee for Appeals consists of three principal leaders of the Critical Side, namely the Partners' Counsellor, who is supremely concerned with the dues of each individual Partner or group of Partners against the Partnership as a whole, the Chief Registrar and the Internal Auditor, the two other Heads of the Critical Side whose functions are least likely to give rise to friction and are most confined to the ascertainment of facts.

The quorum is three, each regular member being represented, if necessary, by a deputy of his own appointment from his own Department.

NEED OF SOME LIMIT TO APPEALING

709. Possibility of appeal may be very highly desirable but it must not be too open to misuse. In some cases the appellant may have little or nothing to lose by appealing. In that case he will tend to try his luck however faint the hope may be. He may even appeal without any hope at all. He may simply do so from a desire to revenge himself in some way or for. the satisfaction of airing what he feels to be a grievance.

It seems therefore desirable that between the Chairman's own necessarily limited time and strength and the theoretically possible stream of appeals from a Partnership that contains already 12,000 members and that may be destined to become vastly larger, there shall be some filter to separate the appeals that the Chairman ought to consider from those that he need not.

The Central Council is always free to communicate with the Chairman of the Partnership if they feel that some result of the Partnership's organisation is so seriously unsatisfactory that they ought to do so.

CHAIRMAN'S PROCEDURE IN CASES POSSIBLY DANGEROUS TO HIS OWN TENURE

710. In some cases of appeal to himself the Chairman might take legal advice whether, if he refused the appeal, a Court of Law would be likely to hold that the refusal was a breach of the Constitution of the Partnership.

As well or instead he might in some case of extraordinary difficulty request the Central Council to express their own opinion upon it. If he then adopted that opinion, a Court of Law would presumably he very reluctant to decide that in so doing the Chairman had failed in his own undertaking to maintain the Partnership's Constitution and presumably, if the Chairman asked for the Council's advice, he would not decide against it unless his legal advisers felt very sure that the answer of the Council was in fact contrary to the Partnership's Constitution.

This is the extreme view of the possible ultimate development of the Partnership's methods of securing democratisation—devolution—and of incidentally keeping the holder of the position of chief individual responsibility, the Chairmanship of the Central Board, as free as possible from avoidable calls upon his time and strength that have got to be sufficient for his part in the partnership; no matter how large the partnership may eventually become, and that must therefore be used as economically as possible, since, the larger the partnership, the more will it tend to be necessary that anything, that has got to be done by the Chairman himself, shall be done with ample time for study and thought and with a mind sufficiently fresh and sufficiently free from preoccupation of any kind.

TO VOTE OR NOT TO VOTE

711. The substitution of groups for individuals in matters of more than a certain importance may not always involve a taking of votes. In some cases, of which the Chairman's Conference is one and the British Cabinet is said to be another, organisation may be—and in the Partnership has always tended to be—based upon the Roman idea that in some matters it is expedient that power and responsibility shall be concentrated upon one person but that it shall be specifically his or her duty to ascertain one or more prescribed opinions before upon his own responsibility he commits himself to whatever course he in the light of that opinion judges to be best.

VALUE OF COMMITTEES FOR CONTINUITY

712. From this it is a natural step to say that in matters of more than a certain gravity senior authorities shall be consulted unless those, who thus confer, are able to reach unanimity.

The Partnership in its recent development to meet the immense growth of its business has extended this idea a good deal. For doing so it has had several reasons.

If in matters of more than a certain importance decisions are taken by a single mind without any close and constant conference, any really intimate cooperation with other minds, and if that single mind ceases more or less suddenly to be available, there is likely to be a grave loss of such continuity as could and should have been achieved.

A decision to pass over Mr. A may have been influenced by an intention to reserve Mr. A for some other position not immediately available for him. If this decision is taken by an individual holder of authority and that authority passes to someone else, this intention in respect of Mr. A may fall right out of sight. Conceivably the original individual might lose sight of it by a mere failure of memory such as could not have occurred if the decision had been the result of discussion between two or more and that discussion had been properly minuted. But the risk is, of course, far greater if individual authority passes from the one individual to another. This danger is avoided if the decisions require the participation of more than one person for then the other persons are necessarily aware of all the considerations upon which the decision was based. Even if the system of record is not so good as it should be, the mere memories of those who voted will be a very substantial safeguard of proper continuity.

BETTER RECORDING AND OTHER ADVANTAGES

713. But committee-work with a good quality of secretary tends to adequacy of record and, where record is adequate, the safeguard of continuity is complete. All the members of the committee can be drowned in the "Titanic" or killed in an aircraft and yet the record will make Mr. A's future almost as safe as possible and will safeguard the Partnership from losing whatever advantage it would derive from that use of Mr. A's availability.

The group system has, of course, also the advantage that, though in many important senses "the best committee is a committee of one", in other very important senses two heads are better than one and three may be better than two. In organisations that make use of majority voting, three is the smallest group that can be used but the Partnership will as far as possible avoid majority voting.

It will say to the group that, if they cannot achieve unanimity, the decision must be taken elsewhere and it will repeat the process up to the highest level of seniority to which it is felt to be practicable that the matter shall be carried, and at that final stage it will concentrate the responsibility upon one pair of shoulders.

THE GENERAL SECRETARYSHIP

714. This institution of the Principal Executive Committee and of the Committee for Appeals to safeguard the Chairman from being overloaded with matters, for which the responsibility ought perhaps not to be laid upon any other one member of the Partnership, led to the creation of a General Secretaryship of which the holder should be appointed by the Chairman and should be responsible to him for the efficiency, so far as that can depend upon secretarial work, of both of

these Committees and of such other individual posts or groups as may come into a similar relation to the Chairman, the secretarial work of the Chairman's own Regular Conferences being one case in point.

As the Partnership develops, the General Secretaryship will presumably develop into a considerable Department with the function of securing that the work of all the meetings within its field is so thoroughly prepared that the meetings are as short as they well can be and that the proceedings are so thoroughly recorded and the records so well indexed that the work, when done, has the fullest possible effect and general usefulness.

The General Secretary may, I think, become one of the most important of the members of the Central Management. In a very real sense he will be to the principal individual posts and the various groups, that together constitute the Partnership's Central Management, what an engineer is to a ship's machinery. He will keep the whole thing running smoothly, with proper connections between one engine and another, proper fuel in the way of properly prepared agenda-papers and so on. The present (the first) holder of this post graduated at Oxford with second-class honours in History. He came into the Partnership in January 1938.

CHAPTER 39

RESULTS UP TO 1948 CONSIDERED AFRESH

715.   THROUGHOUT the putting together of this book I have found it very difficult to hold any satisfactory line between the aim of making it sufficiently useful to Partners seeking in it guidance upon matters of their own procedure and the quite different aim of making available to outside readers a general description of our main ideas and of our experience so far.

For the Partnership's internal purposes the book will certainly have to be supplemented by others and I propose accordingly to let it end here, though perhaps such criticisms, as are invited in the preface, may add some pages to future editions.

716.   As the Partnership stands to-day, what has it really achieved for its members? It has already (without counting 1947/48 for which the figures are not yet settled) provided for Partnership Benefit and for pension-fund £1,125,696, besides a great deal more in holiday-pay, sick-pay, help in special need of various kinds, clubs and so forth beyond the general custom even of good employers of the ordinary profit-seeking sort.

PARTNERSHIP BENEFIT, THE PENSION FUND, FREE INSURANCE AND AMENITIES

717.   Twenty-three years have passed since Partnership Benefit began to be distributed regularly. During seven of them the flow was stopped by the war. In the other sixteen the average rate was twelve per cent., that is to say over six weeks' additional earnings upon a full year's work and proportionately for those who joined the Partnership after that year began.

For the whole twenty-three years, war and all, the average rate has been eight per cent. but that is of little significance because such a complete stoppage seems unlikely ever to happen except because of a world-war or for some reason almost equally extraordinary.

Before the war, the largest amount, that was thus distributed in any one year, was £62,565 in 1937. At that time none of this distributable profit was going to a pension-fund. The accumulation of that fund began from the 1st February 1941. Now, that is to say after seven years, it is £726,107. For this last year, 1947/48, the appropriation was £210,038. Of this total £73,000 was the last of certain arrears that the war had delayed.

Henceforward the pension-requirement will leave more available for distribution as Partnership Benefit.

In the same year the Partnership spent upon free insurance against exceptional need (chiefly sick-pay) £52,741. It is impossible to know how much of this sick-pay was beyond the ordinary practice of good employers in business of the same kind but the figure is certainly large. Besides this the Partnership spent in this same year upon education, country-clubs, music, dancing and other collective amenities about £50,000.

718.   For reasons of Law the pension-appropriation has to be made before the end of January. It will be some weeks before we shall know what amount of distributable profit will remain for Partnership Benefit.

The pay-sheet, upon which the distribution has to be made, is now so large that to distribute Partnership Benefit to the extent of one per cent. requires about £27,000. Nevertheless, although according to our elaborate system of budgeting the pension-fund, the free insurance and the amenities were going to absorb, as they did, from the earnings of this last year about £313,000, we were confident until very lately that the distribution of Partnership Benefit would be eight per cent., that is to say just about four weeks' additional pay upon a full year's work.

The new purchase-tax, however, under the November Budget reduced by about £40,000 the profit that had been expected from the sales of the specially important month of December and, as we have had at the same time another and rather heavier disappointment, it may be that the specially heavy appropriation to the pension-fund will leave available for distribution as Partnership Benefit no more than about £135,000 i.e. five per cent. of the pay-sheet upon which that distribution will have to be made.

In that case the total receipts, present and prospective (pension-fund) of the Partners from the earnings of this last year over and above their ordinary contractual remuneration and individual bonuses for services considered to deserve such special reward will have been approximately £448,000.

719.   For seven consecutive years from 1924 to 1930 inclusive the rate, at which the Partnership Benefit itself was distributed, was never less than fifteen per cent. For three out of four consecutive years (1925 to 1928 inclusive), it was twenty per cent. and in the fourth twenty-three.

To make the comparison quite accurate account would have to be taken of the fact that in those years I was making to the Partnership an interest-free loan of some capital that they have since paid out and that has been in the main replaced by Partnership Benefit capital upon which there is an interest-charge of about five per cent. On the other hand, we should have to take account also of the fact that in those years much of the earnings of John Lewis and Company were not coming to the

Partnership at all but were going to my father or to my brother, while my share was being taxed as one separate income before it could pass from me to the members of the Partnership. We should have to take account also of the fact that a good deal of the capital, that has been paid out to me in respect of the Deferred Bonds, has been lent back to the Partnership and again without interest.

In any case, all these things would, I think, on balance affect the Partnership Benefit by no more than about one per cent, if so much. I always hoped that the Partnership would, as in the event it has, grow so fast and so far that, as the repayment of my original interest-free loan proceeded, the interest-charge upon the new capital, by which my own would be replaced, would be thus light in its effect upon the. Partnership Benefit.

720. All of these distributions were, as aforesaid, on top of large expenditure upon what in this book is called free insurance against exceptional need and also of large expenditure upon country-clubs and other collective amenities. It is impossible to prove that the Partnership's members were getting at the same time as good or better pay in the ordinary sense than they would ordinarily have got for equivalent work elsewhere. I am, however, sure that was so and for the recent past it happens that in these last two days we have received in this respect information that is at present confidential but that will, I understand, be published shortly.

It shows that in the period under review (the two and a half years from the beginning of 1945 until the middle of 1947) the Partnership was employing in proportion to its turnover a staff substantially larger than the average of the many businesses of the same kind from which the information had been obtained. Many hands proverbially make light work. Nevertheless the Partnership's average rate of pay to each member of that larger staff was substantially higher than the general average.

721. The information shows also that during that period the numbers of the Partnership were increasing almost exactly three times as fast as the average for the very large group of similar businesses in question.

This last figure was a complete surprise to us. It seems to show that in this period our general reputation and high pay-rates have made a really significant difference to our recruiting-power. It should be observed that for several years before the period in question and during the period itself there had been no distribution of Partnership Benefit. The first since the war has been made in this present winter.

It is, I think, reasonably certain that the fact, that the Partnership's rate of recruitment has been almost exactly three times as great as the average for businesses of the same kind, was due not to the prospective resumption of distribution of Partnership Benefit but partly to favourable general reputation and for the rest to the fact that the particular pay-rates, that concerned those recruits, i.e. those of the Rank and File, were attractively high.

This is important because the fact, that in most of those kinds of business, in which the Partnership is engaged at present, pay-rates are a matter of individual bargaining, makes it easy for some Partners to persuade themselves that whatever they get from the Partnership otherwise than in contractual remuneration is to some extent offset by adverse difference in that contractual remuneration itself.

722. The Partnership takes great pains to be well-informed in these matters and I believe that none of my colleagues, who are specially well placed to judge, have ever doubted that those Partners, who have thought and talked like this and still do so, were and are simply wrong. As a general rule, however, there is no such means of proving that as in respect of the recent past we have now got in this confidential information. If they were not confidential, I should very gladly give the figures here.

As a matter of fact, according to the same statistics the Partnership's expenditure upon managerial remuneration was notably lower but we do not yet know in what sense this term "managerial" was used. So far as it goes, however, this low expenditure upon management, coupled with the figures of recruiting, seems to be virtually conclusive evidence that the pay-rates, to which the Partnership has been adding its large expenditure upon free insurance against exceptional need and upon amenities and upon its pension-fund and finally upon Partnership Benefit, were themselves not merely quite as high as but actually considerably above the general contemporary rates of similar businesses.

I say nothing of the present abnormal taxation because we should have to set against that the present inflation of prices. The bombing, however, of so very much of our floor-space, including far the most important of all our individual businesses, is only too real an adverse factor.

All this suggests that the persistent attainment in the years between 1920 and 1930 of Partnership Benefit at the rate of about twenty per cent., that is to say about ten weeks' extra pay upon a full year's work, was not due to any merely temporary conditions and it is interesting to notice that, if the Partnership's present pay-sheet were at the average proportion to turnover shown in the confidential figures of which I have been speaking, we should now be distributing Partnership Benefit at more than fifteen per cent. on top of the pension-prospect that did not exist before the war.

CONSEQUENCES TO ECONOMIC EFFICIENCY

723. In those years the Partnership was much handicapped for discovering how to get from its members in return for what it gave

to them a full proportion of additional efficiency in the service of its customers and therefore a still further increase in the earnings of its members. Up to 1929 our field of operations was restricted to the comparatively small business of Peter Jones and thereafter before the real economic potentialities of the system could be demonstrated, so far as this particular partnership might have succeeded in doing that, there came, first, the great world depression of 1930 and then the succession of sudden opportunities, that we felt that we should be wrong to let slip, of great expansions that lowered drastically the rate of Partnership Benefit because they produced immediate great increases of the pay-sheet without proportionate immediate increases of the profit.

For all these reasons, though there are hopeful symptoms that to me seem important, as for example the general friendliness to newcomers, the good manners in war-time, certain features of our recruiting and certain figures of unexplained wastage, our system's real economic potentialities for the service of the general community upon the one hand and of the workers upon the other are still much more matters of conjecture, much more disputable, than otherwise they might have been by now. But in my own view the Partnership has now at last reached a scale of operations that may be considered to be full, though early, maturity for our particular enterprise. If that is so, then, so far as general conditions in this country may allow, we should begin now to see how far Producer-Cooperatives of this general type may be the answer to one of the great problems of our modern civilisation, how to make our working-lives as fruitful for ourselves and in all other ways as happy as they ought to be and so make ourselves work as well as for our own sakes we should.

APPENDIX A

THE TRUST SETTLEMENT OF 1929

This is a settlement made the Eighteenth day of April One thousand nine hundred and twenty-nine BETWEEN JOHN SPEDAN LEWIS of Oxford Street London W. Esquire (hereinafter called "the Settlor") of the one part and the said JOHN SPEDAN LEWIS, SARAH BEATRICE MARY LEWIS also of Oxford Street aforesaid and CECIL JAMES HERBERT HUNTER[1] of 51 Hampton Road Teddington in the County of Middlesex (hereinafter called "the Trustees" which expression shall include the Trustees or Trustee for the time being hereof) of the other part WHEREAS:

(i)   The Settlor is absolutely entitled to Seven hundred thousand fully paid Ordinary Shares of One Pound each in the Capital of John Lewis and Company Limited Eighty three thousand and sixty-six Preference Shares and Thirty-six thousand nine hundred and forty-two Ordinary Shares of One Pound each in the capital of Peter Jones Limited and Six thousand nine hundred and ninety-five Ordinary Shares of the Odney Estate Limited and being desirous of making such provisions as are hereinafter contained for the benefit of the employees of the Trading Companies as hereinafter defined has transferred such shares into the joint names of the Trustees in anticipation of the execution of these presents.

(ii)   The Settlor after due consideration has resolved that subject only to the provisions of Clause 15 hereof the Settlement hereby made shall be irrevocable.

(iii)   In furtherance of the purposes of these presents the Settlor is about to cause to be registered under the Companies Acts 1908 to 1928 a Company (hereinafter called "the Partnership Company") under the name of The John Lewis Partnership Limited[2] with a capital of Three hundred and twelve thousand Pounds divided into Three hundred thousand Preferred Ordinary Shares each of One Pound carrying a fixed Cumulative Preferential Dividend at the rate of Seven and one-half per cent. and Twelve thousand Deferred Ordinary Shares each of One Pound limited in respect of any year to a dividend at the rate of Ten Pounds per cent. per annum for the year.

1   Replaced in 1936 by Rear-Admiral Cloudesley Varyl Robinson (now Sir Varyl Robinson, K.C.B.)

2   Now John Lewis Partnership Limited.

NOW THIS DEED WITNESSETH that it is hereby agreed and declared as follows:

1.   IN this Deed where the context so admits :

(A)   The expression "the Reversioner" means the Settlor or other the person persons or corporation for the time being entitled under this Deed (whether by assignment or otherwise) in reversion expectant on the determination of the Settlement Period as hereinafter defined.

(B)   The expression "the Trading Companies" means and includes John Lewis and Company Limited Peter Jones Limited and The Odney Estate Limited and any other company or companies which the Reversioner may from time to time hereafter by deed nominate and appoint to be a member or members of the class of trading companies for the purposes of this Deed (Provided that no such nomination or appointment shall be effective in the case of any company unless and until shares of such company carrying voting rights sufficient in the aggregate to ensure the passing of a special resolution of such company shall have been transferred to or vested in the Trustees upon the trusts hereof).

(c)   The expression "the shares" means and includes the shares hereby settled and any other shares in the trading companies or any of them which may at any time hereafter be transferred to or vested in the Trustees upon the trusts hereof whether in addition to or in substitution for or by way of bonus on any shares previously held by them;

(D)   The expression "employees" and "employee" mean and include any persons or person of either sex employed by the trading companies or any of them in regular service of any description at an hourly weekly quarterly monthly or yearly wage or salary with or without commission including any secretaries or assistant secretaries so employed but excluding:

a)   Directors or Managing Directors unless apart from their tenure of such office they are duly qualified as employees under the foregoing provisions of this definition and

b)   Persons employed in service of a temporary or non-recurrent nature.

PROVIDED that in the case of any employee within the foregoing definition who is also a Director or Managing Director the remuneration received by him by virtue of such office shall not be taken into account in calculating his salary for the purposes of this Deed.

AND PROVIDED further that in case any question arises as to whether any person is or is not an employee within the foregoing definition the decision of the Trustees on such question shall be final and conclusive and binding on all persons interested hereunder.

(E) The expression "salary" includes wages.

(F) Words importing the masculine gender include the feminine and words importing the singular number include the plural and *vice versa.*

(G) The expression "the Settlement Period" means the period until the expiration of Twenty-one years from the death of the last survivor of the issue now living of his late Majesty King Edward VII or until at any time during such last mentioned period that shall have been a consecutive period of not less than three calendar months during which there shall have been in existence no Trading Company within the foregoing definition.

(H) Year means a calendar year from the First day of January to the Thirty-first day of December.

2. DURING the Settlement Period the Trustees shall subject to the provisions of Clause 15 hereof stand possessed of the Shares IN TRUST to receive the dividends thereon and in the first place to pay to the Settlor one equal fifth part of each such dividend and to apply the remaining four equal fifth parts thereof (hereinafter called "the Benefit Fund") in manner following that is to say: —

(i) In the first place the Trustees shall out of the Benefit Fund to the extent and subject as hereinafter provided provide for and pay the Cumulative Dividends at the rate of Seven and one-half per cent. per annum upon the Preferred Ordinary Shares of the Partnership Company for the time being issued so far as such dividends shall not be paid by and out of the income of the Partnership Company.

(ii) The Trustees shall subject as hereinafter mentioned distribute the balance of the Benefit Fund arising in each year amongst all the employees who were in the service of any of the Trading Companies on the last day of the preceding year and the legal personal representatives of any employees who died in the service of any of the Trading Companies during that year in such shares that each such employee or his legal personal representatives as the case may be shall receive an amount bearing the same proportion to the total sum distributed as the amount of salary and commission earned by such employee during such preceding year bears to the total aggregate amount of salary and commission earned during such preceding year by all such employees except that any fraction of a pound sterling which would otherwise be payable to any employee upon any distribution shall not be payable to, him but shall be carried forward and added to and treated for all purposes as forming part of the Benefit Fund arising in the year next following PROVIDED ALWAYS that no employee unless exempted from the operation of this proviso under the power for this purpose hereinafter contained shall be qualified to participate in any distribution of the Benefit Fund unless he shall have applied all the sums paid to him upon any previous distribution within Fourteen days after the payment thereof respectively or such extended time (if any) as the Trustees may for special reasons think fit to allow in subscribing for and paying up in full (either at par or with such premium (if any) as the Partnership Company may from time to time prescribe shares in the Partnership Company which shall be either Preferred Ordinary Shares of the class mentioned above or shares of such other classes or class (other than the said Deferred Shares) whether ranking in priority or subsequently to or *pari passu* with the said Preferred Ordinary Shares and whether conferring greater equal or inferior rights as to dividend and other matters as may from time to time be made available for this purpose by the Partnership Company and any employee excluded from participation by the operation of this proviso shall be deemed not be an employee for any of the purposes of these presents. AND PROVIDED further that no employee shall for the purpose of any distribution be deemed to be an employee if at the date of such distribution he shall be an undischarged bankrupt or shall have done or suffered any other act or thing whereby if he had been absolutely entitled to participate therein he would have been prevented from receiving his share or any part thereof for his own sole benefit. AND PROVIDED further that if and so often as any employee of any of the Trading Companies shall at the time of any distribution of the Benefit Fund be indebted to such Company on any account whatsoever such company may by notice in writing to the Trustees direct that the whole or such part as such notice may prescribe of the share in the Benefit Fund payable to such employee shall in lieu of being paid to him be paid to such company in or towards satisfaction of such indebtedness and the Trustees shall pay the same to such company accordingly and such notice shall be a complete protection to the Trustees and should it subsequently be shown that no such indebtedness existed such employee shall not have any right to recover any sum so paid either from the Benefit Fund or from the Trustees but shall be left to such remedy (if any) as he may have against such company as aforesaid.

3.   FOR the purpose of giving effect to the provisions of Paragraph 2 (i) of these presents the following provisions shall apply that is to say (A) The Trustees shall out of the Benefit Fund arising in any year pay the fixed

Cumulative Preferential Dividend upon the Preferred Ordinary Shares of the Partnership Company for the preceding year and all arrears thereof accrued down to that year so far as the same shall not have been actually paid by the Partnership Company out of its own moneys within three months after the expiration of such preceding year or in the case of such arrears by the Trustees out of the Benefit Fund arising in any previous year (B) The Trustees may if they think fit out of the Benefit Fund arising in any year retain a fund by way of provision for part or all of the fixed Preferential Dividend upon the said Preferred Ordinary Shares for the year then current and any sum so retained shall for all the purposes of these presents be dealt with as if it had formed part of the Benefit Fund arising in the following year.

4. FOR the purposes of these presents the Benefit Fund arising in any year shall include the proper proportion of all final dividends actually made payable in such year by the Company declaring the same and any interim dividend declared by any company in respect of any trading year shall be deemed to have been actually made payable simultaneously with the final dividend declared by the same company in respect of the same year and if no such final dividend is declared then at the end of two calendar months after the expiration of the same year.

5. FROM and after the determination of the Settlement Period the Trustees shall stand possessed of the shares and any investments or property representing the same or any of them IN TRUST for the Settlor absolutely.

6. A statement in writing signed by the Secretary of any of the Trading Companies purporting to contain the names of the persons who were on the Thirty-first day of December of any year the employees of such company within the meaning of these presents and the amount of salary and commission earned by any employee during any year or the names of any employees who died during any year or of the legal personal representatives of any deceased employee shall so far as regards the protection of the Trustees be sufficient evidence of the matters stated therein and the Trustees shall be entitled to assume that no person not named in such a statement was in fact an employee at the relevant date.

7. (i)   The Trustees may in their discretion upon the recommendation of any Council or Committee which appears to them fairly to represent the views of the majority of the employees for the time being from time to time and at any time exclude any employee either wholly or partially

from participation in any distribution of the Benefit Fund.

(ii)   In the event of an employee being wholly excluded under this clause from participation in any distribution of the Benefit Fund he shall be treated for all the purposes of Clause 2 (ii) hereof as having earned no salary or commission during the year preceding that in which the Benefit Fund arises.

(iii)   In the event of an employee being partially excluded under this clause from participation in any distribution of the Benefit Fund he shall be treated for all the purposes of Clause 2 (ii) hereof as having earned during the year preceding that in which the Benefit Fund arises such proportion of the salary and commission earned by him during such preceding year as the Trustees may determine.

8. (i)   Subject to the provisions of these presents excluding Directors and Managing Directors in respect of their remuneration as such the Reversioners may from time to time and at any time by notice in writing to the Trustees direct that (A) any person employed by any of the Trading Companies but not an employee within the foregoing definition or (B) any employee who shall for any reason (including exclusion under Clause 7 hereof) have become excluded from participation in any distribution of the Benefit Fund shall participate in any such distribution on the footing that he earned during the year preceding that in which the Benefit Fund arises such amount of salary and commission (not exceeding the amount actually earned by him during such preceding year) as such notice shall specify and in such case such person employed or employee as aforesaid shall be included in such distribution and shall be treated for all the purposes of Clause 2 (ii) hereof as an employee who earned the amount of salary and commission so specified during such preceding year.

(ii)   Without prejudice to the generality of the foregoing power the Reversioner may from time to time and at any time give to any employee a written authority to retain any sums paid to him on any distribution of the Benefit Fund without applying the same in manner provided by Clause 2 (ii) hereof and every such authority shall to the extent mentioned therein exempt such employee from the operation of the first proviso to Clause 2 (ii) aforesaid. Notice in writing of every such authority shall be given by the Reversioner to the Trustees.

9. THE Trustees shall not incur any liability by paying any share in any dividend to an employee who shall have become disqualified from receiving the same under any of the provisions hereof unless they have actual notice of the facts giving rise to such disqualification although by making proper enquiries they might have ascertained such facts.

10.   SUBJECT to the provisions of Clause 15 hereof the Trustees shall not during the Settlement Period sell or dispose of the shares or any of them PROVIDED as follows: —

(i)   In the event of any of the Trading Companies being wound up in pursuance of a scheme of amalgamation absorption or reconstruction whereunder shares in any other company which is or becomes one of the Trading Companies are issued in substitution for the shares held by the Trustees in the Company so wound up by the Trustees shall accept such substituted shares in lieu of the shares held by them in the company so wound up and shall stand possessed thereof upon the trusts and with and subject to the powers and provisions applicable hereunder to the shares for which they were substituted.

(ii)   In the event of any of the Trading Companies being wound up otherwise than in pursuance of any such scheme as is mentioned in Sub-clause (i) of this clause the Settlement Period shall as regards the shares of that company be deemed to have come to an end and the Trustees shall stand possessed of such shares upon trust for the Settlor accordingly.

11. THE Trustees may from time to time consult with the Reversioner as to the manner in which the voting powers attached to the shares or any of them is to be exercised and may exercise the same in accordance with such directions as may be given by the Reversioner from time to time and a written direction from the Reversioner as to any exercise of such voting powers shall be a complete protection to the Trustees complying therewith notwithstanding that such compliance may bring about the determination of the Settlement Period or otherwise prejudicially affect the interests of the employees hereunder.

12. ANY moneys forming part of the Benefit Fund which are not immediately required for the purposes of these presents may be invested by the Trustees in any manner for the time being authorised by law for the investment of trust moneys or may be left on current or deposit account at any bank and any income arising from any such moneys shall

be treated as part of the Benefit Fund in such year as the Trustees shall think expedient.

13.   ANY Trustee for the time being hereof being a solicitor or other professional person shall be entitled to charge and be paid all his usual professional or other charges for all work and business done and time spent by him or his firm in relation to the trusts hereof including work and business done and time spent on matters which a Trustee not being a solicitor or other professional person might have attended to personally.

14.   the power of appointing a new Trustee or new Trustees hereof shall be vested in the Reversioner.

15.   (i)   Notwithstanding anything hereinbefore contained the Trustees shall as and when directed in writing so to do by the Settlor raise by mortgage or charge of all or any of the shares such sum or sums not exceeding in the whole the sum of Two hundred thousand Pounds as the Settlor shall at any time or from time to time by such direction require and shall pay every sum so raised to the Settlor or as he shall direct.

(ii)   Every such mortgage or charge shall override and take effect in priority to all the trusts powers and provisions hereinbefore declared so far as regards the shares comprised therein.

(iii)   In the event of any sum or sums being so raised as aforesaid the Trustees shall during the residue of the Settlement Period or any shorter period during which any such mortgage or charge shall be outstanding in priority to the trusts powers and provisions hereinbefore contained (but subject and without prejudice to the rights powers and remedies of any mortgagee or chargee so far as regards the shares comprised in his mortgage or charge and the dividends thereon) apply the dividends received by them on the shares either

(A) FIRST in paying all interest due and payable on any sum or sums so raised as aforesaid and for the time being outstanding SECONDLY in making such provision (if any) as the Trustees shall in their absolute discretion think proper for the due payment of any accruing or future interest on any sum or sums so raised as aforesaid and THIRDLY in making such provision (if any) as the Trustees shall in their absolute discretion think proper (whether by payments on account of principal or by establishing and contributing to a sinking fund) for the redemption of the shares comprised in any such mortgage or charge or

(B) In the event of any such sum or sums as aforesaid being repayable by instalments FIRST in paying all instalments of principal and interest due and payable in respect thereof and SECONDLY in making such provision (if any) for payment of future instalments of principal and interest as the Trustees shall in their absolute discretion think fit.

AND subject to such payment and provision as aforesaid the balance of the dividends received by the Trustees on the shares shall be dealt with and applied as hereinbefore provided.

(iv)   In the event of the shares or any of them being sold by any mortgagee or chargee thereof:

(A) If by reason of any such sale the shares in any of the Trading Companies remaining subject to the Trusts hereof shall be so reduced as to cease to carry voting rights sufficient in the aggregate to ensure the passing of a special resolution of such company then and in such case the Reversioner may by deed executed at any time before the shares in such company subject to the trusts hereof shall once more carry voting rights sufficient as aforesaid declare that such company shall cease to be a Trading Company for the purposes of this Deed and thereupon such company shall as from the date of such deed cease to be a member of the class of Trading Companies hereunder.

(B) In the event of any company ceasing to be a member of the class of Trading Companies under the foregoing provisions of this clause any of the shares in such company remaining subject to the trusts hereof shall thenceforth during the residue of the Settlement Period be held by the Trustees in trust either to retain the same as actually invested so long as the Trustees shall think fit without being responsible for loss or at the discretion of the Trustees to sell the same or any of them and to invest the proceeds in any manner for the time being authorised by law for the investment of trust moneys and to pay one equal fifth part of the income of such shares and of the investments and property from time to time representing the same to the Settlor and to apply the remaining four equal fifth parts of such income as part of the Benefit Fund in such years as the Trustees shall think expedient.

(c) Any surplus proceeds of the sale of any of such shares by any mortgagee or chargee received by the Trustees shall be invested by the Trustees in any manner for the time being authorised by law for the investment of trust moneys and during the residue of the Settlement Period one equal fifth part of any income arising therefrom shall be paid to the Settlor and the remaining four equal fifth parts of such income shall be applied as part of the Benefit Fund in such years as the Trustees shall think expedient.

(v)   Every such mortgage or charge shall be in such form as the Trustees shall in their absolute and uncontrolled discretion think proper.

IN WITNESS whereof the Settlor and the Trustees have hereunto set their respective hands and seals the day and year first above written.

Signed Sealed and Delivered
  by the above-named JOHN
  SPEDAN LEWIS in the presence
  of GEOFFREY S. CONWAY,
    277, Oxford Street, W.1,
        Secretary.

} JOHN SPEDAN LEWIS (L.S.)

Signed Sealed and Delivered
  by the above-named JOHN
  SPEDAN LEWIS in the presence
  of GEOFFREY S. CONWAY,
    277, Oxford Street, W.1,
        Secretary.

} JOHN SPEDAN LEWIS (L.S.)

Signed Sealed and Delivered
  by the above-named SARAH
  BEATRICE MARY LEWIS in the
  presence of
  GEOFFREY S. CONWAY,
    277, Oxford Street, W.1,
        Secretary.

} SARAH BEATRICE MARY LEWIS (L.S.)

Signed Sealed and Delivered by
  the above-named CECIL JAMES
  HERBERT HUNTER in the
  presence of
  GEOFFREY S. CONWAY,
    277, Oxford Street, W.1,
        Secretary.

} CECIL JAMES HERBERT HUNTER (L.S.)

APPENDIX B

DRAFT ARTICLES OF THE CONSTITUTION OF THE JOHN LEWIS PARTNERSHIP

These draft Articles, as they stand, are the result of an effort to reduce them to their absolute core. Recent indications from the Partnership's lawyers suggest that they may have to be altered somewhat to meet the technical legal requirements of the impending second Settlement in Trust. But, if that happens, the intentions will be the same and, so far as the changes may reduce the content of the Articles as they stand, we shall have to do our best to secure the same results by some supplementary provisions.

I. THE CONSTITUTION

The John Lewis Partnership shall be governed in accordance with the Articles hereinafter set out and with such by-laws rules and regulations as the Chairman of the Central Board shall from time to time in writing determine.

IA. AMENDMENT OF THE CONSTITUTION

The Articles of the Constitution of the Partnership may be amended, cancelled or replaced by others to any extent by an agreement between a majority of the whole of the Council and the Chairman but neither the Council nor the Chairman shall be under any obligation to justify a withholding of that consent.

The Rules and Regulations may at any time be changed by the Chairman of the Central Board who shall have power to delegate his authority to any Partner or body of Partners. Any alteration in the Rules and Regulations shall be brought to the notice of all Partners by publication at the earliest moment in THE GAZETTE of the John Lewis Partnership or by other sufficient means.

2. THE PARTNERSHIP'S BEHAVIOUR TO THE GENERAL COMMUNITY

The Partnership shall endeavour constantly to keep on a high level of good citizenship its behaviour as a group within the general community.

3. THE PARTNERSHIP'S BEHAVIOUR TO ITS CUSTOMERS

The Partnership shall endeavour constantly to give to all of its Customers service at least as good as the best otherwise available to them and in as many cases as possible service so much better as to secure their custom.

4. THE PARTNERSHIP'S BEHAVIOUR TO ITS SUPPLIERS

The Partnership shall finance itself as in the judgment of its Central Board shall be ultimately best for its own efficiency and shall punctiliously keep faith with all owners of capital of which it accepts charge. Any failure to provide sufficiently for the punctuality of any payment due to them shall be a failure on the part of the Chairman of the Board in his undertaking to maintain the Partnership's Constitution and shall entitle the Trustees thereof to exercise their powers under the sixth of these Articles and under Article   of the Memorandum and Articles of Association of the Trustee Company* to declare the Chairmanship vacant and to make a fresh appointment thereto.

With other commodities or services, whereof likewise the supply does not make the supplier a member of the Partnership, the Partnership shall supply itself as in the judgment of the Chairman or of his properly appointed representative shall be likewise ultimately best for its own efficiency and with all of those suppliers the Partnership shall likewise punctiliously keep faith and shall endeavour constantly to make dealings with itself advantageous and pleasant to them in all proper ways.

5. THE PARTNERSHIP'S BEHAVIOUR TO ITS OWN MEMBERS

The Partnership's ultimate aim shall be the happiness in every way of all its Members with among them no more inequality in any respect whatever than shall seem to be necessary to the Partnership's efficiency in the service of the general community. This efficiency shall be the utmost possible without overstrain of body or mind for workers of first-rate ability for the posts they are undertaking to fill. To a newcomer, whose contractual remuneration from the Partnership during that time will not be more than half of its contemporary highest, the Partnership may ensure employment for any period not exceeding three years in all, the employment being terminable by payment in lieu of notice of not more than the contractual remuneration for the unexpired remainder of the term of the engagement but in all other cases the Partnership shall reserve to itself power to close without cause assigned any individual membership by the giving of not more than twelve months' notice or half-pay in lieu of that notice or of any unexpired remainder thereof.

6. THE PARTNERSHIP'S BEHAVIOUR TO COMPETITORS IN ITS BUSINESS

The behaviour of the Partnership to competitors in its business shall be as friendly as may be compatible with the utmost vigour of fair competition.

* This Company has not yet been incorporated.

7. PRINCIPAL AUTHORITY IN THE AFFAIRS OF THE PARTNERSHIP

Principal authority in the affairs of the Partnership shall be divided between a Council, the Board of Directors of John Lewis Partnership Limited (the Central Board) and the Chairman of that Board. Of the Council two-thirds at least shall be elected yearly by secret ballot of all those members of the Partnership who are not members of the Council by virtue of their office in the Partnership or by other appointment. The remaining members of the Council, being not more than one-third of the whole, shall be the holders in the business of the Partnership of positions to which for the time the Chairman of the Central Board shall attach membership of the Council or shall be such other members of the Partnership as for the time the Chairman of the Central Board shall appoint to be members of the Council.

The Council after its election shall first of all appoint one of its own members to be during its pleasure its President. The President having assumed office, the Council shall next appoint during the Council's pleasure three Partners (who shall be the Trustees of the Constitution of the Partnership) none of whom shall be the Chairman or the Deputy Chairman of the Central Board or any person nominated by the Chairman for appointment as a Director of the Central Board or the Partnership's General Inspector, Chief Registrar, Internal Auditor, Financial Adviser or Partners' Counsellor, to be Directors of John Lewis Partnership Trust Limited and shall nominate five other Partners for appointment by the Trustees as Directors of John Lewis Partnership Limited.

A Partner appointed by the Council to be a Trustee of the Constitution shall be appointed forthwith by the Chairman of the Trustee Company a member of the Board of Directors of the Trustee Company. The twelve members of the Central Board shall be appointed by the Trustees of the Second Settlement in accordance with the terms thereof.

The Central Board, in addition to their statutory functions as Directors of John Lewis Partnership Limited, shall by their decision in certain cases and by their advice in other cases operate the system of budgetary control whereby the Partnership shall con duct its business. In the operation of that system the Board shall decide what estimate the Partnership shall adopt of its revenues for the future period under consideration and what shall be provided therefrom for impersonal expenditure necessary to the achievement of that revenue.

The word "impersonal" shall here mean all expenditure by the Partnership that will not accrue to any individual member of the Partnership in any way whatever, either for his separate property, whether by way of contractual remuneration or by way of contractual or non-contractual pension or by way of expectation of such pension or by way of provision that the Partnership shall make for free insurance of its members against exceptional misfortune and that will not alternatively accrue to any Partner by way of amenities to be enjoyed collectively, those amenities being provided expressly and not merely incidental to provision necessary to the Partnership's business or by any other way whatsoever.

In the Constitution of the Partnership all such expenditure accruing to Partners for their own advantage in any way whatsoever shall be reckoned "personal" and shall be made by the Partnership as the Chairman in his discharge of his duty under the Partnership's Constitution shall direct.

The Central Board in any exercise of their aforesaid powers shall if three of their Directors nominated for appointment by the Trustees as such by the Council so demand consult and ascertain the opinion of the Council in the following two cases. First, if the Board propose to commit the Partnership to liquidating more than five per cent. of its fixed assets as those stood on the first day of the Board's year of office or at any later date therein, and, second, if the Board propose to commit the Partnership to increasing its total capital by more than five per cent. thereof otherwise than by accumulation of profits of its own business.

The Chairman shall cause the Partnership to place monies at the disposal of the Council to the extent of one per cent. at least of the total amount that in the previous year the Partnership paid out to its members by way of remuneration for their services together with any amount that in respect of that same year was appropriated to the pension fund and also any amount that in respect of that same year was distributed to the members of the Partnership either by way of free insurance against exceptional misfortune or by way of general Partnership Benefit. The Council furthermore, except that they shall not appropriate any of it to their own personal benefit, shall make at their absolute discretion any use that they shall consider to be good for the Partnership of these monies.

The Council may furthermore with or without any preliminary enquiry of the Board or of the Chairman discuss any matter whatsoever and make any suggestion that they shall see fit to the Central Board or to the Chairman. Any enquiry from the Council shall be answered by the Central Board or by the Chairman only so far as in their respective judgments shall be expedient for the Partnership.

The Chairman upon taking office shall give the Partnership written assurance of his having considered carefully its Constitution and the Partnership's latest edition of the book published, in connection with the completion of its foundation by the making in 1948 of the second irrevocable settlement in trust and that his acceptance of appointment to the Chair is upon those terms and that to the utmost of his ability he will maintain the Constitution and promote in every way the welfare of the Partnership and during his continuance in office will undertake no official responsibilities of any kind outside the Partnership without the consent of the Central Council and that failure on his part to maintain the Constitution will give the Trustees power to exercise their powers under Article† of the Memorandum and Articles of John Lewis Partnership Trust Limited.

8. JOHN LEWIS PARTNERSHIP TRUST FOR PENSIONS

The Partnership shall maintain the Pension Scheme in accordance with the Rules of the Committee for Management of the John Lewis Partnership Pensions Trust* and any proper amendment thereof.

9. INTERPRETATION

(1) The 1929 Settlement means the Settlement dated the 18th day of April 1929 and made between John Spedan Lewis of the one part and the said John Spedan Lewis, Sarah Beatrice Mary Lewis and Cecil James Herbert Hunter of the other part.

(2) The Second Settlement means the Settlement dated the day of 194 and made between John Spedan Lewis of the one part and

(3) The "Partnership" means the general body of employees as defined in the 1929 Settlement.

(4) A "Partner" means any person employed by a trading Company as defined in the 1929 Settlement and includes the Chairman and Deputy Chairman of the Trustee Company.

(5) The Trust Company means John Lewis Partnership Trust Limited.

(6) The Central Board means the Board of John Lewis Partnership Limited.

(7) The Constitution means the above written Articles of the Constitution of the John Lewis Partnership and all Rules and Regulations properly made thereunder.

(8) The Trustees means the three Partners nominated by the Council to be Directors of the Trustee Company and Trustees of the Constitution.

* See Appendix C.
† This Company has not yet been incorporated.

APPENDIX C

RULES OF THE JOHN LEWIS PARTNERSHIP
TRUST FOR PENSIONS

1.   THIS scheme shall be known as the John Lewis Partnership Trust for Pensions and shall come into operation as from the first day of February 1941.

DEFINITIONS

2.   In these rules the headings shall not affect the construction and unless inconsistent with the subject or context the following words and expressions shall have the following meanings :

(a)   "The Scheme" means this scheme and includes any variation thereof from time to time in force under the power to vary it hereinafter contained.

(b)   "The Central Company" means John Lewis Partnership Limited.

(c)   "The Central Board" means the Board of Directors of the Central Company.

(d)   "The Council" means the Central Council of the John Lewis Partnership appointed or elected in accordance with the current constitution of that Partnership.

(e)   "Constituent Company" means the Central Company or any Company or firm which is directly or indirectly controlled by allied to or associated with the Central Company and which the Central Company and the Council jointly declare to be or at the material time to have been within the Partnership.

(f)   "Subscribing Company" means a Constituent Company which complies with Rule 13.

(g)   "The Trustee" means John Lewis Partnership Pensions Trust Limited or other the Trustee or Trustees for the time being of the Fund.

(h)   "The Committee" means the Committee for the time being and consisting of three persons nominated from time to time by the Central Board and two persons elected annually by the Council.

(i)   "The Trust Deed" means the Trust Deed dated 30th January 1942, and made between the Central Company of the first part John Lewis & Company Limited of the second part, Suburban & Provincial Stores Limited of the third part, and John Lewis Partnership Pensions Trust Limited of the fourth part.

(j) "The Fund" means the fund established as at and from the first day of February 1941 by the Trust Deed and shall include all contributions made to and all moneys and property from time to time subject to the Scheme. All such contributions moneys and property shall constitute one fund the whole of which shall be applicable and shall be liable for the payment thereout of all moneys and benefits payable under or in respect of the Scheme.

(k) "The Rules" means and includes these Rules and any variations and additions to or substitutions for the same respectively which may from time to time be duly made.

(l) "Member" means and includes every past present and future member of the Partnership that is to say employee of a Constituent Company who, in accordance with and subject to the Rules, shall become and for the time being be a Member of the Scheme and also all persons who having been Members shall for the time being be entitled to receive pensions hereunder.

(m) "Pension" means superannuation allowances payable in monthly instalments or otherwise of which a Member is assured, on retirement or which the Committee may grant under the provisions of the Scheme.

(n) "Pensionable Date" means the date on which a Member at or after attaining the age of 60 if a man or 55 if a woman retires or is dismissed from the employment of a Constituent Company or having attained the age of 60 or 55 as the case may be and being still in the employment of a Constituent Company dies.

(o) "Pay" means the remuneration for the time being paid to members by or properly chargeable to a Constituent Company in respect of Members by way of pay including such bonuses commissions and other payments of any kind as are treated as commercial remuneration for the purpose of calculating what is known to the Constituent Companies as Partnership Benefit (but excluding Partnership Benefit itself) except in such particular cases or class of cases and to such extent and for such period or periods as the Central Company by notice in writing addressed to the Committee may for the time being and from time to time prescribe.

(p) "Dependants" means such person or persons who in the opinion of the Committee is or are in any way dependent upon a Member.

(q) "Service" means service in respect of which the Member shall have been entitled to receive pay or other remuneration or any part thereof whilst serving either (I) a Subscribing Company or (II) a Constituent Company which is not a Subscribing Company provided that a Subscribing Company has been properly charged with the whole or any part of his pay and shall not (unless the Committee in their absolute discretion otherwise decide) include any period or periods during which the employee (whilst remaining in the employment of the Company) has for any reason been absent from his employment and has not for any such period or periods been entitled to receive pay or other remuneration or any part thereof. Service or employment with more than one Constituent Company shall be included.

(r)   Words implying the masculine gender include the feminine gender and words implying the singular shall include the plural or vice versa.

THE FUND

3.   The Fund will consist of:

a)   The Contributions of the Constituent Companies under the Scheme.

b)   interest and dividends payable on the investments of the Fund.

c)   any other moneys or property which may be paid or transferred from any source from time to time for the purposes of the Fund, whether by way of donations, gifts, legacies, or otherwise.

MEMBERSHIP

4.   All Members of the John Lewis Partnership who work with any constituent Company are eligible to membership of the Scheme. Subject to the Provisions of these Rules all of them on attaining if a man the age of thirty or if a woman the age of twenty-five and having worked with any Constituent Company for fifteen years before or after the 1st February 1941 shall be admissible to benefit under the Scheme. Employment by a Constituent Company prior to its becoming a Constituent Company shall, unless in a particular case the Committee in its absolute discretion decides otherwise, count towards the completion of the said period of fifteen years. For the purpose of this Rule service includes whole-time National service of a Member during the National Emergency commencing on the 3rd September 1939 so long as a Constituent Company is under a legal obligation to re-employ such Member upon the termination of his National Service.

5.   It is a condition of membership of the Scheme that every Member agrees to be bound in all respects by the Rules for the time being in force.

BENEFITS

6.   Subject as herein provided there shall be assured to every member on the pensionable date a pension at the rate of one-sixtieth of his total pay

for his service as defined in Rule 2 (q) for all years of service up to a total of thirty. Unless in individual cases the committee in its absolute discretion shall decide otherwise no pay earned by a man before his thirtieth or by a woman before her twenty-fifth birthday shall be taken into account. If the years of service with any Subscribing Company and subsequent to those birthdays be more than thirty, then the rate of pension shall be fixed by reference to those thirty years in respect of which pay was highest.

7. Nothing herein shall prevent the Committee with the previous consent of the Central Company and of the Council from granting a pension of such an amount as the Committee shall think just (a) to a Member who while not fulfilling all or any of the conditions of the. Scheme in respect of age or length of service is in the judgment of the Committee deserving of special consideration either (i) on account of ill-health or (ii) for any other reason at any time during a period of ten years prior to the pensionable date or (b) to a Member who after the pensionable date renders part time service to a Constituent Company.

8. Subject to the funds required to be reserved for the payment of current and pending pensions the Committee with the previous consent of the Central Company and of the Council shall have power to direct the Trustee:

(a) To provide additional pensions for Members who are or have been employed by a Subscribing Company but who are not qualified under the provisions of the Scheme provided that the Committee may take into account length of service with a Constituent Company before the date referred to in Rule I or before a Constituent Company became a Subscribing Company but no such additional pension shall exceed an amount equal to one half of the average yearly pay received by any Member in respect of service with a Constituent Company.

(b) To pay a pension to the dependants of a Member who has died whilst in the service of a Constituent Company and who has served at least five years with a Subscribing Company. Such pension if less than five shillings per week to be commutable by the payment of such lump sum as the actuary may certify to be its equivalent.

9. So long as any "means" qualification shall be attached to the right to receive any outside pension or benefit whether from the State or not, the pension payable to any Member out of the Fund shall be reduced by such an amount (if any) as will qualify him for the maximum outside pension or benefit which he would be entitled to receive for the time being if he received no pension under these Rules. Provided however that in no case shall the combined amount of the outside pension or benefit and the

pension payable under these Rules be less than the amount of the pension provided for in Rules 6 and 8.

10. The Central Board and the Council may jointly in their absolute discretion direct the Trustee to withhold or reduce by such amount as they decide the pension or other benefits which might otherwise have been received by a member of the Scheme who being qualified by age and service either is dismissed or retires in order to escape dismissal from his employment on grounds involving fraud or misconduct or has or is subsequently found to have defrauded a Constituent Company or to have made a false statement with regard to his age or any other material particular when obtaining employment with any Constituent Company or has, in the opinion of the Trustee, brought discredit upon the John Lewis Partnership.

11. If any person in receipt of a pension or other benefit shall without first obtaining the permission of the Committee engage in or carry on either as principal or as agent and either directly or indirectly any business of any kind such pension shall cease to be payable. Such permission may at any time be revoked by the Committee.

12. Every member at the pensionable date may, subject to the approval of the Committee, convert a portion of his or her pension, not exceeding one-half into a life pension for his or her wife or husband or other dependant commencing at his or her death and of such amount as shall be certified by the Actuary to require the same financial provision from the Fund as the proportion of the pension converted would have required.

CONTRIBUTIONS

13. In order to become a Subscribing Company a Constituent Company shall pay to the Trustee a sum equal to five per cent. of the total amount paid by it in respect of pay as defined by Rule 2 (o) during each financial year for all service as defined in Rule 2 (q) and payment of such sum or of an amount approximately as nearly as possible to such sum shall be made by the Constituent Company to the Trustee before the end of each trading year and any further amount necessary to complete such sum shall be paid to or refunded by the Trustee as the case may be, as soon as the Auditors of the Constituent Company have certified the accounts of that Company for the relevant trading year. Failure to pay such sum or approximate amount before the end of each trading period or within thirty days thereafter will disqualify the Constituent Company from being a Subscribing Company in respect of such trading period.

13A. In addition to the payments provided for by Rule 13, a Subscribing

Company may, before the end of any trading year, pay to the Trustee a further sum which sum shall be deemed to be a payment in respect of such previous financial year or years when the Subscribing Company was not a Subscribing Company as the Subscribing Company shall declare in writing to the Trustee at the time of paying such further sum and the Subscribing Company shall thereupon be deemed for the purpose of these Rules to have been a Subscribing Company in respect of such previous financial year or years and the sum paid shall be divided into (a) a notional amount deemed to have been paid pursuant to Rule 13 and (b) interest thereon at the rate of three and one-half per cent. per annum from the date of notional payment until the date of actual payment.

13B.   In addition to the payment provided for by Rule 13 a Subscribing Company may before the end of any trading year with the previous consent of the Central Board pay to the Trustee:

    (a)   A sum in excess of the sum required to be paid by Rule 13 but not exceeding a further five per cent. of the total amount paid by it in respect of pay as defined by Rule 2 (o) for the current financial year and the pensions payable by Rule 6 shall be increased proportionately by the sums paid pursuant to this Rule, but so that the total pension of any member shall not exceed two-thirds of the highest pay for any of the five years of service immediately preceding retirement.

    (b)   Without prejudice to the provisions of Rule 8 (a) an additional sum not exceeding the amount certified by the Actuary as required to provide additional pensions for a qualified member or members so that his or their total pensions shall not exceed two-thirds of the highest pay for any of the five years immediately before leaving the Partnership and thereupon such additional pensions shall be assured to all such members, and shall be payable at the pensionable date or if they have previously left the service of the Partnership, at age 60 for a man or 55 if a woman, always provided their right to pension has not been forfeited under Rule 10.

ACCOUNTS AND AUDIT

14.   The Committee shall cause true accounts to be kept of the assets and liability of the Fund and of all sums of money received and expended and the matters in respect of which such receipts and expenditure have taken place and shall cause records to be kept of the members and of the contributions made by the Subscribing Companies and of all other facts proper or necessary to be recorded.

15.   Once at least in every year the accounts of the Fund shall be examined a Balance Sheet thereof prepared and the correctness of the Balance Sheet

ascertained by Auditors who shall from time to time be appointed by the Trustee and the Council. In default of agreement upon an Auditor there shall be two Auditors of whom one shall be appointed by the Trustee and the other by the Council. A copy of the Balance Sheet together with the Auditors' Report thereon and the report of the Committee as to the state of the Fund shall be published in the Partnership Gazette, or otherwise so as to be easily accessible to all Members.

ANNUAL VALUATION

16. (a) Within six months of the close of each financial year of the Fund the Trustee shall direct the Actuary to make actuarial valuation of the Fund and its assets and liabilities (including estimated risks and contributions if any) and for that purpose all necessary accounts and information shall be furnished by the Trustee and the Central Company to the Actuary. Such valuation shall take into account (inter alia) all Members who have become admissible to benefit under Rule 4 but shall not take into account Members who have not completed fifteen years service as defined by these Rules.

(b) If any such valuation shall show a surplus beyond the requirements of the Fund the Committee shall direct the Trustee to use such surplus for one or more of the following purposes:

(i) In establishing a Reserve Fund which may at any subsequent date be applied in meeting any deficiency in the Fund.

(ii) In reducing by such amount and for such period or periods as the Actuary shall advise the future contributions to be made to the Fund by Subscribing Companies.

(iii) In increasing as provided in Rule 8 and by such amount or amounts and for such period or periods as the Actuary shall advise the benefits and pensions payable out of the Fund.

(c) If any such valuation shall show a deficiency in the Fund such deficiency shall so far as possible be met out of any moneys for the time being standing to the credit of the Reserve Fund and in so far as such moneys shall not be sufficient to make good such deficiency first by reducing the pensions and benefits provided for by Rule 8 and then by reducing to the extent required the pensions and benefits provided for by Rule 6 and such reductions shall be of such extent and made in such manner and for such period or periods as the Actuary shall certify to be necessary.

(d) The Trustee or the Committee shall be entitled to make or direct to be made an actuarial valuation of the Fund at any other time or times including the time provided by this Rule.

MANAGEMENT

17.   The Scheme will be managed by the Committee. The Committee may meet together for the despatch of business adjourn or otherwise regulate their meetings as they think fit. Subject as provided by Rule 26 questions arising at any meeting shall be decided by a majority of votes and in the case of an equality of votes the Chairman shall have a second or casting vote. The Chairman may and on the requisition of the Central Company or the Trustee the Secretary shall at any time summon a meeting of the Committee. The quorum necessary for the transaction of the business of the Committee shall be three which must include one nominated and one elected member of the Committee. If any Member of the Committee fail to attend three consecutive meetings of which he shall have been given proper notice, the Central Board or the Council, as the case may be, may terminate his membership of the Committee and may nominate or elect for the remainder of the year another member in his place. The Chairman of the Committee shall be such Member of the Committee as the Committee shall for the time being and from time to time appoint to hold that office. The Committee shall from time to time appoint a Secretary who may also be a Member of the Committee.

18.   The cost and expenses of managing and administering the Scheme shall be paid out of the Fund. The Scheme will for the time being be administered from the registered office of the Central Company at 13 Holles Street, London, W.1 and notice of any change in the place of administration will be given in the Partnership Gazette.

GENERAL PROVISIONS

19.   Pensions are to be regarded as strictly personal and shall not be assigned, charged or alienated in any way and no payments thereof shall be made if the Member shall be adjudged a bankrupt or make or attempt to make any arrangement or composition with his creditors having the effect of a charge upon or alienation of his pension or any part thereof, or has assigned, charged or has attempted to assign or charge the same or if any act or offence has been done or happened which would have the effect of depriving him of his right to receive the pension or any part thereof. The Committee shall have full discretion as to the payment or application of any forfeited pension to or for the benefit of any Member or his dependants.

20.   The Pension shall accrue from day to day but unless otherwise agreed with the pensioner shall be paid by the Trustee by monthly instalments upon the last day of each month unless such last day shall fall upon a Sunday, in which case the payment shall be made on the previous

working day. All pensions shall be paid in such manner and in such places as the Committee shall decide. The Committee may in any case or cases and at such time or times as they think fit require to be furnished with evidence of the life of the person to or in respect of whom the Pension is payable and may withhold payment of such pension until such evidence has been supplied.

21. When a member dies any amount which may then or thereafter be due in respect of him from the Fund shall be paid to or expended for the benefit of the member's dependants in such manner as the Committee shall in their absolute discretion think fit. No benefits which under the Rules shall on the death or in respect of any period after the death of a member be payable in respect of such member shall form part of the deceased member's estate and neither the deceased member's legal personal representatives nor any person claiming in right of him shall have any claim to such benefits or any part thereof.

22. In the event of a member who has become qualified for or is in receipt of a pension or other benefits from the Scheme becoming in the opinion of the Committee incapacitated by reason of failure of health to manage his own affairs or to sign documents or for any reason unfit to receive his pension, the Committee may from time to time at their discretion direct the Trustee to pay or expend the pension or other benefits to or for the benefit of his dependants in such manner as the Committee shall think fit or if such member is in an Institution or Home may at their discretion authorise the payment of so much of the pension or other benefits as they think fit to that Institution or Home for his maintenance.

23. Nothing in the Trust Deed or the Rules shall in any way affect the right of a Constituent Company to determine the employment of any member at any time.

24. The Committee may at their discretion treat intermittent periods of employment with a Constituent Company as continuous employment.

25. The Committee may if they think fit require any member to furnish to the Committee such evidence as they may require as to his date of birth and may direct the Trustee to pay out of the Fund the costs of obtaining such evidence.

26. All money for the time being subject to the Trusts of the Fund and not required for immediate payment shall be invested in the name

of the Trustee in such investments as the Committee shall from time to time, and for the time being in its absolute discretion think fit. These investments may include loans, with or without security, and freehold and leasehold investments and mortgages of any kind. These investments are not limited to investments for the time being authorised by law for the investment of trust funds, provided that at least four of the five members of the Committee must previously approve of any investments not for the time being authorised by law for the investment of Trust Funds.

27.   The Trustee may from time to time if it thinks desirable or expedient in the interest of the Scheme borrow from a Constituent Company or from any other person such sums of money and upon such terms and conditions in all respects as it thinks fit and may secure the repayment thereof by mortgages or charges of all or any of the property for the time being constituting the Fund.

28.   No decision or exercise of a power by the Trustee or the Committee shall be invalidated or questioned on the ground that the Directors of the Trustee or the Committee or any of them had a direct or other personal interest in the result of such decision or exercise of such power.

29.   It shall not be obligatory upon the Trustee or the Committee to enforce payment of any contributions or other moneys payable under the Scheme. The Trustee and the Committee shall be indemnified by the Central Company against any loss which they may suffer in the bona fide execution of their duties or services under the scheme.

30.   The Trustee shall from time to time appoint a Member of the Institute of Actuaries approved by the Committee to be the Actuary of the Fund.

31.   Subject to the consent of the Central Board and of the Council the Committee may vary the Scheme or any of its provisions or Rules as it may from time to time think fit provided that no variation of the Scheme or alteration of the Rules shall be made which would enable any of the moneys of the Fund to be paid to a Constituent Company or alter the main purpose of the Scheme from that of providing pensions for members on retirement.

32.   The Committee shall have power to take over and administer any other existing pension scheme of a Constituent Company and to direct the Trustee to hold the funds of such Scheme upon the trusts of such

scheme (if any) provided that the Actuary shall previously certify such Scheme to be, in his opinion, sound.

DETERMINATION OF SCHEME

33. If an order shall be made or an effective Resolution passed for the winding up of a Constituent Company (except for the purpose of reconstruction or amalgamation) or if a Constituent Company shall cease to carry on business or shall cease to be either directly or indirectly controlled by allied to or associated with the Central Company or if the Central Company shall give notice to a Constituent Company that in the opinion of the Central Company it is necessary or expedient that the employees of such Constituent Company should become members of some other pension or like benefit Scheme. Then upon the happening of such events or upon the giving of such notice the membership of such of the employees of such Company (hereinafter called "the retiring Company") as are members of the Scheme (hereinafter called "the retiring Members") shall cease and the liability of the retiring Company to contribute to the Fund shall cease and the Trustee shall cause an actuarial valuation of the Fund as at the date of such cessation of membership of the Fund to be prepared by the Actuary and the proportion of the Fund and the investments and moneys representing the same (after deducting the amount ascertained upon such valuation to be required to meet pensions or other benefits then payable out of the Fund to former employees of the Retiring Company entitled to such pensions or other benefits at the date of such cessation of membership) which shall be ascertained upon such valuation to be applicable to the retiring members shall be applied by the Trustee in making payments in cash to or in the purchase of annuities for the retiring Members in accordance with their interests therein as certified by the Actuary.

34. Nothing in the preceding Rule contained shall affect the right of the former employees of a retiring Company to continue to receive out of the Fund the pensions or benefits assured to them prior to the date of such retirement by such retiring Company.

35. Upon the determination of the trusts of the Fund for any cause whatsoever the Fund shall be wound up and the liability of the Constituent Companies to contribute to the Fund shall cease and the Trustee shall realise the Fund and the investments for the time being representing the same and shall apply the proceeds and any unapplied income:

    (a) In paying the cost charges and expenses of winding up the Fund and other expenses properly payable thereout.

(b)   Subject thereto in making full and adequate provision as far as the Trustee is able by the purchase of annuities or otherwise in such manner as the Committee may think expedient for the maintenance and future payment and satisfaction of all pensions payable out of the Fund at the date of such winding up.

(c)   Subject thereto in applying the surplus, if any, in the purchase of annuities carrying no surrender or loan value in making payments in lieu of or in commutation of such annuities for persons entitled in anticipation to pension benefits out of the Fund regard being had to their respective prospects of becoming entitled to pensions had the Fund continued in existence and to their respective interests therein as certified by the Actuary.

(d)   Subject thereto in paying any surplus to the Commissioners for the National Debt.

INDEX

COMPILED BY LESLIE S. SHAW